M000009064

FREE Test Taking Tips DVD Offer

To help us better serve you, we have developed a Test Taking Tips DVD that we would like to give you for FREE. **This DVD covers world-class test taking tips that you can use to be even more successful when you are taking your test.**

All that we ask is that you email us your feedback about your study guide. Please let us know what you thought about it – whether that is good, bad or indifferent.

To get your **FREE Test Taking Tips DVD**, email freedvd@studyguideteam.com with "FREE DVD" in the subject line and the following information in the body of the email:

a. The title of your study guide.

b. Your product rating on a scale of 1-5, with 5 being the highest rating.

c. Your feedback about the study guide. What did you think of it?

d. Your full name and shipping address to send your free DVD.

If you have any questions or concerns, please don't hesitate to contact us at freedvd@studyguideteam.com.

Thanks again!

CBEST Prep Book

Study Guide and Practice Exam Questions for the California Basic Educational Skills Test [3rd Edition]

TPB Publishing

Written and edited by TPB Publishing.

ISBN 13: 9781628458756
ISBN 10: 1628458755

Table of Contents

Quick Overview

As you draw closer to taking your exam, effective preparation becomes more and more important. Thankfully, you have this study guide to help you get ready. Use this guide to help keep your studying on track and refer to it often.

This study guide contains several key sections that will help you be successful on your exam. The guide contains tips for what you should do the night before and the day of the test. Also included are test-taking tips. Knowing the right information is not always enough. Many well-prepared test takers struggle with exams. These tips will help equip you to accurately read, assess, and answer test questions.

A large part of the guide is devoted to showing you what content to expect on the exam and to helping you better understand that content. In this guide are practice test questions so that you can see how well you have grasped the content. Then, answer explanations are provided so that you can understand why you missed certain questions.

Don't try to cram the night before you take your exam. This is not a wise strategy for a few reasons. First, your retention of the information will be low. Your time would be better used by reviewing information you already know rather than trying to learn a lot of new information. Second, you will likely become stressed as you try to gain a large amount of knowledge in a short amount of time. Third, you will be depriving yourself of sleep. So be sure to go to bed at a reasonable time the night before. Being well-rested helps you focus and remain calm.

Be sure to eat a substantial breakfast the morning of the exam. If you are taking the exam in the afternoon, be sure to have a good lunch as well. Being hungry is distracting and can make it difficult to focus. You have hopefully spent lots of time preparing for the exam. Don't let an empty stomach get in the way of success!

When travelling to the testing center, leave earlier than needed. That way, you have a buffer in case you experience any delays. This will help you remain calm and will keep you from missing your appointment time at the testing center.

Be sure to pace yourself during the exam. Don't try to rush through the exam. There is no need to risk performing poorly on the exam just so you can leave the testing center early. Allow yourself to use all of the allotted time if needed.

Remain positive while taking the exam even if you feel like you are performing poorly. Thinking about the content you should have mastered will not help you perform better on the exam.

Once the exam is complete, take some time to relax. Even if you feel that you need to take the exam again, you will be well served by some down time before you begin studying again. It's often easier to convince yourself to study if you know that it will come with a reward!

Test-Taking Strategies

1. Predicting the Answer

When you feel confident in your preparation for a multiple-choice test, try predicting the answer before reading the answer choices. This is especially useful on questions that test objective factual knowledge. By predicting the answer before reading the available choices, you eliminate the possibility that you will be distracted or led astray by an incorrect answer choice. You will feel more confident in your selection if you read the question, predict the answer, and then find your prediction among the answer choices. After using this strategy, be sure to still read all of the answer choices carefully and completely. If you feel unprepared, you should not attempt to predict the answers. This would be a waste of time and an opportunity for your mind to wander in the wrong direction.

2. Reading the Whole Question

Too often, test takers scan a multiple-choice question, recognize a few familiar words, and immediately jump to the answer choices. Test authors are aware of this common impatience, and they will sometimes prey upon it. For instance, a test author might subtly turn the question into a negative, or he or she might redirect the focus of the question right at the end. The only way to avoid falling into these traps is to read the entirety of the question carefully before reading the answer choices.

3. Looking for Wrong Answers

Long and complicated multiple-choice questions can be intimidating. One way to simplify a difficult multiple-choice question is to eliminate all of the answer choices that are clearly wrong. In most sets of answers, there will be at least one selection that can be dismissed right away. If the test is administered on paper, the test taker could draw a line through it to indicate that it may be ignored; otherwise, the test taker will have to perform this operation mentally or on scratch paper. In either case, once the obviously incorrect answers have been eliminated, the remaining choices may be considered. Sometimes identifying the clearly wrong answers will give the test taker some information about the correct answer. For instance, if one of the remaining answer choices is a direct opposite of one of the eliminated answer choices, it may well be the correct answer. The opposite of obviously wrong is obviously right! Of course, this is not always the case. Some answers are obviously incorrect simply because they are irrelevant to the question being asked. Still, identifying and eliminating some incorrect answer choices is a good way to simplify a multiple-choice question.

4. Don't Overanalyze

Anxious test takers often overanalyze questions. When you are nervous, your brain will often run wild, causing you to make associations and discover clues that don't actually exist. If you feel that this may be a problem for you, do whatever you can to slow down during the test. Try taking a deep breath or counting to ten. As you read and consider the question, restrict yourself to the particular words used by the author. Avoid thought tangents about what the author *really* meant, or what he or she was *trying* to say. The only things that matter on a multiple-choice test are the words that are actually in the question. You must avoid reading too much into a multiple-choice question, or supposing that the writer meant something other than what he or she wrote.

5. No Need for Panic

It is wise to learn as many strategies as possible before taking a multiple-choice test, but it is likely that you will come across a few questions for which you simply don't know the answer. In this situation, avoid panicking. Because most multiple-choice tests include dozens of questions, the relative value of a single wrong answer is small. As much as possible, you should compartmentalize each question on a multiple-choice test. In other words, you should not allow your feelings about one question to affect your success on the others. When you find a question that you either don't understand or don't know how to answer, just take a deep breath and do your best. Read the entire question slowly and carefully. Try rephrasing the question a couple of different ways. Then, read all of the answer choices carefully. After eliminating obviously wrong answers, make a selection and move on to the next question.

6. Confusing Answer Choices

When working on a difficult multiple-choice question, there may be a tendency to focus on the answer choices that are the easiest to understand. Many people, whether consciously or not, gravitate to the answer choices that require the least concentration, knowledge, and memory. This is a mistake. When you come across an answer choice that is confusing, you should give it extra attention. A question might be confusing because you do not know the subject matter to which it refers. If this is the case, don't eliminate the answer before you have affirmatively settled on another. When you come across an answer choice of this type, set it aside as you look at the remaining choices. If you can confidently assert that one of the other choices is correct, you can leave the confusing answer aside. Otherwise, you will need to take a moment to try to better understand the confusing answer choice. Rephrasing is one way to tease out the sense of a confusing answer choice.

7. Your First Instinct

Many people struggle with multiple-choice tests because they overthink the questions. If you have studied sufficiently for the test, you should be prepared to trust your first instinct once you have carefully and completely read the question and all of the answer choices. There is a great deal of research suggesting that the mind can come to the correct conclusion very quickly once it has obtained all of the relevant information. At times, it may seem to you as if your intuition is working faster even than your reasoning mind. This may in fact be true. The knowledge you obtain while studying may be retrieved from your subconscious before you have a chance to work out the associations that support it. Verify your instinct by working out the reasons that it should be trusted.

8. Key Words

Many test takers struggle with multiple-choice questions because they have poor reading comprehension skills. Quickly reading and understanding a multiple-choice question requires a mixture of skill and experience. To help with this, try jotting down a few key words and phrases on a piece of scrap paper. Doing this concentrates the process of reading and forces the mind to weigh the relative importance of the question's parts. In selecting words and phrases to write down, the test taker thinks about the question more deeply and carefully. This is especially true for multiple-choice questions that are preceded by a long prompt.

9. Subtle Negatives

One of the oldest tricks in the multiple-choice test writer's book is to subtly reverse the meaning of a question with a word like *not* or *except*. If you are not paying attention to each word in the question, you can easily be led astray by this trick. For instance, a common question format is, "Which of the following is...?" Obviously, if the question instead is, "Which of the following is not...?," then the answer will be quite different. Even worse, the test makers are aware of the potential for this mistake and will include one answer choice that would be correct if the question were not negated or reversed. A test taker who misses the reversal will find what he or she believes to be a correct answer and will be so confident that he or she will fail to reread the question and discover the original error. The only way to avoid this is to practice a wide variety of multiple-choice questions and to pay close attention to each and every word.

10. Reading Every Answer Choice

It may seem obvious, but you should always read every one of the answer choices! Too many test takers fall into the habit of scanning the question and assuming that they understand the question because they recognize a few key words. From there, they pick the first answer choice that answers the question they believe they have read. Test takers who read all of the answer choices might discover that one of the latter answer choices is actually *more* correct. Moreover, reading all of the answer choices can remind you of facts related to the question that can help you arrive at the correct answer. Sometimes, a misstatement or incorrect detail in one of the latter answer choices will trigger your memory of the subject and will enable you to find the right answer. Failing to read all of the answer choices is like not reading all of the items on a restaurant menu: you might miss out on the perfect choice.

11. Spot the Hedges

One of the keys to success on multiple-choice tests is paying close attention to every word. This is never truer than with words like almost, most, some, and sometimes. These words are called "hedges" because they indicate that a statement is not totally true or not true in every place and time. An absolute statement will contain no hedges, but in many subjects, the answers are not always straightforward or absolute. There are always exceptions to the rules in these subjects. For this reason, you should favor those multiple-choice questions that contain hedging language. The presence of qualifying words indicates that the author is taking special care with his or her words, which is certainly important when composing the right answer. After all, there are many ways to be wrong, but there is only one way to be right! For this reason, it is wise to avoid answers that are absolute when taking a multiple-choice test. An absolute answer is one that says things are either all one way or all another. They often include words like *every*, *always*, *best*, and *never*. If you are taking a multiple-choice test in a subject that doesn't lend itself to absolute answers, be on your guard if you see any of these words.

12. Long Answers

In many subject areas, the answers are not simple. As already mentioned, the right answer often requires hedges. Another common feature of the answers to a complex or subjective question are qualifying clauses, which are groups of words that subtly modify the meaning of the sentence. If the question or answer choice describes a rule to which there are exceptions or the subject matter is complicated, ambiguous, or confusing, the correct answer will require many words in order to be expressed clearly and accurately. In essence, you should not be deterred by answer choices that seem excessively long. Oftentimes, the author of the text will not be able to write the correct answer without offering some qualifications and modifications. Your job is to read the answer choices thoroughly and completely and to select the one that most accurately and precisely answers the question.

13. Restating to Understand

Sometimes, a question on a multiple-choice test is difficult not because of what it asks but because of how it is written. If this is the case, restate the question or answer choice in different words. This process serves a couple of important purposes. First, it forces you to concentrate on the core of the question. In order to rephrase the question accurately, you have to understand it well. Rephrasing the question will concentrate your mind on the key words and ideas. Second, it will present the information to your mind in a fresh way. This process may trigger your memory and render some useful scrap of information picked up while studying.

14. True Statements

Sometimes an answer choice will be true in itself, but it does not answer the question. This is one of the main reasons why it is essential to read the question carefully and completely before proceeding to the answer choices. Too often, test takers skip ahead to the answer choices and look for true statements. Having found one of these, they are content to select it without reference to the question above. Obviously, this provides an easy way for test makers to play tricks. The savvy test taker will always read the entire question before turning to the answer choices. Then, having settled on a correct answer choice, he or she will refer to the original question and ensure that the selected answer is relevant. The mistake of choosing a correct-but-irrelevant answer choice is especially common on questions related to specific pieces of objective knowledge. A prepared test taker will have a wealth of factual knowledge at his or her disposal, and should not be careless in its application.

15. No Patterns

One of the more dangerous ideas that circulates about multiple-choice tests is that the correct answers tend to fall into patterns. These erroneous ideas range from a belief that B and C are the most common right answers, to the idea that an unprepared test-taker should answer "A-B-A-C-A-D-A-B-A." It cannot be emphasized enough that pattern-seeking of this type is exactly the WRONG way to approach a multiple-choice test. To begin with, it is highly unlikely that the test maker will plot the correct answers according to some predetermined pattern. The questions are scrambled and delivered in a random order. Furthermore, even if the test maker was following a pattern in the assignation of correct answers, there is no reason why the test taker would know which pattern he or she was using. Any attempt to discern a pattern in the answer choices is a waste of time and a distraction from the real work of taking the test. A test taker would be much better served by extra preparation before the test than by reliance on a pattern in the answers.

FREE DVD OFFER

Don't forget that doing well on your exam includes both understanding the test content and understanding how to use what you know to do well on the test. We offer a completely FREE Test Taking Tips DVD that covers world class test taking tips that you can use to be even more successful when you are taking your test.

All that we ask is that you email us your feedback about your study guide. To get your **FREE Test Taking Tips DVD**, email freedvd@studyguideteam.com with "FREE DVD" in the subject line and the following information in the body of the email:

- The title of your study guide.
- Your product rating on a scale of 1-5, with 5 being the highest rating.
- Your feedback about the study guide. What did you think of it?
- Your full name and shipping address to send your free DVD.

Introduction to the CBEST

Function of the Test

The California Basic Educational Skills Test (CBEST) was created by the government of the state of California as a way for teacher candidates to demonstrate proficiency in reading, writing, and mathematics. Individuals applying for their first California teaching credential, applying for admission to certain teacher preparation and credentialing programs, or seeking employment in a California school district or educational agency must meet the California Basic Skills Requirement. The California legislature has established eight different ways to meet this requirement, such as achieving certain scores on various tests, one of which is to pass the CBEST. The state of Nevada has also adopted the CBEST as a way to meet certain Nevada licensing requirements.

CBEST scores are generally used only for California and Nevada teacher licensing, credentialing and hiring. In the 2014-2015 school year, 32,890 individuals took the CBEST for the first time. 22,847 of these first-time test takers passed, for a passing rate of 69.5%. The passing rate over the last five years has ranged from 69.5% to 71.4%. Of the three sections, reading and math are generally a bit easier to pass, with passing rates of around 80%, while writing is a bit more difficult, with a passing rate around 73%. (http://www.ctc.ca.gov/commission/agendas/2016-04/2016-04-5C.pdf).

Test Administration

The computer-based version of the CBEST is offered year-round by appointment, Monday through Saturday, excluding certain holidays, at Pearson VUE testing centers. The paper-based version is available on a more limited basis, usually around five times per school year. Individuals who do not pass must wait 45 days to attempt the CBEST again on computer, or may attempt the test again on any scheduled paper-administered test day.

All CBEST test sites are wheelchair-accessible. Individuals with documented disabilities may receive additional accommodations such as allowance of a medical device in the testing room, additional breaks, and use of tools such as a magnifying glass or straight edge. Individuals seeking such accommodation should complete and submit an Alternative Testing Arrangements Request Form along with appropriate documentation prior to their scheduled test date. The form must be submitted each time a student seeking accommodations takes the CBEST exam.

Test Format

A CBEST testing session will last four hours. Test takers may elect to take one, two, or all three of the sections offered. The reading section is made up of questions designed to assess the test takers ability to comprehend information in written passages, tables, and graphs. The mathematics section is primarily comprised of word problems to be solved without the use of a calculator. The writing section is composed of two essays, one in which the test taker is asked to analyze a given situation or statement and one in which the test taker is asked to describe a personal experience.

A summary of the content of the CBEST is as follows:

Section	Subsection	Approx # of Questions
Reading	Critical analysis and evaluation	20
	Comprehension and research skills	30
Mathematics	Estimation, measurement, and statistical principles	15
	Computation and problem solving	17
	Numerical and graphic relationships	17
Writing	Essay	2

Scoring

Scoring on the reading and math sections is done by calculating a raw score based on the number of correct answers with no penalty for guessing incorrectly and converting that raw score to a scaled score between 20 and 80. Similarly, the essays in the writing section are given a score between 1 and 4 by two readers for each of the two essays. The total raw score (between 4 and 16) is then converted to a scaled score between 20 and 80.

Test takers may pass the CBEST by *either* earning a scaled score on each section of at least 41, *or* earning a scaled score on each section of at least 37 and a total scaled score of at least 123. As discussed, the passing rate on individual sections ranges from the mid-70s to around 80%, and the overall passing rate hovers around 70%.

Reading

Critical Analysis and Evaluation

Comparison and Contrast

One writing device authors use is *comparison and contrast.* When authors take two objects and show how they are alike or similar, a comparison is being made. When authors take the same two objects and show how they differ, they are contrasting them. Comparison and contrast essays are most commonly written in nonfiction form. The Venn diagram below presents some of the common words or phrases used when comparing or contrasting objects.

Compare and Contrast Venn Diagram

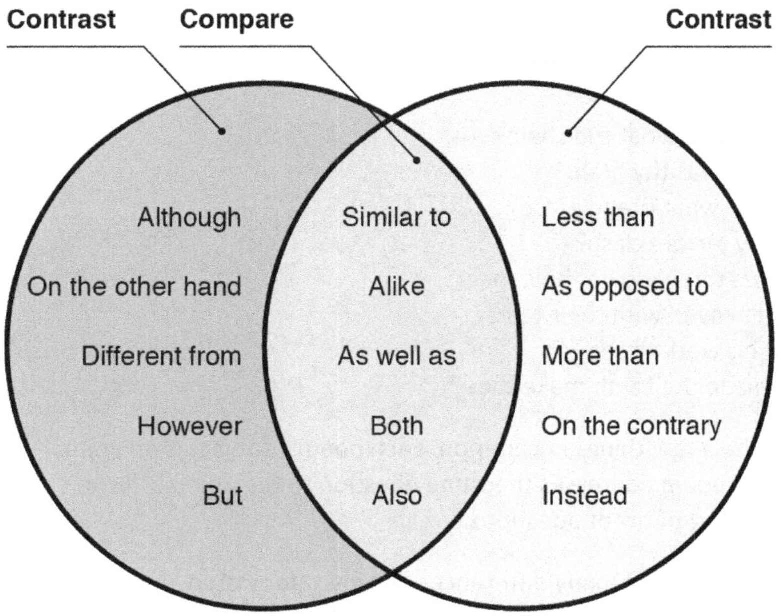

In order to understand the relationship between ideas, readers need to be able to *compare* and *contrast*. Comparing two things means identifying their similarities, while contrasting two things means finding their differences. Consider the following excerpt from "The Lamb" by William Blake:

> Little lamb, who made thee?
> Dost thou know who made thee,
> Gave thee life, and bid thee feed
> By the stream and o'er the mead;
> Gave thee clothing of delight,
> Softest clothing, woolly, bright;
> Gave thee such a tender voice,
> Making all the vales rejoice?
> Little lamb, who made thee?
> Dost thou know who made thee?

Consider that poem alongside an excerpt from another work by Blake called "The Tyger."

> Tyger! Tyger! burning bright
> In the forests of the night,
> What immortal hand or eye
> Could frame thy fearful symmetry?
> [...]
> What the hammer? what the chain?
> In what furnace was thy brain?
> What the anvil? what dread grasp
> Dare its deadly terrors clasp?
> When the stars threw down their spears,
> And watered heaven with their tears,
> Did he smile his work to see?
> Did he who made the Lamb make thee?

These poems have quite a few things in common. Each poem's subject is an animal—a lamb and a tiger, respectively—and each poem addresses the same question to the animal: "Who created you?" In fact, both poems are formed primarily of questions.

However, the poems also exhibit many differences. It's easy, for instance, to contrast the tone and word choice in each poem. Whereas "The Lamb" uses words with positive and gentle connotations to create a tone of innocence and serenity, "The Tyger" gives a completely different impression. Some strongly connotative words that stand out include "night," "fearful," and "deadly terrors," all of which contribute to a tone that's tense and full of danger.

When taken together, then, the two poems address the same question—who created the world and all of its creatures?—from two different perspectives. "The Lamb" considers all of the sweet and delightful things that exist, leaving "The Tyger" to ponder the problem of why evil exists. In fact, Blake relies on the contrast between the two poems to fully communicate his dilemma over the paradox of creation—"Did he who make the Lamb make thee?" Although the poems present a strong contrast to one another, it's also possible to find similarities in their subject matter.

Authors often intentionally use contrast in order to ask readers to delve deeper into the qualities of the two things being compared. When an author deliberately places two things (characters, settings, etc.)

side-by-side for readers to compare, it's known as *juxtaposition*. An example of juxtaposition can be found in Emily Bronte's *Wuthering Heights*, a novel in which the protagonist Cathy is caught in a love triangle between two romantic interests, Heathcliff and Edgar Linton, who are complete opposites. Cathy compares her feelings for each man in her memorable speech:

> *My love for Linton is like the foliage in the woods: time will change it, I'm well aware, as winter changes the trees. My love for Heathcliff resembles the eternal rocks beneath: a source of little visible delight, but necessary. Nelly, I* ***am*** *Heathcliff! He's always, always in my mind: not as a pleasure, any more than I am always a pleasure to myself, but as my own being.*

When these two characters are placed next to each other, it's easier for readers to grasp their notable characteristics. Edgar is gentle and sophisticated in comparison to Heathcliff, who is rough and wild. Here, Cathy also juxtaposes her feelings about each character. Her love for Edgar is fresh and harmless, like the new spring leaves on trees; but come winter, it will fade away. Her love for Heathcliff might be less conventionally appealing, like the rocks that form the earth; but, just like those rocks, that love forms the foundation of Cathy's being and is essential to her life. By juxtaposing these two men, Cathy is better able to express her thoughts about them.

Synthesize Information Across Multiple Sources

In any academic endeavor, it's essential to look to *many* sources of information to get a comprehensive and well-rounded view of the subject matter. Getting information from multiple texts, though, requires readers to synthesize their content—that is, to combine ideas from various sources and express it in an organized way.

In order to synthetize information, readers first need to understand the relationship between the different sources. One way to do so is comparing and contrasting, as described above. Comparison and contrast is also useful in evaluating non-literary sources. For example, if readers want to learn more about a controversial issue, they might decide to read articles from both sides of the argument, compare differences in the arguments on each side, and identify any areas of overlap or agreement. This will allow readers to arrive at a more balanced conclusion.

In addition to synthesizing information from persuasive sources with different opinions, readers can also combine information from different types of texts—for example, from entertaining and informative texts. Readers who are interested in medieval religious life in Europe, for instance, might read a text on medieval history by modern academics; a sociological research article about the role of religion in society; and a piece of literature from the Middle Ages such as Chaucer's *The Canterbury Tales*. By reading fiction written in that time period, readers can look at one writer's perspective on religious activities in their world; and by reading non-fiction texts by modern researchers, readers can further enhance their background knowledge of the subject.

Main Ideas and Supporting Details

Topics and main ideas are critical parts of writing. The **topic** is the subject matter of the piece. An example of a topic would be *the use of cell phones in a classroom*.

The **main idea** is what the writer wants to say about that topic. A writer may make the point that the use of cell phones in a classroom is a serious problem that must be addressed in order for students to learn better. Therefore, the topic is cell phone usage in a classroom, and the main idea is that it's *a* *serious problem needing to be addressed.* The topic can be expressed in a word or two, but the main idea should be a complete thought.

An author will likely identify the topic immediately within the title or the first sentence of the passage. The main idea is usually presented in the introduction. In a single passage, the main idea may be identified in the first or last sentence, but it will most likely be directly stated and easily recognized by the reader. Because it is not always stated immediately in a passage, it's important that readers carefully read the entire passage to identify the main idea.

The main idea should not be confused with the thesis statement. A **thesis statement** is a clear statement of the writer's specific stance and can often be found in the introduction of a nonfiction piece. The thesis is a specific sentence (or two) that offers the direction and focus of the discussion.

In order to illustrate the main idea, a writer will use **supporting details**, which provide evidence or examples to help make a point. Supporting details are typically found in nonfiction pieces that seek to inform or persuade the reader.

In the example of cell phone usage in the classroom, where the author's main idea is to show the seriousness of this problem and the need to "unplug", supporting details would be critical for effectively making that point. Supporting details used here might include statistics on a decline in student focus and studies showing the impact of digital technology usage on students' attention spans. The author could also include testimonies from teachers surveyed on the topic.

It's important that readers evaluate the author's supporting details to be sure that they are credible, provide evidence of the author's point, and directly support the main idea. Although shocking statistics grab readers' attention, their use may provide ineffective information in the piece. Details like this are crucial to understanding the passage and evaluating how well the author presents his or her argument and evidence.

Also remember that when most authors write, they want to make a point or send a message. This point or message of a text is known as the theme. Authors may state themes explicitly, like in *Aesop's Fables*. More often, especially in modern literature, readers must infer the theme based on text details. Usually after carefully reading and analyzing an entire text, the theme emerges. Typically, the longer the piece, the more themes you will encounter, though often one theme dominates the rest, as evidenced by the author's purposeful revisiting of it throughout the passage.

Author's Intent

No matter the genre or format, all authors are writing to persuade, inform, entertain, or express feelings. Often, these purposes are blended, with one dominating the rest. It's useful to learn to recognize the author's intent.

Persuasive writing is used to persuade or convince readers of something. It often contains two elements: the argument and the counterargument. The argument takes a stance on an issue, while the counterargument pokes holes in the opposition's stance. Authors rely on logic, emotion, and writer credibility to persuade readers to agree with them. If readers are opposed to the stance before reading, they are unlikely to adopt that stance. However, those who are undecided or committed to the same stance are more likely to agree with the author.

Informative writing tries to teach or inform. Workplace manuals, instructor lessons, statistical reports and cookbooks are examples of informative texts. Informative writing is usually based on facts and is often void of emotion and persuasion. Informative texts generally contain statistics, charts, and graphs. Though most informative texts lack a persuasive agenda, readers must examine the text carefully to determine whether one exists within a given passage.

Stories or narratives are designed to entertain. When you go to the movies, you often want to escape for a few hours, not necessarily to think critically. Entertaining writing is designed to delight and engage the reader. However, sometimes this type of writing can be woven into more serious materials, such as persuasive or informative writing to hook the reader before transitioning into a more scholarly discussion.

Emotional writing works to evoke the reader's feelings, such as anger, euphoria, or sadness. The connection between reader and author is an attempt to cause the reader to share the author's intended emotion or tone. Sometimes in order to make a piece more poignant, the author simply wants readers to feel the same emotions that the author has felt. Other times, the author attempts to persuade or manipulate the reader into adopting his stance. While it's okay to sympathize with the author, be aware of the individual's underlying intent.

Identifying Modes of Writing

Distinguishing Between Common Modes of Writing

To distinguish between the common modes of writing, it is important to identify the primary purpose of the work. This can be determined by considering what the author is trying to say to the reader. Although there are countless different styles of writing, all written works tend to fall under four primary categories: argumentative/persuasive, informative expository, descriptive, and narrative.

The table below highlights the purpose, distinct characteristics, and examples of each rhetorical mode.

Writing Mode	Purpose	Distinct Characteristics	Examples
Argumentative	To persuade	Opinions, loaded or subjective language, evidence, suggestions of what the reader should do, calls to action	Critical reviews Political journals Letters of recommendation Cover letters Advertising
Informative	To teach or inform	Objective language, definitions, instructions, factual information	Business and scientific reports Textbooks Instruction manuals News articles Personal letters Wills Informative essays Travel guides Study guides
Descriptive	To deliver sensory details to the reader	Heavy use of adjectives and imagery, language that appeals to any of the five senses	Poetry Journal entries Often used in narrative mode
Narrative	To tell a story, share an experience, entertain	Series of events, plot, characters, dialogue, conflict	Novels Short stories Novellas Anecdotes Biographies Epic poems Autobiographies

Identifying Common Types of Writing

The following steps help to identify examples of common types within the modes of writing:

1. Identifying the audience—to whom or for whom the author is writing
2. Determining the author's purpose—why the author is writing the piece
3. Analyzing the word choices and how they are used

To demonstrate, the following passage has been marked to illustrate *the addressee*, the author's purpose, and word choices:

> *To Whom It May Concern*:
>
> I am extraordinarily excited to be applying to the Master of Environmental Science program at Australian National University. I believe the richness in biological and cultural diversity, as well as Australia's close proximity to the Great Barrier Reef, would provide a deeply fulfilling

educational experience. *I am writing to express why I believe I would be an excellent addition to the program.*

While in college, I participated in a three-month public health internship in Ecuador, where I spent time both learning about medicine in a third world country and also about the Ecuadorian environment, including the Amazon Jungle and the Galápagos Islands. My favorite experience through the internship, besides swimming with sea lions in San Cristóbal, was helping to neutralize parasitic potable water and collect samples for analysis in Puyo.

Though my undergraduate studies related primarily to the human body, I took several courses in natural science, including a year of chemistry, biology, and physics as well as a course in a calculus. I am confident that my fundamental knowledge in these fields will prepare me for the science courses integral to the Masters of Environmental Science.

Having identified the *addressee*, it is evident that this selection is a letter of some kind. Further inspection into the author's purpose, seen in *bold*, shows that the author is trying to explain why he or she should be accepted into the environmental science program, which automatically places it into the argumentative mode as the writer is trying to persuade the reader to agree and to incite the reader into action by encouraging the program to accept the writer as a candidate. In addition to revealing the purpose, the use of emotional language—extraordinarily, excellent, deeply fulfilling, favorite experience, confident—illustrates that this is a persuasive piece. It also provides evidence for why this person would be an excellent addition to the program—his/her experience in Ecuador and with scientific curriculum.

The following passage presents an opportunity to solidify this method of analysis and practice the steps above to determine the mode of writing:

The biological effects of laughter have long been an interest of medicine and psychology. Laughing is often speculated to reduce blood pressure because it induces feelings of relaxation and elation. Participating students watched a series of videos that elicited laughter, and their blood pressure was taken before and after the viewings. An average decrease in blood pressure was observed, though resulting p-values attest that the results were not significant.

This selection contains factual and scientific information, is devoid of any adjectives or flowery descriptions, and is not trying to convince the reader of any particular stance. Though the audience is not directly addressed, the purpose of the passage is to present the results of an experiment to those who would be interested in the biological effects of laughter—most likely a scientific community. Thus, this passage is an example of informative writing.

Below is another passage to help identify examples of the common writing modes, taken from *The Endeavor Journal of Sir Joseph Banks*:

10th May 1769 – THE ENGLISH CREW GET TAHITIAN NAMES

We have now got the Indian name of the Island, Otahite, so therefore for the future I shall call it. As for our own names the Indians find so much dificulty in pronouncing them that we are forcd to indulge them in calling us what they please, or rather what they say when they attempt to pronounce them. I give here the List: Captn Cooke *Toote*, Dr Solander *Torano*, Mr Hicks *Hete*, Mr Gore *Toárro*, Mr Molineux *Boba* from his Christian name Robert, Mr Monkhouse *Mato*, and myself *Tapáne*. In this manner they have names for almost every man in the ship.

This extract contains no elements of an informative or persuasive intent and does not seem to follow any particular line of narrative. The passage gives a list of the different names that the Indians have given the crew members, as well as the name of an island. Although there is no context for the selection, through the descriptions, it is clear that the author and his comrades are on an island trying to communicate with the native inhabitants. Hence, this passage is a journal that reflects the descriptive mode.

These are only a few of the many examples that can be found in the four primary modes of writing.

Determining the Appropriate Mode of Writing

The author's *primary purpose* is defined as the reason an author chooses to write a selection, and it is often dependent on his or her *audience*. A biologist writing a textbook, for example, does so to communicate scientific knowledge to an audience of people who want to study biology. An audience can be as broad as the entire global population or as specific as women fighting for equal rights in the bicycle repair industry. Whatever the audience, it is important that the author considers its demographics—age, gender, culture, language, education level, etc.

If the author's purpose is to persuade or inform, he or she will consider how much the intended audience knows about the subject. For example, if an author is writing on the importance of recycling to anyone who will listen, he or she will use the informative mode—including background information on recycling—and the argumentative mode—evidence for why it works, while also using simple diction so that it is easy for everyone to understand. If, on the other hand, the writer is proposing new methods for recycling using solar energy, the audience is probably already familiar with standard recycling processes and will require less background information, as well as more technical language inherent to the scientific community.

If the author's purpose is to entertain through a story or a poem, he or she will need to consider whom he/she is trying to entertain. If an author is writing a script for a children's cartoon, the plot, language, conflict, characters, and humor would align with the interests of the age demographic of that audience. On the other hand, if an author is trying to entertain adults, he or she may write content not suitable for children. The author's purpose and audience are generally interdependent.

Understanding the Task, Purpose, and Audience

Identifying the Task, Purpose, and Intended Audience

An author's *writing style*—the way in which words, grammar, punctuation, and sentence fluidity are used—is the most influential element in a piece of writing, and it is dependent on the purpose and the audience for whom it is intended. Together, a writing style and mode of writing form the foundation of a written work, and a good writer will choose the most effective mode and style to convey a message to readers.

Writers should first determine what they are trying to say and then choose the most effective mode of writing to communicate that message. Different writing modes and *word choices* will affect the tone of a piece—that is, its underlying attitude, emotion, or character. The argumentative mode may utilize words that are earnest, angry, passionate, or excited whereas an informative piece may have a sterile, germane, or enthusiastic tone. The tones found in narratives vary greatly, depending on the purpose of the writing. *Tone* will also be affected by the audience—teaching science to children or those who may be uninterested would be most effective with enthusiastic language and exclamation points whereas teaching science to college students may take on a more serious and professional tone, with fewer charged words and punctuation choices that are inherent to academia.

Sentence fluidity—whether sentences are long and rhythmic or short and succinct—also affects a piece of writing as it determines the way in which a piece is read. Children or audiences unfamiliar with a subject do better with short, succinct sentence structures as these break difficult concepts up into shorter points. A period, question mark, or exclamation point is literally a signal for the reader to stop and takes more time to process. Thus, longer, more complex sentences are more appropriate for adults or educated audiences as they can fit more information in between processing time.

The amount of *supporting detail* provided is also tailored to the audience. A text that introduces a new subject to its readers will focus more on broad ideas without going into greater detail whereas a text that focuses on a more specific subject is likely to provide greater detail about the ideas discussed.

Writing styles, like modes, are most effective when tailored to their audiences. Having awareness of an audience's demographic is one of the most crucial aspects of properly communicating an argument, a story, or a set of information.

Choosing the Most Appropriate Type of Writing

Before beginning any writing, it is imperative that a writer have a firm grasp on the message he or she wishes to convey and how he or she wants readers to be affected by the writing. For example, does the author want readers to be more informed about the subject? Does the writer want readers to agree with his or her opinion? Does the writer want readers to get caught up in an exciting narrative? The following steps are a guide to determining the appropriate type of writing for a task, purpose, and audience:

1. Identifying the purpose for writing the piece
2. Determining the audience
3. Adapting the writing mode, word choices, tone, and style to fit the audience and the purpose

It is important to distinguish between a work's purpose and its main idea. The essential difference between the two is that the *main idea* is what the author wants to communicate about the topic at hand whereas the *primary purpose* is why the author is writing in the first place. The primary purpose is what will determine the type of writing an author will choose to utilize, not the main idea, though the two are related. For example, if an author writes an article on the mistreatment of animals in factory farms and, at the end, suggests that people should convert to vegetarianism, the main idea is that vegetarianism would reduce the poor treatment of animals. The primary purpose is to convince the reader to stop eating animals. Since the primary purpose is to galvanize an audience into action, the author would choose the argumentative writing mode.

The next step is to consider to whom the author is appealing as this will determine the type of details to be included, the diction to be used, the tone to be employed, and the sentence structure to be used. An audience can be identified by considering the following questions:

- What is the purpose for writing the piece?
- To whom is it being written?
- What is their age range?
- Are they familiar with the material being presented, or are they just being newly introduced to it?
- Where are they from?
- Is the task at hand in a professional or casual setting?
- Is the task at hand for monetary gain?

These are just a few of the numerous considerations to keep in mind, but the main idea is to become as familiar with the audience as possible. Once the audience has been understood, the author can then adapt the writing style to align with the readers' education and interests. The audience is what determines the *rhetorical appeal* the author will use—ethos, pathos, or logos. *Ethos* is a rhetorical appeal to an audience's ethics and/or morals. Ethos is most often used in argumentative and informative writing modes. *Pathos* is an appeal to the audience's emotions and sympathies, and it is found in argumentative, descriptive, and narrative writing modes. *Logos* is an appeal to the audience's logic and reason and is used primarily in informative texts as well as in supporting details for argumentative pieces. Rhetorical appeals are discussed in depth in the informational texts and rhetoric section of the test.

If the author is trying to encourage global conversion to vegetarianism, he or she may choose to use all three rhetorical appeals to reach varying personality types. Those who are less interested in the welfare of animals but are interested in facts and science would relate more to logos. Animal lovers would relate better to an emotional appeal. In general, the most effective works utilize all three appeals.

Finally, after determining the writing mode and rhetorical appeal, the author will consider word choice, sentence structure, and tone, depending on the purpose and audience. The author may choose words that convey sadness or anger when speaking about animal welfare if writing to persuade, or he or she will stick to dispassionate and matter-of-fact tones, if informing the public on the treatment of animals in factory farms. If the author is writing to a younger or less-educated audience, he or she may choose to shorten and simplify sentence structures and word choice. If appealing to an audience with more expert knowledge on a particular subject, writers will more likely employ a style of longer sentences and more complex vocabulary.

Depending on the task, the author may choose to use a first person, second person, or third person point of view. First person and second person perspectives are inherently more casual in tone, including the author and the reader in the rhetoric, while third person perspectives are often seen in more professional settings.

Evaluating the Effectiveness of a Piece of Writing

An effective and engaging piece of writing will cause the reader to forget about the author entirely. Readers will become so engrossed in the subject, argument, or story at hand that they will almost identify with it, readily adopting beliefs proposed by the author or accepting all elements of the story as believable. On the contrary, poorly written works will cause the reader to be hyperaware of the author, doubting the writer's knowledge of a subject or questioning the validity of a narrative. Persuasive or expository works that are poorly researched will have this effect, as well as poorly planned stories with significant plot holes. An author must consider the task, purpose, and audience to sculpt a piece of writing effectively.

When evaluating the effectiveness of a piece, the most important thing to consider is how well the purpose is conveyed to the audience through the mode, use of rhetoric, and writing style.

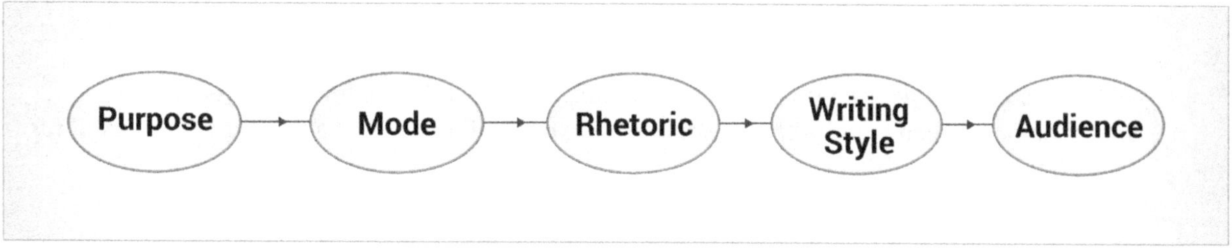

The purpose must pass through these three aspects for effective delivery to the audience. If any elements are not properly considered, the reader will be overly aware of the author, and the message will be lost. The following is a checklist for evaluating the effectiveness of a piece:

- Does the writer choose the appropriate writing mode—argumentative, narrative, descriptive, informative—for his or her purpose?
- Does the writing mode employed contain characteristics inherent to that mode?
- Does the writer consider the personalities/interests/demographics of the intended audience when choosing rhetorical appeals?
- Does the writer use appropriate vocabulary, sentence structure, voice, and tone for the audience demographic?
- Does the author properly establish himself/herself as having authority on the subject, if applicable?
- Does the piece make sense?

Another thing to consider is the medium in which the piece was written. If the medium is a blog, diary, or personal letter, the author may adopt a more casual stance towards the audience. If the piece of writing is a story in a book, a business letter or report, or a published article in a journal or if the task is to gain money or support or to get published, the author may adopt a more formal stance. Ultimately, the writer will want to be very careful in how he or she addresses the reader.

Finally, the effectiveness of a piece can be evaluated by asking how well the purpose was achieved. For example, if students are assigned to read a persuasive essay, instructors can ask whether the author influences students' opinions. Students may be assigned two differing persuasive texts with opposing perspectives and be asked which writer was more convincing. Students can then evaluate what factors contributed to this—for example, whether one author uses more credible supporting facts, appeals more effectively to readers' emotions, presents more believable personal anecdotes, or offers stronger counterargument refutation. Students can then use these evaluations to strengthen their own writing skills.

Inferences in a Text

Readers should be able to make *inferences*. Making an inference requires the reader to read between the lines and look for what is *implied* rather than what is directly stated. That is, using information that is known from the text, the reader is able to make a logical assumption about information that is *not* directly stated but is probably true. Read the following passage:

> "Hey, do you wanna meet my new puppy?" Jonathan asked.
>
> "Oh, I'm sorry but please don't—" Jacinta began to protest, but before she could finish, Jonathan had already opened the passenger side door of his car and a perfect white ball of fur came bouncing towards Jacinta.
>
> "Isn't he the cutest?" beamed Jonathan.
>
> "Yes—achoo!—he's pretty—aaaachooo!!—adora—aaa—aaaachoo!" Jacinta managed to say in between sneezes. "But if you don't mind, I—I—achoo!—need to go inside."

Which of the following can be inferred from Jacinta's reaction to the puppy?

a. she hates animals
b. she is allergic to dogs
c. she prefers cats to dogs
d. she is angry at Jonathan

An inference requires the reader to consider the information presented and then form their own idea about what is probably true. Based on the details in the passage, what is the best answer to the question? Important details to pay attention to include the tone of Jacinta's dialogue, which is overall polite and apologetic, as well as her reaction itself, which is a long string of sneezes. Answer choices (a) and (d) both express strong emotions ("hates" and "angry") that are not evident in Jacinta's speech or actions. Answer choice (c) mentions cats, but there is nothing in the passage to indicate Jacinta's feelings about cats. Answer choice (b), "she is allergic to dogs," is the most logical choice—based on the fact that she began sneezing as soon as a fluffy dog approached her, it makes sense to guess that Jacinta might be allergic to dogs. So even though Jacinta never directly states, "Sorry, I'm allergic to dogs!" using the clues in the passage, it is still reasonable to guess that this is true.

Making inferences is crucial for readers of literature because literary texts often avoid presenting complete and direct information to readers about characters' thoughts or feelings, or they present this information in an unclear way, leaving it up to the reader to interpret clues given in the text. In order to make inferences while reading, readers should ask themselves:

- What details are being presented in the text?
- Is there any important information that seems to be missing?
- Based on the information that the author *does* include, what else is probably true?
- Is this inference reasonable based on what is already known?

Apply Information

A natural extension of being able to make an inference from a given set of information is also being able to apply that information to a new context. This is especially useful in non-fiction or informative writing. Considering the facts and details presented in the text, readers should consider how the same information might be relevant in a different situation. The following is an example of applying an inferential conclusion to a different context:

> Often, individuals behave differently in large groups than they do as individuals. One example of this is the psychological phenomenon known as the bystander effect. According to the bystander effect, the more people who witness an accident or crime occur, the less likely each individual bystander is to respond or offer assistance to the victim. A classic example of this is the murder of Kitty Genovese in New York City in the 1960s. Although there were over thirty witnesses to her killing by a stabber, none of them intervened to help Kitty or contact the police.

Considering the phenomenon of the bystander effect, what would probably happen if somebody tripped on the stairs in a crowded subway station?

a. Everybody would stop to help the person who tripped
b. Bystanders would point and laugh at the person who tripped
c. Someone would call the police after walking away from the station
d. Few if any bystanders would offer assistance to the person who tripped

This question asks readers to apply the information they learned from the passage, which is an informative paragraph about the bystander effect. According to the passage, this is a concept in psychology that describes the way people in groups respond to an accident—the more people are present, the less likely any one person is to intervene. While the passage illustrates this effect with the example of a woman's murder, the question asks readers to apply it to a different context—in this case, someone falling down the stairs in front of many subway passengers. Although this specific situation is not discussed in the passage, readers should be able to apply the general concepts described in the paragraph. The definition of the bystander effect includes any instance of an accident or crime in front of a large group of people. The question asks about a situation that falls within the same definition, so the general concept should still hold true: in the midst of a large crowd, few individuals are likely to actually respond to an accident. In this case, answer choice (d) is the best response.

Identifying the Position and Purpose

When it comes to authors' writings, readers should always identify a position or stance. No matter how objective a piece may seem, assume the author has preconceived beliefs. Reduce the likelihood of accepting an invalid argument by looking for multiple articles on the topic, including those with varying opinions. If several opinions point in the same direction, and are backed by reputable peer-reviewed sources, it's more likely the author has a valid argument. Positions that run contrary to widely held beliefs and existing data should invite scrutiny. There are exceptions to the rule, so be a careful consumer of information.

Though themes, symbols, and motifs are buried deep within the text and can sometimes be difficult to infer, an author's purpose is usually obvious from the beginning. There are four purposes of writing: to inform, to persuade, to describe, and to entertain. Informative writings present facts in an accessible way. Persuasive writing appeals to emotions and logic to inspire the reader to adopt a specific stance. Be wary of this type of writing, as it often lacks objectivity. Descriptive writing is designed to paint a picture in the reader's mind, while writings that entertain are often narratives designed to engage and delight the reader.

The various writing styles are usually blended, with one purpose dominating the rest. For example, a persuasive piece might begin with a humorous tale to make readers more receptive to the persuasive message, or a recipe in a cookbook designed to inform might be preceded by an entertaining anecdote that makes the recipe more appealing.

Writing Devices

Authors use a variety of writing devices throughout texts. Below is a list of some writing devices authors use in their writing.

- Comparison and Contrast
- Cause and Effect
- Analogy
- Point of View
- Transitional Words and Phrases

Let's look at each device individually.

Comparison and Contrast

One writing device authors use is comparison and contrast. Comparison is when authors take objects and show how they are the same. Contrast is when authors take objects and show how they differ. Comparison and contrast essays are mostly written in nonfiction form. There are common words used when authors compare or contrast. The list below will show you some of these words:

Comparison Words:

- Similar to
- Alike
- As well as
- Both

Contrast Words:

- Although
- On the other hand
- Different from
- However
- As opposed to
- More than
- Less than
- On the contrary

Cause and Effect

Cause and effect is a common writing device. A cause is why something happens. An effect is something that happens because of the cause. Many times, authors use key words to show cause and effect, such as *because, so, therefore, without, now, then,* and *since*. For example: "Because of the sun shower, a rainbow appeared." In this sentence, due to the sun shower (the cause), a rainbow appeared (the effect).

Analogy

An analogyis a comparison between two things. Sometimes the two things are very different from one another. Authors often use analogiesto add meaning and make ideas relatable in texts. There are two types of analogies: metaphors and similes. Metaphors compare two things that are not similar. Similes also compare two unlike things but use the words *like* or *as*. For example, "In the library, students are asked to be as quiet as a mouse." Clearly, students and mice are very different. However, when students are asked to be as quiet as a mouse, readers understand that they are being asked to be absolutely silent.

Point of View

Point of view is the viewpoint in which authors tell stories. Authors usually tell stories in either the first or third person. If an author writes in the first person, they are a character within a story telling about their own experiences. The pronouns *I* and *we* are used when writing in the first person. If an author writes in the third person, the narrator is telling the story from an outside perspective. The author is not a character in the story, but rather tells about the characters' actions and dialogues. Pronouns such as *he, she, it,* and *they* are used in texts written in the third person. Point of view will be addressed in more detail in a subsequent section.

Transitional Words and Phrases

There are approximately 200 transitional words and phrases that are commonly used in the English language. Below are lists of common transition words and phrases.

Time	**Example**	**Compare**	**Contrast**	**Addition**	**Logical Relationships**	**Steps**
After	for example	likewise	however	and	if	first
before	in fact	also	yet	also	then	second
during	for instance		but	furthermore	therefore	last
in the middle				moreover	as a result	
					since	

Transitional words and phrases are important writing devices. They connect sentences and paragraphs. Transitional words and phrases help writing to make more sense. They provide clearer meaning to readers.

Understanding the Effect of Word Choice

An author's choice of words—also referred to as *diction*—helps to convey his or her meaning in a particular way. Through diction, an author can convey a particular tone—e.g., a humorous tone, a serious tone—in order to support the thesis in a meaningful way to the reader.

Connotation and Denotation

Connotation is when an author chooses words or phrases that invoke ideas or feelings other than their literal meaning. An example of the use of connotation is the word *cheap*, which suggests something is poor in value or negatively describes a person as reluctant to spend money. When something or someone is described this way, the reader is more inclined to have a particular image or feeling about it or him/her. Thus, connotation can be a very effective language tool in creating emotion and swaying opinion. However, connotations are sometimes hard to pin down because varying emotions can be associated with a word. Generally, though, connotative meanings tend to be fairly consistent within a specific cultural group.

Denotation refers to words or phrases that mean exactly what they say. It is helpful when a writer wants to present hard facts or vocabulary terms with which readers may be unfamiliar. Some examples of denotation are the words *inexpensive* and *frugal*. *Inexpensive* refers to the cost of something, not its value, and *frugal* indicates that a person is conscientiously watching his or her spending. These terms do not elicit the same emotions that *cheap* does. Authors sometimes choose to use both, but what they choose and when they use it is what critical readers need to differentiate. One method isn't inherently better than the other; however, one may create a better effect, depending upon an author's intent. If, for example, an author's purpose is to inform, to instruct, and to familiarize readers with a difficult subject, his or her use of connotation may be helpful. However, it may also undermine credibility and confuse readers. An author who wants to create a credible, scholarly effect in his or her text would most likely use denotation, which emphasizes literal, factual meaning and examples.

Technical Language

Test takers and critical readers alike should be very aware of technical language used within informational text. *Technical language* refers to terminology that is specific to a particular industry and is best understood by those specializing in that industry. This language is fairly easy to differentiate, since it will most likely be unfamiliar to readers. It's critical to be able to define technical language either by the author's written definition, through the use of an included glossary—if offered—or through context clues that help readers clarify word meaning.

Identifying Rhetorical Strategies

Rhetoric refers to an author's use of particular strategies, appeals, and devices to persuade an intended audience. The more effective the use of rhetoric, the more likely the audience will be persuaded.

Determining an Author's Point of View

A *rhetorical strategy*—also referred to as a *rhetorical mode*—is the structural way an author chooses to present his/her argument. Though the terms noted below are similar to the organizational structures noted earlier, these strategies do not imply that the entire text follows the approach. For example, a cause and effect organizational structure is solely that, nothing more. A persuasive text may use cause and effect as a strategy to convey a singular point. Thus, an argument may include several of the strategies as the author strives to convince his or her audience to take action or accept a different point of view. It's important that readers are able to identify an author's thesis and position on the topic in order to be able to identify the careful construction through which the author speaks to the reader. The following are some of the more common rhetorical strategies:

- *Cause and effect*—establishing a logical correlation or causation between two ideas
- *Classification/division*—the grouping of similar items together or division of something into parts
- *Comparison/contrast*—the distinguishing of similarities/differences to expand on an idea
- *Definition*—used to clarify abstract ideas, unfamiliar concepts, or to distinguish one idea from another
- *Description*—use of vivid imagery, active verbs, and clear adjectives to explain ideas

- *Exemplification*—the use of examples to explain an idea
- *Narration*—anecdotes or personal experience to present or expand on a concept
- *Problem/Solution*—presentation of a problem or problems, followed by proposed solution(s)

Rhetorical Strategies and Devices

A *rhetorical device* is the phrasing and presentation of an idea that reinforces and emphasizes a point in an argument. A rhetorical device is often quite memorable. One of the more famous uses of a rhetorical device is in John F. Kennedy's 1961 inaugural address: "Ask not what your country can do for you, ask what you can do for your country." The contrast of ideas presented in the phrasing is an example of the rhetorical device of antimetabole. Some other common examples are provided below, but test takers should be aware that this is not a complete list.

Device	Definition	Example
Allusion	A reference to a famous person, event, or significant literary text as a form of significant comparison	"We are apt to shut our eyes against a painful truth, and listen to the song of that siren till she transforms us into beasts." Patrick Henry
Anaphora	The repetition of the same words at the beginning of successive words, phrases, or clauses, designed to emphasize an idea	"We shall not flag or fail. We shall go on to the end. We shall fight in France, we shall fight on the seas and oceans, we shall fight with growing confidence ... we shall fight in the fields and in the streets, we shall fight in the hills. We shall never surrender." Winston Churchill
Understatement	A statement meant to portray a situation as less important than it actually is to create an ironic effect	"The war in the Pacific has not necessarily developed in Japan's favor." Emperor Hirohito, surrendering Japan in World War II
Parallelism	A syntactical similarity in a structure or series of structures used for impact of an idea, making it memorable	"A penny saved is a penny earned." Ben Franklin
Rhetorical question	A question posed that is not answered by the writer though there is a desired response, most often designed to emphasize a point	"Can anyone look at our reduced standing in the world today and say, 'Let's have four more years of this?'" Ronald Reagan

Understanding Methods Used to Appeal to a Specific Audience

Rhetorical Appeals

In an argument or persuasive text, an author will strive to sway readers to an opinion or conclusion. To be effective, an author must consider his or her intended audience. Although an author may write text for a general audience, he or she will use methods of appeal or persuasion to convince that audience. Aristotle asserted that there were three methods or modes by which a person could be persuaded. These are referred to as *rhetorical appeals*.

The three main types of rhetorical appeals are shown in the following graphic.

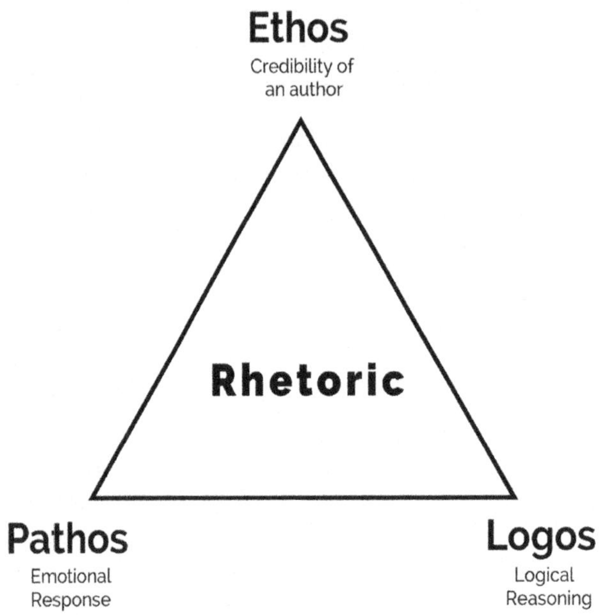

Ethos, also referred to as an *ethical appeal*, is an appeal to the audience's perception of the writer as credible (or not), based on their examination of their ethics and who the writer is, his/her experience or incorporation of relevant information, or his/her argument. For example, authors may present testimonials to bolster their arguments. The reader who critically examines the veracity of the testimonials and the credibility of those giving the testimony will be able to determine if the author's use of testimony is valid to his or her argument. In turn, this will help the reader determine if the author's thesis is valid. An author's careful and appropriate use of technical language can create an overall knowledgeable effect and, in turn, act as a convincing vehicle when it comes to credibility. Overuse of technical language, however, may create confusion in readers and obscure an author's overall intent.

Pathos, also referred to as a *pathetic* or *emotional appeal*, is an appeal to the audience's sense of identity, self-interest, or emotions. A critical reader will notice when the author is appealing to pathos through anecdotes and descriptions that elicit an emotion such as anger or pity. Readers should also beware of factual information that uses generalization to appeal to the emotions. While it's tempting to believe an author is the source of truth in his or her text, an author who presents factual information as universally true, consistent throughout time, and common to all groups is using *generalization*. Authors who exclusively use generalizations without specific facts and credible sourcing are attempting to sway readers solely through emotion.

Logos, also referred to as a *logical appeal*, is an appeal to the audience's ability to see and understand the logic in a claim offered by the writer. A critical reader has to be able to evaluate an author's arguments for validity of reasoning and for sufficiency when it comes to argument.

Counterarguments and Evaluating Arguments

If an author presents a differing opinion or a counterargument in order to refute it, the reader should consider how and why this information is being presented. It is meant to strengthen the original argument and shouldn't be confused with the author's intended conclusion, but it should also be considered in the reader's final evaluation.

Authors can also use bias if they ignore the opposing viewpoint or present their side in an unbalanced way. A strong argument considers the opposition and finds a way to refute it. Critical readers should look for an unfair or one-sided presentation of the argument and be skeptical, as a bias may be present. Even if this bias is unintentional, if it exists in the writing, the reader should be wary of the validity of the argument. Readers should also look for the use of stereotypes, which refer to specific groups. Stereotypes are often negative connotations about a person or place, and should always be avoided. When a critical reader finds stereotypes in a piece of writing, they should be critical of the argument, and consider the validity of anything the author presents. Stereotypes reveal a flaw in the writer's thinking and may suggest a lack of knowledge or understanding about the subject.

In general, readers should always heed attention to whether an author's ideas or stated facts are relevant to the argument or counterargument posed in the reading. Those that are irrelevant can cloud the argument or weaken it. In much the same way, critical readers are able to identify whether statements in a reading strengthen or weaken the author's argument.

Authors want you to accept their assertions and arguments as true but critical readers evaluate the strength of the argument instead of simply taking it at face value and accepting it as the truth or only point of view. All arguments need two parts: the claim and the supporting evidence or rationale. The claim *is* the argument. It asserts an opinion, idea, point of view, or conclusion. The supporting evidence is the rationale, assumptions, beliefs, as well as the factual evidence in support of the stated claim. The supporting evidence is what gives readers the information necessary to accept or reject the stated claim. Critical readers should assess the argument in its entirety by evaluating the claims and conclusions themselves, the process of reasoning, and the accuracy of the evidence. For example, arguments are weaker and should be skeptically considered when the supporting evidence is highly opinionated, biased, or derived from sources that are not credible. Authors should cite where statistics and other stated facts were found. Lastly, the support for a claim should be pertinent to it and consistent with the other statements and evidence.

Opinions, Facts, and Fallacies

As mentioned previously, authors write with a purpose. They adjust their writing for an intended audience. It is the readers' responsibility to comprehend the writing style or purpose of the author. When readers understand a writer's purpose, they can then form their own thoughts about the text(s) regardless of whether their thoughts are the same as or different from the author's. The following section will examine different writing tactics that authors use, such as facts versus opinions, bias and stereotypes, appealing to the readers' emotions, and fallacies (including false analogies, circular reasoning, false dichotomy, and overgeneralization).

Facts Versus Opinions

Readers need to be aware of the writer's purpose to help discern facts and opinions within texts. A *fact* is a piece of information that is true. It can either prove or disprove claims or arguments presented in texts. Facts cannot be changed or altered. For example, the statement: *Abraham Lincoln was assassinated on April 15, 1865*, is a fact. The date and related events cannot be altered.

Authors not only present facts in their writing to support or disprove their claim(s), but they may also express their opinions. Authors may use factsto support their own opinions, especially in a persuasive text; however, that does not make their opinions facts. An *opinion* is a belief or view formed about something that is not necessarily based on the truth. Opinions often express authors' personal feelings about a subject and use words like *believe, think,* or *feel.* For example, the statement: *Abraham Lincoln was the best president who has ever lived*, expresses the writer's opinion. Not all writers or readers agree or disagree with the statement. Therefore, the statement can be altered or adjusted to express opposing or supporting beliefs, such as "Abraham Lincoln was the worst president who has ever lived" or "I also think Abraham Lincoln was a great president."

When authors include facts and opinions in their writing, readers may be less influenced by the text(s). Readers need to be conscious of the distinction between facts and opinions while going through texts. Not only should the intended audience be vigilant in following authors' thoughts versus valid information, readers need to check the source of the facts presented. Facts should have reliable sources derived from credible outlets like almanacs, encyclopedias, medical journals, and so on.

Bias and Stereotypes

Not only can authors state facts or opinions in their writing, they sometimes intentionally or unintentionally show bias or portray a stereotype. A *bias* is when someone demonstrates a prejudice in favor of or against something or someone in an unfair manner. When an author is biased in his or her writing, readers should be skeptical despite the fact that the author's bias may be correct. For example, two athletes competed for the same position. One athlete is related to the coach and is a mediocre athlete, while the other player excels and deserves the position. The coach chose the less talented player who is related to him for the position. This is a biased decision because it favors someone in an unfair way.

Similar to a bias, a *stereotype* shows favoritism or opposition but toward a specific group or place. Stereotypes create an oversimplified or overgeneralized idea about a certain group, person, or place. For example,

> Women are horrible drivers.

This statement basically labels *all* women as horrible drivers. While there may be some terrible female drivers, the stereotype implies that *all* women are bad drivers when, in fact, not *all* women are. While many readers are aware of several vile ethnic, religious, and cultural stereotypes, audiences should be cautious of authors' flawed assumptions because they can be less obvious than the despicable examples that are unfortunately pervasive in society.

Appealing to the Readers' Emotions

Authors write to captivate the attention of their readers. Oftentimes, authors will appeal to their readers' emotions to convince or persuade their audience, especially in when trying to win weak arguments that lack factual evidence. Authors may tell sob stories or use bandwagon approaches in their writing to tap into the readers' emotions. For example, "Everyone is voting yes" or "He only has two months to live" are statements that can tug at the heartstrings of readers. Authors may use other tactics, such as name-calling or advertising, to lead their readers into believing something is true or false. These emotional pleas are clear signs that the authors do not have a favorable point and that they are trying to distract the readers from the fact that their argument is factually weak.

Fallacies

A fallacy is a mistaken belief or faulty reasoning, otherwise known as a *logical fallacy.* It is important for readers to recognize logical fallacies because they discredit the author's message. Readers should continuously self-question as they go through a text to identify logical fallacies. Readers cannot simply complacently take information at face value. There are six common types of logical *fallacies:*

1. False analogy
2. Circular reasoning
3. False dichotomy
4. Overgeneralization
5. Slippery slope
6. Hasty generalization

Each of the six logical fallacies are reviewed individually.

False Analogy

A *false analogy* is when the author assumes two objects or events are alike in all aspects despite the fact that they may be vastly different. Authors intend on making unfamiliar objects relatable to convince readers of something. For example, the letters *A* and *E* are both vowels; therefore, *A* = *E*. Readers cannot assume that because *A* and *E* are both vowels that they perform the same function in words or independently. If authors tell readers, *A* = *E*, then that is a false analogy. While this is a simple example, other false analogies may be less obvious.

Circular reasoning

Circular reasoning is when the reasoning is decided based upon the outcome or conclusion and then vice versa. Basically, those who use circular reasoning start out with the argument and then use false logic to try to prove it, and then, in turn, the reasoning supports the conclusion in one big circular pattern. For example, consider the two thoughts, "I don't have time to get organized" and "My disorganization is costing me time." Which is the argument? What is the conclusion? If there is not time to get organized, will more time be spent later trying to find whatever is needed? In turn, if so much time is spent looking for things, there is not time to get organized. The cycle keeps going in an endless series. One problem affects the other; therefore, there is a circular pattern of reasoning.

False dichotomy

A *false dichotomy,* also known as a false dilemma, is when the author tries to make readers believe that there are only two options to choose from when, in fact, there are more. The author creates a false sense of the situation because he or she wants the readers to believe that his or her claim is the most logical choice. If the author does not present the readers with options, then the author is purposefully limiting what readers may believe. In turn, the author hopes that readers will believe that his or her point of view is the most sensible choice. For example, in the statement: *you either love running, or you are lazy*, the fallacy lies in the options of loving to run or being lazy. Even though both statements do not necessarily have to be true, the author tries to make one option seem more appealing than the other.

Overgeneralization

An *overgeneralization* is a logical fallacy that occurs when authors write something so extreme that it cannot be proved or disproved. Words like *all, never, most,* and *few* are commonly used when an overgeneralization is being made. For example,

> All kids are crazy when they eat sugar; therefore, my son will not have a cupcake at the birthday party.

Not *all* kids are crazy when they eat sugar, but the extreme statement can influence the readers' points of view on the subject. Readers need to be wary of overgeneralizations in texts because authors may try to sneak them in to sway the readers' opinions.

Slippery slope

A *slippery slope* is when an author implies that something will inevitably happen as a result of another action. A slippery slope may or may not be true, even though the order of events or gradations may seem logical. For example, in the children's book *If You Give a Mouse a Cookie*, the author goes off on tangents such as "If you give a mouse a cookie, he will ask for some milk. When you give him the milk, he'll probably ask you for a straw." The mouse in the story follows a series of logical events as a result of a previous action. The slippery slope continues on and on throughout the story. Even though the mouse made logical decisions, it very well could have made a different choice, changing the direction of the story.

Hasty generalization

A *hasty generalization* is when the reader comes to a conclusion without reviewing or analyzing all the evidence. It is never a good idea to make a decision without all the information, which is why hasty generalizations are considered fallacies. For example, if two friends go to a hairdresser and give the hairdresser a positive recommendation, that does not necessarily mean that a new client will have the same experience. Two referrals is not quite enough information to form an educated and well-formed conclusion.

Overall, readers should carefully review and analyze authors' arguments to identify logical fallacies and come to sensible conclusions.

Drawing Conclusions

When drawing conclusions about texts or passages, readers should do two main things: 1) Use the information that they already know and 2) Use the information they have learned from the text or passage. Authors write with an intended purpose, and it is the readers' responsibility to understand and form logical conclusions of authors' ideas. It is important to remember that the readers' conclusions should be supported by information directly from the text. Readers cannot simply form conclusions based off of only information they already know.

There are several ways readers can draw conclusions from authors' ideas and points to consider when doing so, such as text evidence, text credibility, and directly stated information versus implications.

Text Evidence

Text evidence is the information readers find in a text or passage that supports the main idea or point(s) in a story. In turn, text evidence can help readers draw conclusions about the text or passage. The information should be taken directly from the text or passage and placed in quotation marks. Text evidence provides readers with information to support ideas about the text or passage so that they simply do not just rely on their own thoughts. Details should be precise, descriptive, and factual. Statistics are a great piece of text evidencebecause it provides readers with exact numbers and not just a generalization. For example, instead of saying "Asia has a larger population than Europe," authors could provide detailed information such as "In Asia there are over 7 billion people, whereas in Europe there are a little over 750 million." More definitive information provides better evidence to readers to help support their conclusions about texts or passages.

Text Credibility

Credible sources are important when drawing conclusions because readers need to be able to trust what they are reading. Authors should always use credible sources to help gain the trust of their readers. A text is *credible* when it is believable and the author is objective and unbiased. If readers do not trust authors' words, they may simply dismiss the text completely. For example, if an author writes a persuasive essay, he or she is outwardly trying to sway readers' opinions to align with his or her own, providing readers with the liberty to do what they please with the text. Readers may agree or disagree with the author, which may, in turn, lead them to believe that the author is credible or not credible. Also, readers should keep in mind the source of the text. If readers review a journal about astronomy, would a more reliable source be a NASA employee or a plumber? Overall, text credibility is important when drawing conclusions because readers want reliable sources that support the decisions they have made about the author's ideas.

Directly Stated Information Versus Implications

Engaged readers should constantly self-question while reviewing texts to help them form conclusions. Self-questioning is when readers review a paragraph, page, passage, or chapter and ask themselves, "Did I understand what I read?," "What was the main event in this section?," "Where is this taking place?," and so on. Authors can provide clues or pieces of evidence throughout a text or passage to guide readers toward a conclusion. This is why active and engaged readers should read the text or passage in its entirety before forming a definitive conclusion. If readers do not gather all the necessary pieces of evidence, then they may jump to an illogical conclusion.

At times, authors directly state conclusions while others simply imply them. Of course, it is easier if authors outwardly provide conclusions to readers because this does not leave any information open to interpretation. However, implications are things that authors do not directly state but can be assumed based off of information they provided. If authors only imply what may have happened, readers can form a menagerie of ideas for conclusions. For example, in the statement: *Once we heard the sirens, we hunkered down in the storm shelter*, the author does not directly state that there was a tornado, but clues such as "sirens" and "storm shelter" provide insight to the readers to help form that conclusion.

Style, Tone, and Mood

Style, tone, and mood are often thought to be the same thing. Though they're closely related, there are important differences to keep in mind. The easiest way to do this is to remember that style "creates and affects" tone and mood. More specifically, style is how the writer uses words to create the desired tone and mood for their writing.

Style

Style can include any number of technical writing choices. A few examples of style choices include:

- Sentence Construction: When presenting facts, does the writer use shorter sentences to create a quicker sense of the supporting evidence, or do they use longer sentences to elaborate and explain the information?

- Technical Language: Does the writer use jargon to demonstrate their expertise in the subject, or do they use ordinary language to help the reader understand things in simple terms?

- Formal Language: Does the writer refrain from using contractions such as *won't* or *can't* to create a more formal tone, or do they use a colloquial, conversational style to connect to the reader?

- Formatting: Does the writer use a series of shorter paragraphs to help the reader follow a line of argument, or do they use longer paragraphs to examine an issue in great detail and demonstrate their knowledge of the topic?

On the test, examine the writer's style and how their writing choices affect the way the text comes across.

Tone

Tone refers to the writer's attitude toward the subject matter. Tone is usually explained in terms of a work of fiction. For example, the tone conveys how the writer feels about their characters and the situations in which they're involved. Nonfiction writing is sometimes thought to have no tone at all; however, this is incorrect.

A lot of nonfiction writing has a neutral tone, which is an important tone for the writer to take. A neutral tone demonstrates that the writer is presenting a topic impartially and letting the information speak for itself. On the other hand, nonfiction writing can be just as effective and appropriate if the tone isn't neutral. For instance, take this example involving seat belts:

> Seat belts save more lives than any other automobile safety feature. Many studies show that airbags save lives as well; however, not all cars have airbags. For instance, some older cars don't. Furthermore, air bags aren't entirely reliable. For example, studies show that in 15% of accidents airbags don't deploy as designed, but, on the other hand, seat belt malfunctions are extremely rare. The number of highway fatalities has plummeted since laws requiring seat belt usage were enacted.

In this passage, the writer mostly chooses to retain a neutral tone when presenting information. If the writer would instead include their own personal experience of losing a friend or family member in a car accident, the tone would change dramatically. The tone would no longer be neutral and would show that the writer has a personal stake in the content, allowing them to interpret the information in a different way. When analyzing tone, consider what the writer is trying to achieve in the text and how they *create* the tone using style.

Mood

Mood refers to the feelings and atmosphere that the writer's words create for the reader. Like tone, many nonfiction texts can have a neutral mood. To return to the previous example, if the writer would choose to include information about a person they know being killed in a car accident, the text would suddenly carry an emotional component that is absent in the previous example. Depending on how they present the information, the writer can create a sad, angry, or even hopeful mood. When analyzing the mood, consider what the writer wants to accomplish and whether the best choice was made to achieve that end.

Point of View

As mentioned, point of view is an important writing device to consider. In fiction writing, point of view refers to who tells the story or from whose perspective readers are observing as they read. In non-fiction writing, the *point of view* refers to whether the author refers to himself/herself, his/her readers, or chooses not to mention either. Whether fiction or nonfiction, the author will carefully consider the impact the perspective will have on the purpose and main point of the writing.

- *First-person point of view*: The story is told from the writer's perspective. In fiction, this would mean that the main character is also the narrator. First-person point of view is easily recognized by the use of personal pronouns such as *I*, *me*, *we*, *us*, *our*, *my*, and *myself.*
- *Third-person point of view*: In a more formal essay, this would be an appropriate perspective because the focus should be on the subject matter, not the writer or the reader. Third-person point of view is recognized by the use of the pronouns *he*, *she*, *they*, and *it*. In fiction writing, third person point of view has a few variations.
- *Third-person limited* point of view refers to a story told by a narrator who has access to the thoughts and feelings of just one character.
- In *third-person omniscient* point of view, the narrator has access to the thoughts and feelings of all the characters.
- In *third-person objective* point of view, the narrator is like a fly on the wall and can see and hear what the characters do and say, but does not have access to their thoughts and feelings.
- *Second-person point of view*: This point of view isn't commonly used in fiction or non-fiction writing because it directly addresses the reader using the pronouns *you*, *your*, and *yourself.* Second-person perspective is more appropriate in direct communication, such as business letters or emails.

Point of View	**Pronouns Used**
First person	I, me, we, us, our, my, myself
Second person	You, your, yourself
Third person	He, she, it, they

Consistency

Whatever style, tone, point of view, and mood the writer uses, good writing should remain consistent throughout. If the writer chooses to include the tragic, personal experience above, it would affect the style, tone, and mood of the entire text. It would seem out of place for such an example to be used in the middle of a neutral, measured, and analytical text. To adjust the rest of the text, the writer needs to make additional choices to remain consistent. For example, the writer might decide to use the word *tragedy* in place of the more neutral *fatality*, or they could describe a series of car-related deaths as an *epidemic*. Adverbs and adjectives such as *devastating* or *horribly* could be included to maintain this consistent attitude toward the content. When analyzing writing, look for sudden shifts in style, tone, and mood, and consider whether the writer would be wiser to maintain the prevailing strategy.

Comprehension and Context

Topic Versus the Main Idea

It is very important to know the difference between the topic and the main idea of the text. Even though these two are similar because they both present the central point of a text, they have distinctive differences. A *topic* is the subject of the text; it can usually be described in a one- to two-word phrase and appears in the simplest form. On the other hand, the *main idea* is more detailed and provides the author's central point of the text. It can be expressed through a complete sentence and is often found in the beginning, middle, or end of a paragraph. In most nonfiction books, the first sentence of the passage usually (but not always) states the main idea. Review the passage below to explore the topic versus the main idea.

Cheetahs

> *Cheetahs are one of the fastest mammals on the land, reaching up to 70 miles an hour over short distances. Even though cheetahs can run as fast as 70 miles an hour, they usually only have to run half that speed to catch up with their choice of prey. Cheetahs cannot maintain a fast pace over long periods of time because their bodies will overheat. After a chase, cheetahs need to rest for approximately 30 minutes prior to eating or returning to any other activity.*

In the example above, the topic of the passage is "Cheetahs" simply because that is the subject of the text. The main idea of the text is "Cheetahs are one of the fastest mammals on the land but can only maintain a fast pace for shorter distances." While it covers the topic, it is more detailed and refers to the text in its entirety. The text continues to provide additional details called *supporting details,* which will be discussed in the next section.

Supporting Details

Supporting details help readers better develop and understand the main idea. Supporting details answer questions like *who, what, where, when, why,* and *how*. Different types of supporting details include examples, facts and statistics, anecdotes, and sensory details.

Persuasive and informative texts often use supporting details. In persuasive texts, authors attempt to make readers agree with their points of view, and supporting details are often used as "selling points." If authors make a statement, they need to support the statement with evidence in order to adequately persuade readers. Informative texts use supporting details such as examples and facts to inform readers. Review the previous "Cheetahs" passage to find examples of supporting details.

Cheetahs

> *Cheetahs are one of the fastest mammals on the land, reaching up to 70 miles an hour over short distances. Even though cheetahs can run as fast as 70 miles an hour, they usually only have to run half that speed to catch up with their choice of prey. Cheetahs cannot maintain a fast pace over long periods of time because their bodies will overheat. After a chase, cheetahs need to rest for approximately 30 minutes prior to eating or returning to any other activity.*

In the example, supporting details include:

1. Cheetahs reach up to 70 miles per hour over short distances.
2. They usually only have to run half that speed to catch up with their prey.
3. Cheetahs will overheat if they exert a high speed over longer distances.
4. Cheetahs need to rest for 30 minutes after a chase.

Look at the diagram below (applying the cheetah example) to help determine the hierarchy of topic, main idea, and supporting details.

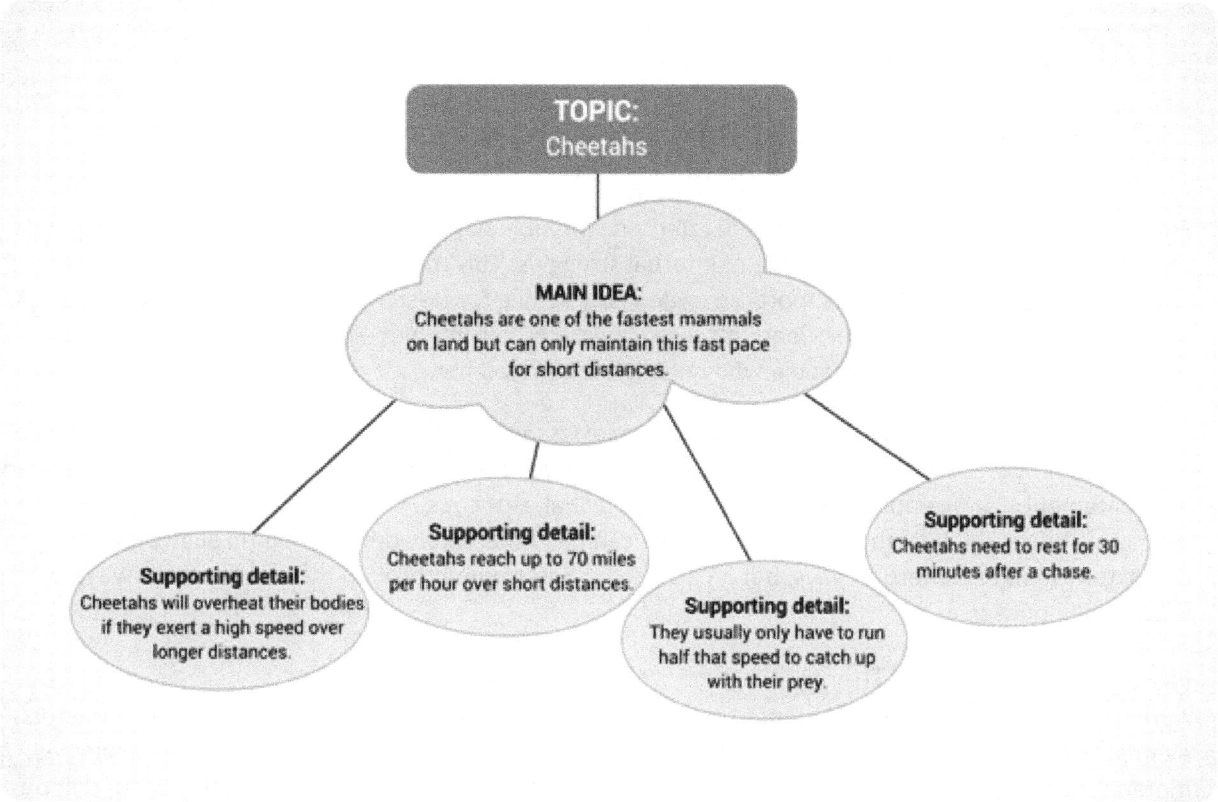

Understanding the Development of Themes

Identifying Theme or Central Message

The *theme* is the central message of a fictional work, whether that work is structured as prose, drama, or poetry. It is the heart of what an author is trying to say to readers through the writing, and theme is largely conveyed through literary elements and techniques.

In literature, a theme can often be determined by considering the over-arching narrative conflict within the work.

Though there are several types of conflicts and several potential themes within them, the following are the most common:

- *Individual against the self*—relevant to themes of self-awareness, internal struggles, pride, coming of age, facing reality, fate, free will, vanity, loss of innocence, loneliness, isolation, fulfillment, failure, and disillusionment
- *Individual against nature*— relevant to themes of knowledge vs. ignorance, nature as beauty, quest for discovery, self-preservation, chaos and order, circle of life, death, and destruction of beauty
- *Individual against society*— relevant to themes of power, beauty, good, evil, war, class struggle, totalitarianism, role of men/women, wealth, corruption, change vs. tradition, capitalism, destruction, heroism, injustice, and racism
- *Individual against another individual*— relevant to themes of hope, loss of love or hope, sacrifice, power, revenge, betrayal, and honor

For example, in Hawthorne's *The Scarlet Letter*, one possible narrative conflict could be the individual against the self, with a relevant theme of internal struggles. This theme is alluded to through characterization—Dimmesdale's moral struggle with his love for Hester and Hester's internal struggles with the truth and her daughter, Pearl. It's also alluded to through plot—Dimmesdale's suicide and Hester helping the very townspeople who initially condemned her.

Sometimes, a text can convey a *message* or *universal lesson*—a truth or insight that the reader infers from the text, based on analysis of the literary and/or poetic elements. This message is often presented as a statement. For example, a potential message in Shakespeare's *Hamlet* could be "Revenge is what ultimately drives the human soul." This message can be immediately determined through plot and characterization in numerous ways, but it can also be determined through the setting of Norway, which is bordering on war.

How Authors Develop Theme

Authors employ a variety of techniques to present a theme. They may compare or contrast characters, events, places, ideas, or historical or invented settings to speak thematically. They may use analogies, metaphors, similes, allusions, or other literary devices to convey the theme. An author's use of diction, syntax, and tone can also help convey the theme. Authors will often develop themes through the development of characters, use of the setting, repetition of ideas, use of symbols, and through contrasting value systems. Authors of both fiction and nonfiction genres will use a variety of these techniques to develop one or more themes.

Regardless of the literary genre, there are commonalities in how authors, playwrights, and poets develop themes or central ideas.

Authors often do research, the results of which contributes to theme. In prose fiction and drama, this research may include real historical information about the setting the author has chosen or include elements that make fictional characters, settings, and plots seem realistic to the reader. In nonfiction, research is critical since the information contained within this literature must be accurate and, moreover, accurately represented.

In fiction, authors presen[illegible]t that will contribute to the overall theme. In fiction, this conflict may involve the sto[illegible]me trouble within characters that needs resolution. In nonfiction, this conflict may b[illegible]planation or commentary on factual people and events.

Authors will sometimes use character motivation to convey theme, such as in the example from *Hamlet* regarding revenge. In fiction, the characters an author creates will think, speak, and act in ways that effectively convey the theme to readers. In nonfiction, the characters are factual, as in a biography, but authors pay particular attention to presenting those motivations to make them clear to readers.

Authors also use literary devices as a means of conveying theme. For example, the use of moon symbolism in Mary Shelley's *Frankenstein* is significant as its phases can be compared to the phases that the Creature undergoes as he struggles with his identity.

The selected point of view can also contribute to a work's theme. The use of first-person point of view in a fiction or non-fiction work engages the reader's response differently than third person point of view. The central idea or theme from a first-person narrative may differ from a third-person limited text.

In literary nonfiction, authors usually identify the purpose of their writing, which differs from fiction, where the general purpose is to entertain. The purpose of nonfiction is usually to inform, persuade, or entertain the audience. The stated purpose of a non-fiction text will drive how the central message or theme, if applicable, is presented.

Authors identify an audience for their writing, which is critical in shaping the theme of the work. For example, the audience for J.K. Rowling's *Harry Potter* series would be different than the audience for a biography of George Washington. The audience an author chooses to address is closely tied to the purpose of the work. The choice of an audience also drives the choice of language and level of diction an author uses. Ultimately, the intended audience determines the level to which that subject matter is presented and the complexity of the theme.

Summarizing and Paraphrasing a Passage

As an aid to drawing conclusions, outlining the information contained in the passage should be a familiar skill to readers. An effective outline will reveal the structure of the passage and will lead to solid conclusions. An effective outline will have a title that refers to the basic subject of the text though the title needs not recapitulate the main idea. In most outlines, the main idea will be the first major section. Each major idea of the passage will be established as the head of a category. For instance, the most common outline format calls for the main ideas of the passage to be indicated with Roman numerals. In an effective outline of this kind, each of the main ideas will be represented by a Roman numeral and none of the Roman numerals will designate minor details or secondary ideas. Moreover, all supporting ideas and details should be placed in the appropriate place on the outline. An outline does not need to include every detail listed in the text, but the outline should feature all of those that are central to the argument or message. Each of these details should be listed under the appropriate main idea.

Ideas from a text can also be organized using graphic organizers. A graphic organizer is a way to simplify information and take key points from the text. A graphic organizer such as a timeline may have an event listed for a corresponding date on the timeline while an outline may have an event listed under a key point that occurs in the text. Each reader needs to create the type of graphic organizer that works the best for him or her in terms of being able to recall information from a story. Examples include a *spider-map,* which takes a main idea from the story and places it in a bubble with supporting points branching off the main idea. An *outline* is useful for diagramming the main and supporting points of the entire story, and a *Venn diagram* classifies information as separate or overlapping.

A helpful tool is the ability to summarize the information that you have read in a paragraph or passage format. This process is similar to creating an effective outline. First, a summary should accurately define the main idea of the passage though the summary does not need to explain this main idea in exhaustive detail. The summary should continue by laying out the most important supporting details or arguments from the passage. All of the significant supporting details should be included, and none of the details included should be irrelevant or insignificant. Also, the summary should accurately report all of these details. Too often, the desire for brevity in a summary leads to the sacrifice of clarity or accuracy. Summaries are often difficult to read because they omit all of the graceful language, digressions, and asides that distinguish great writing. However, an effective summary should contain much the same message as the original text.

Paraphrasing is another method that the reader can use to aid in comprehension. When paraphrasing, one puts what they have read into their words by rephrasing what the author has written, or one "translates" all of what the author shared into their words by including as many details as they can.

Outlining

As mentioned, an *outline* is a system used to organize writing. When reading texts, outlining is important because it helps readers organize important information in a logical pattern using Roman numerals. Usually, outlines start out with the main idea(s) and then branch out into subgroups or subsidiary thoughts or subjects. Not only do outlines provide a visual tool for readers to reflect on how events, characters, settings, or other key parts of the text or passage relate to one another, but they can also lead readers to a stronger conclusion. The sample below demonstrates what a general outline looks like.

I. Main Topic 1
    a. Subtopic 1
    b. Subtopic 2
        1. Detail 1
        2. Detail 2
II. Main Topic 2
    a. Subtopic 1
    b. Subtopic 2
        1. Detail 1
        2. Detail 2

Summarizing

At the end of a text or passage, it is important to summarize what the readers read. *Summarizing* is a strategy in which readers determine what is important throughout the text or passage, shorten those ideas, and rewrite or retell it in their own words. A summary should identify the main idea of the text or passage. Important details or supportive evidence should also be accurately reported in the summary. If writers provide irrelevant details in the summary, it may cloud the greater meaning of the text or passage. When summarizing, writers should not include their opinions, quotes, or what they thought the author should have said. A clear summary provides clarity of the text or passage to the readers.

The following checklist lists items that writers should include in a summary:

Summary Checklist

1. Title of the story
2. Someone: Who is or are the main character(s)?
3. Wanted: What did the character(s) want?
4. But: What was the problem?
5. So: How did the character(s) solve the problem?
6. Then: How did the story end? What was the resolution?

Paraphrasing

Another strategy readers can use to help them fully comprehend a text or passage is *paraphrasing.* Paraphrasing is when readers take the author's words and put them into their own words. When readers and writers paraphrase, they need to avoid copying the text—that is plagiarism. It is also important to include as many details as possible when restating the facts. Not only will this help readers and writers recall information, but by putting the information into their own words, they demonstrate if they fully comprehend the text or passage. The example below shows an original text and how to paraphrase it.

> *Original Text: Fenway Park is home to the beloved Boston Red Sox. The stadium opened on April 20, 1912. The stadium currently seats over 37,000 fans, many of whom travel from all over the country to experience the iconic team and nostalgia of Fenway Park.*
>
> *Paraphrased: On April 20, 1912, Fenway Park opened. Home to the Boston Red Sox, the stadium now seats over 37,000 fans. Many spectators travel to watch the Red Sox and experience the spirit of Fenway Park.*

Paraphrasing, summarizing, and quoting can often cross paths with one another. The chart below shows the similarities and differences between the three strategies:

PARAPHRASING	SUMMARIZING	QUOTING
Uses own words	Puts main ideas into own words	Uses words that are identical to text
References original source	References original source	Requires quotation marks
Uses own sentences	Shows important ideas of source	Uses author's words and ideas

Identifying Logical Conclusions

Determining conclusions requires being an active reader, as a reader must make a prediction and analyze facts to identify a conclusion. A reader should identify key words in a passage to determine the logical conclusion or determination that flows from the information presented. Consider the passage below:

> Lindsay, covered in flour, moved around the kitchen frantically. Her mom yelled from another room, "Lindsay, we're going to be late!

You can conclude that Lindsay's next steps are to finish baking, clean herself up, and head off somewhere with her baked goods. Notice that the conclusion cannot be verified factually. Many conclusions are not spelled out specifically in the text, thus they have to be identified and drawn out by the reader.

Context Clues

Context clues help readers understand unfamiliar words, and thankfully, there are many types.

Synonyms are words or phrases that have nearly, if not exactly, the same meaning as other words or phrases

> *Large* boxes are needed to pack *big* items.

Antonyms are words or phrases that have opposite definitions. Antonyms, like synonyms, can serve as context clues, although more cryptically.

> *Large* boxes are not needed to pack *small* items.

Definitions are sometimes included within a sentence to define uncommon words.

> They practiced the *rumba*, a *type of dance*, for hours on end.

Explanations provide context through elaboration.

> Large boxes holding items weighing over 60 pounds were stacked in the corner.

Here's an example of *contrast*:

> These *minute* creatures were much different than the *huge* mammals that the zoologist was accustomed to dealing with.

Understanding the Use of Affixes, Context, and Syntax

Affixes

Individual words are constructed from building blocks of meaning. An *affix* is an element that is added to a root or stem word that can change the word's meaning.

For example, the stem word *fix* is a verb meaning *to repair*. When the ending *–able* is added, it becomes the adjective *fixable*, meaning "capable of being repaired." Adding *un–* to the beginning changes the word to *unfixable*, meaning "incapable of being repaired." In this way, affixes attach to the word stem to create a new word and a new meaning. Knowledge of affixes can assist in deciphering the meaning of unfamiliar words.

Affixes are also related to inflection. *Inflection* is the modification of a base word to express a different grammatical or syntactical function. For example, countable nouns such as *car* and *airport* become plural with the addition of *–s* at the end: *cars* and *airports*.

Verb tense is also expressed through inflection. *Regular verbs*—those that follow a standard inflection pattern—can be changed to past tense using the affixes *–ed*, *–d*, or *–ied*, as in *cooked* and *studied*. Verbs can also be modified for continuous tenses by using *–ing*, as in *working* or *exploring*. Thus, affixes are used not only to express meaning but also to reflect a word's grammatical purpose.

A *prefix* is an affix attached to the beginning of a word. The meanings of English prefixes mainly come from Greek and Latin origins. The chart below contains a few of the most commonly used English prefixes.

Prefix	**Meaning**	**Example**
a-	Not	amoral, asymptomatic
anti-	Against	antidote, antifreeze
auto-	Self	automobile, automatic
circum-	Around	circumference, circumspect
co-, com-, con-	Together	coworker, companion
contra-	Against	contradict, contrary
de-	negation or reversal	deflate, deodorant
extra-	outside, beyond	extraterrestrial, extracurricular
in-, im-, il-, ir-	Not	impossible, irregular
inter-	Between	international, intervene
intra-	Within	intramural, intranet
mis-	Wrongly	mistake, misunderstand
mono-	One	monolith, monopoly
non-	Not	nonpartisan, nonsense
pre-	Before	preview, prediction
re-	Again	review, renew
semi-	Half	semicircle, semicolon
sub-	Under	subway, submarine
super-	Above	superhuman, superintendent
trans-	across, beyond, through	trans-Siberian, transform
un-	Not	unwelcome, unfriendly

While the addition of a prefix alters the meaning of the base word, the addition of a *suffix* may also affect a word's part of speech. For example, adding a suffix can change the noun *material* into the verb *materialize* and back to a noun again in *materialization*.

Suffix	Part of Speech	Meaning	Example
-able, -ible	adjective	having the ability to	honorable, flexible
-acy, -cy	noun	state or quality	intimacy, dependency
-al, -ical	adjective	having the quality of	historical, tribal
-en	verb	to cause to become	strengthen, embolden
-er, -ier	adjective	comparative	happier, longer
-est, -iest	adjective	superlative	sunniest, hottest
-ess	noun	female	waitress, actress
-ful	adjective	full of, characterized by	beautiful, thankful
-fy, -if[illegible]	verb	to cause, to come to be	liquefy, intensify
-is[illegible]	noun	doctrine, belief, action	Communism, Buddhism
-ive, [illegible]	adjective	having the quality of	creative, innovative
-ize	verb	to convert into, to subject to	Americanize, dramatize
-less	adjective	without, missing	emotionless, hopeless
-ly	adverb	in the manner of	quickly, energetically
-ness	noun	quality or state	goodness, darkness
-ous, -ious, -eous	adjective	having the quality of	spontaneous, pious
-ship	noun	status or condition	partnership, ownership
-tion	noun	action or state	renovation, promotion
-y	adjective	characterized by	smoky, dreamy

Through knowledge of prefixes and suffixes, a student's vocabulary can be instantly expanded with an understanding of *etymology*—the origin of words. This, in turn, can be used to add sentence structure variety to academic writing.

Context Clues

Familiarity with common prefixes, suffixes, and root words assists tremendously in unraveling the meaning of an unfamiliar word and making an educated guess as to its meaning. However, some words do not contain many easily-identifiable clues that point to their meaning. In this case, rather than looking at the elements within the word, it is useful to consider elements around the word—i.e., its context. *Context* refers to the other words and information within the sentence or surrounding sentences that indicate the unknown word's probable meaning. The following sentences provide context for the potentially-unfamiliar word *quixotic*:

> Rebecca had never been one to settle into a predictable, ordinary life. Her quixotic personality led her to leave behind a job with a prestigious law firm in Manhattan and move halfway around the world to pursue her dream of becoming a sushi chef in Tokyo.

A reader unfamiliar with the word *quixotic* doesn't have many clues to use in terms of affixes or root meaning. The suffix *–ic* indicates that the word is an adjective, but that is it. In this case, then, a reader would need to look at surrounding information to obtain some clues about the word. Other adjectives in the passage include *predictable* and *ordinary*, things that Rebecca was definitely not, as indicated by

"Rebecca had never been one to settle." Thus, a first clue might be that *quixotic* means the opposite of predictable.

The second sentence doesn't offer any other modifier of *personality* other than *quixotic*, but it does include a story that reveals further information about her personality. She had a stable, respectable job, but she decided to give it up to follow her dream. Combining these two ideas together, then—unpredictable and dream-seeking—gives the reader a general idea of what *quixotic* probably means. In fact, the root of the word is the character Don Quixote, a romantic dreamer who goes on an impulsive adventure.

While context clues are useful for making an approximate definition for newly-encountered words, these types of clues also come in handy when encountering common words that have multiple meanings. The word *reservation* is used differently in each the following sentences:

A. That restaurant is booked solid for the next month; it's impossible to make a reservation unless you know somebody.

B. The hospital plans to open a branch office inside the reservation to better serve Native American patients who cannot easily travel to the main hospital fifty miles away.

C. Janet Clark is a dependable, knowledgeable worker, and I recommend her for the position of team leader without reservation.

All three sentences use the word to express different meanings. In fact, most words in English have more than one meaning—sometimes meanings that are completely different from one another. Thus, context can provide clues as to which meaning is appropriate in a given situation. A quick search in the dictionary reveals several possible meanings for *reservation*:

1. An exception or qualification
2. A tract of public land set aside, such as for the use of American Indian tribes
3. An arrangement for accommodations, such as in a hotel, on a plane, or at a restaurant

Sentence A mentions a restaurant, making the third definition the correct one in this case. In sentence B, some context clues include Native Americans, as well as the implication that a reservation is a place—"inside the reservation," both of which indicate that the second definition should be used here. Finally, sentence C uses *without reservation* to mean "completely" or "without exception," so the first definition can be applied here.

Using context clues in this way can be especially useful for words that have multiple, widely varying meanings. If a word has more than one definition and two of those definitions are the opposite of each other, it is known as an *auto-antonym*—a word that can also be its own antonym. In the case of auto-antonyms, context clues are crucial to determine which definition to employ in a given sentence. For example, the word *sanction* can either mean "to approve or allow" or "a penalty." Approving and penalizing have opposite meanings, so *sanction* is an example of an auto-antonym.

The following sentences reflect the distinction in meaning:

A. In response to North Korea's latest nuclear weapons test, world leaders have called for harsher sanctions to punish the country for its actions.

B. The general has sanctioned a withdrawal of troops from the area.

A context clue can be found in sentence A, which mentions "to punish." A punishment is similar to a penalty, so sentence A is using the word *sanction* according to this definition.

Other examples of auto-antonyms include *oversight*—"to supervise something" or "a missed detail"), *resign*—"to quit" or "to sign again, as a contract," and *screen*—"to show" or "to conceal." For these types of words, recognizing context clues is an important way to avoid misinterpreting the sentence's meaning.

Syntax

Syntax refers to the arrangement of words, phrases, and clauses to form a sentence. Knowledge of syntax can also give insight into a word's meaning. The section above considered several examples using the word *reservation* and applied context clues to determine the word's appropriate meaning in each sentence. Here is an example of how the placement of a word can impact its meaning and grammatical function:

> A. The development team has reserved the conference room for today.
>
> B. Her quiet and reserved nature is sometimes misinterpreted as unfriendliness when people first meet her.

In addition to using *reserved* to mean different things, each sentence also uses the word to serve a different grammatical function. In sentence A, *reserved* is part of the verb phrase *has reserved*, indicating the meaning "to set aside for a particular use." In sentence B, *reserved* acts as a modifier within the noun phrase "her quiet and reserved nature." Because the word is being used as an adjective to describe a personality characteristic, it calls up a different definition of the word—"restrained or lacking familiarity with others." As this example shows, the function of a word within the overall sentence structure can allude to its meaning. It is also useful to refer to the earlier chart about suffixes and parts of speech as another clue into what grammatical function a word is serving in a sentence.

Analyzing Nuances of Word Meaning and Figures of Speech

By now, it should be apparent that language is not as simple as one word directly correlated to one meaning. Rather, one word can express a vast array of diverse meanings, and similar meanings can be expressed through different words. However, there are very few words that express exactly the same meaning. For this reason, it is important to be able to pick up on the nuances of word meaning.

Many words contain two levels of meaning: connotation and denotation as discussed previously in the informational texts and rhetoric section. A word's *denotation* is its most literal meaning—the definition that can readily be found in the dictionary. A word's *connotation* includes all of its emotional and cultural associations.

In literary writing, authors rely heavily on connotative meaning to create mood and characterization. The following are two descriptions of a rainstorm:

> A. The rain slammed against the windowpane and the wind howled through the fireplace. A pair of hulking oaks next to the house cast eerie shadows as their branches trembled in the wind.
>
> B. The rain pattered against the windowpane and the wind whistled through the fireplace. A pair of stately oaks next to the house cast curious shadows as their branches swayed in the wind.

Description A paints a creepy picture for readers with strongly emotional words like *slammed*, connoting force and violence. *Howled* connotes pain or wildness, and *eerie* and *trembled* connote fear. Overall, the connotative language in this description serves to inspire fear and anxiety.

However, as can be seen in description B, swapping out a few key words for those with different connotations completely changes the feeling of the passage. *Slammed* is replaced with the more cheerful *pattered*, and *hulking* has been swapped out for *stately*. Both words imply something large, but *hulking* is more intimidating whereas *stately* is more respectable. *Curious* and *swayed* seem more playful than the language used in the earlier description. Although both descriptions represent roughly the same situation, the nuances of the emotional language used throughout the passages create a very different sense for readers.

Selective choice of connotative language can also be extremely impactful in other forms of writing, such as editorials or persuasive texts. Through connotative language, writers reveal their biases and opinions while trying to inspire feelings and actions in readers:

> A. Parents won't stop complaining about standardized tests.
>
> B. Parents continue to raise concerns about standardized tests.

Readers should be able to identify the nuance in meaning between these two sentences. The first one carries a more negative feeling, implying that parents are being bothersome or whiny. Readers of the second sentence, though, might come away with the feeling that parents are concerned and involved in their children's education. Again, the aggregate of even subtle cues can combine to give a specific emotional impression to readers, so from an early age, students should be aware of how language can be used to influence readers' opinions.

Another form of non-literal expression can be found in *figures of speech*. As with connotative language, figures of speech tend to be shared within a cultural group and may be difficult to pick up on for learners outside of that group. In some cases, a figure of speech may be based on the literal denotation of the words it contains, but in other cases, a figure of speech is far removed from its literal meaning. A case in point is *irony*, where what is said is the exact opposite of what is meant:

> The new tax plan is poorly planned, based on faulty economic data, and unable to address the financial struggles of middle class families. Yet legislators remain committed to passing this brilliant proposal.

When the writer refers to the proposal as brilliant, the opposite is implied—the plan is "faulty" and "poorly planned." By using irony, the writer means that the proposal is anything but brilliant by using the word in a non-literal sense.

Another figure of speech is *hyperbole*—extreme exaggeration or overstatement. Statements like, "I love you to the moon and back" or "Let's be friends for a million years" utilize hyperbole to convey a greater depth of emotion, without literally committing oneself to space travel or a life of immortality.

Figures of speech may sometimes use one word in place of another. *Synecdoche*, for example, uses a part of something to refer to its whole. The expression "Don't hurt a hair on her head!" implies protecting more than just an individual hair, but rather her entire body. "The art teacher is training a class of Picassos" uses Picasso, one individual notable artist, to stand in for the entire category of talented artists. Another figure of speech using word replacement is *metonymy*, where a word is replaced with something closely associated to it. For example, news reports may use the word "Washington" to refer to the American government or "the crown" to refer to the British monarch.

Figurative Language

Literary texts also employ rhetorical devices. Figurative language like simile and metaphor is a type of rhetorical device commonly found in literature. In addition to rhetorical devices that play on the *meanings* of words, there are also rhetorical devices that use the *sounds* of words. These devices are most often found in poetry but may also be found in other types of literature and in non-fiction writing like speech texts.

Alliteration and *assonance* are both varieties of sound repetition. Other types of sound repetition include: anaphora, repetition that occurs at the beginning of the sentences; epiphora, repetition occurring at the end of phrases; antimetatabolee, repetition of words in reverse order; and antiphrasis, a form of denial of an assertion in a text.

Alliteration refers to the repetition of the first sound of each word. Recall Robert Burns' opening line:

> My love is like a red, red rose

This line includes two instances of alliteration: "love" and "like" (repeated *L* sound), as well as "red" and "rose" (repeated *R* sound). Next, assonance refers to the repetition of vowel sounds, and can occur anywhere within a word (not just the opening sound). Here is the opening of a poem by John Keats:

> When I have fears that I may cease to be
>
> Before my pen has glean'd my teeming brain

Assonance can be found in the words "fears," "cease," "be," "glean'd," and "teeming," all of which stress the long *E* sound. Both alliteration and assonance create a harmony that unifies the writer's language.

Another sound device is *onomatopoeia*, or words whose spelling mimics the sound they describe. Words such as "crash," "bang," and "sizzle" are all examples of onomatopoeia. Use of onomatopoetic language adds auditory imagery to the text.

Readers are probably most familiar with the technique of *pun*. A pun is a play on words, taking advantage of two words that have the same or similar pronunciation. Puns can be found throughout Shakespeare's plays, for instance:

> Now is the winter of our discontent
> Made glorious summer by this son of York

These lines from *Richard III* contain a play on words. Richard III refers to his brother, the newly crowned King Edward IV, as the "son of York," referencing their family heritage from the house of York. However, while drawing a comparison between the political climate and the weather (times of political trouble were the "winter," but now the new king brings "glorious summer"), Richard's use of the word "son" also implies another word with the same pronunciation, "sun"—so Edward IV is also like the sun, bringing light, warmth, and hope to England. Puns are a clever way for writers to suggest two meanings at once.

Some examples of figurative language are included in the following graphic.

	Definition	Example
Simile	Compares two things using "like" or "as"	Her hair was like gold.
Metaphor	Compares two things as if they are the same	He was a giant teddy bear.
Idiom	Using words with predictable meanings to create a phrase with a different meaning	The world is your oyster.
Alliteration	Repeating the same beginning sound or letter in a phrase for emphasis	The busy baby babbled.
Personification	Attributing human characteristics to an object or an animal	The house glowered menacingly with a dark smile.
Foreshadowing	Giving an indication that something is going to happen later in the story	I wasn't aware at the time, but I would come to regret those words.
Symbolism	Using symbols to represent ideas and provide a different meaning	The ring represented the bond between us.
Onomatopoeia	Using words that imitate sound	The tire went off with a bang and a crunch.
Imagery	Appealing to the senses by using descriptive language	The sky was painted with red and pink and streaked with orange.
Hyperbole	Using exaggeration not meant to be taken literally	The girl weighed less than a feather.

Figurative language can be used to give additional insight into the theme or message of a text by moving beyond the usual and literal meaning of words and phrases. It can also be used to appeal to the senses of readers and create a more in-depth story.

Transitional Words and Phrases

There are approximately 200 transitional words and phrases that are commonly used in the English language. Below are lists of common transition words and phrases used throughout transitions.

Time
After
Before
During
In the middle

Example About to be Given
For example
In fact
For instance

Compare
Likewise
Also

Contrast
However
Yet
But

Addition
And
Also
Furthermore
Moreover

Logical Relationships
If
Then
Therefore
As a result
Since

Steps in a Process
First
Second
Last

Transitional words and phrases are important writing devices because they connect sentences and paragraphs. Transitional words and phrases present logical order to writing and provide more coherent meaning to readers.

Transition words can be categorized based on the relationships they create between ideas:

- General order: signaling elaboration of an idea to emphasize a point—e.g., for example, for instance, to demonstrate, including, such as, in other words, that is, in fact, also, furthermore, likewise, and, truly, so, surely, certainly, obviously, doubtless
- Chronological order: referencing the time frame in which main event or idea occurs—e.g., before, after, first, while, soon, shortly thereafter, meanwhile
- *Numerical order/order of importance*: indicating that related ideas, supporting details, or events will be described in a sequence, possibly in order of importance—e.g., *first, second, also, finally, another, in addition, equally important, less importantly, most significantly, the main reason, last but not least*
- *Spatial order*: referring to the space and location of something or where things are located in relation to each other—e.g., *inside, outside, above, below, within, close, under, over, far, next to, adjacent to*
- Cause and effect order: signaling a causal relationship between events or ideas—e.g., thus, therefore, since, resulted in, for this reason, as a result, consequently, hence, for, so
- Compare and contrast order: identifying the similarities and differences between two or more objects, ideas, or lines of thought—e.g., like, as, similarly, equally, just as, unlike, however, but, although, conversely, on the other hand, on the contrary
- Summary order: indicating that a particular idea is coming to a close—e.g., in conclusion, to sum up, in other words, ultimately, above all

Research and Reference Skills

Identifying Information in an Index or Table of Contents

An index is an alphabetical listing of topics, such as people, works, or concepts that appear at the end of expository materials like textbooks, cookbooks, and repair manuals. When these key words are used in paragraphs, they sometimes appear in bold writing to indicate their importance and let the reader know that they're found in the index as well.

Index listings often discard articles like *a*, *an*, and *the*. Additionally, authors will be listed by their last names, not first. Topics may be further divided into subtopics. If you start by looking for the most basic topics first, you can quickly acquire information. For example, when looking for a cookie recipe in a cookbook, first find the word *cookie* in the index and then examine the indented list of cookie-related topics located directly beneath the original heading.

Some textbooks have multiple indexes arranged by different subjects. If, for instance, you're dealing with a weighty literature textbook, you might find one index that lists authors and another devoted to concepts. The lengthier the book, the more likely you are to find this format.

While an index is typically found at the end of a book, a table of contents is found at the beginning to help readers quickly locate information. A table of contents is arranged differently, however, because it provides a chronological listing of each chapter and a corresponding page number. Each entry may also include a description, summary statement, or objective.

When students first receive a textbook, they should take time to preview the table of contents to create a framework for mentally organizing information. By classifying the contents, the reader creates mental schemas and becomes more likely to retain the information longer.

Using Text Features

Text features are used to bring clarity or to affect the meaning of it. Sometimes a publication will follow a certain style guide/manual of style, which is a set of standards for how to write and format a publication. Some examples are APA, MLA, and the Chicago Manual of Style. If the publication is following one of those standards then the text features will be in accordance with that style guide.

Writers can come up with their own uses for text features based on what they feel is best. However, text features are generally used for a specific purpose. It's important to catch on to that purpose to maximize comprehension.

A clear layout is essential for good reader comprehension. Even with the use of many text features, the text needs to be laid out in a clear, consistent manner.

Bolding, Italics, and Underlining

Bolding, italics, and underlining are all used to make words stand out. **Bolded** words are often key concepts and can usually be found in summary statements at the end of chapters and in indexes. *Italics* can be used to identify words of another language or to add extra emphasis to a word or phrase. Writers will sometime place words in italics when the word is being referred to as the word itself. Quotation marks or italics can be used for this, as long as there is consistency. Italics are also used to represent a character's thoughts.

> Entering Jessica's room, Jessica's mom stepped over a pile of laundry, a stack of magazines, and a pile of dishes. *My messy daughter*, she thought, shaking her head.

Text can be <u>underlined</u> for a number of reasons, but generally it's to indicate a key term or important point.

Color can also be a text feature, as different color text can be used to make certain parts stand out or to indicate that a new section is beginning. Even if something is in black & white, the text may be in different shades of grey.

Formatting

In addition, formatting—such as indentation or bullet points—helps to clearly present content. Content may also be left justified, centered, or right justified:

Left Justified

Centered

Right Justified

Text is often centered to stand out and catch the reader's eye.

Analyzing Headings and Subheadings

Headings and subheadings are used in writing to organize discussions and allow the reader to find information quickly. Headings show a complete change in thought. Subheadings, which fall below headings, show different aspects of the same topic. For instance, if you saw the title *Government* and the heading *Forms of Government*, you might see the subheadings *Monarchy*, *Oligarchy*, *Democracy*, *Socialism*, and *Totalitarianism*.

Note the headings that got you to this point:

Reading

Research and Reference Skills

Using Text Features

Analyzing Headings and Subheadings

As well as providing organization and structure, headings and subheadings also put more white space on a page, which places less strain on the reader's eyes. It's a good idea to skim a document and get familiar with headings and subheadings. Write down the title, headings, and subheadings before you begin reading to provide structure to your notes and thoughts.

Locating Where in a Reading That Specific Information Can Be Found

Readers are often looking for specific information in a text. Perhaps they need to answer a reflective question about a reading they have completed and need to refer back to the text to find certain supporting details. Alternatively, they be scanning a new text for a particular piece of information and do not want to have to read the whole thing to find what they are looking for. In such instances, readers need to be able to location the place in the given reading, such as the chapter, paragraph, or table, where such information can be found. In informational texts, the table of context and the index are great tools to help in this task. Some narrative pieces contain chapter titles that can clue readers into what may occur in that chapter. Likewise, in instances where readers have already read the text, these headings can jog their memories about what occurred in that chapter so they can identify if that chapter likely contains what they are looking for.

Research studies published in journals, for example, scientific experiments, typically have a structured format. Once readers understand the structure and what sorts of information found in each section of the study, they can quickly and relatively easily hone in on the information they desire. After the title and list of authors, the study begins with an *abstract,* which is essentially a short summary of the research: the purpose and hypothesis of the study, the methodology employed, and the findings and their meanings. The abstract is usually offset from the rest of the report in a smaller font or different formatting. It is a good place to get a quick snapshot of the gist of the study.

The first section of main part of the report is the *introduction.* The introduction identifies the problem, or the need for the research. It sometimes contains a brief literature review of prior research pertaining to the issue and what gaps or issues existed in such studies. In this way, it sets the context for the current study and the hypothesis. The *methods* section details the approach used in the study – the steps that were followed and the subjects and materials used. The data analysis procedures are also described. In the next section, *results,* the findings are summarized and often displayed in tabular and graphic form. Statistical findings and relationships between the variables and groups are reported, particularly those pertaining to the hypothesis. The final section is the *discussion.* This section reports the results in narrative form and evaluates the significance of the findings. It often also discusses the study's strengths and weaknesses and the need for future research.

Text Structure

Depending on what the author is attempting to accomplish, certain formats or text structures work better than others. For example, a sequence structure might work for narration but not when identifying similarities and differences between dissimilar concepts. Similarly, a comparison-contrast structure is not useful for narration. It's the author's job to put the right information in the correct format.

Readers should be familiar with the five main literary structures:

1. *Sequence* structure (sometimes referred to as the order structure) is when the order of events proceed in a predictable order. In many cases, this means the text goes through the plot elements: exposition, rising action, climax, falling action, and resolution. Readers are introduced to characters, setting, and conflict in the exposition. In the rising action, there's an increase in tension and suspense. The climax is the height of tension and the point of no return. Tension decreases during the falling action. In the resolution, any conflicts presented in the exposition are solved, and the story concludes. An informative text that is structured sequentially will often go in order from one step to the next.

2. In the *problem-solution* structure, authors identify a potential problem and suggest a solution. This form of writing is usually divided into two paragraphs and can be found in informational texts. For example, cell phone, cable, and satellite providers use this structure in manuals to help customers troubleshoot or identify problems with services or products.

3. When authors want to discuss similarities and differences between separate concepts, they arrange thoughts in a *comparison-contrast* paragraph structure. Venn diagrams are an effective graphic organizer for comparison-contrast structures because they feature two overlapping circles that can be used to organize similarities and differences. A comparison-contrast essay organizes one paragraph based on similarities and another based on differences. A comparison-contrast essay can also be arranged with the similarities and differences of individual traits addressed within individual paragraphs. Words such as *however*, *but*, and *nevertheless* help signal a contrast in ideas.

4. *Descriptive* writing structure is designed to appeal to your senses. Much like an artist who constructs a painting, good descriptive writing builds an image in the reader's mind by appealing to the five senses: sight, hearing, taste, touch, and smell. However, overly descriptive writing can become tedious; sparse descriptions can make settings and characters seem flat. Good authors strike a balance by applying descriptions only to passages, characters, and settings that are integral to the plot.

5. Passages that use the *cause and effect* structure are simply asking *why* by demonstrating some type of connection between ideas. Words such as *if*, *since*, *because*, *then*, or *consequently* indicate relationship. By switching the order of a complex sentence, the writer can rearrange the emphasis on different clauses. Saying *"If Sheryl is late, we'll miss the dance"* is different from saying "We'll miss the dance if Sheryl is late." One emphasizes Sheryl's tardiness while the other emphasizes missing the dance. Paragraphs can also be arranged in a cause and effect format. Since the format—before and after—is sequential, it is useful when authors wish to discuss the impact of choices. Researchers often apply this paragraph structure to the scientific method.

Identifying Information from a Graph or Table

Texts may have graphic representations to help illustrate and visually support assertions made. For example, graphs can be used to express samples or segments of a population or demonstrate growth or decay. Readers should also learn to use graphs and tables to draw logical conclusions, generalizations, or identify implied relationships. Three of the most popular graph formats included in texts are line graphs, bar graphs, and pie charts.

Line graphs rely on a horizontal X-axis and a vertical Y-axis to establish baseline values. Dots are plotted where the horizontal and vertical axes intersect, and those dots are connected with lines. Compared to bar graphs or pie charts, line graphs are more useful for looking at the past and present and predicting future outcomes. For instance, a potential investor would look for stocks that demonstrated steady growth over many decades when examining the stock market. Note that severe spikes up and down indicate instability, while line graphs that display a slow but steady increase may indicate good returns.

Here's an example of a bar graph:

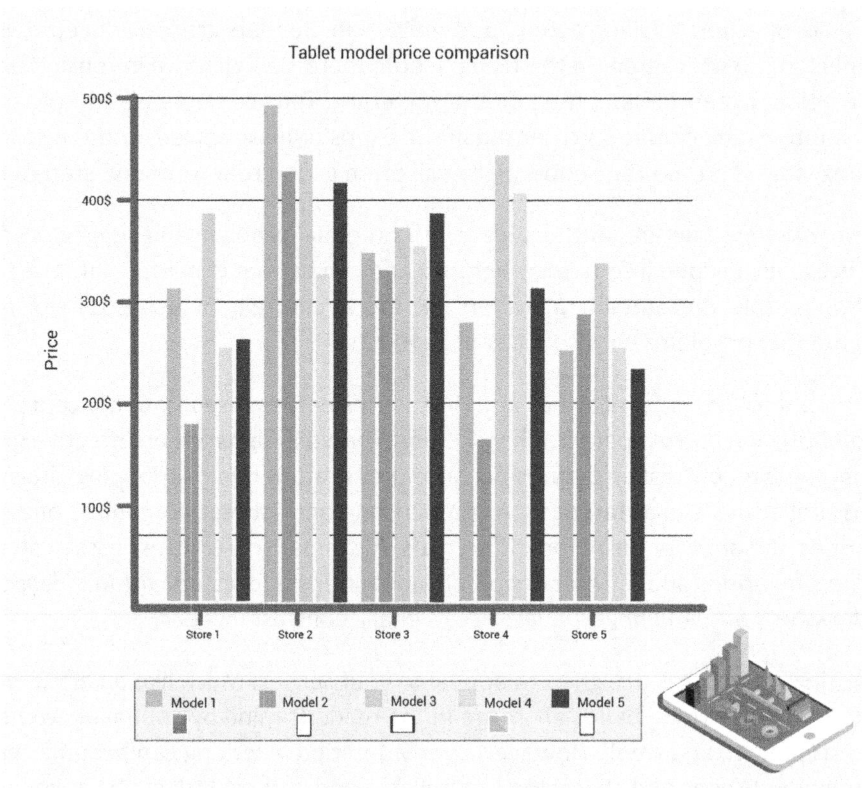

Bar graphs are usually displayed on a vertical Y-axis. The bars themselves can be two- or three-dimensional, depending on the designer's tastes. Unlike a line graph, which shows the fluctuation of only one variable, the X-axis on a bar graph is excellent for making comparisons, because it shows differences between several variables. For instance, if a consumer wanted to buy a new tablet, she could narrow the selection down to a few choices by using a bar graph to plot the prices side by side. The tallest bar would be the most expensive tablet, the shortest bar would be the cheapest.

A pie chart is divided into wedges that represent a numerical piece of the whole. Pie charts are useful for demonstrating how different categories add up to 100 percent. However, pie charts are not useful in comparing dissimilar items. High schools tend to use pie charts to track where students end up after graduation. Each wedge, for instance, might be labeled *vocational school*, *two-year college*, *four-year college*, *workforce*, or *unemployed*. By calculating the size of each wedge, schools can offer classes in the same ratios as where students will end up after high school. Pie charts are also useful for tracking finances. Items such as car payments, insurance, rent, credit cards, and entertainment would each get their own wedge proportional to the amount spent in a given time period. If one wedge is inordinately bigger than the rest, or if a wedge is expendable, it might be time to create a new financial strategy.

Practice Questions

Questions 1-4 are based on the following passage.

Smoking is Terrible

Smoking tobacco products is terribly destructive. A single cigarette contains over 4,000 chemicals, including 43 known carcinogens and 400 deadly toxins. Some of the most dangerous ingredients include tar, carbon monoxide, formaldehyde, ammonia, arsenic, and DDT. Smoking can cause numerous types of cancer including throat, mouth, nasal cavity, esophageal, gastric, pancreatic, renal, bladder, and cervical cancer.

Cigarettes contain a drug called nicotine, one of the most addictive substances known to man. Addiction is defined as a compulsion to seek the substance despite negative consequences. According to the National Institute of Drug Abuse, nearly 35 million smokers expressed a desire to quit smoking in 2015; however, more than 85 percent of those who struggle with addiction will not achieve their goal. Almost all smokers regret picking up that first cigarette. You would be wise to learn from their mistake if you have not yet started smoking.

According to the U.S. Department of Health and Human Services, 16 million people in the United States presently suffer from a smoking-related condition and nearly nine million suffer from a serious smoking-related illness. According to the Centers for Disease Control and Prevention (CDC), tobacco products cause nearly six million deaths per year. This number is projected to rise to over eight million deaths by 2030. Smokers, on average, die ten years earlier than their nonsmoking peers.

In the United States, local, state, and federal governments typically tax tobacco products, which leads to high prices. Nicotine users who struggle with addiction sometimes pay more for a pack of cigarettes than for a few gallons of gas. Additionally, smokers tend to stink. The smell of smoke is all-consuming and creates a pervasive nastiness. Smokers also risk staining their teeth and fingers with yellow residue from the tar.

Smoking is deadly, expensive, and socially unappealing. Clearly, smoking is not worth the risks.

1. Which of the following best describes the passage?
    a. Narrative
    b. Persuasive
    c. Expository
    d. Technical
    e. Informative

2. Which of the following statements most accurately summarizes the passage?
   a. Almost all smokers regret picking up that first cigarette.
   b. Tobacco is deadly, expensive, and socially unappealing, and smokers would be much better off kicking the addiction.
   c. In the United States, local, state, and federal governments typically tax tobacco products, which leads to high prices.
   d. Tobacco products shorten smokers' lives by ten years and kill more than six million people per year.
   e. Tobacco is less healthy than many alternatives.

3. The author would be most likely to agree with which of the following statements?
   a. Smokers should only quit cold turkey and avoid all nicotine cessation devices.
   b. Other substances are more addictive than tobacco.
   c. Smokers should quit for whatever reason that gets them to stop smoking.
   d. People who want to continue smoking should advocate for a reduction in tobacco product taxes.
   e. Smokers don't have the desire to quit and often don't see their smoking as a bad habit.

4. Which of the following represents an opinion statement on the part of the author?
   a. According to the Centers for Disease Control and Prevention (CDC), tobacco products cause nearly six million deaths per year.
   b. Nicotine users who struggle with addiction sometimes pay more for a pack of cigarettes than a few gallons of gas.
   c. They also risk staining their teeth and fingers with yellow residue from the tar.
   d. Additionally, smokers tend to stink. The smell of smoke is all-consuming and creates a pervasive nastiness.
   e. Smokers, on average, die ten years earlier than their nonsmoking peers.

Questions 5-7 are based on the following passage.

George Washington emerged out of the American Revolution as an unlikely champion of liberty. On June 14, 1775, the Second Continental Congress created the Continental Army, and John Adams, serving in the Congress, nominated Washington to be its first commander. Washington fought under the British during the French and Indian War, and his experience and prestige proved instrumental to the American war effort. Washington provided invaluable leadership, training, and strategy during the Revolutionary War. He emerged from the war as the embodiment of liberty and freedom from tyranny.

After vanquishing the heavily favored British forces, Washington could have pronounced himself as the autocratic leader of the former colonies without any opposition, but he famously refused and returned to his Mount Vernon plantation. His restraint proved his commitment to the fledgling state's republicanism. Washington was later unanimously elected as the first American president. But it is Washington's farewell address that cemented his legacy as a visionary worthy of study.

In 1796, President Washington issued his farewell address by public letter. Washington enlisted his good friend, Alexander Hamilton, in drafting his most famous address. The letter expressed Washington's faith in the Constitution and rule of law. He encouraged his fellow Americans to put aside partisan differences and establish a national union. Washington warned Americans against meddling in foreign affairs and entering military alliances. Additionally, he stated his opposition to national political parties, which he considered partisan and counterproductive.

Americans would be wise to remember Washington's farewell, especially during presidential elections when politics hits a fever pitch. They might want to question the political institutions that were not planned by the Founding Fathers, such as the nomination process and political parties themselves.

5. Which of the following statements is logically based on the information contained in the passage above?
   a. George Washington's background as a wealthy landholder directly led to his faith in equality, liberty, and democracy.
   b. George Washington would have opposed America's involvement in the Second World War.
   c. George Washington would not have been able to write as great a farewell address without the assistance of Alexander Hamilton.
   d. George Washington would probably not approve of modern political parties.
   e. George Washington would likely befriend former President Barack Obama.

6. Which of the following statements is the best description of the author's purpose in writing this passage about George Washington?
   a. To caution American voters about being too political during election times because George Washington would not have agreed with holding elections.
   b. To introduce George Washington to readers as a historical figure worthy of study
   c. To note that George Washington was more than a famous military hero
   d. To convince readers that George Washington is a hero of republicanism and liberty
   e. To inform American voters about a Founding Father's sage advice on a contemporary issue and explain its applicability to modern times

7. In which of the following materials would the author be the most likely to include this passage?
   a. A history textbook
   b. An obituary
   c. A fictional story
   d. A newspaper editorial
   e. A research journal

Questions 8-12 are based on the following passage.

Christopher Columbus is often credited for discovering America. This is incorrect. First, it is impossible to "discover" something where people already live; however, Christopher Columbus did explore places in the New World that were previously untouched by Europe, so the term “explorer” would be more accurate. Another correction must be made, as well: Christopher Columbus was not the first European explorer to reach the present day Americas! Rather, it was Leif Erikson who first came to the New World and contacted the natives, nearly five hundred years before Christopher Columbus.

Leif Erikson, the son of Erik the Red (a famous Viking outlaw and explorer in his own right), was born in either 970 or 980, depending on which historian you seek. His own family, though, did not raise Leif, which was a Viking tradition. Instead, one of Erik's prisoners taught Leif reading and writing, languages, sailing, and weaponry. At age 12, Leif was considered a man and returned to his family. He killed a man during a dispute shortly after his return, and the council banished the Erikson clan to Greenland.

In 999, Leif left Greenland and traveled to Norway where he would serve as a guard to King Olaf Tryggvason. It was there that he became a convert to Christianity. Leif later tried to return home with the intention of taking supplies and spreading Christianity to Greenland, however his ship was blown off course and he arrived in a strange new land: present day Newfoundland, Canada.

When he finally returned to his adopted homeland Greenland, Leif consulted with a merchant who had also seen the shores of this previously unknown land we now know as Canada. The son of the legendary Viking explorer then gathered a crew of 35 men and set sail. Leif became the first European to touch foot in the New World as he explored present-day Baffin Island and Labrador, Canada. His crew called the land Vinland since it was plentiful with grapes.

During their time in present-day Newfoundland, Leif's expedition made contact with the natives whom they referred to as Skraelings (which translates to "wretched ones" in Norse). There are several secondhand accounts of their meetings. Some contemporaries described trade between the peoples. Other accounts describe clashes where the Skraelings defeated the Viking explorers with long spears, while still others claim the Vikings dominated the natives. Regardless of the circumstances, it seems that the Vikings made contact of some kind. This happened around 1000, nearly five hundred years before Columbus famously sailed the ocean blue.

Eventually, in 1003, Leif set sail for home and arrived at Greenland with a ship full of timber.

In 1020, seventeen years later, the legendary Viking died. Many believe that Leif Erikson should receive more credit for his contributions in exploring the New World.

8. Which of the following best describes how the author generally presents the information?
   a. Chronological order
   b. Comparison-contrast
   c. Cause-effect
   d. Conclusion-premises
   e. Spatial order

9. Which of the following is an opinion, rather than historical fact, expressed by the author?
   a. Leif Erikson was definitely the son of Erik the Red; however, historians debate the year of his birth.
   b. Leif Erikson's crew called the land Vinland since it was plentiful with grapes.
   c. Leif Erikson deserves more credit for his contributions in exploring the New World.
   d. Leif Erikson explored the Americas nearly five hundred years before Christopher Columbus.
   e. Leif's expedition made contact with the natives whom they referred to as Skraelings.

10. Which of the following most accurately describes the author's main conclusion?
   a. Leif Erikson is a legendary Viking explorer.
   b. Leif Erikson deserves more credit for exploring America hundreds of years before Columbus.
   c. Spreading Christianity motivated Leif Erikson's expeditions more than any other factor.
   d. Leif Erikson contacted the natives nearly five hundred years before Columbus.
   e. Leif Erikson discovered the Americas.

11. Which of the following best describes the author’s intent in the passage?
   a. To entertain
   b. To inform
   c. To alert
   d. To suggest
   e. To share

12. Which of the following can be logically inferred from the passage?
   a. The Vikings disliked exploring the New World.
   b. Leif Erikson's banishment from Iceland led to his exploration of present-day Canada.
   c. Leif Erikson never shared his stories of exploration with the King of Norway.
   d. Historians have difficulty definitively pinpointing events in the Vikings' history.
   e. Christopher Columbus knew of Leif Erikson's explorations

Questions 13-17 are based on the chart following a brief introduction to the topic.

The American Civil War was fought from 1861 to 1865. It is the only civil war in American history. While the South's secession was the initiating event of the war, the conflict grew out of several issues like slavery and differing interpretations of individual state rights. General Robert E. Lee led the Confederate Army for the South for the duration of the conflict (although other generals held command positions over individual battles, as you will see next). The North employed a variety of lead generals, but Ulysses S. Grant finished the war as the victorious general. There were more American casualties in the Civil War than any other military conflict in American history.

Civil War Casualties by Battle (approximate)					
Battle	**Date**	**Union General**	**Confederate General**	**Union Casualties**	**Confederate Casualties**
Gettysburg	July 1863	George Meade	Robert E. Lee	23,049	28,063
Chancellorsville	May 1863	Joseph Hooker	Robert E. Lee	17,304	13,460
Shiloh	April 1862	Ulysses S. Grant	Albert Sydney Johnston	13,047	10,669
Cold Harbor	May 1864	Ulysses S. Grant	Robert E. Lee	12,737	4,595
Atlanta	July 1864	William T. Sherman	John Bell Hood	3,722	5,500

13. In which of the following battles were there more Confederate casualties than Union casualties?
   a. The one in May 1864
   b. Chancellorsville
   c. The one in April 1862
   d. Shiloh
   e. Atlanta

14. Which one of the following battles occurred first?
   a. Cold Harbor
   b. Chancellorsville
   c. Atlanta
   d. Shiloh
   e. Gettysburg

15. Robert E. Lee did not lead the Confederate forces in which one of the following battles?
   a. Atlanta
   b. The one in May 1863
   c. Cold Harbor
   d. Gettysburg
   e. The one in May 1864

16. In which of the following battles did the Union casualties exceed the Confederate casualties by the greatest number?
   a. Cold Harbor
   b. Chancellorsville
   c. Atlanta
   d. Shiloh
   e. Gettysburg

17. The total number of American casualties suffered at the battle of Gettysburg is about double the total number of casualties suffered at which one of the following battles?
   a. Cold Harbor
   b. Chancellorsville
   c. Atlanta
   d. Shiloh
   e. Cannot be determined with the information provided

Questions 18 and 19 are based on the graphic that follows a brief introduction to the topic.

The United States Constitution directs Congress to conduct a census of the population to determine the country's population and demographic information. The United States Census Bureau carries out the survey. In 1790, then Secretary of State Thomas Jefferson conducted the first census, and the most recent U.S. census was in 2010. The next U.S. census will be the first to be issued primarily through the Internet.

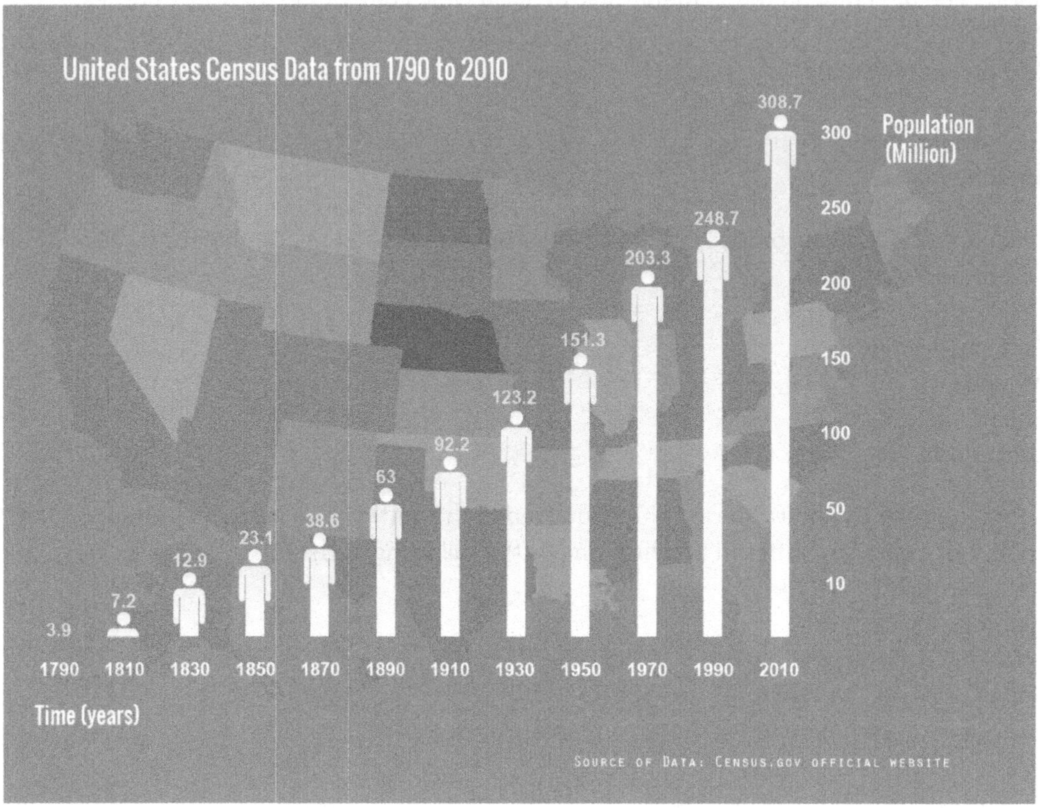

18. In which of the following years was the United States population less than it was in 1930?
    a. 1950
    b. 1970
    c. 2010
    d. 1990
    e. 1910

19. In what year did the population increase the most during a twenty-year interval?
    a. From 1930 to 1950
    b. From 1950 to 1970
    c. From 1970 to 1990
    d. From 1990 to 2010
    e. From 1790 to 1810

Questions 20-22 are based on the graphic following a brief introduction to the topic.

A food chain is a diagram used by biologists to better understand ecosystems. It represents the interrelationships between different plants and animals. The energy is derived from the sun and converted into stored energy by plants through photosynthesis, which travels up the food chain. The energy returns to the ecosystem after the organisms die and decompose back into the Earth. This process is an endless cycle.

In food chains, living organisms are grouped into categories called primary producers and consumers, which come in multiple tiers. For example, secondary consumers feed on primary consumers, while tertiary consumers feed on secondary consumers. Apex predators are the animals at the top of the food chain. They are the highest category consumer in an ecosystem, and apex predators do not have natural predators.

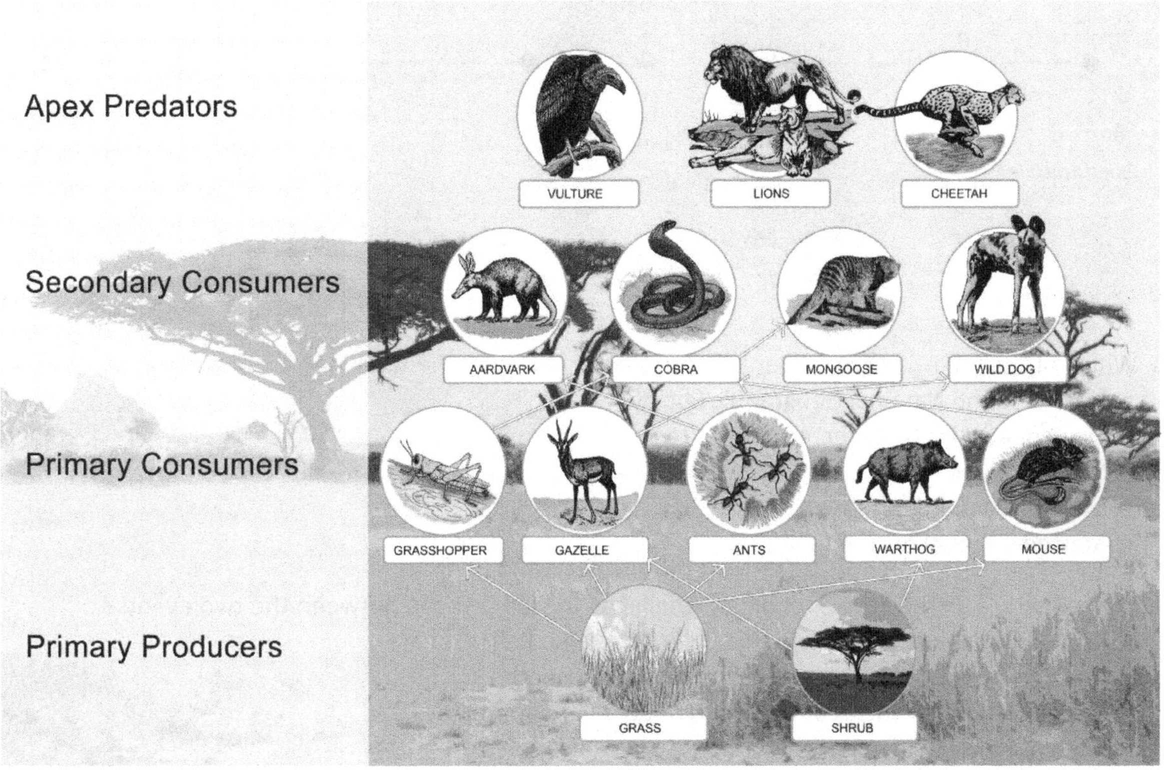

20. Which of the following eats primary producers according to the food chain diagram?
    a. Cobra
    b. Gazelle
    c. Wild dog
    d. Aardvark
    e. Grass

21. Which of the following animals has no natural predators according to the food chain diagram?
    a. Grass
    b. Cobra
    c. Mongoose
    d. Aardvark
    e. Vulture

22. Which of the following is something that the mongoose would eat?
    a. Shrub
    b. Aardvark
    c. Vulture
    d. Mouse
    e. Lion

Questions 23-26 are based on the timeline of the life of Alexander Graham Bell.

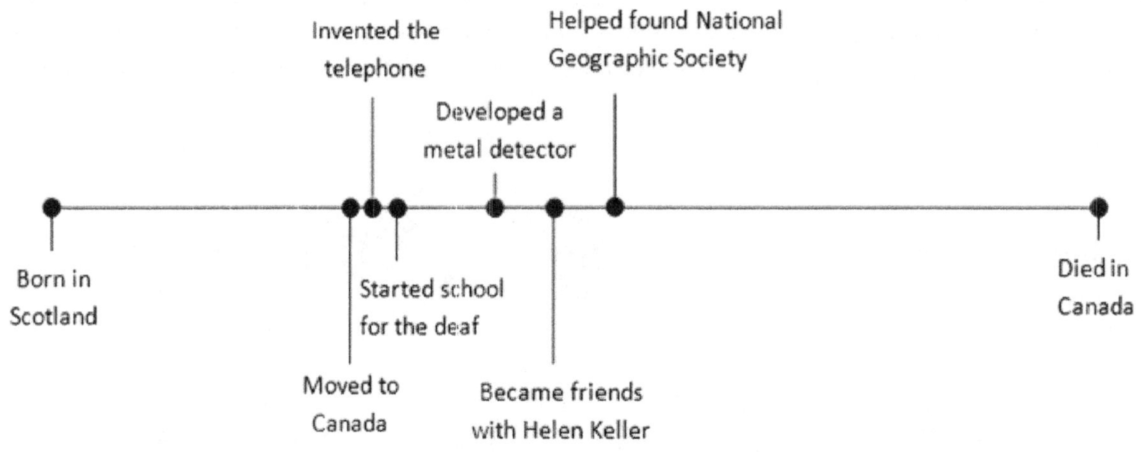

23. Which of the following is the event that occurred fourth on the timeline?
    a. Helped found National Geographic Society
    b. Developed a metal detector
    c. Moved to Canada
    d. Became friends with Helen Keller
    e. Started a school for the deaf

24. Of the pairings in the answer choices, which has the longest gap between the two events?
    a. Moved to Canada and Became friends with Helen Keller
    b. Became friends with Helen Keller and Died in Canada
    c. Started school for the deaf and Developed a metal detector
    d. Born in Scotland and Started school for the deaf
    e. Developed a metal detector and Became friends with Helen Keller

25. Which one of the following statements is accurate based on the timeline?
    a. Bell did nothing significant after he helped found the National Geographic Society.
    b. Bell started a school for the deaf in Canada.
    c. Bell lived in at least two countries.
    d. Developing a metal detector allowed Bell to meet Helen Keller.
    e. Bell was born and died in the same place.

26. Which one of the following events occurred most recently?
    a. Bell's invention of the telephone
    b. Bell's founding of the school
    c. Bell's birth
    d. Bell's move to Canada
    e. Bell's founding the National Geographic Society

Questions 27 and 28 are based on the following graph of high school students.

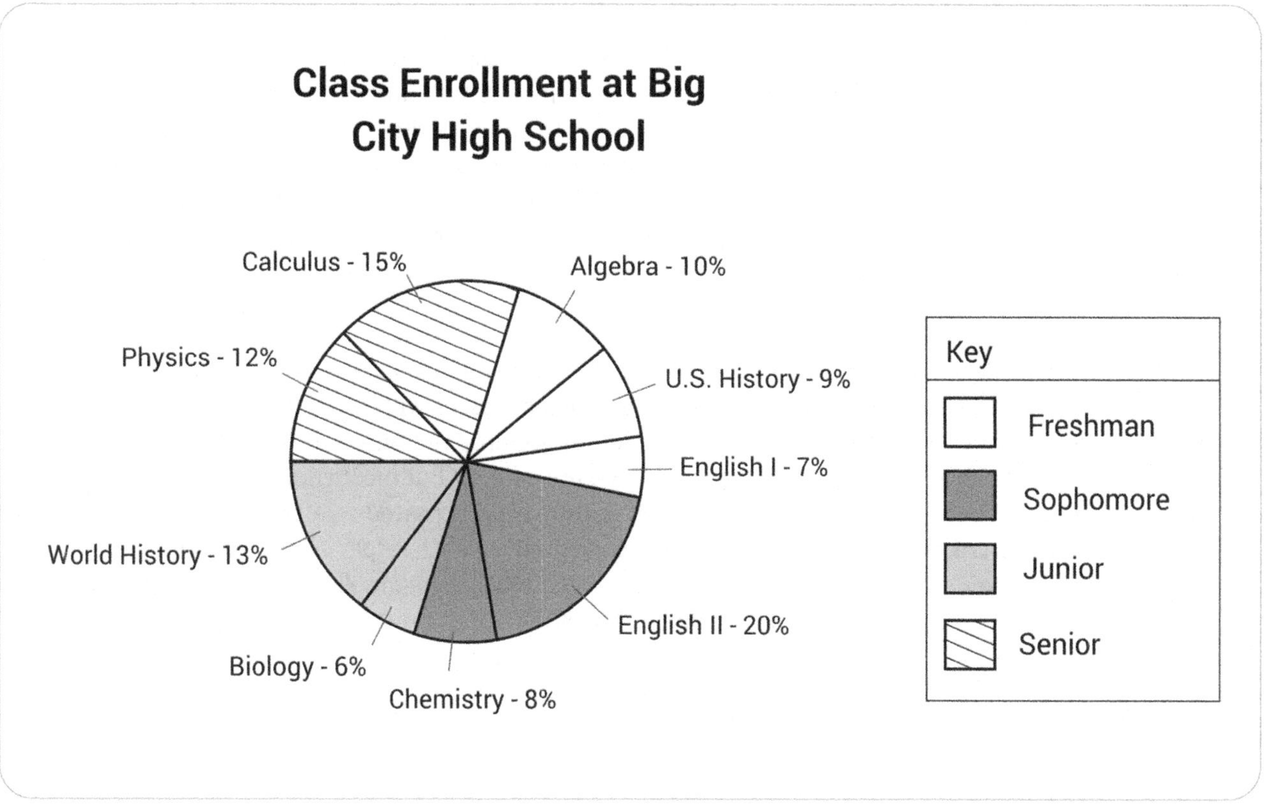

27. Which grade level has the most students in it?
    a. Freshman
    b. Sophomore
    c. Junior
    d. Senior
    e. It cannot be determined from the graph

28. What percent of the school is made up of freshman?
    a. 26%
    b. 27%
    c. 28%
    d. 29%
    e. 31

Questions 29-34 are based on the following passage:

When researchers and engineers undertake a large-scale scientific project, they may end up making discoveries and developing technologies that have far wider uses than originally intended. This is especially true in NASA, one of the most influential and innovative scientific organizations in America. NASA *spinoff technology* refers to innovations originally developed for NASA space projects that are now used in a wide range of different commercial fields. Many consumers are unaware that products they are buying are based on NASA research! Spinoff technology proves that it is worthwhile to invest in science research because it could enrich people's lives in unexpected ways.

The first spinoff technology worth mentioning is baby food. In space, where astronauts have limited access to fresh food and fewer options about their daily meals, malnutrition is a serious concern. Consequently, NASA researchers were looking for ways to enhance the nutritional value of astronauts' food. Scientists found that a certain type of algae could be added to food, improving the food's neurological benefits. When experts in the commercial food industry learned of this algae's potential to boost brain health, they were quick to begin their own research. The nutritional substance from algae then developed into a product called life's DHA, which can be found in over 90% of infant food sold in America.

Another intriguing example of a spinoff technology can be found in fashion. People who are always dropping their sunglasses may have invested in a pair of sunglasses with scratch resistant lenses—that is, it's impossible to scratch the glass, even if the glasses are dropped on an abrasive surface. This innovation is incredibly advantageous for people who are clumsy, but most shoppers don't know that this technology was originally developed by NASA. Scientists first created scratch resistant glass to help protect costly and crucial equipment from getting scratched in space, especially the helmet visors in space suits. However, sunglasses companies later realized that this technology could be profitable for their products, and they licensed the technology from NASA.

29. What is the main purpose of this article?
    a. To advise consumers to do more research before making a purchase
    b. To persuade readers to support NASA research
    c. To tell a narrative about the history of space technology
    d. To define and describe instances of spinoff technology
    e. To entertain readers with an engaging narrative

30. What is the organizational structure of this article?
    a. A general definition followed by more specific examples
    b. A general opinion followed by supporting arguments
    c. An important moment in history followed by chronological details
    d. A popular misconception followed by counterevidence
    e. An interweaving of comparisons and contrasts

31. Why did NASA scientists research algae?
    a. They already knew algae was healthy for babies.
    b. They were interested in how to grow food in space.
    c. They were looking for ways to add health benefits to food.
    d. They hoped to use it to protect expensive research equipment.
    e. They wanted to find a good use for the excessive algae near the laboratory.

32. What does the word "neurological" mean in the second paragraph?
    a. Related to the body
    b. Related to the brain
    c. Related to vitamins
    d. Related to technology
    e. Related to birth

33. Why does the author mention space suit helmets?
    a. To give an example of astronaut fashion
    b. To explain where sunglasses got their shape
    c. To explain how astronauts protect their eyes
    d. To give an example of valuable space equipment
    e. Because people on Earth need helmets as well

34. Which statement would the author probably NOT agree with?
    a. Consumers don't always know the history of the products they are buying.
    b. Sometimes new innovations have unexpected applications.
    c. It is difficult to make money from scientific research.
    d. Space equipment is often very expensive.
    e. NASA has made more of an impact than simply exploring space.

Questions 35-40 are based on the following passage.

This excerpt is an adaptation of Robert Louis Stevenson's The Strange Case of Dr. Jekyll and Mr. Hyde.

"Did you ever come across a protégé of his—one Hyde?" He asked.

"Hyde?" repeated Lanyon. "No. Never heard of him. Since my time."

That was the amount of information that the lawyer carried back with him to the great, dark bed on which he tossed to and fro until the small hours of the morning began to grow large. It was a night of little ease to his toiling mind, toiling in mere darkness and besieged by questions.

Six o'clock struck on the bells of the church that was so conveniently near to Mr. Utterson's dwelling, and still he was digging at the problem. Hitherto it had touched him on the intellectual side alone; but now his imagination also was engaged, or rather enslaved; and as he lay and tossed in the gross darkness of the night in the curtained room, Mr. Enfield's tale went by before his mind in a scroll of lighted pictures. He would be aware of the great field of lamps in a nocturnal city; then of the figure of a man walking swiftly; then of a child running from the doctor's; and then these met, and that human Juggernaut trod the child down and passed on regardless of her screams. Or else he would see a room in a rich house, where his friend lay asleep, dreaming and smiling at his dreams; and then the door of that room would be opened, the curtains of the bed plucked apart, the sleeper recalled, and, lo! There would stand by his side a figure to whom power was given, and even at that dead hour he must rise and do its bidding. The figure in these two phrases haunted the lawyer all night; and if at anytime he dozed over, it was but to see it glide more stealthily through sleeping houses, or move the more swiftly, and still the more smoothly, even to dizziness, through wider labyrinths of lamplighted city, and at every street corner crush a child and leave her screaming. And still the figure had no face by which he might know it; even in his dreams it had no face, or one that baffled him and melted before his eyes; and thus there it was that there sprung up and grew apace in the lawyer's mind a singularly strong, almost an inordinate, curiosity to behold the features of the real Mr. Hyde. If he could but once set eyes on him, he thought the mystery would lighten and perhaps roll altogether away, as was the habit of mysterious things when well examined. He might see a reason for his friend's strange preference or bondage, and even for the startling clauses of the will. And at least it would be a face worth seeing: the face of a man who was without bowels of mercy: a face which had but to show itself to raise up, in the mind of the unimpressionable Enfield, a spirit of enduring hatred.

From that time forward, Mr. Utterson began to haunt the door in the by street of shops. In the morning before office hours, at noon when business was plenty of time scarce, at night under the face of the full city moon, by all lights and at all hours of solitude or concourse, the lawyer was to be found on his chosen post.

"If he be Mr. Hyde," he had thought, "I should be Mr. Seek."

35. What is the purpose of the use of repetition in the following passage?

> It was a night of little ease to his toiling mind, toiling in mere darkness and besieged by questions.

a. It serves as a demonstration of the mental state of Mr. Lanyon.
b. It is reminiscent of the church bells that are mentioned in the story.
c. It mimics Mr. Utterson's ambivalence.
d. It emphasizes Mr. Utterson's anguish in failing to identify Hyde's whereabouts.
e. It accentuates how easy it is to get lost in the city.

36. What is the setting of the story in this passage?

a. In the city
b. On the countryside
c. In a jail
d. In a mental health facility
e. Inside of a church

37. What can one infer about the meaning of the word "Juggernaut" from the author's use of it in the passage?

a. It is an apparition that appears at daybreak.
b. It scares children.
c. It is associated with space travel.
d. Mr. Utterson finds it soothing.
e. It lives deep in the ocean.

38. What is the definition of the word *haunt* in the following passage?

> From that time forward, Mr. Utterson began to haunt the door in the by street of shops. In the morning before office hours, at noon when business was plenty of time scarce, at night under the face of the full city moon, by all lights and at all hours of solitude or concourse, the lawyer was to be found on his chosen post.

a. To levitate
b. To constantly visit
c. To terrorize
d. To daunt
e. A ghost or spirit

39. The phrase *labyrinths of lamplighted city* contains an example of what?
a. Hyperbole
b. Simile
c. Juxtaposition
d. Alliteration
e. Metaphor

40. What can one reasonably conclude from the final comment of this passage?

> "If he be Mr. Hyde," he had thought, "I should be Mr. Seek."

a. The speaker is considering a name change.
b. The speaker is experiencing an identity crisis.
c. The speaker has mistakenly been looking for the wrong person.
d. The speaker intends to continue to look for Hyde.
e. The speaker has decided to befriend Hyde.

Questions 41-46 are based on the following passage.

Dana Gioia argues in his article that poetry is dying, now little more than a limited art form confined to academic and college settings. Of course, poetry remains healthy in the academic setting, but the idea of poetry being limited to this academic subculture is a stretch. New technology and social networking alone have contributed to poets and other writers' work being shared across the world. YouTube has emerged to be a major asset to poets, allowing live performances to be streamed to billions of users. Even now, poetry continues to grow and voice topics that are relevant to the culture of our time. Poetry is not in the spotlight as it may have been in earlier times, but it's still a relevant art form that continues to expand in scope and appeal.

Furthermore, Gioia's argument does not account for live performances of poetry. Not everyone has taken a poetry class or enrolled in university—but most everyone is online. The Internet is a perfect launching point to get all creative work out there. An example of this was the performance of Buddy Wakefield's *Hurling Crowbirds at Mockingbars*. Wakefield is a well-known poet who has published several collections of contemporary poetry. One of my favorite works by Wakefield is *Crowbirds*, specifically his performance at New York University in 2009. Although his reading was a campus event, views of his performance online number in the thousands. His poetry attracted people outside of the university setting.

Naturally, the poem's popularity can be attributed both to Wakefield's performance and the quality of his writing. *Crowbirds* touches on themes of core human concepts such as faith, personal loss, and growth. These are not ideas that only poets or students of literature understand, but all human beings: "You acted like I was hurling crowbirds at mockingbars / and abandoned me for not making sense. / Evidently, I don't experience things as rationally as you do" (Wakefield 15-17). Wakefield weaves together a complex description of the perplexed and hurt emotions of the speaker undergoing a separation from a romantic interest. The line "You acted like I was hurling crowbirds at mockingbars" conjures up an image of someone confused, seemingly out of their mind . . . or in the case of the speaker, passionately trying to grasp at a relationship that is fading. The speaker is looking back and finding the words that described how he wasn't making sense. This poem is particularly human and gripping in its message, but the entire effect of the poem is enhanced through the physical performance.

At its core, poetry is about addressing issues/ideas in the world. Part of this is also addressing the perspectives that are exiguously considered. Although the platform may look different, poetry continues to have a steady audience due to the emotional connection the poet shares with the audience.

41. Which one of the following best explains how the passage is organized?
   a. The author begins with a long definition of the main topic, and then proceeds to prove how that definition has changed over the course of modernity.
   b. The author presents a puzzling phenomenon and uses the rest of the passage to showcase personal experiences in order to explain it.
   c. The author contrasts two different viewpoints, then builds a case showing preference for one over the other.
   d. The passage is an analysis of another theory in which the author has no stake in.
   e. The passage is a summary of a main topic from its historical beginnings to its contemplated end.

42. The author of the passage would likely agree most with which of the following?
   a. Buddy Wakefield is a genius and is considered at the forefront of modern poetry.
   b. Poetry is not irrelevant; it is an art form that adapts to the changing time while containing its core elements.
   c. Spoken word is the zenith of poetic forms and the premier style of poetry in this decade.
   d. Poetry is on the verge of vanishing from our cultural consciousness.
   e. Poetry is a writing art. While poetry performances are useful for introducing poems, the act of reading a poem does not contribute to the piece overall.

43. Which one of the following words, if substituted for the word *exiguously* in the last paragraph, would LEAST change the meaning of the sentence?
   a. Indolently
   b. Inaudibly
   c. Interminably
   d. Infrequently
   e. Impecunious

44. Which of the following is most closely analogous to the author's opinion of Buddy Wakefield's performance in relation to modern poetry?

a. Someone's refusal to accept that the Higgs Boson will validate the Standard Model.
b. An individual's belief that soccer will lose popularity within the next fifty years.
c. A professor's opinion that poetry contains the language of the heart, while fiction contains the language of the mind.
d. An individual's assertion that video game violence was the cause of the Columbine shootings.
e. A student's insistence that psychoanalysis is a subset of modern psychology.

45. What is the primary purpose of the passage?

a. To educate readers on the development of poetry and describe the historical implications of poetry in media.
b. To disprove Dana Gioia's stance that poetry is becoming irrelevant and is only appreciated in academia.
c. To inform readers of the brilliance of Buddy Wakefield and to introduce them to other poets that have influence in contemporary poetry.
d. To prove that Gioia's article does have some truth to it and to shed light on its relevance to modern poetry.
e. To recount the experience of watching a live poetry performance and to look forward to future performances.

46. What is the author's main reason for including the quote in the passage?

a. To give an example of speaking meter, the writing style of spoken word poets.
b. To demonstrate that people are still writing poetry even if the medium has changed in current times.
c. To prove that poets still have an audience to write for even if the audience looks different than from centuries ago.
d. To illustrate the complex themes poets continue to address, which still draw listeners and appreciation.
e. To open up opportunity to disprove Gioia's views.

Questions 47-50 are based upon the following passage.

This excerpt is adapted from Mineralogy --- Encyclopedia International, Grolier

Mineralogy is the science of minerals, which are the naturally occurring elements and compounds that make up the solid parts of the universe. Mineralogy is usually considered in terms of materials in the Earth, but meteorites provide samples of minerals from outside the Earth.

A mineral may be defined as a naturally occurring, homogeneous solid, inorganically formed, with a definite chemical composition and an ordered atomic arrangement. The qualification *naturally occurring* is essential because it is possible to reproduce most minerals in the laboratory. For example, evaporating a solution of sodium chloride produces crystal indistinguishable from those of the mineral halite, but such laboratory-produced crystals are not minerals.

A *homogeneous solid* is one consisting of a single kind of material that cannot be separated into simpler compounds by any physical method. The requirement that a mineral be solid eliminates gases and liquids from consideration. Thus ice is a mineral (a very common one, especially at high altitudes and latitudes) but water is not. Some mineralogists dispute this restriction and would consider both water and native mercury (also a liquid) as minerals.

The restriction of minerals to *inorganically formed* substances eliminates those homogenous solids produced by animals and plants. Thus, the shell of an oyster and the pearl inside, though both consist of calcium carbonate indistinguishable chemically or physically from the mineral aragonite, are not usually considered minerals.

The requirement of a *definite chemical composition* implies that a mineral is a chemical compound, and the composition of a chemical compound is readily expressed by a formula. Mineral formulas may be simple or complex, depending upon the number of elements present and the proportions in which they are combined.

Minerals are crystalline solids, and the presence of an *ordered atomic arrangement* is the criterion of the crystalline state. Under favorable conditions of formation the ordered atomic arrangement is expressed in the external crystal form. In fact, the presence of an ordered atomic arrangement and crystalline solids was deduced from the external regularity of crystals by a French mineralogist, Abbé R. Haüy, early in the 19th century.

47. According to the text, an object or substance must have all of the following criteria to be considered a mineral except for?

   a. Be naturally occurring
   b. Be a homogeneous solid
   c. Be organically formed
   d. Have a definite chemical composition
   e. Be reproducible in the lab

48. What is the definition of the word "homogeneous" as it appears in the following passage?

"A homogeneous solid is one consisting of a single kind of material that cannot be separated into simpler compounds by any physical method."

   a. Made of similar substances
   b. Differing in some areas
   c. Having a higher atomic mass
   d. Lacking necessary properties
   e. A hybrid between a solid and a liquid

49. The suffix -logy refers to?

   a. The properties of
   b. The chemical makeup of
   c. The study of
   d. The classification of
   e. The methods of

50. The author included the counterargument in the following passage to achieve which following effect?

The requirement that a mineral be solid eliminates gases and liquids from consideration. Thus, ice is a mineral (a very common one, especially at high altitudes and latitudes) but water is not. Some mineralogists dispute this restriction and would consider both water and native mercury (also a liquid) as minerals.

a. To complicate the subject matter
b. To express a bias
c. To point to the fact that there are differing opinions in the field of mineralogy concerning the characteristics necessary to determine whether a substance or material is a mineral
d. To create a new subsection of minerals
e. To strengthen his or her argument and the persuasiveness of the text

Answer Explanations

1. B: This passage is persuasive writing, which hopes to change someone's beliefs based on an appeal to reason or emotion. The author is aiming to convince the reader that smoking is terrible. Persuasive is another term for argumentative. They use health, price, and beauty in their argument against smoking, so Choice *B*, persuasive, is the correct answer. Narrative, Choice *A*, means a written account of connected events. Think of narrative writing as a story. Choice *C*, expository writing, generally seeks to explain or describe some phenomena, whereas Choice *D*, technical writing, includes directions, instructions, and/or explanations. Choice *E*, informative writing, may be an appealing choice since this passage is informative in some ways, but informative texts should be very objective in their language.

2. B: The author is clearly opposed to tobacco. He cites disease and deaths associated with smoking. He points to the monetary expense and aesthetic costs. Choices *A* and *C* are wrong because they do not summarize the passage but rather are each just a premise. Choice *D* is wrong because, while these statistics are a premise in the argument, they do not represent a summary of the piece. Choice *B* is the correct answer because it states the three critiques offered against tobacco and expresses the author's conclusion. Choice *E* is wrong because alternatives to smoking are not even addressed in the passage.

3. C: We are looking for something the author would agree with, so it will almost certainly be anti-smoking or an argument in favor of quitting smoking. Choice *A* is wrong because the author does not speak against means of cessation. Choice *B* is wrong because the author does not reference other substances but does speak of how addictive nicotine, a drug in tobacco, is. Choice *D* is wrong because the author certainly would not encourage reducing taxes to encourage a reduction of smoking costs, thereby helping smokers to continue the habit. Choice *E* is wrong because the author states that according to the National Institute of Drug Abuse, nearly 35 million smokers expressed a desire to quit smoking in 2015. If the author had used the word "only" instead of "nearly" (and perhaps if the number was a lot lower) that would have changed the argument. Choice *C* is correct because the author is definitely attempting to persuade smokers to quit smoking.

4. D: Here, we are looking for an opinion of the author's rather than a fact or statistic. Choice *A* is wrong because quoting statistics from the Centers of Disease Control and Prevention is stating facts, not opinions. Choice *B* is wrong because it expresses the fact that cigarettes sometimes cost more than a few gallons of gas. It would be an opinion if the author said that cigarettes were not affordable. Choice *C* is incorrect because yellow stains are a known possible adverse effect of smoking. Choice *E* is incorrect because decreased life expectancy for smokers is a known fact because of the health problems it can create. Choice *D* is correct as an opinion because smell is subjective. Some people might like the smell of smoke, they might not have working olfactory senses, and/or some people might not find the smell of smoke akin to "pervasive nastiness," so this is the expression of an opinion. Thus, Choice *D* is the correct answer.

5. D: Although Washington was from a wealthy background, the passage does not say that his wealth led to his republican ideals, so Choice *A* is not supported. Choice *B* also does not follow from the passage. Washington's warning against meddling in foreign affairs does not mean that he would oppose wars of every kind, so Choice *B* is wrong. Choice *C* is also unjustified since the author does not indicate that Alexander Hamilton's assistance was absolutely necessary. Choice *E* is incorrect because we don't know which particular presidents Washington would befriend. Choice *D* is correct because the farewell address clearly opposes political parties and partisanship. The author then notes that presidential elections often hit a fever pitch of partisanship. Thus, it follows that George Washington would not approve of modern political parties and their involvement in presidential elections.

6. E: The author finishes the passage by applying Washington's farewell address to modern politics, so the purpose probably includes this application. Choice *A* does focus on modern politics, but it is incorrect. The passage does not state that it is the election process itself that George Washington would oppose; in fact, it mentions that he was also elected. Choice *B* is wrong because George Washington is already a well-established historical figure; furthermore, the passage does not seek to introduce him. Choice *C* is wrong because the author is not fighting a common perception that Washington was merely a military hero. Choice *D* is wrong because the author is not convincing readers. Persuasion does not correspond to the passage. Choice *E* states the primary purpose.

7. D: Choices *A* and *E* are wrong because the last paragraph is not appropriate for a history textbook nor a research journal, both which should be strictly objective and research-based. Choice *B* is false because the piece is not a notice or announcement of Washington's death. Choice *C* is clearly false because it is not fiction, but a historical writing. Choice *D* is correct. The passage is most likely to appear in a newspaper editorial because it cites information relevant and applicable to the present day, a popular format in editorials.

8. D: The passage does not proceed in chronological order since it begins by pointing out Leif Erikson's explorations in America so Choice *A* does not work. Although the author compares and contrasts Erikson with Christopher Columbus, this is not the main way the information is presented; therefore, Choice *B* does not work. Neither does Choice *C* because there is no mention of or reference to cause and effect in the passage. However, the passage does offer a conclusion (Leif Erikson deserves more credit) and premises (first European to set foot in the New World and first to contact the natives) to substantiate Erikson's historical importance. Thus, Choice *D* is correct. Choice *E* is incorrect because spatial order refers to the space and location of something or where things are located in relation to each other.

9. C: Choice *A* is wrong because it describes facts: Leif Erikson was the son of Erik the Red and historians debate Leif's date of birth. These are not opinions. Choice *B* is wrong; that Erikson called the land Vinland is a verifiable fact as is Choice *D* because he did contact the natives almost 500 years before Columbus. Choice *E* is also a fact and the passage mentions that there are several secondhand accounts (evidence) of their meetings. Choice *C* is the correct answer because it is the author's opinion that Erikson deserves more credit. That, in fact, is his conclusion in the piece, but another person could argue that Columbus or another explorer deserves more credit for opening up the New World to exploration. Rather than being an incontrovertible fact, it is a subjective value claim.

10. B: Choice *A* is wrong because the author aims to go beyond describing Erikson as a mere legendary Viking. Choice *C* is wrong because the author does not focus on Erikson's motivations, let alone name the spreading of Christianity as his primary objective. Choice *D* is wrong because it is a premise that Erikson contacted the natives 500 years before Columbus, which is simply a part of supporting the author's conclusion. Choice *E* is incorrect because the author states at the beginning that he or she believes it can't be considered "discovering" if people already lived there. Choice *B* is correct because, as stated in the previous answer, it accurately identifies the author's statement that Erikson deserves more credit than he has received for being the first European to explore the New World.

11. B: Choice *A* is wrong because the author is not in any way trying to entertain the reader. Choice *D* is wrong because he goes beyond a mere suggestion; "suggest" is too vague. Choice *E* is wrong for the same reason. Although the author is certainly trying to alert the readers of Leif Erikson's unheralded accomplishments, the nature of the writing does not indicate the author would be satisfied with the reader merely knowing of Erikson's exploration (Choice *C*). Rather, the author would want the reader to be informed about it, which is more substantial (Choice *B*).

12. D: Choice *A* is wrong because the author never addresses the Vikings' state of mind or emotions. Choice *B* is wrong because the author does not elaborate on Erikson's exile and whether he would have become an explorer if not for his banishment. Choice *C* is wrong because there is not enough information to support this premise. It is unclear whether Erikson informed the King of Norway of his finding. Although it is true that the King did not send a follow-up expedition, he could have simply chosen not to expend the resources after receiving Erikson's news. It is not possible to logically infer whether Erikson told him. Choice *E* is incorrect because the passage does not mention anything about Columbus' awareness of Erikson's travels. Choice *D* is correct because there are two examples—Leif Erikson's date of birth and what happened during the encounter with the natives—of historians having trouble pinning down important details in Viking history.

13. E: The question asks which of the battles in the chart that are listed in this question had more Confederate casualties than Union casualties. There were more Confederate casualties than Union casualties at the Battles of Gettysburg and Atlanta. Of the two, only Atlanta is listed as an answer choice out of the battles explicitly listed or referred to by their dates. Thus, *E*, Atlanta, is the correct answer.

14. D: The question is asking you to find where the dates are located in the table and to identify the earliest battle. Answer D, Shiloh, occurred in April 1862 and no other battle listed on the table happened until May 1863. Choice *E*, Gettysburg, is listed first but did not occur first.

15. A: Robert E. Lee led the Confederate army in all battles listed on the table, except Shiloh and Atlanta. Looking at the dates and corresponding battles, as well as the battle explicitly listed, Shiloh is not listed as a choice, therefore Atlanta, option *A* is the correct answer.

16. A: This question is asking you to compare the Union and Confederate casualties and find the one listed where the Union casualties most exceeded the Confederate ones. At Cold Harbor, there were approximately 8,142 more Union casualties than Confederate. At Chancellorsville, there were approximately 3,844 more Union casualties. At Atlanta and Gettysburg, the number of Confederate casualties exceeded the Union number, so neither of these can be the correct answer. At Shiloh, there were approximately 2,378 more Union casualties. Thus, the number of Union casualties most greatly exceeding the Confederate number was at Cold Harbor, making *A*, Cold Harbor, the correct answer.

17. D: To calculate the total American casualties, we combine the Union and Confederate casualties since it was a civil war with Americans on both sides, so Choice *E* is incorrect. There were approximately 51,112 (Union + Confederate losses) American casualties at Gettysburg; thus, the correct answer will be a battle with approximately 25,556 casualties, which is half of that number. Shiloh is the closest with a total of 23,716 casualties, making *D* the correct answer.

18. E: The correct answer choice is *E,* 1910. There are two ways to arrive at the correct answer. You could find the five answer choices on the graph, or you could have identified that the population never dips at any point. Thus, the correct answer needs to be the only answer choice that is earlier in time than the others, Choice *E*.

19. D: The population increased the most between 1990 and 2010. The question is asking you to identify the rate of change for each interval. Between 1790 to 1810, the population increased by about 3.3 million. Between 1930 and 1950, the population increased by approximately 28 million. Between 1950 and 1970, the population increased by approximately 52 million. Between 1970 and 1990, the population increased by approximately 45 million. Between 1990 and 2010, the population increased by approximately 60 million. Thus, *D* is the correct answer. The slope is also the steepest in this interval, which represents its higher increase.

20. B: Primary producers make up the base of the food chain, so the correct answer will be in the level just above: a primary consumer. The cobra, wild dog, and aardvark are all secondary consumers. The gazelle is a primary consumer, so ***B*** is the correct answer. Grass *is* a primary producer, making *E* incorrect.

21. E: According to the passage preceding the food chain, the apex predators do not have natural predators. So, the question is really asking which of the answer choices is an apex predator. The cobra, mongoose, and aardvark are all secondary consumers. Grass is a primary producer. The vulture is an apex predator; thus, a vulture has no natural predators, making *E* the correct answer.

22. D: A mongoose is a secondary consumer; thus, the mongoose consumes primary consumers. The shrub is a primary producer. The aardvark is a secondary consumer. The vulture and the lion are apex predators. The mouse is a primary consumer, so Choice *D* is the correct answer.

23. E: This question is testing whether you realize how a timeline illustrates information in chronological order from left to right. "Started school for the deaf" is fourth on the timeline from the left, which means that it is the fourth event on the timeline. Thus, Choice *E* is the correct answer.

24. B: This question is asking you to determine the length of time between the pairs of events listed as answer choices. Events in timelines are arranged proportional to time. To determine the answer to this question, one must find the largest space between two events. Visually, this can be seen between the events of befriending Helen Keller and dying in Canada. Thus, Choice *B* is the correct answer.

25. C: This question is testing whether you can discern accurate conclusions from a timeline. Although the incorrect answer choices can seem correct, they cannot be confirmed from the information presented on the timeline. Choice *A* is incorrect; while it may be reasonable to assume that the timeline documents all major life events, we do not know for certain that Bell did not engage in any notable activities after founding the National Geographic Society. Choice *B* is incorrect because the timeline does not confirm that the school was in Canada; Bell actually started it in the United States. Choice *D* is incorrect because nothing on the timeline shows causation between the two events. Choice *E* is incorrect because the timeline states he was born in Scotland and died in Canada. Choice *C* is the only verifiable statement based on the timeline. Thus, *C* is the correct answer.

26. E: The founding of the National Geographic Society is the event listed farthest to the right of the events in the answer choices. This means it occurred most recently. Thus, *E* is the correct answer.

27. B: The sophomore class is made up of English II and Chemistry and encompasses 28% of the students. Freshman only make up 26% of the students, while Seniors make up 27%, and Juniors make up 19%.

28. A: To find this add up the percent of Algebra, US History, and English I. This comes up to 26%.

29. D: To define and describe instances of spinoff technology. This is an example of a purpose question—*why* did the author write this? The article contains facts, definitions, and other objective information without telling a story or arguing an opinion. In this case, the purpose of the article is to inform the reader. The only answer choice that is related to giving information is answer Choice *D*: to define and describe.

30. A: A general definition followed by more specific examples. This organization question asks readers to analyze the structure of the essay. The topic of the essay is about spinoff technology; the first paragraph gives a general definition of the concept, while the following two paragraphs offer more detailed examples to help illustrate this idea.

31. C: They were looking for ways to add health benefits to food. This reading comprehension question can be answered based on the second paragraph—scientists were concerned about astronauts' nutrition and began researching useful nutritional supplements. Choice *A* in particular is not true because it reverses the order of discovery (first NASA identified algae for astronaut use, and then it was further developed for use in baby food).

32. B: Related to the brain. This vocabulary question could be answered based on the reader's prior knowledge; but even for readers who have never encountered the word "neurological" before, the passage does provide context clues. The very next sentence talks about "this algae's potential to boost brain health," which is a paraphrase of "neurological benefits." From this context, readers should be able to infer that "neurological" is related to the brain.

33. D: To give an example of valuable space equipment. This purpose question requires readers to understand the relevance of the given detail. In this case, the author mentions "costly and crucial equipment" before mentioning space suit visors, which are given as an example of something that is very valuable. *A* is not correct because fashion is only related to sunglasses, not to NASA equipment. *B* can be eliminated because it is simply not mentioned in the passage. While *C* seems like it could be a true statement, it is also not relevant to what is being explained by the author. A similar thing could be said about *E*. The passage does not talk about helmet use on Earth.

34. C: It is difficult to make money from scientific research. The article gives several examples of how businesses have been able to capitalize on NASA research, so it is unlikely that the author would agree with this statement. Evidence for the other answer choices can be found in the article: *A*, the author mentions that "many consumers are unaware that products they are buying are based on NASA research"; *B* is a general definition of spinoff technology; *D* is mentioned in the final paragraph, and *E* is mentioned in the opening paragraph and is a theme throughout.

35. D: It emphasizes Mr. Utterson's anguish in failing to identify Hyde's whereabouts. Context clues indicate that Choice *D* is correct because the passage provides great detail of Mr. Utterson's feelings about locating Hyde. Choice *A* does not fit because there is no mention of Mr. Lanyon's mental state. Choice *B* is incorrect; although the text does make mention of bells, Choice *B* is not the *best* answer overall. Choice *C* is incorrect because the passage clearly states that Mr. Utterson was determined, not unsure. While the passage mentions "labyrinths of lamplighted city", this is a minor detail and not the main focus of the passage, so Choice *E* is incorrect.

36. A: In the city. The word *city* appears in the passage several times, thus establishing the location for the reader.

37. B: It scares children. The passage states that the Juggernaut causes the children to scream. Choices *A* and *D* don't apply because the text doesn't mention either of these instances specifically. Choices *C* and *E* are incorrect because there is nothing in the text that mentions space travel or oceans.

38. B: To constantly visit. The mention of *morning*, *noon*, and *night* make it clear that the word *haunt* refers to frequent appearances at various locations. Choice *A* doesn't work because the text makes no mention of levitating. Choices *C* and *D* are not correct because the text makes mention of Mr. Utterson's anguish and disheartenment because of his failure to find Hyde but does not make mention of Mr. Utterson's feelings negatively affecting anyone else. While "a ghost or spirit" is a common definition of the word *haunt*, that is not how it is being used in the passage, so Choice *E* is incorrect.

39. D: This is an example of alliteration. Choice *D* is the correct answer because of the repetition of the *L*-words. Hyperbole is an exaggeration, so Choice *A* doesn't work. No comparison is being made, so no simile or metaphor is being used, thus eliminating Choices *B, C,* and *E*.

40. D: The speaker intends to continue to look for Hyde. Choices *A* and *B* are not possible answers because the text doesn't refer to any name changes or an identity crisis, despite Mr. Utterson's extreme obsession with finding Hyde. The text also makes no mention of a mistaken identity or wanting to make friends when referring to Hyde, so Choices *C* and *E* are also incorrect.

41. C: The author contrasts two different viewpoints, then builds a case showing preference for one over the other. Choice *A* is incorrect because the introduction does not contain an impartial definition, but rather another's opinion. Choice *B* is incorrect. There is no puzzling phenomenon given, as the author doesn't mention any peculiar cause or effect that is in question regarding poetry. Choice *D* does contain another's viewpoint at the beginning of the passage; however, to say that the author has no stake in this argument is incorrect; the author uses personal experiences to build their case. Finally, Choice *E* is incorrect because there is no description of the history of poetry offered within the passage.

42. B: Choice *B* accurately describes the author's argument in the text—that poetry is not irrelevant. While the author does praise—and even value—Buddy Wakefield as a poet, he or she never heralds him as a genius. Eliminate Choice *A*, as it is an exaggeration. Not only is Choice *C* an exaggerated statement, but the author never mentions spoken word poetry in the text. Choice *D* is wrong because this statement contradicts the writer's argument. Choice *E* can also be eliminated, because the author mentions how performance actually *enhances* poetry and that modern technology is one way poetry remains vital.

43. D: *Exiguously* means not occurring often, or occurring rarely, so Choice *D* would LEAST change the meaning of the sentence. Choice *A*, *indolently*, means unhurriedly, or slow, and does not fit the context of the sentence. Choice *B*, *inaudibly*, means quietly or silently. Choice *C*, *interminably*, means endlessly, or all the time, and is the opposite of the word *exiguously*. Choice *E*, *impecunious,* means impoverished or destitute, and does not fit within the context of the sentence.

44. E: The author of the passage tries to insist that performance poetry is a subset of modern poetry, and therefore prove that modern poetry is not "dying," but thriving on social media for the masses. Choice *A* is incorrect, as the author is not refusing any kind of validation. Choice *B* is incorrect; the author's insistence is that poetry will *not* lose popularity. Choice *C* mimics the topic but compares two different genres, while the author makes no comparison in this passage. Choice *D* is incorrect as well; again, there is no cause or effect the author is trying to prove.

45. B: The author's purpose is to disprove Gioia's article claiming that poetry is a dying art form that only survives in academic settings. In order to prove his argument, the author educates the reader about new developments in poetry (Choice *A*) and describes the brilliance of a specific modern poet (Choice *C*), but these are used to serve as examples of a growing poetry trend that counters Gioia's argument. Choice *D* is incorrect because it contradicts the author's argument. Choice *E* is incorrect because the passage uses the performance as a way to convey the author's point; it's not the focus of the piece. It's also unclear if the author was actually present at the live performance.

46. D: Choice *D* is the best answer. Before the quote, we see the statement, "*Crowbirds* touches on themes of core human concepts such as faith, personal loss, and growth. These are not ideas that only poets or students of literature understand, but all human beings . . ." Choice *D* mentions the quote is used to depict "complex themes," (such as faith, personal loss, and growth) that draw an audience. Choice *D* is the most closely aligned answer choice to this statement. We can eliminate Choice *A*. "Speaking meter" doesn't exist and isn't mentioned in the passage. The author does mention that although poetry's medium is changing, people are still writing poetry (Choice *B*). However, this is a conclusion of the passage and isn't a direct reason the author includes the quote. Choice *C* is also mentioned as a concluding argument: "poetry continues to have a steady audience," but it is not the reason why the author includes the quote. Finally, Choice *E* is incorrect; the author of the passage opposed Gioia's argument in the first paragraph.

47. C: The text mentions all of the listed properties of minerals except the instance of minerals being organically formed. Objects or substances must be naturally occurring, must be a homogeneous solid, and must have a definite chemical composition in order to be considered a mineral.

48. A: Choice *A* is the correct answer because the prefix "homo" means same. Choice *B* is incorrect because "differing in some areas" would be linked to the root word "hetero," meaning "different" or "other."

49: C: Choice *C* is the correct answer because *-logy* refers to the study of a particular subject matter.

50: C: Choice *C* is the correct answer because the counterargument is necessary to point to the fact that researchers don't always agree with findings. Choices *A* and *B* are incorrect because the counterargument isn't overcomplicated or expressing bias, but simply stating an objective dispute. Choice *D* is incorrect because the counterargument is not used to persuade readers to create a new subsection of minerals.

Mathematics

Estimation, Measurement, & Statistics

Measurement Systems and Standard Units of Measure

The American Measuring System

The measuring system used today in the United States developed from the British units of measurement during colonial times. The most typically used units in this customary system are those used to measure weight, liquid volume, and length, whose common units are found below. In the customary system, the basic unit for measuring weight is the ounce (oz); there are 16 ounces (oz) in 1 pound (lb) and 2000 pounds in 1 ton. The basic unit for measuring liquid volume is the ounce (oz); 1 ounce is equal to 2 tablespoons (tbsp) or 6 teaspoons (tsp), and there are 8 ounces in 1 cup, 2 cups in 1 pint (pt), 2 pints in 1 quart (qt), and 4 quarts in 1 gallon (gal). For measurements of length, the inch (in) is the base unit; 12 inches make up 1 foot (ft), 3 feet make up 1 yard (yd), and 5280 feet make up 1 mile (mi). However, as there are only a set number of units in the customary system, with extremely large or extremely small amounts of material, the numbers can become awkward and difficult to compare.

Common Customary Measurements		
Length	**Weight**	**Capacity**
1 foot = 12 inches	1 pound = 16 ounces	1 cup = 8 fluid ounces
1 yard = 3 feet	1 ton = 2,000 pounds	1 pint = 2 cups
1 yard = 36 inches		1 quart = 2 pints
1 mile = 1,760 yards		1 quart = 4 cups
1 mile = 5,280 feet		1 gallon = 4 quarts
		1 gallon = 16 cups

The Metric System

Aside from the United States, most countries in the world have adopted the metric system embodied in the International System of Units (SI). The three main SI base units used in the metric system are the meter (m), the kilogram (kg), and the liter (L); meters measure length, kilograms measure mass, and liters measure volume.

These three units can use different prefixes, which indicate larger or smaller versions of the unit by powers of ten. This can be thought of as making a new unit which is sized by multiplying the original unit in size by a factor.

These prefixes and associated factors are:

Metric Prefixes			
Prefix	**Symbol**	**Multiplier**	**Exponential**
giga	G	1,000,000,000	10^9
mega	M	1,000,000	10^6
kilo	k	1,000	10^3
hecto	h	100	10^2
deca	da	10	10^1
no prefix		1	10^0
deci	d	0.1	10^{-1}
centi	c	0.01	10^{-2}
milli	m	0.001	10^{-3}
micro	µ	0.000001	10^{-6}
nano	n	0.000000001	10^{-9}

The correct prefix is then attached to the base. Some examples:

1 milliliter equals .001 liters.
1,000,000,000 nanometers equals 1 meter.
1 kilogram equals 1,000 grams.

Choosing the Appropriate Measuring Unit

Some units of measure are represented as square or cubic units depending on the solution. For example, perimeter is measured in units, area is measured in square units, and volume is measured in cubic units.

Also be sure to use the most appropriate unit for the thing being measured. A building's height might be measured in feet or meters while the length of a nail might be measured in inches or centimeters. Additionally, for SI units, the prefix should be chosen to provide the most succinct available value. For example, the mass of a bag of fruit would likely be measured in kilograms rather than grams or milligrams, and the length of a bacteria cell would likely be measured in micrometers rather than centimeters or kilometers.

Conversions

Converting measurements in different units between the two systems can be difficult because they follow different rules. The best method is to look up an English to Metric system conversion factor and then use a series of equivalent fractions to set up an equation to convert the units of one of the measurements into those of the other.

The table below lists some common conversion values that are useful for problems involving measurements with units in both systems:

English System	Metric System
1 inch	2.54 cm
1 foot	0.3048 m
1 yard	0.914 m
1 mile	1.609 km
1 ounce	28.35 g
1 pound	0.454 kg
1 fluid ounce	29.574 mL
1 quart	0.946 L
1 gallon	3.785 L

Consider the example where a scientist wants to convert 6.8 inches to centimeters. The table above is used to find that there are 2.54 centimeters in every inch, so the following equation should be set up and solved:

$$\frac{6.8\ in}{1} \times \frac{2.54\ cm}{1\ in} = 17.272\ cm$$

Notice how the inches in the numerator of the initial figure and the denominator of the conversion factor cancel out. (This equation could have been written simply as $6.8\ in \times 2.54\ cm = 17.272\ cm$, but it was shown in detail to illustrate the steps). The goal in any conversion equation is to set up the fractions so that the units you are trying to convert from cancel out and the units you desire remain.

For a more complicated example, consider converting 2.15 kilograms into ounces. The first step is to convert kilograms into grams and then grams into ounces. Note that the measurement you begin with does not have to be put in a fraction.

So in this case, 2.15 kg is by itself although it's technically the numerator of a fraction:

$$2.15\ kg \times \frac{1000g}{kg} = 2150\ g$$

Then, use the conversion factor from the table to convert grams to ounces:

$$2150g \times \frac{1\ oz}{28.35g} = 75.8\ oz$$

Perimeter and Area

Perimeter is the measurement of a distance around something or the sum of all sides of a polygon. Think of perimeter as the length of the boundary, like a fence. In contrast, **area** is the space occupied by a defined enclosure, like a field enclosed by a fence.

When thinking about perimeter, think about walking around the outside of something. When thinking about area, think about the amount of space or **surface area** something takes up.

Squares

The perimeter of a square is measured by adding together all of the sides. Since a square has four equal sides, its perimeter can be calculated by multiplying the length of one side by 4. Thus, the formula is $P = 4 \times s$, where s equals one side. For example, the following square has side lengths of 5 meters:

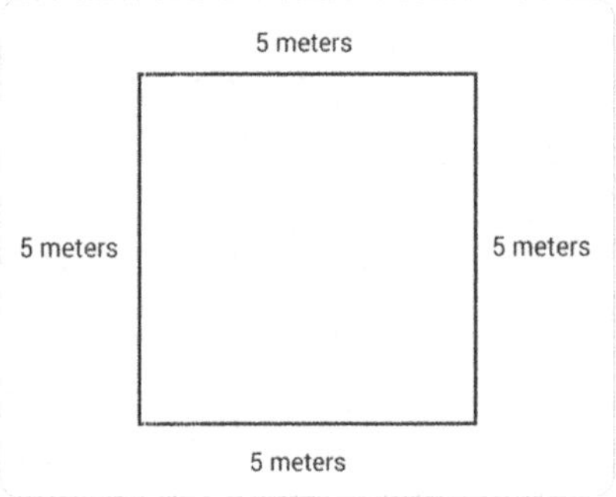

The perimeter is 20 meters because 4 times 5 is 20.

The area of a square is the length of a side squared. For example, if a side of a square is 7 centimeters, then the area is 49 square centimeters. The formula for this example is $A = s^2 = 7^2 = 49$ square centimeters. An example is if the rectangle has a length of 6 inches and a width of 7 inches, then the area is 42 square inches:

$$A = lw = 6(7) = 42 \text{ square inches}$$

Rectangles

Like a square, a rectangle's perimeter is measured by adding together all of the sides. But as the sides are unequal, the formula is different. A rectangle has equal values for its lengths (long sides) and equal values for its widths (short sides), so the perimeter formula for a rectangle is:

$$P = l + l + w + w = 2l + 2w$$

l equals length
w equals width

The area is found by multiplying the length by the width, so the formula is $A = l \times w$.

For example, if the length of a rectangle is 10 inches and the width 8 inches, then the perimeter is 36 inches because:

$$P = 2l + 2w = 2(10) + 2(8) = 20 + 16 = 36 \text{ inches}$$

Triangles

A triangle's perimeter is measured by adding together the three sides, so the formula is $P = a + b + c$, where $a, b,$ and c are the values of the three sides. The area is the product of one-half the base and height so the formula is:

$$A = \frac{1}{2} \times b \times h$$

It can be simplified to:

$$A = \frac{bh}{2}$$

The base is the bottom of the triangle, and the height is the distance from the base to the peak. If a problem asks to calculate the area of a triangle, it will provide the base and height.

For example, if the base of the triangle is 2 feet and the height 4 feet, then the area is 4 square feet. The following equation shows the formula used to calculate the area of the triangle:

$$\text{A} = \frac{1}{2}\text{bh} = \frac{1}{2}(2)(4) = 4 \text{ square feet}$$

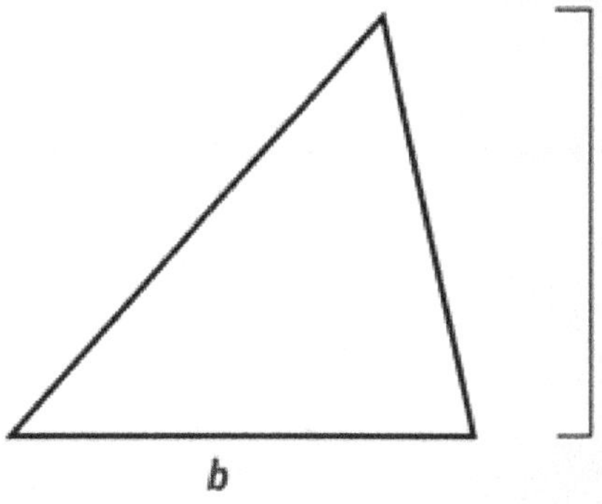

Circles

A circle's perimeter—also known as its circumference—is measured by multiplying the diameter by π.

Diameter is the straight line measured from one end to the direct opposite end of the circle.

π is referred to as pi and is equal to 3.14 (with rounding).

So the formula is $\pi \times d$.

This is sometimes expressed by the formula $C = 2 \times \pi \times r$, where r is the radius of the circle. These formulas are equivalent, as the radius equals half of the diameter.

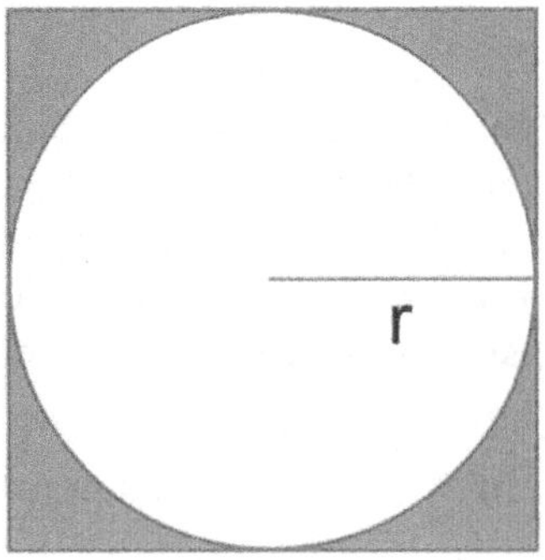

The area of a circle is calculated through the formula $A = \pi \times r^2$. The test will indicate either to leave the answer with π attached or to calculate to the nearest decimal place, which means multiplying by 3.14 for π.

Parallelograms

Similar to triangles, the height of the parallelogram is measured from one base to the other at a 90° angle (or perpendicular).

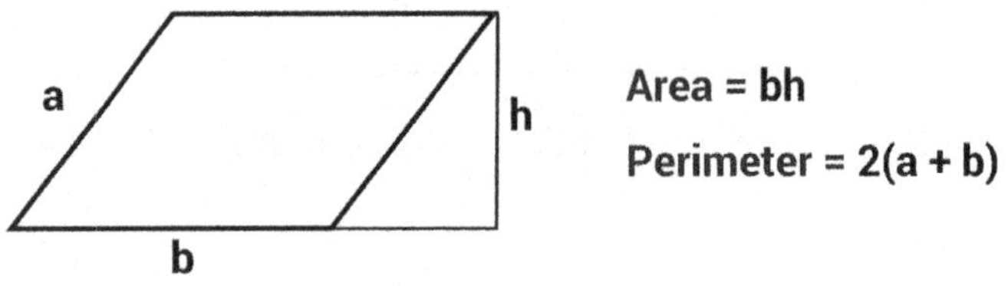

Trapezoid

The area of a trapezoid can be calculated using the formula: $A = \frac{1}{2} \times h(b_1 + b_2)$, where h is the height and b_1 and b_2 are the parallel bases of the trapezoid.

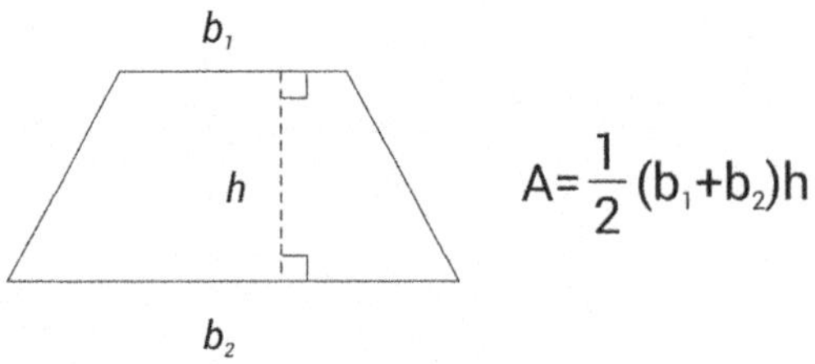

Irregular Shapes

The perimeter of an irregular polygon is found by adding the lengths of all of the sides. In cases where all of the sides are given, this will be very straightforward, as it will simply involve finding the sum of the provided lengths. Other times, a side length may be missing and must be determined before the perimeter can be calculated. Consider the example below:

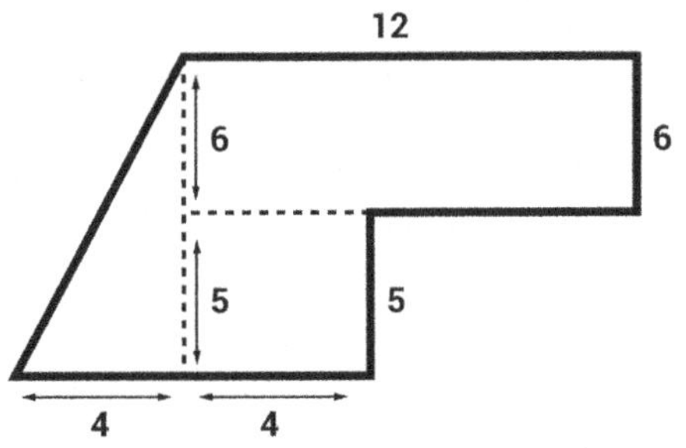

All of the side lengths are provided except for the angled side on the left. Test takers should notice that this is the hypotenuse of a right triangle. The other two sides of the triangle are provided (the base is 4 and the height is 6 + 5 = 11). The Pythagorean Theorem can be used to find the length of the hypotenuse, remembering that $a^2 + b^2 = c^2$.

Substituting the side values provided yields:

$$(4)^2 + (11)^2 = c^2$$

Therefore:

$$c = \sqrt{16 + 121} = 11.7$$

Finally, the perimeter can be found by adding this new side length with the other provided lengths to get the total length around the figure:

$$4 + 4 + 5 + 8 + 6 + 12 + 11.7 = 50.7$$

Although units are not provided in this figure, remember that reporting units with a measurement is important.

The area of irregular polygons is found by decomposing, or breaking apart, the figure into smaller shapes. When the area of the smaller shapes is determined, the area of the smaller shapes will produce the area of the original figure when added together. Consider the earlier example:

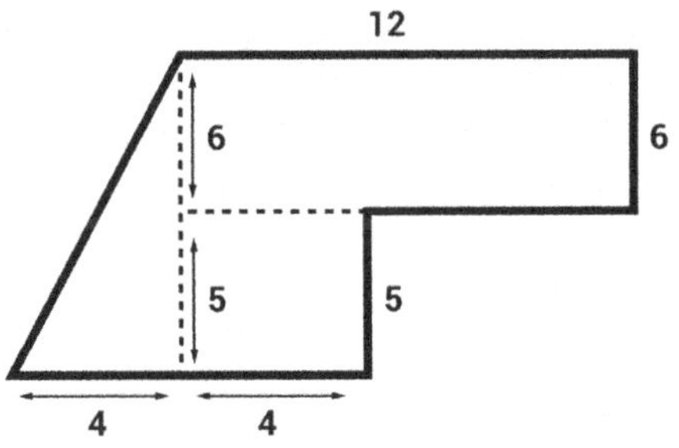

The irregular polygon is decomposed into two rectangles and a triangle. The area of the large rectangles ($A = l \times w \rightarrow A = 12 \times 6$) is 72 square units. The area of the small rectangle is 20 square units ($A = 4 \times 5$). The area of the triangle ($A = \frac{1}{2} \times b \times h \rightarrow A = \frac{1}{2} \times 4 \times 11$) is 22 square units. The sum of the areas of these figures produces the total area of the original polygon:

$$A = 72 + 20 + 22 \rightarrow A = 114 \text{ square units}$$

Here's another example:

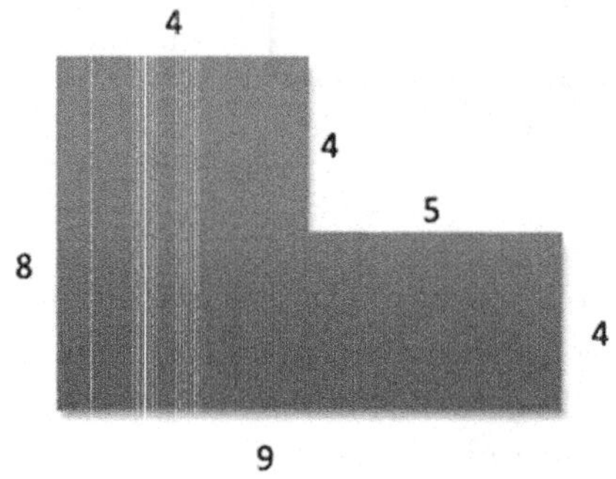

This irregular polygon is decomposed into two rectangles. The area of the large rectangle ($A = l \times w \rightarrow A = 8 \times 4$) is 32 square units. The area of the small rectangle is 20 square units ($A = 4 \times 5$). The sum of the areas of these figures produces the total area of the original polygon:

$$A = 32 + 20 \rightarrow A = 52 \text{ square units}$$

Estimating Time

Estimation is finding a value that is close to a solution but is not the exact answer. For example, if there are values in the thousands to be multiplied, then each value can be estimated to the nearest thousand and the calculation performed. This value provides an approximate solution that can be determined very quickly.

When estimating, it's often convenient to **round** a number, which means to give an approximate figure to make it easier to compare amounts or perform mental math. Round up when the digit is 5 or more. The digit used to determine the rounding, and all subsequent digits, become 0, and the selected place value is increased by 1. Here are some examples:

75 rounded to the nearest ten is 80
380 rounded to the nearest hundred is 400
22.697 rounded to the nearest hundredth is 22.70

Round down when rounding on any digit that is below 5. The rounded digit, and all subsequent digits, becomes 0, and the preceding digit stays the same. Here are some examples:

92 rounded to the nearest ten is 90
839 rounded to the nearest hundred is 800
22.643 rounded to the nearest hundredth is 22.64

The same estimation strategies and techniques used when working with standard math problems can be employed when working with real-life situations. Estimation is frequently used in calculations involving money, such as for determining if one has enough money for a purchase, how much one needs to save weekly to buy a desired product, or how much a restaurant bill will sum to.

Another equally effective application of estimation—albeit a bit more difficult and less straightforward—involves time. Many people find it helpful to estimate the length of time it will take them to complete a given task or perform some function. This enables them to budget their time and energy effectively and develop a schedule or timeline by which projects and activities should be addressed. Estimating one's time is especially helpful for work-related objectives, to set reasonable expectations and meet required deadlines accordingly.

When estimating time, the same principles of rounding can be used, but now there is context behind the rounding. In other words, there is a specific meaning to what is being rounded (hours, minutes, seconds, days, etc.). This context needs to be considered when making the estimation and the rounding rules are typically not as formal and strict as those used in standard math calculations. For example, to round a number when performing regular mathematical calculations, the place value is specified. Then, as mentioned, the digit to its right is looked at. For example, if rounding to the nearest hundreds place, the digit in the tens place is used. If it is a 0, 1, 2, 3, or 4, the digit being rounded to is left alone. If it is a 5, 6, 7, 8 or 9, the digit being rounded to is increased by one.

All other digits before the decimal point are then changed to zeros, and the digits in decimal places are dropped. In contrast, there are no explicitly defined rules for rounding time. Two people may round time differently or the same person might round the same time differently depending on the situation. For example, it is 1:10pm, one person may say it is "around 1" and another might say it is "going on 1:30." Similarly, if someone is going on vacation in 24 days, he or she might say the vacation is in three weeks. If, instead, that person has been dieting for that length of time but have not seen results, he or she may say, "I've been dieting for about a month and still haven't lost a pound!" Although some of these estimations are more accurate than others, since formal rules don't exist, none are necessarily "wrong."

In general, estimating time is more complicated than estimation involved in mathematical computations because it not only involves rounding numbers and the normal mathematical techniques, but also the awareness or forethought about how long a certain task will likely take to complete. For example, if working with a team to design a new logo for a company, one has to try to imagine the realistic, but potential, factors that will affect the projected timeline (i.e., How long might meetings take with the other team members? Will a compromise or agreement be reached easily or does there tend to be a lot of stubbornness surrounding one's idea? What is the process like for logo approval?).

With that said, as one becomes more experienced in a given job position or more self-aware over time, his or her ability to estimate the time needed for various work-related objectives or other life functions will improve. In these cases, time estimations can be instrumental in establishing functional schedules and realistic timelines.

Estimating Prior to Calculating

Prior to performing operations and calculating the answer to a problem involving addition, subtraction, multiplication, or division, it is helpful to estimate the result. Doing so will enable the test taker to determine whether his or her computed answer is logical within the context of a given problem and prevent careless errors. For example, it is unfortunately common under the pressure of a testing situation for test takers to inadvertently perform the incorrect operation or make a simple calculation error on an otherwise easy math problem. By quickly estimating the answer by eyeballing the numbers, rounding if needed, and performing some simple mental math, test takers can establish an approximate expected outcome before calculating the specific answer. The derived result after computation can then be evaluated by its nearness to the expected answer. This is performed by approximating given values to perform mental math. Numbers should be rounded to the nearest value possible to check the initial results.

As mentioned, sometimes when performing operations such as multiplying numbers, the result can be estimated by rounding. For example, to estimate the value of 11.2×2.01, each number can be rounded to the nearest integer. This will yield a result of 22.

Rounding numbers helps with estimation because it changes the given number to a simpler, although less accurate, number than the exact given number. Rounding allows for easier calculations, which estimate the results of using the exact given number. The accuracy of the estimate and ease of use depends on the place value to which the number is rounded. First, the place value is specified. Then, the digit to its right is looked at. For example, if rounding to the nearest hundreds place, the digit in the tens place is used. If it is a zero, one, 2, 3, or 4, the digit being rounded to is left alone. If it is a 5, 6, 7, 8 or 9, the digit being rounded to is increased by one. All other digits before the decimal point are then changed to zeros, and the digits in decimal places are dropped. If a decimal place is being rounded to, all digits that come after are just dropped.

For example, if 845,231.45 was to be rounded to the nearest thousands place, the answer would be 845,000. The 5 would remain the same due to the 2 in the hundreds place. Also, if 4.567 were to be rounded to the nearest tenths place, the answer would be 4.6. The 5 increased to 6 due to the 6 in the hundredths place, and the rest of the decimal is dropped.

Mental math should always be considered as problems are worked through, and the ability to work through problems in one's head helps save time. If a problem is simple enough, such as $15 + 3 = 18$, it should be completed mentally. The ability to do this will increase once addition and subtraction in higher place values are grasped. Also, mental math is important in multiplication and division. The times tables multiplying all numbers from 1 to 12 should be memorized. This will allow for division within those numbers to be memorized as well. For example, we should know easily that $121 \div 11 = 11$ because it should be memorized that $11 \times 11 = 121$.

Here is the multiplication table to be memorized:

x	1	2	3	4	5	6	7	8	9	10	11	12	13	14	15
1	1	2	3	4	5	6	7	8	9	10	11	12	13	14	15
2	2	4	6	8	10	12	14	16	18	20	22	24	26	28	30
3	3	6	9	12	15	18	21	24	27	30	33	36	39	42	45
4	4	8	12	16	20	24	28	32	36	40	44	48	52	56	60
5	5	10	15	20	25	30	35	40	45	50	55	60	65	70	75
6	6	12	18	24	30	36	42	48	54	60	66	72	78	84	90
7	7	14	21	28	35	42	49	56	63	70	77	84	91	98	105
8	8	16	24	32	40	48	56	64	72	80	88	96	104	112	120
9	9	18	27	36	45	54	63	72	81	90	99	108	117	126	135
10	10	20	30	40	50	60	70	80	90	100	110	120	130	140	150
11	11	22	33	44	55	66	77	88	99	110	121	132	143	154	165
12	12	24	36	48	60	72	84	96	108	120	132	144	156	168	180
13	13	26	39	52	65	78	91	104	117	130	143	156	169	182	195
14	14	28	42	56	70	84	98	112	126	140	154	168	182	196	210
15	15	30	45	60	75	90	105	120	135	150	165	180	195	210	225

The values along the diagonal of the table consist of **perfect squares**. A perfect square is a number that represents a product of two equal integers.

Estimating Absolute and Relative Error in the Numerical Answer to a Problem

Once a result is determined to be logical within the context of a given problem, the result should be evaluated by its nearness to the expected answer. This is performed by approximating given values to perform mental math. Numbers should be rounded to the nearest value possible to check the initial results.

Consider the following example: A problem states that a customer is buying a new sound system for their home. The customer purchases a stereo for $435, 2 speakers for $67 each, and the necessary cables for $12. The customer chooses an option that allows him to spread the costs over equal payments for 4 months. How much will the monthly payments be?

After making calculations for the problem, a student determines that the monthly payment will be $145.25. To check the accuracy of the results, the student rounds each cost to the nearest ten ($440 + 70 + 70 + 10$) and determines that the total is approximately $590. Dividing by 4 months gives an approximate monthly payment of $147.50. Therefore, the student can conclude that the solution of $145.25 is very close to what should be expected.

When rounding, the place-value that is used in rounding can make a difference. Suppose the student had rounded to the nearest hundred for the estimation. The result ($400 + 100 + 100 + 0 = 600;\ 600 \div 4 = 150$) will show that the answer is reasonable but not as close to the actual value as rounding to the nearest ten.

When considering the accuracy of estimates, the error in the estimated solution can be shown as absolute and relative. **Absolute error** tells the actual difference between the estimated value and the true, calculated value. The **relative error** tells how large the error is in relation to the true value. There may be two problems where the absolute error of the values (the estimated one and the calculated one) is 10. For one problem, this may mean the relative error in the estimate is very small because the estimated value is 15,000, and the true value is 14,990. Ten in relation to the true value of 15,000 is small: 0.06%. For the other problem, the estimated value is 50, and the true value is 40. In this case, the absolute error of 10 means a high relative error because the true value is smaller. The relative error is 10/40 = 0.25 or 25%.

Statistical Principles

Performing Arithmetic Operations on Basic Statistical Data

The field of statistics describes relationships between quantities that are related, but not necessarily in a deterministic manner. For example, a graduating student's salary will often be higher when the student graduates with a higher GPA, but this is not always the case. Likewise, people who smoke tobacco are more likely to develop lung cancer, but, in fact, it is possible for non-smokers to develop the disease as well. **Statistics** describes these kinds of situations, where the likelihood of some outcome depends on the starting data.

Descriptive statistics involves analyzing a collection of data to describe its broad properties such average (or mean), what percent of the data falls within a given range, and other such properties. An example of this would be taking all of the test scores from a given class and calculating the average test score. **Inferential statistics** attempts to use data about a subset of some population to make inferences about the rest of the population. An example of this would be taking a collection of students who received tutoring and comparing their results to a collection of students who did not receive tutoring, then using that comparison to try to predict whether the tutoring program in question is beneficial.

To be sure that inferences have a high probability of being true for the whole population, the subset that is analyzed needs to resemble a miniature version of the population as closely as possible. For this reason, statisticians like to choose random samples from the population to study, rather than picking a specific group of people based on some similarity. For example, studying the incomes of people who live in Portland does not tell anything useful about the incomes of people who live in Tallahassee.

Ratios and Proportions

A **ratio** is a comparison of two quantities in a particular order. Example: If there are 14 computers in a lab, and the class has 20 students, there is a student to computer ratio of 20 to 14, commonly written as 20:14. Ratios are normally reduced to their smallest whole number representation, so 20:14 would be reduced to 10:7 by dividing both sides by 2.

A **proportion** is a relationship between two quantities that dictates how one changes when the other changes. A direct proportion describes a relationship in which a quantity increases by a set amount for every increase in the other quantity, or decreases by that same amount for every decrease in the other quantity. Example: Assuming a constant driving speed, the time required for a car trip increases as the distance of the trip increases. The distance to be traveled and the time required to travel are directly proportional.

Inverse proportion is a relationship in which an increase in one quantity is accompanied by a decrease in the other, or vice versa. Example: the time required for a car trip decreases as the speed increases, and increases as the speed decreases, so the time required is inversely proportional to the speed of the car.

Solving for x in a Proportion

Solve for *x* in this proportion: $\frac{10}{15} = \frac{x}{30}$.

There are two ways to solve for *x*.

Method 1: Cross multiply; then, solve for x.

$$\frac{10}{15} = \frac{x}{30}$$

$$10(30) = 15(x)$$

$$300 = 15x$$

$$300 \div 15 = 15x \div 15$$

$$x = 20$$

Method 2: Notice that 30 is twice as much as 15, so *x* should be twice as much as 10. Therefore, $x = 10 \times 2 = 20$.

Mean, Median, and Mode

The **center** of a set of data (statistical values) can be represented by its mean, median, or mode. These are sometimes referred to as **measures of central tendency**.

Mean

Suppose that you have a set of data points and some description of the general properties of this data need to be found.

The first property that can be defined for this set of data is the **mean**. This is the same as average. To find the mean, add up all the data points, then divide by the total number of data points. For example, suppose that in a class of 10 students, the scores on a test were 50, 60, 65, 65, 75, 80, 85, 85, 90, 100. Therefore, the average test score will be:

$$\frac{50 + 60 + 65 + 65 + 75 + 80 + 85 + 85 + 90 + 100}{10} = 75.5$$

The mean is a useful number if the distribution of data is normal (more on this later), which roughly means that the frequency of different outcomes has a single peak and is roughly equally distributed on both sides of that peak. However, it is less useful in some cases where the data might be split or where there are some **outliers**. Outliers are data points that are far from the rest of the data. For example, suppose there are 10 executives and 90 employees at a company. The executives make $1000 per hour, and the employees make $10 per hour.

Therefore, the average pay rate will be:

$$\frac{\$1000 \times 10 + \$10 \times 90}{100} = \$109 \text{ per hour}$$

In this case, this average is not very descriptive since it's not close to the actual pay of the executives or the employees.

Median

Another useful measurement is the **median**. In a data set, the median is the point in the middle. The middle refers to the point where half the data comes before it and half comes after, when the data is recorded in numerical order. For instance, these are the speeds of the fastball of a pitcher during the last inning that he pitched (in order from least to greatest):

90, 92, 93, 93, 95, 96, 97, 97, 97

There are nine total numbers, so the middle or *median* number is the 5th one, which is 95.

In cases where the number of data points is an even number, then the average of the two middle points is taken. In the previous example of test scores, the two middle points are 75 and 80. Since there is no single point, the average of these two scores needs to be found. The average is:

$$\frac{75 + 80}{2} = 77.5$$

The median is generally a good value to use if there are a few outliers in the data. It prevents those outliers from affecting the "middle" value as much as when using the mean.

Since an outlier is a data point that is far from most of the other data points in a data set, this means an outlier also is any point that is far from the median of the data set. The outliers can have a substantial effect on the mean of a data set, but they usually do not change the median or mode, or do not change them by a large quantity. For example, consider the data set (3, 5, 6, 6, 6, 8). This has a median of 6 and a mode of 6, with a mean of $\frac{34}{6} \approx 5.67$. Now, suppose a new data point of 1000 is added so that the data set is now (3, 5, 6, 6, 6, 8, 1000). This does not change the median or mode, which are both still 6. However, the average is now $\frac{1034}{7}$, which is approximately 147.7. In this case, the median and mode will be better descriptions for most of the data points.

The reason for outliers in a given data set is a complicated problem. It is sometimes the result of an error by the experimenter, but often they are perfectly valid data points that must be taken into consideration.

Mode

One additional measure to define for *X* is the **mode.** This is the data point that appears most frequently. If two or more data points all tie for the most frequent appearance, then each of them is considered a mode. In the case of the test scores, where the numbers were 50, 60, 65, 65, 75, 80, 85, 85, 90, 100, there are two modes: 65 and 85.

A data set may have a single mode, multiple modes, or no mode. If different values repeat equally as often, multiple modes exist. If no value repeats, no mode exists. Consider the following data sets:

- A: 7, 9, 10, 13, 14, 14
- B: 37, 44, 33, 37, 49, 44, 51, 34, 37, 33, 44
- C: 173, 154, 151, 168, 155

Set A has a mode of 14. Set B has modes of 37 and 44. Set C has no mode.

The range of a data set is the difference between the highest and the lowest values in the set. The range can be considered the span of the data set. To determine the range, the smallest value in the set is subtracted from the largest value. The ranges for the data sets A, B, and C above are calculated as follows: A: $14 - 7 = 7$; B: $51 - 33 = 18$; C: $173 - 151 = 22$.

Changing all values of a data set in a consistent way produces predictable changes in the measures of the center and range of the set. A linear transformation changes the original value into the new value by either adding a given number to each value, multiplying each value by a given number, or both. Adding (or subtracting) a given value to each data point will increase (or decrease) the mean, median, and any modes by the same value. However, the range will remain the same due to the way that range is calculated. Multiplying (or dividing) a given value by each data point will increase (or decrease) the mean, median, and any modes, and the range by the same factor.

Consider the following data set, call it set *P*, representing the price of different cases of soda at a grocery store: $4.25, $4.40, $4.75, $4.95, $4.95, $5.15. The mean of set *P* is $4.74. The median is $4.85. The mode of the set is $4.95. The range is $0.90. Suppose the state passes a new tax of $0.25 on every case of soda sold. The new data set, set *T*, is calculated by adding $0.25 to each data point from set *P*. Therefore, set *T* consists of the following values: $4.50, $4.65, $5.00, $5.20, $5.20, $5.40. The mean of set *T* is $4.99. The median is $5.10. The mode of the set is $5.20. The range is $.90. The mean, median and mode of set *T* is equal to $0.25 added to the mean, median, and mode of set *P*. The range stays the same.

Now suppose, due to inflation, the store raises the cost of every item by 10 percent. Raising costs by 10 percent is calculated by multiplying each value by 1.1. The new data set, set *I*, is calculated by multiplying each data point from set *T* by 1.1. Therefore, set *I* consists of the following values: $4.95, $5.12, $5.50, $5.72, $5.72, $5.94. The mean of set *I* is $5.49. The median is $5.61. The mode of the set is $5.72. The range is $0.99. The mean, median, mode, and range of set *I* is equal to 1.1 multiplied by the mean, median, mode, and range of set *T* because each increased by a factor of 10 percent.

Quartiles and Percentiles

The **first quartile** of a set of data *X* refers to the largest value from the first ¼ of the data points. In practice, there are sometimes slightly different definitions that can be used, such as the median of the first half of the data points (excluding the median itself if there are an odd number of data points). The term also has a slightly different use: when it is said that a data point lies in the first quartile, it means it is less than or equal to the median of the first half of the data points. Conversely, if it lies *at* the first quartile, then it is equal to the first quartile.

When it is said that a data point lies in the **second quartile**, it means it is between the first quartile and the median.

The **third quartile** refers to data that lies between ½ and ¾ of the way through the data set. Again, there are various methods for defining this precisely, but the simplest way is to include all of the data that lie between the median and the median of the top half of the data.

Data that lies in the **fourth quartile** refers to all of the data above the third quartile.

Percentiles may be defined in a similar manner to quartiles. Generally, this is defined in the following manner:

If a data point lies *in the n-th percentile*, this means it lies in the range of the first *n*% of the data.

If a data point lies *at* the *n*-th percentile, then it means that *n*% of the data lies below this data point.

Standard Deviation

Given a data set X consisting of data points $(x_1, x_2, x_3, \dots x_n)$, the **variance** of X is defined to be:

$$\frac{\sum_{i=1}^{n}(x_i - \bar{X})^2}{n}$$

This means that the variance of X is the average of the squares of the differences between each data point and the mean of X. In the formula, $\bar{X}$ is the mean of the values in the data set, and x_i represents each individual value in the data set. The sigma notation indicates that the sum should be found with n being the number of values to add together. $i = 1$ means that the values should begin with the first value.

Given a data set X consisting of data points $(x_1, x_2, x_3, \dots x_n)$, the **standard deviation** of X is defined to be:

$$s_x = \sqrt{\frac{\sum_{i=1}^{n}(x_i - \bar{X})^2}{n}}$$

In other words, the standard deviation is the square root of the variance.

Both the variance and the standard deviation are measures of how much the data tend to be spread out. When the standard deviation is low, the data points are mostly clustered around the mean. When the standard deviation is high, this generally indicates that the data are quite spread out, or else that there are a few substantial outliers.

As a simple example, compute the standard deviation for the data set (1, 3, 3, 5). First, compute the mean, which will be:

$$\frac{1+3+3+5}{4} = \frac{12}{4} = 3$$

Now, find the variance of X with the formula:

$$\sum_{i=1}^{4}(x_i - \bar{X})^2 = (1-3)^2 + (3-3)^2 + (3-3)^2 + (5-3)^2$$

$$-2^2 + 0^2 + 0^2 + 2^2 = 8$$

Therefore, the variance is $\frac{8}{4} = 2$. Taking the square root, the standard deviation will be $\sqrt{2}$.

Note that the standard deviation only depends upon the mean, not upon the median or mode(s). Generally, if there are multiple modes that are far apart from one another, the standard deviation will be high. A high standard deviation does not always mean there are multiple modes, however.

Choosing an Appropriate Measure of Central Tendency

Measures of central tendency, namely mean, median, and mode, describe characteristics of a set of data. Specifically, they are intended to represent a *typical* value in the set by identifying a central position of the set. Depending on the characteristics of a specific set of data, different measures of central tendency are more indicative of a typical value in the set.

When a data set is grouped closely together with a relatively small range and the data is spread out somewhat evenly, the mean is an effective indicator of a typical value in the set. Consider the following data set representing the height of sixth grade boys in inches: 61 inches, 54 inches, 58 inches, 63 inches, 58 inches. The mean of the set is 58.8 inches. The data set is grouped closely (the range is only 9 inches) and the values are spread relatively evenly (three values below the mean and two values above the mean). Therefore, the mean value of 58.8 inches is an effective measure of central tendency in this case.

When a data set contains a small number of values either extremely large or extremely small when compared to the other values, the mean is not an effective measure of central tendency. Consider the following data set representing annual incomes of homeowners on a given street: $71,000; $74,000; $75,000; $77,000; $340,000. The mean of this set is $127,400. This figure does not indicate a typical value in the set, which contains four out of five values between $71,000 and $77,000. The median is a much more effective measure of central tendency for data sets such as these. Finding the middle value diminishes the influence of outliers, or numbers that may appear out of place, like the $340,000 annual income. The median for this set is $75,000 which is much more typical of a value in the set.

The mode of a data set is a useful measure of central tendency for categorical data when each piece of data is an option from a category. Consider a survey of 31 commuters asking how they get to work with results summarized below.

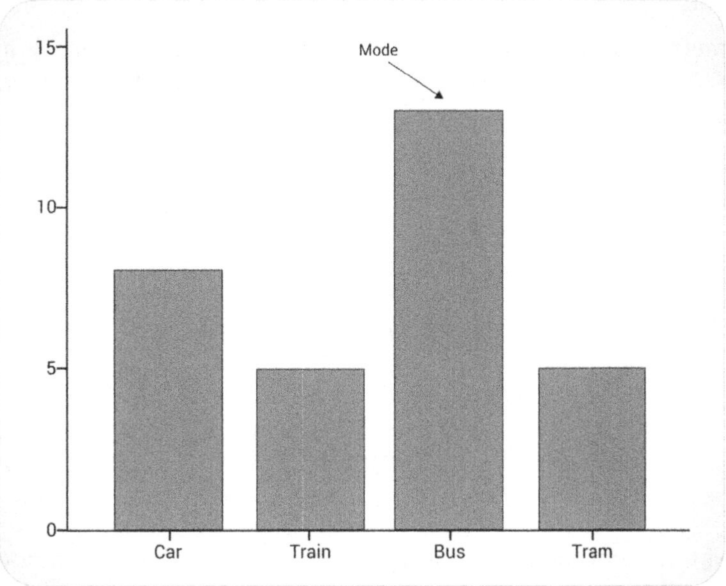

The mode for this set represents the value, or option, of the data that repeats most often. This indicates that the bus is the most popular method of transportation for the commuters.

Common Features of a Data Set

As mentioned, a set of data can be described in terms of its center, spread, shape and any unusual features. The **center** of a data set can be measured by its mean, median, or mode. The **spread** of a data set refers to how far the data points are from the center (mean or median). The spread can be measured by the range or the quartiles and interquartile range. A data set with data points clustered around the center will have a small spread. A data set covering a wide range will have a large spread.

When a data set is displayed as a histogram or frequency distribution plot, the shape indicates if a sample is normally distributed, symmetrical, or has measures of skewness or kurtosis. When graphed, a data set with a normal distribution will resemble a bell curve.

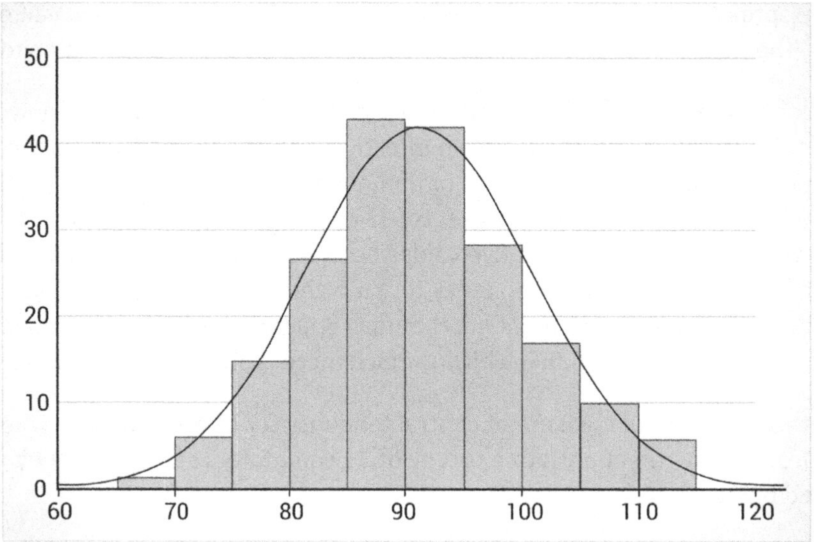

If the data set is **symmetrical**, each half of the graph when divided at the center is a mirror image of the other. If the graph has fewer data points to the right, the data is **skewed right**. If it has fewer data points to the left, the data is **skewed left**.

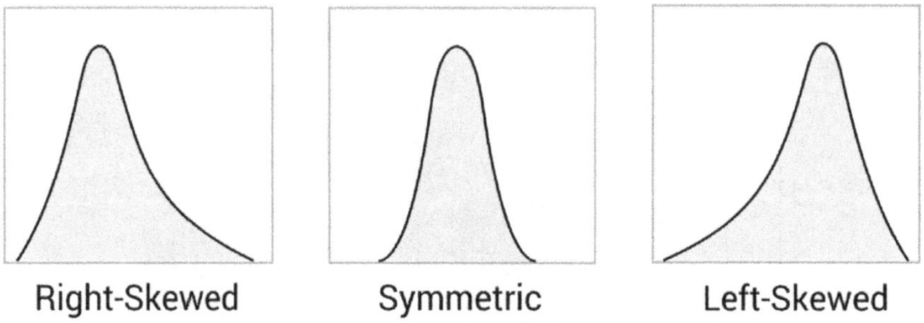

Kurtosis is a measure of whether the data is heavy-tailed with a high number of outliers, or light-tailed with a low number of outliers.

A description of a data set should include any unusual features such as gaps or outliers. A **gap** is a span within the range of the data set containing no data points. An **outlier** is a data point with a value either extremely large or extremely small when compared to the other values in the set.

The Basic Principles of Probability and Predicting the Likeliness of a Particular Outcome

Independent and Dependent Events

Probability is a measure of how likely an event is to occur. Probability is written as a fraction or decimal between zero and one. If an event has a probability of zero, the event will never occur. If an event has a probability of one, the event will definitely occur. If the probability of an event is closer to zero, the event is unlikely to occur. If the probability of an event is closer to one, the event is more likely to occur. For example, a probability of $\frac{1}{2}$ means that the event is equally as likely to occur as it is not to occur. An example of this is tossing a coin. To calculate the probability of an event, the number of favorable outcomes is divided by the number of total outcomes. For example, suppose you have 2 raffle tickets out of 20 total tickets sold. The probability that you win the raffle is calculated:

$$\frac{number\ of\ favorable\ outcomes}{total\ numberof\ outcomes} = \frac{2}{20} = \frac{1}{10} \text{ (always reduce fractions)}$$

Therefore, the probability of winning the raffle is $\frac{1}{10}$ or 0.1.

Chance is the measure of how likely an event is to occur, written as a percent. If an event will never occur, the event has a 0% chance. If an event will certainly occur, the event has a 100% chance. If an event will sometimes occur, the event has a chance somewhere between 0% and 100%. To calculate chance, probability is calculated and the fraction is converted to a percent.

The probability of multiple events occurring can be determined by multiplying the probability of each event. For example, suppose you flip a coin with heads and tails, and roll a six-sided dice numbered one through six. To find the probability that you will flip heads AND roll a two, the probability of each event is determined and those fractions are multiplied. The probability of flipping heads is $\frac{1}{2}\left(\frac{1\ side\ with\ heads}{2\ sides\ total}\right)$ and the probability of rolling a two is:

$$\frac{1}{6}\left(\frac{1\ side\ with\ a\ 2}{6\ total\ sides}\right)$$

The probability of flipping heads AND rolling a 2 is:

$$\frac{1}{2} \times \frac{1}{6} = \frac{1}{12}$$

The above scenario with flipping a coin and rolling a die is an example of independent events. Independent events are circumstances in which the outcome of one event does not affect the outcome of the other event. Conversely, dependent events are ones in which the outcome of one event affects the outcome of the second event. Consider the following scenario: a bag contains 5 black marbles and 5 white marbles. What is the probability of picking 2 black marbles without replacing the marble after the first pick?

The probability of picking a black marble on the first pick is:

$$\frac{5}{10}\left(\frac{5\ black\ marbles}{10\ total\ marbles}\right)$$

Assuming that a black marble was picked, there are now 4 black marbles and 5 white marbles for the second pick. Therefore, the probability of picking a black marble on the second pick is:

$$\frac{4}{9}\left(\frac{4\ black\ marbles}{9\ total\ marbles}\right)$$

To find the probability of picking two black marbles, the probability of each is multiplied:

$$\frac{5}{10} \times \frac{4}{9} = \frac{20}{90} = \frac{2}{9}$$

Conditional Probabilities

An outcome occasionally lies within some range of possibilities *B*, and the probability that the outcomes also lie within some set of possibilities *A* needs to be figured. This is called a **conditional probability**. It is written as $P(A|B)$, which is read "the probability of *A* given *B*." The general formula for computing conditional probabilities is:

$$P(A|B) = \frac{P(A \cap B)}{P(B)}$$

However, when dealing with uniform probability distributions, simplify this a bit. Write $|A|$ to indicate the number of outcomes in *A*. Then, for uniform probability distributions, write $P(A|B) = \frac{|A \cap B|}{|B|}$ (recall that $A \cap B$ means "*A* intersect *B*," and consists of all of the outcomes that lie in both *A* and *B*). This means that all possible outcomes do not need to be known. To see why this formula works, suppose that the set of outcomes *X* is $(x_1, x_2, x_3, \dots x_n)$, so that $|X| = n$. Then, for a uniform probability distribution, $P(A) = \frac{|A|}{n}$. However, this means:

$$(A|B) = \frac{P(A \cap B)}{P(B)} = \frac{\frac{|A \cap B|}{n}}{\frac{|B|}{n}} = \frac{|A \cap B|}{|B|}$$

(since the *n*'s cancel out)

For example, suppose a die is rolled, and it is known that it will land between 1 and 4. However, how many sides the die has is unknown. Figure the probability that the die is rolled higher than 2. To figure this, $P(3)$ or $P(4)$ does not need to be determined, or any of the other probabilities, since it is known that a fair die has a uniform probability distribution. Therefore, apply the formula $\frac{|A \cap B|}{|B|}$. So, in this case *B* is (1, 2, 3, 4) and $A \cap B$ is (3, 4). Therefore:

$$\frac{|A \cap B|}{|B|} = \frac{2}{4} = \frac{1}{2}$$

Conditional probability is an important concept because, in many situations, the likelihood of one outcome can differ radically depending on how something else comes out. The probability of passing a test given that one has studied all of the material is generally much higher than the probability of passing a test given that one has not studied at all. The probability of a person having heart trouble is much lower if that person exercises regularly. The probability that a college student will graduate is higher when his or her SAT scores are higher, and so on. For this reason, there are many people who are interested in conditional probabilities.

Note that in some practical situations, changing the order of the conditional probabilities can make the outcome very different. For example, the probability that a person with heart trouble has exercised regularly is quite different than the probability that a person who exercises regularly will have heart trouble. The probability of a person receiving a military-only award, given that he or she is or was a soldier, is generally not very high, but the probability that a person being or having been a soldier, given that he or she received a military-only award, is 1.

However, in some cases, the outcomes do not influence one another this way. If the probability of *A* is the same regardless of whether *B* is given; that is, if $P(A|B) = P(A)$, then *A* and *B* are considered **independent**. In this case:

$$P(A|B) = \frac{P(A \cap B)}{P(B)} = P(A)$$

So:

$$P(A \cap B) = P(A)P(B)$$

In fact, if $P(A \cap B) = P(A)P(B)$, it can be determined that $P(A|B) = P(A)$ and $P(A|B) = P(B)$ by working backward. Therefore, *B* is also independent of *A*.

An example of something being independent can be seen in rolling dice. In this case, consider a red die and a green die. It is expected that when the dice are rolled, the outcome of the green die should not depend in any way on the outcome of the red die. Or, to take another example, if the same die is rolled repeatedly, then the next number rolled should not depend on which numbers have been rolled previously. Similarly, if a coin is flipped, then the next flip's outcome does not depend on the outcomes of previous flips.

This can sometimes be counterintuitive, since when rolling a die or flipping a coin, there can be a streak of surprising results. If, however, it is known that the die or coin is fair, then these results are just the result of the fact that over long periods of time, it is very likely that some unlikely streaks of outcomes will occur. Therefore, avoid making the mistake of thinking that when considering a series of independent outcomes, a particular outcome is "due to happen" simply because a surprising series of outcomes has already been seen.

There is a second type of common mistake that people tend to make when reasoning about statistical outcomes: the idea that when something of low probability happens, the outcome is surprising. It would be surprising that something with low probability happened after just one attempt. However, with so much happening all at once, it is easy to see at least something happen in a way that seems to have a very low probability. In fact, a lottery is a good example. The odds of winning a lottery are very small, but the odds that somebody wins the lottery each week are actually fairly high. Therefore, no one should be surprised when some low probability things happen.

Addition Rule

The **addition rule** for probabilities states that the probability of *A* or *B* happening is:

$$P(A \cup B) = P(A) + P(B) - P(A \cap B)$$

Note that the subtraction of $P(A \cap B)$ must be performed, or else it would result in double counting any outcomes that lie in both *A* and in *B*. For example, suppose that a 20-sided die is being rolled. Fred bets that the outcome will be greater than 10, while Helen bets that it will be greater than 4 but less than 15. What is the probability that at least one of them is correct?

We apply the rule $P(A \cup B) = P(A) + P(B) - P(A \cap B)$, where *A* is that outcome *x* is in the range $x > 10$, and *B* is that outcome *x* is in the range:

$$4 < x < 15.\ P(A) = 10 \cdot \frac{1}{20}$$

$$\frac{1}{2}.\ P(B) = 10 \cdot \frac{1}{20} = \frac{1}{2}$$

$P(A \cap B)$ can be computed by noting that $A \cap B$ means the outcome *x* is in the range $10 < x < 15$, so:

$$P(A \cap B) = 4 \cdot \frac{1}{20} = \frac{1}{5}$$

Therefore:

$$P(A \cup B) = P(A) + P(B) - P(A \cap B)$$

$$\frac{1}{2} + \frac{1}{2} - \frac{1}{5} = \frac{4}{5}$$

Note that in this particular example, we could also have directly reasoned about the set of possible outcomes $A \cup B$, by noting that this would mean that *x* must be in the range $5 \leq x$. However, this is not always the case, depending on the given information.

Multiplication Rule

The **multiplication rule** for probabilities states the probability of *A* and *B* both happening is:

$$P(A \cap B) = P(A)P(B|A)$$

As an example, suppose that when Jamie wears black pants, there is a ½ probability that she wears a black shirt as well, and that she wears black pants ¾ of the time. What is the probability that she is wearing both a black shirt and black pants?

To figure this, use the above formula, where *A* will be "Jamie is wearing black pants," while *B* will be "Jamie is wearing a black shirt." It is known that $P(A)$ is ¾. It is also known that $P(B|A) = \frac{1}{2}$. Multiplying the two, the probability that she is wearing both black pants and a black shirt is:

$$P(A)P(B|A) = \frac{3}{4} \cdot \frac{1}{2} = \frac{3}{8}$$

Counting Techniques

There are many counting techniques that can help solve problems involving counting possibilities; the Addition Principle and Multiplication Principle just described are two examples. Counting techniques also involve permutations. A **permutation** is an arrangement of elements in a set for which order must be considered. For example, if three letters from the alphabet are chosen, ABC and BAC are two different permutations. The multiplication rule can be used to determine the total number of possibilities. If each letter can't be selected twice, the total number of possibilities is:

$$26 \times 25 \times 24 = 15{,}600$$

A formula can also be used to calculate this total. In general, the notation $P(n, r)$ represents the number of ways to arrange r objects from a set of n and, the formula is:

$$P(n, r) = \frac{n!}{(n-r)!}$$

In the previous example:

$$P(26, 3) = \frac{26!}{23!} = 15{,}600$$

Contrasting permutations, a **combination** is an arrangement of elements in which order doesn't matter. In this case, ABC and BAC are the same combination. In the previous scenario, there are six permutations that represent each single combination. Therefore, the total number of possible combinations is $15{,}600 \div 6 = 2{,}600$. In general, $C(n, r)$ represents the total number of combinations of n items selected r at a time where order doesn't matter, and the formula is:

$$C(n, r) = \frac{n!}{(n-r)!\ r!}$$

Therefore, the following relationship exists between permutations and combinations:

$$C(n, r) = \frac{P(n, r)}{n!} = \frac{P(n, r)}{P(r, r)}$$

Probability for an event is equal to the number of outcomes in that event divided by the total number of outcomes in the sample space. For example, consider rolling a 6-sided die. The probability of rolling an odd number is $\frac{3}{6}$, or $\frac{1}{2}$, because there are 3 odd numbers on the die.

The **fundamental counting principle** states that if there are *m* possible ways for an event to occur, and *n* possible ways for a second event to occur, there are $m \times n$ possible ways for both events to occur. For example, there are two events that can occur after flipping a coin and six events that can occur after rolling a die, so there are $2 \times 6 = 12$ total possible event scenarios if both are done simultaneously. This principle can be used to find probabilities involving finite sample spaces and independent trials because it calculates the total number of possible outcomes. For this principle to work, the events must be independent of each other.

Using Normal, Binomial, and Exponential Distributions

A **normal distribution** of data follows the shape of a bell curve and the data set's median, mean, and mode are equal. Therefore, 50 percent of its values are less than the mean and 50 percent are greater than the mean. Data sets that follow this shape can be generalized using normal distributions. Normal distributions are described as **frequency distributions** in which the data set is plotted as percentages rather than true data points. A **relative frequency distribution** is one where the y-axis is between zero and 1, which is the same as 0% to 100%.

Within a standard deviation, 68 percent of the values are within 1 standard deviation of the mean, 95 percent of the values are within 2 standard deviations of the mean, and 99.7 percent of the values are within 3 standard deviations of the mean. The number of standard deviations that a data point falls from the mean is called the **z-score.** The formula for the z-score is $Z = \frac{x-\mu}{\sigma}$, where μ is the mean, σ is the standard deviation, and x is the data point. This formula is used to fit any data set that resembles a normal distribution to a standard normal distribution, in a process known as **standardizing.**

Here is a normal distribution with labeled z-scores:

Normal Distribution with Labelled Z-Scores

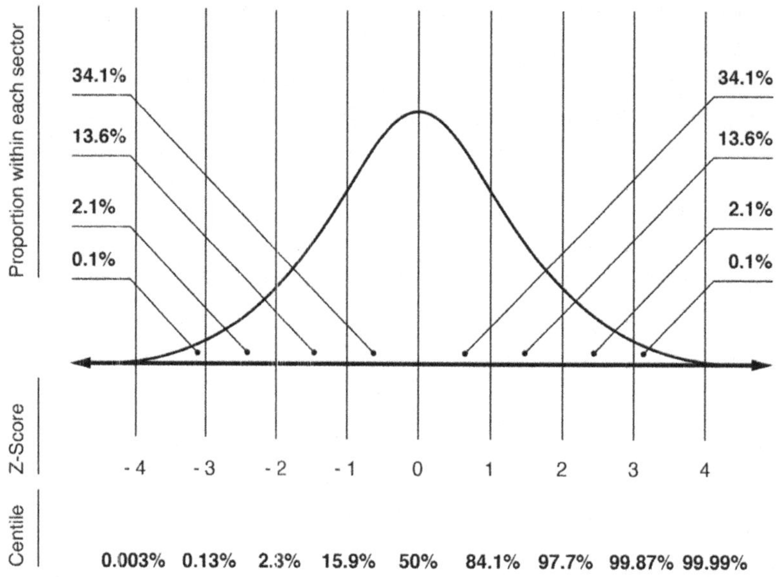

Population percentages can be estimated using normal distributions. For example, the probability that a data point will be less than the mean, or that the z-score will be less than 0, is 50%. Similarly, the probability that a data point will be within 1 standard deviation of the mean, or that the z-score will be between -1 and 1, is about 68.2%. When using a table, the left column states how many standard deviations (to one decimal place) away from the mean the point is, and the row heading states the second decimal place. The entries in the table corresponding to each column and row give the probability, which is equal to the area.

In statistics, a **binomial experiment** is an experiment that has the following properties. The experiment consists of n repeated trial that can each have only one of two outcomes. It can be either a success or a failure. The probability of success, p, is the same in every trial. Each trial is also independent of all other trials. An example of a binomial experiment is rolling a die 10 times with the goal of rolling a 5. Rolling a 5 is a success while any other value is a failure. In this experiment, the probability of rolling a 5 is $\frac{1}{6}$. In any binomial experiment, x is the number of resulting successes, n is the number of trials, p is the probability of success in each trial, and $q = 1 - p$ is the probability of failure within each trial.

The probability of obtaining x successes within n trials is:

$$P(X = x) = \frac{n!}{x!\,(n-x)!} p^x (1-p)^{n-x}$$

With the following being the **binomial coefficient**:

$$\binom{n}{x} = \frac{n!}{x!\,(n-x)!}$$

Within this calculation, $n!$ is n factorial that's defined as:

$$n \times (n-1) \times (n-2) \ldots 1$$

Let's look at the probability of obtaining 2 rolls of a 5 out of the 10 rolls.

Start with $P(X = 2)$, where 2 is the number of successes. Then fill in the rest of the formula with what is known, *n*=10, *x*=2, *p*=1/6, *q*=5/6:

$$P(X = 2) = \left(\frac{10!}{2!\,(10-2)!}\right)\left(\frac{1}{6}\right)^2\left(1 - \frac{1}{6}\right)^{10-2}$$

Which simplifies to:

$$P(X = 2) = \left(\frac{10!}{2!\,8!}\right)\left(\frac{1}{6}\right)^2\left(\frac{5}{6}\right)^8$$

Then solve to get:

$$P(X = 2) = \left(\frac{3628800}{80640}\right)(.0277)(.2325) = .2898$$

A continuous random variable *x* is said to have an exponential distribution if it has probability density function $f(x) = \frac{1}{\beta} e^{-(x-\mu)/\beta}, x \geq \mu;\ \beta > 0.$

The value μ is known as the **location parameter**, and β is the **scale parameter**. Oftentimes, the scale parameter is referred to as λ and is equal to $^1/_\beta$. λ is also referred to as the scale parameter. When $\mu =$

0 and $\beta = 1$, this function is known as the **standard exponential distribution**, and $f(x) = e^{-x}$ for $x \geq 0$. Here is the plot of the exponential probability distribution function:

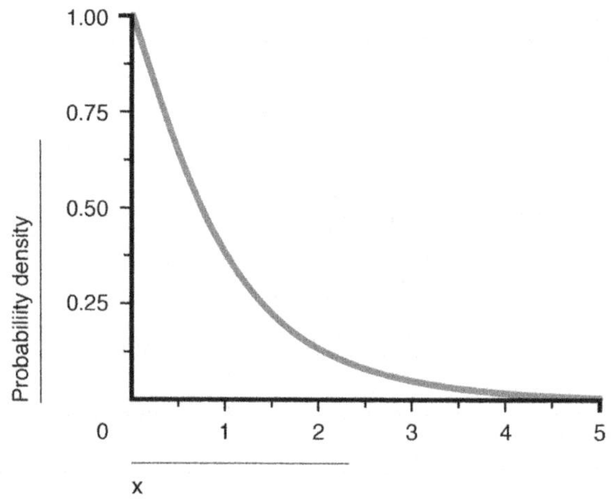

Similarly, the formula for the cumulative distribution function of the exponential function is $F(x) = 1 - e^{-x/\beta}$ for $x \geq 0, \beta > 0$, and here is its plot:

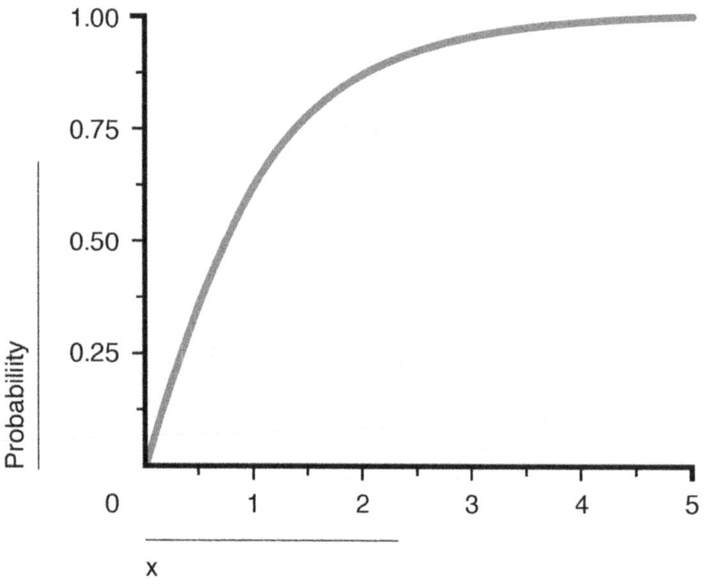

In probability and statistics, exponential distributions are used when the time between events that occur continuously and independently is a constant, average rate. The mean of an exponential distribution is $\beta = \frac{1}{\lambda}$, and its variance is $\beta^2 = \frac{1}{\lambda^2}$. Therefore, if the square root of the variance is taken, it is equal to the mean. Therefore, the standard deviation is equal to the mean.

Consider a rental car counter in which customers arrive at the rate of 20 per hour. The cumulative exponential distribution can be used to find the probability in which the arrival time between consecutive customers is less than 2 minutes. The mean number of customers per hour is 20, and therefore this is the rate of the function, so $\lambda = 20$. Two minutes represents 0.033 hour. Therefore:

$$\text{P(arrival time less than 2 minutes)} = 1 - e^{-(20)(0.033)} = 0.483$$

Therefore, there is a 48.3% chance that the arrival time between consecutive customers is less than 2 minutes.

Calculating Expected Values

The **expected value** of a random variable represents the mean value in either a large sample size or after a large number of trials. According to the law of large numbers, after a large number of trials, the actual mean (and that of the probability distribution) is approximately equal to the expected value. The expected value is a weighted average and is calculated as $E(X) = \sum x_i p_i$, where x_i represents the value of each outcome and p_i represents the probability of each outcome. If all probabilities are equal, the expected value is:

$$E(X) = \frac{x_1 + x_2 + \cdots + x_n}{n}$$

Expected value is often called the **mean of the random variable** and is also a measure of central tendency.

Consider the following situation: A landscaper bids on jobs where she can make a $2,000 profit. The probabilities of getting 1, 2, or 3 jobs per month are shown below in the probability distribution:

Number of Jobs	1	2	3
Probability	0.4	0.5	0.1

Her expected profit per month can be calculated by using the expected value formula. Multiply each probability times the profit in each instance, and sum up those values. This results in the following:

$$E(x) = 2{,}000 \times 0.4 + 4{,}000 \times 0.5 + 6{,}000 \times 0.1$$

$$800 + 2{,}000 + 600 = 3400$$

Therefore, she expects to make, on average, $3,400 per month.

Given a statistical experiment, a theoretical probability distribution can be calculated if the theoretical probabilities are known. The theoretical probabilities are plugged into the formula for both the binomial probability and the expected value. An example of this is any scenario involving rolls of a die or flips of a coin. The theoretical probabilities are known without any observed experiments. Another example of this is finding the theoretical probability distribution for the number of correct answers obtained by guessing a specific number of multiple choice questions on a class exam.

Empirical data is defined as real data. If real data is known, approximations concerning samples and populations can be obtained by working backwards. This scenario is the case where theoretical probabilities are unknown, and experimental data must be used to make decisions. The sample data (including actual probabilities) must be plugged into the formulas for both binomial probability and the expected value. The actual probabilities are obtained using observation and can be seen in a probability distribution. An example of this scenario is determining a probability distribution for the number of televisions per household in the United States, and determining the expected number of televisions per household as well.

Calculating if it's worth it to play a game or make a decision is a critical part of probability theory. Expected values can be calculated in terms of payoff values and deciding whether to make a decision or play a game can be done based on the actual expected value. Applying this theory to gambling and card games is fairly typical. The payoff values in these instances are the actual monetary totals.

Understanding Standardized Test Scores

Students will undoubtedly take several standardized tests throughout their academic career, and it is important for educators to be able to interpret results from these types of exams. Educators should be able to understand an individual student's score relative to the performance of his or her peer group, other students, or the aggregate of all test takers. Moreover, it is helpful to be able to explain this relative evaluation to inquisitive students, parents, and also school administrators. Many schools use their students' standardized test scores as a benchmark of performance for the school's curriculum and instruction in that content area. Additionally, with the importance of standardized test scores in competitive college admissions, many students and parents will likely have questions about scores that educators should be able to answer.

Standardized tests often make use of stanines, percentiles, or "grade-level equivalents" as means to compare an individual student's scores with the other students who attempted the exam. **Stanine** is a portmanteau for "standard nine" because the scores range from the minimum of 1 to the maximum of 9. This number range is further divided into three categories, which qualify an individual's performance relative to group at large. A stanine score of 1, 2, or 3 indicates that the student's raw score was "below average." Obtaining a stanine score of 4, 5, or 6 lands one in the "average" group, and scores of 7, 8, or 9 indicate an "above average" performance. Below average scores may indicate the need for further instruction and practice, and average scores mean that the student is at the same level as the majority of his or her peers.

Percentile scores delve into score comparisons with finer detail than stanine scores because instead of working on gross scale of 1-9, percentile scores range from 1 to 99. This multiplicative delineation of one's relative score allows for a significantly more precise performance comparison. A student's percentile score indicates the percentage of total test takers for whom that student outperformed. For example, a student who scored in the 77th percentile achieved a score that is higher than 77% of the rest of the test cohort. A student's percentile score is different than the percentage of correct responses obtained on the test. Percentile score simply compares one student's score with the scores of all of the other students who took the test. Students whose percentile scores fall below the 50th percentile can be considered below average, as more than half of the other test takers outperformed their test attempt.

Lastly, **grade-level equivalents** are sometimes used in situations where an exam is designed to be at the complexity or competency expected of a certain grade level but is taken by students in other grades. Because students at higher and lower grades than the test's intended grade attempt the exam, it can be challenging to interpret grade-level equivalents. Grade-level equivalents fall along a continuum and are often decimal results. The number to the right of the decimal approximates the number of months into that grade level (to the left of the decimal) for which a student's performance is on par. The school year is assumed to be ten months. For example, a score of 5.2 achieved by a fourth-grade student indicates that his or her raw score was that which a typical fifth grade student would receive two months into the school year.

Computation & Problem Solving

Basic Addition, Subtraction, Multiplication, and Division

Gaining more of something related to addition, while taking something away relates to subtraction. Vocabulary words such as *total, more, less, left,* and *remain* are common when working with these problems. The $+$ sign means plus. This shows that addition is happening. The $-$ sign means minus. This shows that subtraction is happening. The symbols will be important when you write out equations.

Addition

Addition can also be defined in equation form. For example, $4 + 5 = 9$ shows that $4 + 5$ is the same as 9. Therefore, $9 = 9$, and "four plus five equals nine." When two quantities are being added together, the result is called the **sum**. Therefore, the sum of 4 and 5 is 9. The numbers being added, such as 4 and 5, are known as the ***addends.***

Subtraction

Subtraction can also be in equation form. For example, $9 - 5 = 4$ shows that $9 - 5$ is the same as 4 and that "9 minus 5 is 4." The result of subtraction is known as a **difference.** The difference of $9 - 5$ is 4. 4 represents the amount that is left once the subtraction is done. The order in which subtraction is completed does matter. For example, $9 - 5$ and $5 - 9$ do not result in the same answer. $5 - 9$ results in a negative number. So, subtraction does not adhere to the commutative or associative property. The order in which subtraction is completed is important.

Multiplication

Multiplication is when we add equal amounts. The answer to a multiplication problem is called a **product**. Products stand for the total number of items within different groups. The symbol for multiplication is $\times$ or $\cdot$. We say 2×3 or $2 \cdot 3$ means "2 times 3."

As an example, there are three sets of four apples. The goal is to know how many apples there are in total. Three sets of four apples gives $4 + 4 + 4 = 12$. Also, three times four apples gives $3 \times 4 = 12$. Therefore, for any whole numbers *a* and *b*, where *a* is not equal to zero, $a \times b = b + b + \cdots b$, where *b* is added *a* times. Also, $a \times b$ can be thought of as the number of units in a rectangular block consisting of *a* rows and *b* columns. For example, 3×7 is equal to the number of squares in the following rectangle:

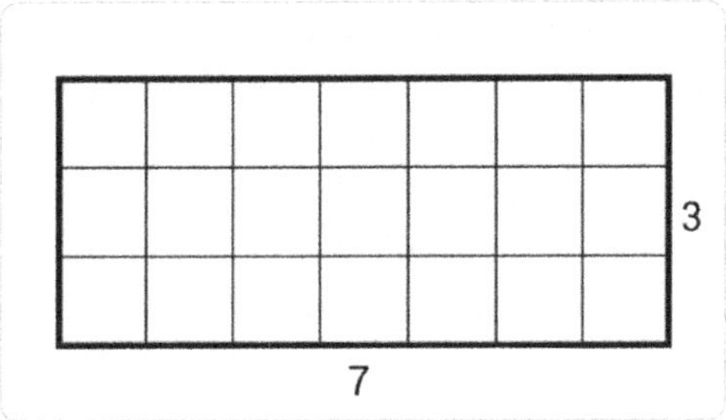

The answer is 21, and there are 21 squares in the rectangle.

With any number times one (for example,$8 \times 1 = 8$) the original amount does not change. Therefore, one is the **multiplicative identity**. For any whole number *a*, $1 \times a = a$. Also, any number multiplied times zero results in zero. Therefore, for any whole number *a*, $0 \times a = 0$.

Another method of multiplication can be done with the use of an **area model**. An area model is a rectangle that is divided into rows and columns that match up to the number of place values within each number. For example, $29 \times 65 = 25 + 4$ and $66 = 60 + 5$. The products of those 4 numbers are found within the rectangle and then summed up to get the answer. The entire process is:

$$(60 \times 25) + (5 \times 25) + (60 \times 4) + (5 \times 4)$$

$$1{,}500 + 240 + 125 + 20 = 1{,}885$$

Here is the actual area model:

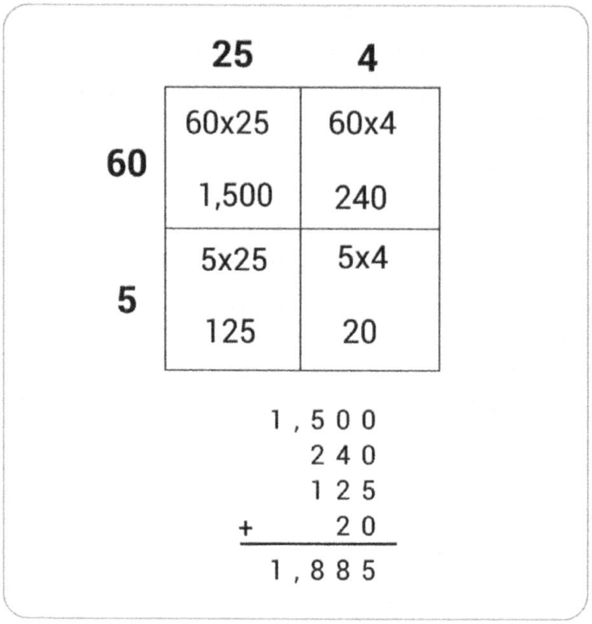

Division

Division is based on dividing a given number into parts. The simplest problem involves dividing a number into equal parts. For example, a pack of 20 pencils is to be divided among 10 children. You would have to divide 20 by 10. In this example, each child would receive 2 pencils.

The symbol for division is $\div$ or /. The equation above is written as $20 \div 10 = 2$, or 20 / 10 = 2. This means "20 divided by 10 is equal to 2." Division can be explained as the following: for any whole numbers *a* and *b,* where *b* is not equal to zero, $a \div b = c$ if and only if $a = b \times c$. This means, division can be thought of as a multiplication problem with a missing part. For instance, calculating $20 \div 10$ is the same as asking the following: "If there are 20 items in total with 10 in each group, how many are in each group?" Therefore, 20 is equal to ten times what value? This question is the same as asking, "If there are 20 items in total with 2 in each group, how many groups are there?" The answer to each question is 2.

In a division problem, *a* is known as the **dividend,** *b* is the **divisor**, and *c* is the **quotient**. Zero cannot be divided into parts. Therefore, for any nonzero whole number $a, 0 \div a = 0$. Also, division by zero is undefined. Dividing an amount into zero parts is not possible.

Harder division involves dividing a number into equal parts, but having some left over. An example is dividing a pack of 20 pencils among 8 friends so that each friend receives the same number of pencils. In this setting, each friend receives 2 pencils. There are 4 pencils leftover. 20 is the dividend, 8 is the divisor, 2 is the quotient, and 4 is known as the **remainder**. Within this type of division problem, for whole numbers *a*, *b*, *c*, and *d*, $a \div b = c$ with a remainder of *d*. This is true if and only if $a = (b \times c) + d$. When calculating $a \div b$, if there is no remainder, *a* is said to be *divisible* by *b*. **Even numbers** are all divisible by the number 2. **Odd numbers** are not divisible by 2. An odd number of items cannot be paired up into groups of 2 without having one item leftover.

Dividing a number by a single digit or two digits can be turned into repeated subtraction problems. An area model can be used throughout the problem that represents multiples of the divisor. For example, the answer to $8580 \div 55$ can be found by subtracting 55 from 8580 one at a time and counting the total number of subtractions necessary.

However, a simpler process involves using larger multiples of 55. First, $100 \times 55 = 5{,}500$ is subtracted from 8,580, and 3,080 is leftover. Next, $50 \times 55 = 2{,}750$ is subtracted from 3,080 to obtain380. $5 \times 55 = 275$ is subtracted from 330 to obtain 55, and finally, $1 \times 55 = 55$ is subtracted from 55 to obtain zero. Therefore, there is no remainder, and the answer is $100 + 50 + 5 + 1 = 156$. Here is a picture of the area model and the repeated subtraction process:

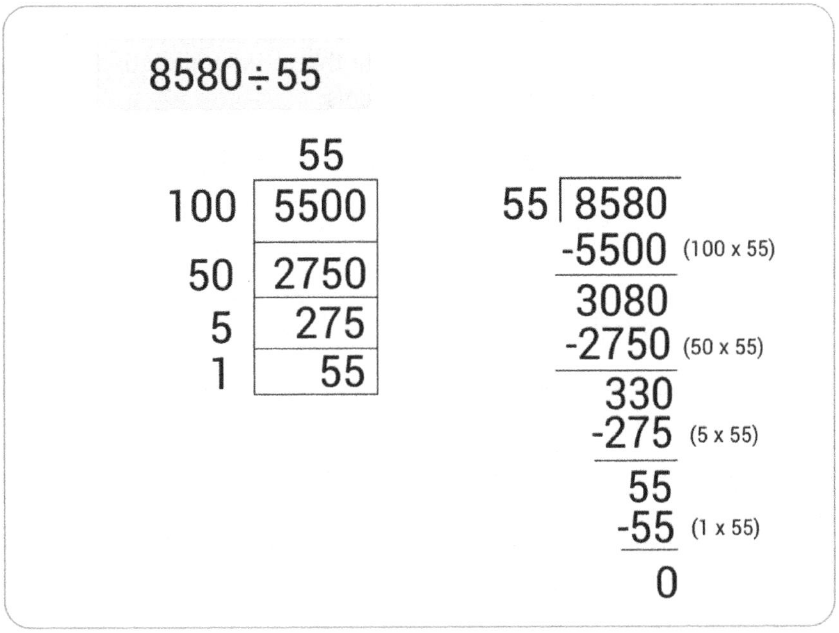

If you want to check the answer of a division problem, multiply the answer times the divisor. This will help you check to see if the dividend is obtained. If there is a remainder, the same process is done, but the remainder is added on at the end to try to match the dividend. In the previous example, $156 \times 64 = 9984$ would be the checking procedure. Dividing decimals involves the same repeated subtraction process. The only difference would be that the subtractions would involve numbers that include values in the decimal places. Lining up decimal places is crucial in this type of problem.

Using Operations in Math and Real-World Problems

Addition and subtraction are “inverse operations.” Adding a number and then subtracting the same number will cancel each other out. This results in the original number, and vice versa. For example, $8 + 7 - 7 = 8$ and $137 - 100 + 100 = 137$.

Multiplication and division are also inverse operations. So, multiplying by a number and then dividing by the same number results in the original number. For example, $8 \times 2 \div 2 = 8$ and $12 \div 4 \times 4 = 12$. Inverse operations are used to work backwards to solve problems. In the case that 7 and a number add to 18, the inverse operation of subtraction is used to find the unknown value ($18 - 7 = 11$). If a school's entire 4th grade was divided evenly into 3 classes each with 22 students, the inverse operation of multiplication is used to determine the total students in the grade ($22 \times 3 = 66$). More scenarios involving inverse operations are listed in the tables below.

Word problems take concepts you learned in the classroom and turn them into real-life situations. Some parts of the problem are known and at least one part is unknown. There are three types of instances in which something can be unknown: the starting point, the change, or the final result. These can all be missing from the information they give you.

For an addition problem, the change is the quantity of a new amount added to the starting point.

For a subtraction problem, the change is the quantity taken away from the starting point.

Regarding addition, the given equation is $3 + 7 = 10$.

The number 3 is the starting point. 7 is the change, and 10 is the result from adding a new amount to the starting point. Different word problems can arise from this same equation, depending on which value is the unknown. For example, here are three problems:

- If a boy had 3 pencils and was given 7 more, how many would he have in total?
- If a boy had 3 pencils and a girl gave him more so that he had 10 in total, how many were given to him?
- A boy was given 7 pencils so that he had 10 in total. How many did he start with?

All three problems involve the same equation. Finding out which part of the equation is missing is the key to solving each word problem. The missing answers would be 10, 7, and 3.

In terms of subtraction, the same three scenarios can occur. The given equation is $6 - 4 = 2$.

The number 6 is the starting point. 4 is the change, and 2 is the new amount that is the result from taking away an amount from the starting point. Again, different types of word problems can arise from this equation. For example, here are three possible problems:

- If a girl had 6 quarters and 2 were taken away, how many would be left over?
- If a girl had 6 quarters, purchased a pencil, and had 2 quarters left over, how many did she pay with?
- If a girl paid for a pencil with 4 quarters and had 2 quarters left over, how many did she have to start with?

The three question types follow the structure of the addition word problems. Finding out whether the starting point, the change, or the final result is missing is the goal in solving the problem. The missing answers would be 2, 4, and 6.

The three addition problems and the three subtraction word problems can be solved by using a picture, a number line, or an algebraic equation. If an equation is used, a question mark can be used to show the number we don't know. For example, $6 - 4 = ?$ can be written to show that the missing value is the result. Using equation form shows us what part of the addition or subtraction problem is missing.

Key words within a multiplication problem involve *times, product, doubled*, and *tripled.* Key words within a division problem involve *split, quotient, divided, shared, groups*, and *half*. Like addition and subtraction, multiplication and division problems also have three different types of missing values.

Multiplication consists of a certain number of groups, with the same number of items within each group, and the total amount within all groups. Therefore, each one of these amounts can be the missing value.

For example, the given equation is $5 \times 3 = 15$.

5 and 3 are interchangeable, so either amount can be the number of groups or the number of items within each group. 15 is the total number of items. Again, different types of word problems can arise from this equation. For example, here are three problems:

- If a classroom is serving 5 different types of apples for lunch and has 3 apples of each type, how many total apples are there to give to the students?
- If a classroom has 15 apples with 5 different types, how many of each type are there?
- If a classroom has 15 apples with 3 of each type, how many types are there to choose from?

Each question involves using the same equation to solve. It is important to decide which part of the equation is the missing value. The answers to the problems are 15, 3, and 5.

Similar to multiplication, division problems involve a total amount, a number of groups having the same amount, and a number of items within each group. The difference between multiplication and division is that the starting point is the total amount. It then gets divided into equal amounts.

For example, the equation is $15 \div 5 = 3$.

15 is the total number of items, which is being divided into 5 different groups. In order to do so, 3 items go into each group. Also, 5 and 3 are interchangeable. So, the 15 items could be divided into 3 groups of 5 items each. Therefore, different types of word problems can arise from this equation. For example, here are three types of problems:

- A boy needs 48 pieces of chalk. If there are 8 pieces in each box, how many boxes should he buy?
- A boy has 48 pieces of chalk. If each box has 6 pieces in it, how many boxes did he buy?
- A boy has partitioned all of his chalk into 8 piles, with 6 pieces in each pile. How many pieces does he have in total?

Each one of these questions involves the same equation. The third question can easily utilize the multiplication equation $8 \times 6 = ?$ instead of division. The answers are 6, 8, and 48.

Adding and Subtracting Positive and Negative Numbers

Some problems require adding positive and negative numbers or subtracting positive and negative numbers. Adding a negative number to a positive one can be thought of a reducing or subtracting from the positive number, and the result should be less than the positive number. For example, adding 8 and -3 is the same is subtracting 3 from 8; the result is 5. This can be visualized by imagining that the positive number (8) represents 8 apples that a student has in her basket. The negative number (-3) indicates the number of apples she is in debt or owes to her friend. In order to pay off her debt and "settle the score," she essentially is in possession of three fewer apples than in her basket (8 – 3 = 5), so she actually has five apples that are hers to keep. Should the negative addend be of higher magnitude than the positive addend (for example -9 + 3), the result will be negative, but "less negative" or closer to zero than the large negative number. This is because adding a positive value, even if relatively smaller, to a negative value, reduces the magnitude of the negative in the total. Considering the apple example again, if the girl owed 9 apples to her friend (-9) but she picked 3 (+3) off a tree and gave them to her friend, she now would only owe him six apples (-6), which reduced her debt burden (her negative number of apples) by three.

Subtracting positive and negative numbers works the same way with one key distinction: subtracting a negative number from a negative number yields a "less negative" or more positive result because again, this can be considered as removing or alleviating some debt. For example, if the student with the apples owed 5 apples to her friend, she essentially has -5 applies. If her mom gives that friend 10 apples on behalf of the girl, she now has removed the need to pay back the 5 apples and surpassed neutral (no net apples owed) and now her friend owes *her* five apples (+5). Stated mathematically: -5 + -10 = +5.

Operations with Fractions, Decimals, and Percentages

Fractions

Fractions are a vital part of mathematics, and their understanding tends to be extremely challenging for students. Too often, steps are learned without understanding why they are being performed. It is important for teachers to make the concept of fractions less abstract and more tangible by providing concrete examples in the classroom. With this solid foundation and a lot of practice, learning will be easier, and success with fractions in later math classes will occur.

A **fraction** is a part of something that is whole. Items such as apples can be cut into parts to help visualize fractions. If an apple is cut into 2 equal parts, each part represents ½ of the apple. If each half is cut into two parts, the apple now is cut into quarters. Each piece now represents ¼ of the apple. In this example, each part is equal because they all have the same size. Geometric shapes, such as circles and squares, can also be utilized in the classroom to help visualize the idea of fractions. For example, a circle can be drawn on the board and divided into 6 equal parts:

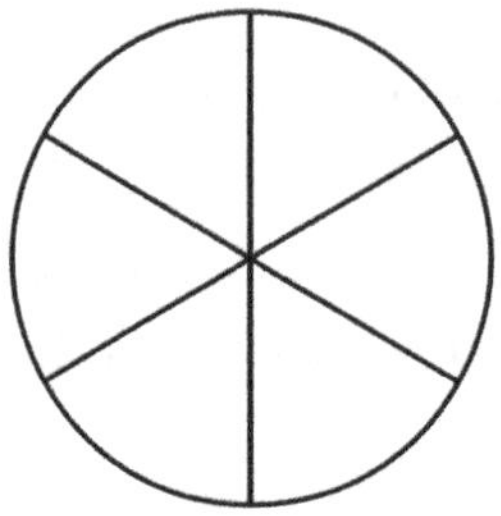

Shading can be used to represent parts of the circle that can be translated into fractions. The top of the fraction, the **numerator,** can represent how many segments are shaded. The bottom of the fraction, the **denominator,** can represent the number of segments that the circle is broken into. A pie is a good analogy to use in this example. If one piece of the circle is shaded, or one piece of pie is cut out, $^1/_6$ of the object is being referred to. An apple, a pie, or a circle can be utilized in order to compare simple fractions. For example, showing that ½ is larger than ¼ and that ¼ is smaller than $^1/_3$ can be accomplished through shading. A **unit fraction** is a fraction in which the numerator is 1, and the denominator is a positive whole number. It represents one part of a whole—one piece of pie.

Imagine that an apple pie has been baked for a holiday party, and the full pie has eight slices. After the party, there are five slices left. How could the amount of the pie that remains be expressed as a fraction? The numerator is 5 since there are 5 pieces left, and the denominator is 8 since there were eight total slices in the whole pie. Thus, expressed as a fraction, the leftover pie totals $\frac{5}{8}$ of the original amount.

Fractions come in three different varieties: proper fractions, improper fractions, and mixed numbers. **Proper fractions** have a numerator less than the denominator, such as $\frac{3}{8}$, but **improper fractions** have a numerator greater than the denominator, such as $\frac{15}{8}$. **Mixed numbers** combine a whole number with a proper fraction, such as $3\frac{1}{2}$. Any mixed number can be written as an improper fraction by multiplying the integer by the denominator, adding the product to the value of the numerator, and dividing the sum by the original denominator. For example:

$$3\frac{1}{2} = \frac{3 \times 2 + 1}{2} = \frac{7}{2}$$

Whole numbers can also be converted into fractions by placing the whole number as the numerator and making the denominator 1. For example, $3 = \frac{3}{1}$.

The bar in a fraction represents division. Therefore $^6/_5$ is the same as $6 \div 5$. In order to rewrite it as a mixed number, division is performed to obtain $6 \div 5 = 1\ R1$. The remainder is then converted into fraction form. The actual remainder becomes the numerator of a fraction, and the divisor becomes the denominator. Therefore $1\ R1$ is written as $1\frac{1}{5}$, a mixed number. A mixed number can also decompose into the addition of a whole number and a fraction. For example,

$$1\frac{1}{5} = 1 + \frac{1}{5} \text{ and } 4\frac{5}{6} = 4 + \frac{1}{6} + \frac{1}{6} + \frac{1}{6} + \frac{1}{6} + \frac{1}{6}$$

Every fraction can be built from a combination of unit fractions.

One of the most fundamental concepts of fractions is their ability to be manipulated by multiplication or division. This is possible since $\frac{n}{n} = 1$ for any non-zero integer. As a result, multiplying or dividing by $\frac{n}{n}$ will not alter the original fraction since any number multiplied or divided by 1 doesn't change the value of that number. Fractions of the same value are known as equivalent fractions. For example, $\frac{2}{8}, \frac{25}{100}$, and $\frac{40}{160}$ are equivalent, as they all equal $\frac{1}{4}$.

Like fractions, or **equivalent fractions**, are the terms used to describe these fractions that are made up of different numbers but represent the same quantity. For example, the given fractions are $^4/_8$ and $^3/_6$. If a pie was cut into 8 pieces and 4 pieces were removed, half of the pie would remain. Also, if a pie was split into 6 pieces and 3 pieces were eaten, half of the pie would also remain. Therefore, both of the fractions represent half of a pie. These two fractions are referred to as like fractions. **Unlike fractions** are fractions that are different and cannot be thought of as representing equal quantities. When working with fractions in mathematical expressions, like fractions should be simplified. Both $^4/_8$ and $^3/_6$ can be simplified into $^1/_2$.

Comparing fractions can be completed through the use of a number line. For example, if $^3/_5$ and $^6/_{10}$ need to be compared, each fraction should be plotted on a number line. To plot $^3/_5$, the area from 0 to 1 should be broken into 5 equal segments, and the fraction represents 3 of them. To plot $^6/_{10}$, the area from 0 to 1 should be broken into 10 equal segments and the fraction represents 6 of them.

It can be seen that $\frac{3}{5} = \frac{6}{10}$

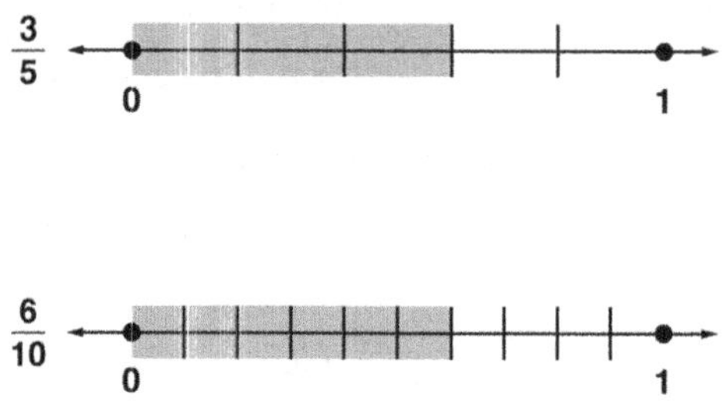

Like fractions are plotted at the same point on a number line. Unit fractions can also be used to compare fractions. For example, if it is known that

$$\frac{4}{5} > \frac{1}{2}$$

and

$$\frac{1}{2} > \frac{4}{10}$$

then it is also known that

$$\frac{4}{5} > \frac{4}{10}$$

Also, converting improper fractions to mixed numbers can be helpful in comparing fractions because the whole number portion of the number is more visible.

Adding and subtracting mixed numbers and fractions can be completed by decomposing fractions into a sum of whole numbers and unit fractions. For example, the given problem is

$$5\frac{3}{7} + 2\frac{1}{7}$$

Decomposing into

$$5 + \frac{1}{7} + \frac{1}{7} + \frac{1}{7} + 2 + \frac{1}{7}$$

This shows that the whole numbers can be added separately from the unit fractions. The answer is:

$$5 + 2 + \frac{1}{7} + \frac{1}{7} + \frac{1}{7} + \frac{1}{7} = 7 + \frac{4}{7} = 7\frac{4}{7}$$

Although many equivalent fractions exist, they are easier to compare and interpret when reduced or simplified. The numerator and denominator of a simple fraction will have no factors in common other than 1. When reducing or simplifying fractions, divide the numerator and denominator by the greatest common factor. A simple strategy is to divide the numerator and denominator by low numbers, like 2, 3, or 5 until arriving at a simple fraction, but the same thing could be achieved by determining the greatest common factor for both the numerator and denominator and dividing each by it. Using the first method is preferable when both the numerator and denominator are even, end in 5, or are obviously a multiple of another number. However, if no numbers seem to work, it will be necessary to factor the numerator and denominator to find the GCF. Let's look at examples:

1) Simplify the fraction $\frac{6}{8}$:

Dividing the numerator and denominator by 2 results in $\frac{3}{4}$, which is a simple fraction.

2) Simplify the fraction $\frac{12}{36}$:

Dividing the numerator and denominator by 2 leaves $\frac{6}{18}$. This isn't a simple fraction, as both the numerator and denominator have factors in common. Dividing each by 3 results in $\frac{2}{6}$, but this can be further simplified by dividing by 2 to get $\frac{1}{3}$. This is the simplest fraction, as the numerator is 1. In cases like this, multiple division operations can be avoided by determining the greatest common factor between the numerator and denominator.

3) Simplify the fraction $\frac{18}{54}$ by dividing by the greatest common factor:

First, determine the factors for the numerator and denominator. The factors of 18 are 1, 2, 3, 6, 9, and 18. The factors of 54 are 1, 2, 3, 6, 9, 18, 27, and 54. Thus, the greatest common factor is 18. Dividing $\frac{18}{54}$ by 18 leaves $\frac{1}{3}$, which is the simplest fraction. This method takes slightly more work, but it definitively arrives at the simplest fraction.

Adding and Subtracting Fractions

Adding and subtracting fractions that have the same denominators involves adding or subtracting the numerators. The denominator will stay the same. Therefore, the decomposition process can be made simpler, and the fractions do not have to be broken into unit fractions.

For example, the given problem is:

$$4\frac{7}{8} - 2\frac{6}{8}$$

The answer is found by adding the answers to both

$$4 - 2 \text{ and } \frac{7}{8} - \frac{6}{8}$$

$$2 + \frac{1}{8} = 2\frac{1}{8}$$

A common mistake would be to add the denominators so that

$$\frac{1}{4} + \frac{1}{4} = \frac{1}{8} \; or \; \frac{2}{8}$$

However, conceptually, it is known that two quarters make a half, so neither one of these are correct.

If two fractions have different denominators, equivalent fractions must be used to add or subtract them. The fractions must be converted into fractions that have common denominators. A **least common denominator** or the product of the two denominators can be used as the common denominator. For example, in the problem $\frac{5}{6} + \frac{2}{3}$, both 6, which is the least common denominator, and 18, which is the product of the denominators, can be used. In order to use 6, $\frac{2}{3}$ must be converted to sixths. A number line can be used to show the equivalent fraction is $\frac{4}{6}$. What happens is that $\frac{2}{3}$ is multiplied times a fractional form of 1 to obtain a denominator of 6. Hence, $\frac{2}{3} \times \frac{2}{2} = \frac{4}{6}$. Therefore, the problem is now $\frac{5}{6} + \frac{4}{6} = \frac{9}{6}$, which can be simplified into $\frac{3}{2}$. In order to use 18, both fractions must be converted into having 18 as their denominator. $\frac{5}{6}$ would have to be multiplied times $\frac{3}{3}$, and $\frac{2}{3}$ would need to be multiplied times $\frac{6}{6}$.The addition problem would be $\frac{15}{18} + \frac{12}{18} = \frac{27}{18}$, which reduces into $\frac{3}{2}$.

It is always possible to find a common denominator by multiplying the denominators. However, when the denominators are large numbers, this method is unwieldy, especially if the answer must be provided in its simplest form. Thus, it's beneficial to find the **least common denominator** of the fractions—the least common denominator is incidentally also the **least common multiple**.

Once equivalent fractions have been found with common denominators, simply add or subtract the numerators to arrive at the answer:

1) $\frac{1}{2} + \frac{3}{4} = \frac{2}{4} + \frac{3}{4} = \frac{5}{4}$

2) $\frac{3}{12} + \frac{11}{20} = \frac{15}{60} + \frac{33}{60} = \frac{48}{60} = \frac{4}{5}$

3) $\frac{7}{9} - \frac{4}{15} = \frac{35}{45} - \frac{12}{45} = \frac{23}{45}$

4) $\frac{5}{6} - \frac{7}{18} = \frac{15}{18} - \frac{7}{18} = \frac{8}{18} = \frac{4}{9}$

Multiplying and Dividing Fractions

Of the four basic operations that can be performed on fractions, the one which involves the least amount of work is multiplication. To multiply two fractions, simply multiply the numerators, multiply the denominators, and place the products as a fraction. Whole numbers and mixed numbers can also be expressed as a fraction, as described above, to multiply with a fraction.

Because multiplication is commutative, multiplying a fraction times a whole number is the same as multiplying a whole number times a fraction. The problem involves adding a fraction a specific number of times. The problem $3 \times \frac{1}{4}$ can be translated into adding the unit fraction 3 times:

$$\frac{1}{4}+\frac{1}{4}+\frac{1}{4}=\frac{3}{4}$$

In the problem $4 \times \frac{2}{5}$, the fraction can be decomposed into $\frac{1}{5}+\frac{1}{5}$ and then added 4 times to obtain $\frac{8}{5}$. Also, both of these answers can be found by just multiplying the whole number times the numerator of the fraction being multiplied.

The whole numbers can be written in fraction form as:

$$\frac{3}{1}\times\frac{1}{4}=\frac{3}{4}$$

$$\frac{4}{1}\times\frac{2}{5}=\frac{8}{5}$$

Multiplying a fraction times a fraction involves multiplying the numerators together separately and the denominators together separately. For example,

$$\frac{3}{8}\times\frac{2}{3}=\frac{3\times 2}{8\times 3}=\frac{6}{24}$$

This can then be reduced to $^1/_4$.

Dividing a fraction by a fraction is actually a multiplication problem. It involves flipping the divisor and then multiplying normally. For example,

$$\frac{22}{5}\div\frac{1}{2}=\frac{22}{5}\times\frac{2}{1}=\frac{44}{5}$$

The same procedure can be implemented for division problems involving fractions and whole numbers. The whole number can be rewritten as a fraction over a denominator of 1, and then division can be completed.

A common denominator approach can also be used in dividing fractions. Considering the same problem, $\frac{22}{5}\div\frac{1}{2}$, a common denominator between the two fractions is 10. $\frac{22}{5}$ would be rewritten as $\frac{22}{5}\times\frac{2}{2}=\frac{44}{10}$, and $\frac{1}{2}$ would be rewritten as $\frac{1}{2}\times\frac{5}{5}=\frac{5}{10}$. Dividing both numbers straight across results in:

$$\frac{44}{10}\div\frac{5}{10}=\frac{^{44}/_5}{^{10}/_{10}}=\frac{^{44}/_5}{1}={}^{44}/_5$$

Many real-world problems will involve the use of fractions. Key words include actual fraction values, such as half, quarter, third, fourth, etc. The best approach to solving word problems involving fractions is to draw a picture or diagram that represents the scenario being discussed, while deciding which type of operation is necessary in order to solve the problem. A phrase such as "one fourth of 60 pounds of coal" creates a scenario in which multiplication should be used, and the mathematical form of the phrase is $\frac{1}{4} \times 60$.

Decimals

The **decimal system** is a way of writing out numbers that uses ten different numerals: 0, 1, 2, 3, 4, 5, 6, 7, 8, and 9. This is also called a "base ten" or "base 10" system. Other bases are also used. For example, computers work with a base of 2. This means they only use the numerals 0 and 1.

The **decimal place** denotes how far to the right of the decimal point a numeral is. The first digit to the right of the decimal point is in the *tenths* place. The next is the **hundredths**. The third is the **thousandths**.

So, 3.142 has a 1 in the tenths place, a 4 in the hundredths place, and a 2 in the thousandths place.

The **decimal point** is a period used to separate the **ones** place from the **tenths** place when writing out a number as a decimal.

A **decimal number** is a number written out with a decimal point instead of as a fraction, for example, 1.25 instead of $\frac{5}{4}$. Depending on the situation, it can sometimes be easier to work with fractions and sometimes easier to work with decimal numbers.

A decimal number is **terminating** if it stops at some point. It is called **repeating** if it never stops but repeats a pattern over and over. It is important to note that every rational number can be written as a terminating decimal or as a repeating decimal.

Addition with Decimals

To add decimal numbers, each number in columns needs to be lined up by the decimal point. For each number being added, the zeros to the right of the last number need to be filled in so that each of the numbers has the same number of places to the right of the decimal. Then, the columns can be added together. Here is an example of 2.45 + 1.3 + 8.891 written in column form:

$$\begin{array}{r} 2.450 \\ 1.300 \\ \underline{+\ 8.891} \end{array}$$

Zeros have been added in the columns so that each number has the same number of places to the right of the decimal.

Added together, the correct answer is 12.641:

$$\begin{array}{r} 2.450 \\ 1.300 \\ \underline{+\ 8.891} \\ 12.641 \end{array}$$

Subtraction with Decimals

Subtracting decimal numbers is the same process as adding decimals. Here is 7.89 – 4.235 written in column form:

$$\begin{array}{r} 7.890 \\ -\ \underline{4.235} \\ 3.655 \end{array}$$

A zero has been added in the column so that each number has the same number of places to the right of the decimal.

Multiplication with Decimals

The simplest way to multiply decimals is to calculate the product as if the decimals are not there, then count the number of decimal places in the original problem. Use that total to place the decimal the same number of places over in your answer, counting from right to left. For example, 0.5 x 1.25 can be rewritten and multiplied as 5 x 125, which equals 625. Then the decimal is added three places from the right for .625.

The final answer will have the same number of decimal *points* as the total number of decimal *places* in the problem. The first number has one decimal place, and the second number has two decimal places. Therefore, the final answer will contain three decimal places:

$$0.5 \times 1.25 = 0.625$$

Division with Decimals

Dividing a decimal by a whole number entails using long division first by ignoring the decimal point. Then, the decimal point is moved the number of places given in the problem.

For example, $6.8 \div 4$ can be rewritten as $68 \div 4$, which is 17. There is one non-zero integer to the right of the decimal point, so the final solution would have one decimal place to the right of the solution. In this case, the solution is 1.7.

Dividing a decimal by another decimal requires changing the divisor to a whole number by moving its decimal point. The decimal place of the dividend should be moved by the same number of places as the divisor. Then, the problem is the same as dividing a decimal by a whole number.

For example, $5.72 \div 1.1$ has a divisor with one decimal point in the denominator. The expression can be rewritten as $57.2 \div 11$ by moving each number one decimal place to the right to eliminate the decimal. The long division can be completed as $572 \div 11$ with a result of 52. Since there is one non-zero integer to the right of the decimal point in the problem, the final solution is 5.2.

In another example, $8 \div 0.16$ has a divisor with two decimal points in the denominator. The expression can be rewritten as $800 \div 16$ by moving each number two decimal places to the right to eliminate the decimal in the divisor. The long division can be completed with a result of 50.

<ins>Percentages</ins>

Think of percentages as fractions with a denominator of 100. In fact, percentage means "per hundred." Problems often require converting numbers from percentages, fractions, and decimals.

The basic percent equation is the following:

$$\frac{is}{of} = \frac{\%}{100}$$

The placement of numbers in the equation depends on what the question asks.

Example 1
Find 40% of 80.

Basically, the problem is asking, "What is 40% of 80?" The 40% is the percent, and 80 is the number to find the percent "of." The equation is:

$$\frac{x}{80} = \frac{40}{100}$$

Solving the equation by cross-multiplication, the problem becomes 100x = 80(40). Solving for x gives the answer: x = 32.

Example 2
What percent of 100 is 20?

The 20 fills in the "is" portion, while 100 fills in the "of." The question asks for the percent, so that will be x, the unknown. The following equation is set up:

$$\frac{20}{100} = \frac{x}{100}$$

Cross-multiplying yields the equation 100x = 20(100). Solving for x gives the answer of 20%.

Example 3
30% of what number is 30?

The following equation uses the clues and numbers in the problem:

$$\frac{30}{x} = \frac{30}{100}$$

Cross-multiplying results in the equation 30(100) = 30x. Solving for x gives the answer x = 100.

<u>Conversions</u>
Decimals and Percentages
Since a percentage is based on "per hundred," decimals and percentages can be converted by multiplying or dividing by 100. Practically speaking, this always amounts to moving the decimal point two places to the right or left, depending on the conversion. To convert a percentage to a decimal, move the decimal point two places to the left and remove the % sign. To convert a decimal to a percentage, move the decimal point two places to the right and add a "%" sign. Here are some examples:

65% = 0.65
0.33 = 33%
0.215 = 21.5%
99.99% = 0.9999
500% = 5.00
7.55 = 755%

Fractions and Percentages

Remember that a percentage is a number per one hundred. So a percentage can be converted to a fraction by making the number in the percentage the numerator and putting 100 as the denominator:

$$43\% = \frac{43}{100}$$

$$97\% = \frac{97}{100}$$

Note that the percent symbol (%) kind of looks like a 0, a 1, and another 0. So think of a percentage like 54% as 54 over 100.

To convert a fraction to a percent, follow the same logic. If the fraction happens to have 100 in the denominator, you're in luck. Just take the numerator and add a percent symbol:

$$\frac{28}{100} = 28\%$$

Otherwise, divide the numerator by the denominator to get a decimal:

$$\frac{9}{12} = 0.75$$

Then convert the decimal to a percentage:

$$0.75 = 75\%$$

Another option is to make the denominator equal to 100. Be sure to multiply the numerator by the same number as the denominator. For example:

$$\frac{3}{20} \times \frac{5}{5} = \frac{15}{100}$$

$$\frac{15}{100} = 15\%$$

Changing Fractions to Decimals

To change a fraction into a decimal, divide the denominator into the numerator until there are no remainders. There may be repeating decimals, so rounding is often acceptable. A straight line above the repeating portion denotes that the decimal repeats.

Example

Express 4/5 as a decimal.

Set up the division problem.

$$5\overline{)4}$$

5 does not go into 4, so place the decimal and add a zero.

$$5\overline{)4.0}$$

5 goes into 40 eight times. There is no remainder.

```
   0 . 8
 5|4 . 0
 - 4 . 0
 -------
       0
```

The solution is 0.8.

Example

Express 33 1/3 as a decimal.

Since the whole portion of the number is known, set it aside to calculate the decimal from the fraction portion.

Set up the division problem.

```
3|1
```

3 does not go into 1, so place the decimal and add zeros. 3 goes into 10 three times.

```
  0 . 3
3|1 . 0
```

This will repeat with a remainder of 1.

```
  0 . 3 3 3
3|1 . 0 0 0
  - 9
  -----
     1 0
    - 9
    ----
     1 0
```

So, we will place a line over the 3 to denote the repetition. The solution is written $0.\overline{3}$.

Changing Decimals to Fractions

To change decimals to fractions, place the decimal portion of the number, the numerator, over the respective place value, the denominator, then reduce, if possible.

Example: Express 0.25 as a fraction.

This is read as twenty-five hundredths, so put 25 over 100. Then reduce to find the solution.

$$\frac{25}{100} = \frac{1}{4}$$

Example: Express 0.455 as a fraction

This is read as four hundred fifty-five thousandths, so put 455 over 1000. Then reduce to find the solution.

$$\frac{455}{1000} = \frac{91}{200}$$

There are two types of problems that commonly involve percentages. The first is to calculate some percentage of a given quantity, where you convert the percentage to a decimal, and multiply the quantity by that decimal. Secondly, you are given a quantity and told it is a fixed percent of an unknown quantity. In this case, convert to a decimal, then divide the given quantity by that decimal.

Example: What is 30% of 760?

Convert the percent into a useable number. "Of" means to multiply.

$$30\% = 0.30$$

Set up the problem based on the givens, and solve.

$$0.30 \times 760 = 228$$

Example: 8.4 is 20% of what number?

Convert the percent into a useable number.

$$20\% = 0.20$$

The given number is a percent of the answer needed, so divide the given number by this decimal rather than multiplying it.

$$\frac{8.4}{0.20} = 42$$

Solving Practical Math Problems

Word problems, or story problems, are math problems that have a real-world context. In word problems, multiple quantities are often provided with a request to find some kind of relation between them. This often will mean that one variable (the dependent variable whose value needs to be found) can be written as a function of another variable (the independent variable whose value can be figured from the given information). The usual procedure for solving these problems is to start by giving each quantity in the problem a variable, and then figuring the relationship between these variables.

For example, suppose a car gets 25 miles per gallon. How far will the car travel if it uses 2.4 gallons of fuel? In this case, *y* would be the distance the car has traveled in miles, and *x* would be the amount of fuel burned in gallons (2.4). Then the relationship between these variables can be written as an algebraic equation, $y = 25x$. In this case, the equation is $y = 25 \times 2.4 = 60$, so the car has traveled 60 miles.

Translating Verbal Relationships into Algebraic Equations or Expressions

When attempting to solve a math problem, it's important to apply the correct algorithm. It is much more difficult to determine what algorithm is necessary when solving word problems, because the necessary operations and equations are typically not provided. In these instances, the test taker must translate the words in the problem into true mathematical statements that can be solved. The following are examples:

Symbol	Phrase
+	Added to; increased by; sum of; more than
−	Decreased by; difference between; less than; take away
×	Multiplied by; 3(4,5…) times as large; product of
÷	Divided by; quotient of; half (third, etc.) of
=	Is; the same as; results in; as much as; equal to
x,t,n, etc.	A number; unknown quantity; value of; variable

Addition and subtraction are **inverse operations**. Adding a number and then subtracting the same number will cancel each other out, resulting in the original number, and vice versa. For example, $8 + 7 - 7 = 8$ and $137 - 100 + 100 = 137$. Similarly, multiplication and division are inverse operations. Therefore, multiplying by a number and then dividing by the same number results in the original number, and vice versa. For example, $8 \times 2 \div 2 = 8$ and $12 \div 4 \times 4 = 12$. Inverse operations are used to work backwards to solve problems. In the case that 7 and a number add to 18, the inverse operation of subtraction is used to find the unknown value ($18 - 7 = 11$). If a school's entire 4th grade was divided evenly into 3 classes each with 22 students, the inverse operation of multiplication is used to determine the total students in the grade ($22 \times 3 = 66$). Additional scenarios involving inverse operations are included in the tables below.

There are a variety of real-world situations in which one or more of the operators is used to solve a problem. The tables below display the most common scenarios.

Addition & Subtraction

	Unknown Result	**Unknown Change**	**Unknown Start**
Adding to	5 students were in class. 4 more students arrived. How many students are in class? $5 + 4 = ?$	8 students were in class. More students arrived late. There are now 18 students in class. How many students arrived late? $8 + ? = 18$ Solved by inverse operations $18 - 8 = ?$	Some students were in class early. 11 more students arrived. There are now 17 students in class. How many students were in class early? $? + 11 = 17$ Solved by inverse operations $17 - 11 = ?$
Taking from	15 students were in class. 5 students left class. How many students are in class now? $15 - 5 = ?$	12 students were in class. Some students left class. There are now 8 students in class. How many students left class? $12 - ? = 8$ Solved by inverse operations $8 + ? = 12 \rightarrow 12 - 8 = ?$	Some students were in class. 3 students left class. Then there were 13 students in class. How many students were in class before? $? - 3 = 13$ Solved by inverse operations $13 + 3 = ?$

	Unknown Total	**Unknown Addends (Both)**	**Unknown Addends (One)**
Putting together/ taking apart	The homework assignment is 10 addition problems and 8 subtraction problems. How many problems are in the homework assignment? $10 + 8 = ?$	Bobby has $9. How much can Bobby spend on candy and how much can Bobby spend on toys? $9 = ? + ?$	Bobby has 12 pairs of pants. 5 pairs of pants are shorts, and the rest are long. How many pairs of long pants does he have? $12 = 5 + ?$ Solved by inverse operations $12 - 5 = ?$

	Unknown Difference	Unknown Larger Value	Unknown Smaller Value
Comparing	Bobby has 5 toys. Tommy has 8 toys. How many more toys does Tommy have than Bobby? $5+?=8$ Solved by inverse operations $8-5=?$ Bobby has \$6. Tommy has \$10. How many fewer dollars does Bobby have than Tommy? $10-6=?$	Tommy has 2 more toys than Bobby. Bobby has 4 toys. How many toys does Tommy have? $2+4=?$ Bobby has 3 fewer dollars than Tommy. Bobby has \$8. How many dollars does Tommy have? $?-3=8$ Solved by inverse operations $8+3=?$	Tommy has 6 more toys than Bobby. Tommy has 10 toys. How many toys does Bobby have? $?+6=10$ Solved by inverse operations $10-6=?$ Bobby has \$5 less than Tommy. Tommy has \$9. How many dollars does Bobby have? $9-5=?$

Multiplication and Division

	Unknown Product	Unknown Group Size	Unknown Number of Groups
Equal groups	There are 5 students, and each student has 4 pieces of candy. How many pieces of candy are there in all? $5\times 4=?$	14 pieces of candy are shared equally by 7 students. How many pieces of candy does each student have? $7\times ?=14$ Solved by inverse operations $14\div 7=?$	If 18 pieces of candy are to be given out 3 to each student, how many students will get candy? $?\times 3=18$ Solved by inverse operations $18\div 3=?$

	Unknown Product	Unknown Factor	Unknown Factor
Arrays	There are 5 rows of students with 3 students in each row. How many students are there? $5\times 3=?$	If 16 students are arranged into 4 equal rows, how many students will be in each row? $4\times ?=16$ Solved by inverse operations $16\div 4=?$	If 24 students are arranged into an array with 6 columns, how many rows are there? $?\times 6=24$ Solved by inverse operations $24\div 6=?$

	Larger Unknown	Smaller Unknown	Multiplier Unknown
Comparing	A small popcorn costs \$1.50. A large popcorn costs 3 times as much as a small popcorn. How much does a large popcorn cost? $1.50 \times 3 = ?$	A large soda costs \$6 and that is 2 times as much as a small soda costs. How much does a small soda cost? $2 \times ? = 6$ Solved by inverse operations $6 \div 2 = ?$	A large pretzel costs \$3 and a small pretzel costs \$2. How many times as much does the large pretzel cost as the small pretzel? $? \times 2 = 3$ Solved by inverse operations $3 \div 2 = ?$

Modeling and Solving Word Problems

Word problems can appear daunting, but don't let the wording intimidate you. No matter the scenario or specifics, the key to answering them is to translate the words into a math problem. Always keep in mind what the question is asking and what operations could lead to that answer.

Some word problems require more than just one simple equation to be written and solved. Consider the following situations and the linear equations used to model them.

Suppose Margaret is 2 miles to the east of John at noon. Margaret walks to the east at 3 miles per hour. How far apart will they be at 3 p.m.? To solve this, *x* would represent the time in hours past noon, and *y* would represent the distance between Margaret and John. Now, noon corresponds to the equation where *x* is 0, so the *y* intercept is going to be 2. It's also known that the slope will be the rate at which the distance is changing, which is 3 miles per hour. This means that the slope will be 3 (be careful at this point: if units were used, other than miles and hours, for *x* and *y* variables, a conversion of the given information to the appropriate units would be required first). The simplest way to write an equation given the *y*-intercept, and the slope is the Slope-Intercept form, is $y = mx + b$. Recall that m here is the slope and *b* is the *y* intercept. So, $m = 3$ and $b = 2$. Therefore, the equation will be $y = 3x + 2$. The word problem asks how far to the east Margaret will be from John at 3 p.m., which means when *x* is 3. So, substitute $x = 3$ into this equation to obtain:

$$y = 3 \cdot 3 + 2 = 9 + 2 = 11$$

Therefore, she will be 11 miles to the east of him at 3 p.m.

For another example, suppose that a box with 4 cans in it weighs 6 lbs., while a box with 8 cans in it weighs 12 lbs. Find out how much a single can weighs. To do this, let *x* denote the number of cans in the box, and *y* denote the weight of the box with the cans in lbs. This line touches two pairs: $(4, 6)$ and (8, 12). A formula for this relation could be written using the two-point form, with $x_1 = 4, y_1 = 6, x_2 = 8, y_2 = 12$. This would yield $\frac{y-6}{x-4} = \frac{12-6}{8-4}$, or $\frac{y-6}{x-4} = \frac{6}{4} = \frac{3}{2}$. However, only the slope is needed to solve this problem, since the slope will be the weight of a single can. From the computation, the slope is $\frac{3}{2}$. Therefore, each can weighs $\frac{3}{2}$ lb.

Solving Simple Algebraic Problems

Linear equations and **linear inequalities** are both comparisons of two algebraic expressions. However, unlike equations in which the expressions are equal, linear inequalities compare expressions that may be unequal. Linear equations typically have one value for the variable that makes the statement true. Linear inequalities generally have an infinite number of values that make the statement true.

When solving a linear equation, the desired result requires determining a numerical value for the unknown **variable**. If given a linear equation involving addition, subtraction, multiplication, or division, working backwards isolates the variable. Addition and subtraction are inverse operations, as are multiplication and division. Therefore, they can be used to cancel each other out.

Since variables are the letters that represent an unknown number, you must solve for that unknown number in single variable problems. The main thing to remember is that you can do anything to one side of an equation as long as you do it to the other.

The first steps to solving linear equations are distributing, if necessary, and combining any like terms on the same side of the equation. Sides of an equation are separated by an **equal sign**. Next, the equation is manipulated to show the variable on one side. Again, whatever is done to one side of the equation must be done to the other side of the equation to remain equal. Inverse operations are then used to isolate the variable and undo the order of operations backwards. Addition and subtraction are undone, then multiplication and division are undone.

For example, solve $4(t-2)+2t-4=2(9-2t)$

Distributing: $4t-8+2t-4=18-4t$

Combining like terms: $6t-12=18-4t$

Adding $4t$ to each side to move the variable: $10t-12=18$

Adding 12 to each side to isolate the variable: $10t=30$

Dividing each side by 10 to isolate the variable: $t=3$

The answer can be checked by substituting the value for the variable into the original equation, ensuring that both sides calculate to be equal.

Linear inequalities express the relationship between unequal values. More specifically, they describe in what way the values are unequal. A value can be greater than (>), less than (<), greater than or equal to (≥), or less than or equal to (≤) another value. $5x+40>65$ is read as *five times a number added to forty is greater than sixty-five.*

When solving a linear inequality, the solution is the set of all numbers that make the statement true. The inequality $x+2\geq 6$ has a solution set of 4 and every number greater than 4 (4.01; 5; 12; 107; etc.). Adding 2 to 4 or any number greater than 4 results in a value that is greater than or equal to 6. Therefore, $x\geq 4$ is the solution set.

To algebraically solve a linear inequality, follow the same steps as those for solving a linear equation. The inequality symbol stays the same for all operations except when multiplying or dividing by a negative number. If multiplying or dividing by a negative number while solving an inequality, the relationship reverses (the sign flips). In other words, > switches to < and vice versa. Multiplying or dividing by a positive number does not change the relationship, so the sign stays the same.

An example is shown below.

Solve $-2x - 8 \leq 22$

Add 8 to both sides: $-2x \leq 30$

Divide both sides by -2: $x \geq -15$

Although linear equations generally have one solution, this is not always the case. If there is no value for the variable that makes the statement true, there is no solution to the equation. Consider the equation:

$$x + 3 = x - 1$$

There is no value for *x* in which adding 3 to the value produces the same result as subtracting one from the value. Conversely, if any value for the variable makes a true statement, the equation has an infinite number of solutions. Consider the equation:

$$3x + 6 = 3(x + 2)$$

Any number substituted for *x* will result in a true statement (both sides of the equation are equal).

By manipulating equations like the two above, the variable of the equation will cancel out completely. If the remaining constants express a true statement (ex. $6 = 6$), then all real numbers are solutions to the equation. If the constants left express a false statement (ex. $3 = -1$), then no solution exists for the equation.

When solving radical and rational equations, extraneous solutions must be accounted for when finding the answers. For example, the equation $\frac{x}{x-5} = \frac{3x}{x+3}$ has two values that create a 0 denominator: $x \neq 5, -3$. When solving for x, these values must be considered because they cannot be solutions. In the given equation, solving for x can be done using cross-multiplication, yielding the equation:

$$x(x + 3) = 3x(x - 5)$$

Distributing results in the quadratic equation yields $x^2 + 3x = 3x^2 - 15x$; therefore, all terms must be moved to one side of the equals sign. This results in $2x^2 - 18x = 0$, which in factored form is $2x(x - 9) = 0$. Setting each factor equal to zero, the apparent solutions are $x = 0$ and $x = 9$. These two solutions are neither 5 nor -3, so they are viable solutions. Neither 0 nor 9 create a 0 denominator in the original equation.

A similar process exists when solving radical equations. One must check to make sure the solutions are defined in the original equations. Solving an equation containing a square root involves isolating the root and then squaring both sides of the equals sign. Solving a cube root equation involves isolating the radical and then cubing both sides. In either case, the variable can then be solved for because there are no longer radicals in the equation.

Solving a linear inequality requires all values that make the statement true to be determined. For example, solving $3x - 7 \geq -13$ produces the solution $x \geq -2$. This means that -2 and any number greater than -2 produces a true statement. Solution sets for linear inequalities will often be displayed using a number line. If a value is included in the set (≥ or ≤), a shaded dot is placed on that value and an arrow extending in the direction of the solutions. For a variable > or ≥ a number, the arrow will point right on a number line, the direction where the numbers increase. If a variable is < or ≤ a number, the arrow will point left on a number line, which is the direction where the numbers decrease. If the value is not included in the set (> or <), an open (unshaded) circle on that value is used with an arrow in the appropriate direction.

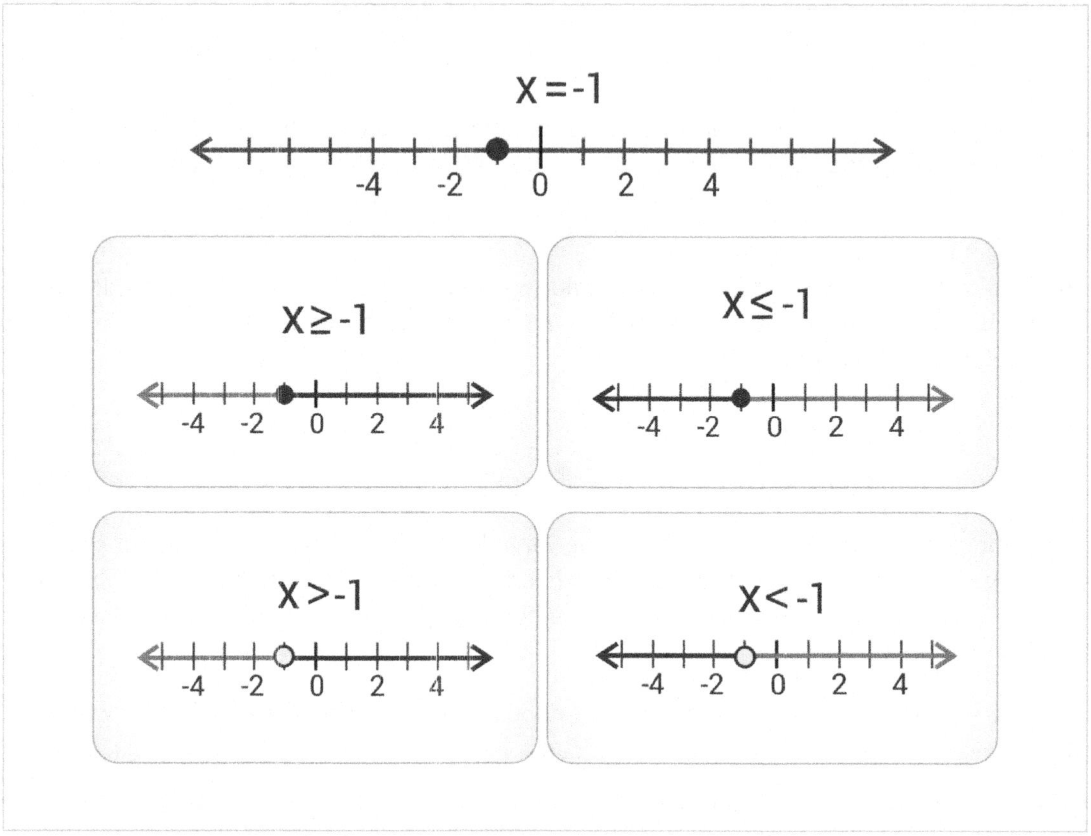

Similar to linear equations, a linear inequality may have a solution set consisting of all real numbers, or can contain no solution. When solved algebraically, a linear inequality in which the variable cancels out and results in a true statement (ex. $7 \geq 2$) has a solution set of all real numbers. A linear inequality in which the variable cancels out and results in a false statement (ex. $7 \leq 2$) has no solution.

Equations and inequalities in two variables represent a relationship. Jim owns a car wash and charges \$40 per car. The rent for the facility is \$350 per month. An equation can be written to relate the number of cars Jim cleans to the money he makes per month. Let x represent the number of cars and y represent the profit Jim makes each month from the car wash. The equation $y = 40x - 350$ can be used to show Jim's profit or loss. Since this equation has two variables, the coordinate plane can be used to show the relationship and predict profit or loss for Jim. The following graph shows that Jim must wash at least nine cars to pay the rent, where $x = 9$. Anything nine cars and above yield a profit shown in the value on the y-axis.

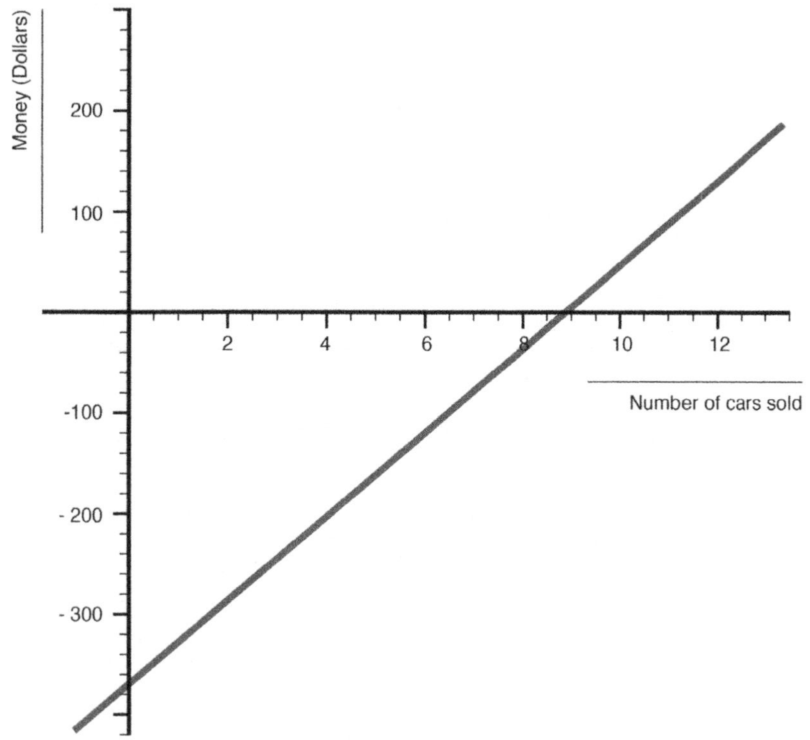

With a single equation in two variables, the solutions are limited only by the situation the equation represents. When two equations or inequalities are used, more constraints are added. For example, in a system of linear equations, there is often—although not always—only one answer. The point of intersection of two lines is the solution. For a system of inequalities, there are infinitely many answers.

The intersection of two solution sets gives the solution set of the system of inequalities. In the following graph, the darker shaded region is where two inequalities overlap. Any set of x and y found in that region satisfies both inequalities. The line with the positive slope is solid, meaning the values on that line are included in the solution. The line with the negative slope is dotted, so the coordinates on that line are not included.

Here's an example:

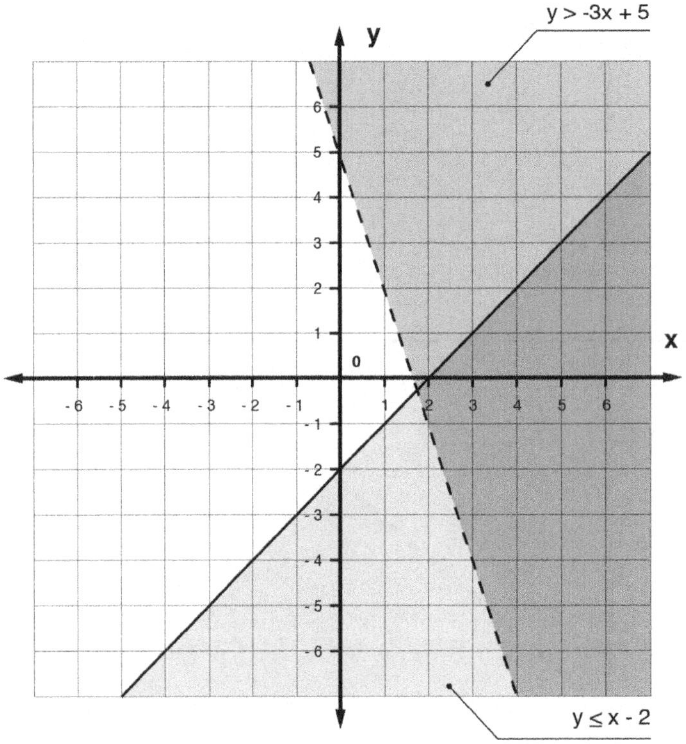

Formulas with two variables are equations used to represent a specific relationship. For example, the formula $d = rt$ represents the relationship between distance, rate, and time. If Bob travels at a rate of 35 miles per hour on his road trip from Westminster to Seneca, the formula $d = 35t$ can be used to represent his distance traveled in a specific length of time. Formulas can also be used to show different roles of the variables, transformed without any given numbers. Solving for r, the formula becomes $\frac{d}{t} = r$. The t is moved over by division so that *rate* is a function of distance and time.

The Problem-Solving Process and Determining If Enough Information Is Provided to Solve a Problem

Overall, the problem-solving process in mathematics involves a step-by-step procedure that one must follow when deciding what approach to take. First, one must understand the problem by deciding what is being sought, then if enough information is given, and what units are necessary in the solution. This is a crucial, but sometimes difficult step. It involves carefully reading the entire problem, identifying (perhaps even underlining) the facts or information that *is* known, and then deciphering the question words to determine what the problem is asking. In this way, math problems require students to be detectives, evaluating the "clues" or facts given in the problem, deciding what the problem is looking for, and evaluating whether sufficient information or "clues" are presented in the problem to solve the posed question.

In general, when solving word problems (also called story problems), it's important to understand what is being asked and to properly set up the initial equation. Always read the entire problem through, and then separate out what information is given in the statement. Decide what you are being asked to find and label each quantity with a variable or constant. Then write an equation to determine the unknown variable. Remember to label answers; sometimes knowing what the answers' units can help eliminate other possible solutions.

When trying to solve any word problem, look for a series of key words indicating addition, subtraction, multiplication, or division to help you determine how to set up the problem:

Addition: add, altogether, together, plus, increased by, more than, in all, sum, and total

Subtraction: minus, less than, difference, decreased by, fewer than, remain, and take away

Multiplication: *times*, *twice*, *of*, *double*, and *triple*

Division: divided by, cut up, half, quotient of, split, and shared equally

If a question asks to give words to a mathematical expression and says "equals," then an = sign must be included in the answer. Similarly, "less than or equal to" is expressed by the inequality symbol ≤, and "greater than or equal" to is expressed as ≥. Furthermore, "less than" is represented by <, and "greater than" is expressed by >.

These strategies are applicable to other question types. For example, calculating salary after deductions, balancing a checkbook, and calculating a dinner bill are common word problems similar to business planning. Just remember to use the correct operations. When a balance is increased, use addition. When a balance is decreased, use subtraction. Common sense and organization are your greatest assets when answering word problems.

For example, suppose the following word problem is encountered:

Walter's Coffee Shop sells a variety of drinks and breakfast treats.

Price List	
Hot Coffee	$2.00
Slow-Drip Iced Coffee	$3.00
Latte	$4.00
Muffin	$2.00
Crepe	$4.00
Egg Sandwich	$5.00

Costs	
Hot Coffee	$0.25
Slow-Drip Iced Coffee	$0.75
Latte	$1.00
Muffin	$1.00
Crepe	$2.00
Egg Sandwich	$3.00

Walter's utilities, rent, and labor costs him $500 per day. Today, Walter sold 200 hot coffees, 100 slow-drip iced coffees, 50 lattes, 75 muffins, 45 crepes, and 60 egg sandwiches. What was Walter's total profit today?

First, it is necessary to establish what is known (the "facts"), what one wants to know, (the question), how to determine the answer (the process), and if there is enough information to solve (sufficient "clues"). The problem clearly asks: "what was Walter's total profit today," so to accurately answer this type of question, the total cost of making his drinks and treats must be calculated, then the total revenue he earned from selling those products must be determined. After arriving at these two totals, the profit is measured found by deducting the total cost from the total revenue.

Now that the question and steps are identified, the provided facts are evaluated. Walter's costs for today:

Item	Quantity	Cost Per Unit	Total Cost
Hot Coffee	200	$0.25	$50
Slow-Drip Iced Coffee	100	$0.75	$75
Latte	50	$1.00	$50
Muffin	75	$1.00	$75
Crepe	45	$2.00	$90
Egg Sandwich	60	$3.00	$180
Utilities, rent, and labor			$500
Total Costs			$1,020

Walter's revenue for today:

Item	Quantity	Revenue Per Unit	Total Revenue
Hot Coffee	200	$2.00	$400
Slow-Drip Iced Coffee	100	$3.00	$300
Latte	50	$4.00	$200
Muffin	75	$2.00	$150
Crepe	45	$4.00	$180
Egg Sandwich	60	$5.00	$300
Total Revenue			$1,530

Walter's Profit = *Revenue* – *Costs* = $1,530 -- $1,020 = $510

In this case, enough information was given in the problem to adequately solve it. If, however, the number of sandwiches and drinks were not provided, or Walter's cost per unit sold, insufficient information would prevent one from arriving at the answer.

Alternative Methods for Solving Mathematical Problems

When solving a math problem, once the question is identified and the clues are evaluated, the plan of action must be determined. In some cases, there might be many options. Therefore, one should begin with one approach and if the strategy does not fit, he or she should move on to another. In some cases, a combination of approaches can be used. A beginning estimate is always useful for comparison once a solution is found. The answer must be reasonable and must fulfill all requirements of the problem.

Presenting students with a variety of methods to solve the same type of math problem empowers each student to select the process that works best for them personally. It can help increase motivation and confidence to tackle difficult math problems. Just as there are different types of learners (visual, kinesthetic, etc.), so too are there particular problem-solving approaches that different students prefer or grasp more easily than others. Skilled mathematicians are versed in multiple methods to tackle various problems, with each method bolstering their toolbox with a strategy that can be employed for ease and efficiency when encountering math work.

Instead of focusing on the "right" way to solve a problem, teachers should strive to present multiple methods and explain the pros, cons, and appropriate applications for each method. For example, when trying to find the zeros in a binomial expression, one might be able to factor the expression, complete the square, use the quadratic equation, or make a rough sketch of the graph and identify the x-intercepts. In some cases, one method may not be possible and another may be "easiest," but by providing students with the various strategies, teachers enable them to be critical thinkers and select the method they deem most appropriate.

The following two examples demonstrate how different methods can be used for the same problem:

Example:

A store is having a spring sale, where everything is 70% off. You have $45.00 to spend. A jacket is regularly priced at $80.00. Do you have enough to buy the jacket and a pair of gloves, regularly priced at $20.00?

There are two ways to approach this.

Method 1:

Set up the equations to find the sale prices: the original price minus the amount discounted.
$80.00 - ($80.00 (0.70)) = sale cost of the jacket.
$20.00 – ($20.00 (0.70)) = sale cost of the gloves.
Solve for the sale cost.
$24.00 = sale cost of the jacket.
$6.00 = sale cost of the gloves.
Determine if you have enough money for both.
$24.00 + $6.00 = total sale cost.
$30.00 is less than $45.00, so you can afford to purchase both.

Method 2:

Determine the percent of the original price that you will pay.
100% – 70% = 30%
Set up the equations to find the sale prices.
$80.00 (0.30) = cost of the jacket.
$20.00 (0.30) = cost of the gloves.
Solve.
$24.00 = cost of the jacket.
$6.00 = cost of the gloves.
Determine if you have enough money for both.
$24.00 + $6.00 = total sale cost.
$30.00 is less than $45.00, so you can afford to purchase both.

Example:

Mary and Dottie team up to mow neighborhood lawns. If Mary mows 2 lawns per hour and the two of them can mow 17.5 lawns in 5 hours, how many lawns does Dottie mow per hour?

Given rate for Mary.

$$Mary = \frac{2\ lawns}{1\ hour}$$

Unknown rate of D for Dottie.

$$Dottie = \frac{D\ lawns}{1\ hour}$$

Given rate for both.

$$Total\ mowed\ together = \frac{17.5\ lawns}{5\ hours}$$

Set up the equation for what is being asked.

$$Mary + Dottie = total\ together.$$

Fill in the givens.

$$2 + D = \frac{17.5}{5}$$

Divide.

$$2 + D = 3.5$$

Subtract 2 from both sides to isolate the variable.

$$2 - 2 + D = 3.5 - 2$$

Solve and label Dottie's mowing rate.

$$D = 1.5\ lawns\ per\ hour$$

Numerical & Graphic Relationships

Relationships in Numerical Data

In some cases, it is useful to compare numerical data and determine the relationship between values. One of the best ways to mathematically compare two values is to compute the percentage difference between the two values. For example, consider a given music shop that had a net profit of $120,000 in the first year of operation and $185,000 over the second year. Rather than simply finding the net difference between the two years (using subtraction), the business owner may want to know by what percentage his profit increased; in other words, how much his profit in the second year increased relative to his first year. In such cases, the percentage change is desired. The following sections provide some guidance for this process.

Percent Increase/Decrease

Problems dealing with percentages may involve an original value, a change in that value, and a percentage change. A problem will provide two pieces of information and ask to find the third. To do so, this formula is used: $\frac{change}{original\ value} \text{ x } 100 = \text{percent change}$. Here's a sample problem:

> Attendance at a baseball stadium has dropped 16% from last year. Last year's average attendance was 40,000. What is this year's average attendance?

Using the formula and information, the change is unknown (*x*), the original value is 40,000, and the percent change is 16%. The formula can be written as: $\frac{x}{40{,}000} \text{ x } 100 = 16$. When solving for *x*, it is determined the change was 6,400. The problem asked for this year's average attendance, so to calculate, the change (6,400) is subtracted from last year's attendance (40,000) to determine this year's average attendance is 33,600.

Percent More Than/Less Than

Percentage problems may give a value and what percent that given value is more than or less than an original unknown value. Here's a sample problem:

> A store advertises that all its merchandise has been reduced by 25%. The new price of a pair of shoes is $60. What was the original price?

This problem can be solved by writing a proportion. Two ratios should be written comparing the cost and the percent of the original cost. The new cost is 75% of the original cost (100% - 25%); and the original cost is 100% of the original cost. The unknown original cost can be represented by *x*. The proportion would be set up as: $\frac{60}{75} = \frac{x}{100}$. Solving the proportion, it is determined the original cost was $80.

The Position of Numbers Relative to Each Other

Place Value of a Digit

Numbers count in groups of 10. That number is the same throughout the set of natural numbers and whole numbers. It is referred to as working within a base 10 numeration system. Only the numbers from zero to 9 are used to represent any number. The foundation for doing this involves **place value**. Numbers are written side by side. This is to show the amount in each place value.

For place value, let's look at how the number 10 is different from zero to 9. It has two digits instead of just one. The one is in the tens' place, and the zero is in the ones' place. Therefore, there is one group of tens and zero ones. 11 has one 10 and one 1. The introduction of numbers from 11 to 19 should be the next step. Each value within this range of numbers consists of one group of 10 and a specific number of leftover ones. Counting by tens can be practiced once the tens column is understood. This process consists of increasing the number in the tens place by one. For example, counting by 10 starting at 17 would result in the next four values being 27, 37, 47, and 57.

A place value chart can be used for understanding and learning about numbers that have more digits. Here is an example of a place value chart:

	MILLIONS			THOUSANDS			ONES			.	DECIMALS		
billions	hundred millions	ten millions	millions	hundred thousands	ten thousands	thousands	hundreds	tens	ones		tenths	hundredths	thousandths

In the number 1,234, there are 4 ones and 3 tens. The 2 is in the hundreds' place, and the one is in the thousands' place. Note that each group of three digits is separated by a comma. The 2 has a value that is 10 times greater than the 3. Every place to the left has a value 10 times greater than the place to its right. Also, each group of three digits is also known as a *period.* 234 is in the ones' period.

The number 1,234 can be written out as *one-thousand, two hundred thirty-four*. The process of writing out numbers is known as the *decimal system*. It is also based on groups of 10. The place value chart is a helpful tool in using this system. In order to write out a number, it always starts with the digit(s) in the highest period. For example, in the number 23,815,467, the 23 is in highest place and is in the millions' period. The number is read *twenty-three million, eight hundred fifteen thousand, four hundred sixty-seven.* Each period is written separately through the use of commas. Also, no "ands" are used within the number. Another way to think about the number 23,815,467 is through the use of an addition problem. For example:

$$23{,}815{,}467 = 20{,}000{,}000 + 3{,}000{,}000 + 800{,}000 + 10{,}000 + 5{,}000 + 400 + 60 + 7$$

This expression is known as *expanded form*. The actual number 23,815,467 is known as being in *standard form*.

In order to compare whole numbers with many digits, place value can be used. In each number to be compared, it is necessary to find the highest place value in which the numbers differ and to compare the value within that place value. For example, $4{,}523{,}345 < 4{,}532{,}456$ because of the values in the ten thousands place. A similar process can be used for decimals. However, number lines can also be used. Tick marks can be placed within two whole numbers on the number line that represent tenths, hundredths, etc. Each number being compared can then be plotted. The value farthest to the right on the number line is the largest.

Comparing, Classifying, and Ordering Real Numbers

A **rational number** is any number that can be written as a fraction or ratio. Within the set of rational numbers, several subsets exist that are referenced throughout the mathematics topics. **Counting numbers** are the first numbers learned as a child. Counting numbers consist of 1,2,3,4, and so on. **Whole numbers** include all counting numbers and zero (0,1,2,3,4,...). **Integers** include counting numbers, their opposites, and zero (...,-3,-2,-1,0,1,2,3,...). **Rational numbers** are inclusive of integers, fractions, and decimals that terminate, or end (1.7, 0.04213) or repeat ($0.136\bar{5}$).

A **number line** typically consists of integers (...3,2,1,0,-1,-2,-3...), and is used to visually represent the value of a rational number. Each rational number has a distinct position on the line determined by comparing its value with the displayed values on the line. For example, if plotting -1.5 on the number line below, it is necessary to recognize that the value of -1.5 is .5 less than -1 and .5 greater than -2. Therefore, -1.5 is plotted halfway between -1 and -2.

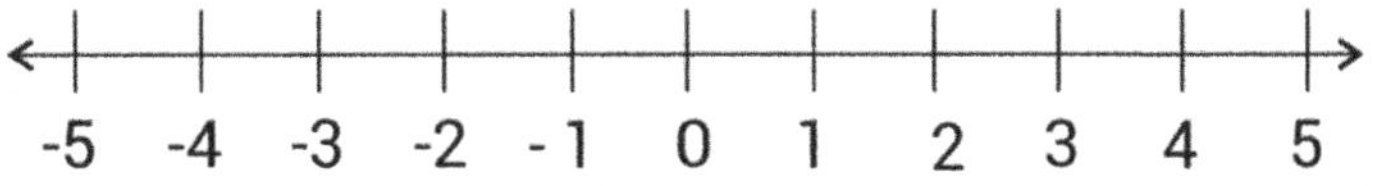

The number system that is used consists of only ten different digits or characters. However, this system is used to represent an infinite number of values. As mentioned, the **place value system** makes this infinite number of values possible. The position in which a digit is written corresponds to a given value. Starting from the decimal point (which is implied, if not physically present), each subsequent place value to the left represents a value greater than the one before it. Conversely, starting from the decimal point, each subsequent place value to the right represents a value less than the one before it.

In accordance with the **base-10 system**, the value of a digit increases by a factor of ten each place it moves to the left. For example, consider the number 7. Moving the digit one place to the left (70), increases its value by a factor of 10 ($7 \times 10 = 70$). Moving the digit two places to the left (700) increases its value by a factor of 10 twice ($7 \times 10 \times 10 = 700$). Moving the digit three places to the left (7,000) increases its value by a factor of 10 three times ($7 \times 10 \times 10 \times 10 = 7{,}000$), and so on.

Conversely, the value of a digit decreases by a factor of ten each place it moves to the right. (Note that multiplying by $\frac{1}{10}$ is equivalent to dividing by 10). For example, consider the number 40. Moving the digit one place to the right (4) decreases its value by a factor of 10 ($40 \div 10 = 4$). Moving the digit two places to the right (0.4), decreases its value by a factor of 10 twice ($40 \div 10 \div 10 = 0.4$) or ($40 \times \frac{1}{10} \times \frac{1}{10} = 0.4$). Moving the digit three places to the right (0.04) decreases its value by a factor of 10 three times ($40 \div 10 \div 10 \div 10 = 0.04$) or ($40 \times \frac{1}{10} \times \frac{1}{10} \times \frac{1}{10} = 0.04$), and so on.

Ordering Numbers

A common question type asks to order rational numbers from least to greatest or greatest to least. The numbers will come in a variety of formats, including decimals, percentages, roots, fractions, and whole numbers. These questions test for knowledge of different types of numbers and the ability to determine their respective values.

Before discussing ordering all numbers, let's start with decimals.

To compare decimals and order them by their value, utilize a method similar to that of ordering large numbers.

The main difference is where the comparison will start. Assuming that any numbers to left of the decimal point are equal, the next numbers to be compared are those immediately to the right of the decimal point. If those are equal, then move on to compare the values in the next decimal place to the right.

For example:

Which number is greater, 12.35 or 12.38?

Check that the values to the left of the decimal point are equal:

$$12 = 12$$

Next, compare the values of the decimal place to the right of the decimal:

$$12.3 = 12.3$$

Those are also equal in value.

Finally, compare the value of the numbers in the next decimal place to the right on both numbers:

12.3**5** and 12.3**8**

Here the 5 is less than the 8, so the final way to express this inequality is:

$$12.35 < 12.38$$

Comparing decimals is regularly exemplified with money because the "cents" portion of money ends in the hundredths place. When paying for gasoline or meals in restaurants, and even in bank accounts, if enough errors are made when calculating numbers to the hundredths place, they can add up to dollars and larger amounts of money over time.

Now that decimal ordering has been explained, let's expand and consider all real numbers. Whether the question asks to order the numbers from greatest to least or least to greatest, the crux of the question is the same—convert the numbers into a common format. Generally, it's easiest to write the numbers as whole numbers and decimals so they can be placed on a number line. Follow these examples to understand this strategy.

1) Order the following rational numbers from greatest to least:

$$\sqrt{36}, 0.65, 78\%, \frac{3}{4}, 7, 90\%, \frac{5}{2}$$

Of the seven numbers, the whole number (7) and decimal (0.65) are already in an accessible form, so concentrate on the other five.

First, the square root of 36 equals 6. (If the test asks for the root of a non-perfect root, determine which two whole numbers the root lies between.) Next, convert the percentages to decimals. A percentage means "per hundred," so this conversion requires moving the decimal point two places to the left, leaving 0.78 and 0.9.

Lastly, evaluate the fractions:

$$\frac{3}{4} = \frac{75}{100} = 0.75\,; \frac{5}{2} = 2\frac{1}{2} = 2.5$$

Now, the only step left is to list the numbers in the request order:

$$7, \sqrt{36}, \frac{5}{2}, 90\%, 78\%, \frac{3}{4}, 0.65$$

2) Order the following rational numbers from least to greatest:

$$2.5, \sqrt{9}, -10.5, 0.853, 175\%, \sqrt{4}, \frac{4}{5}$$

$$\sqrt{9} = 3$$

$$175\% = 1.75$$

$$\sqrt{4} = 2$$

$$\frac{4}{5} = 0.8$$

From least to greatest, the answer is:

$$-10.5, \frac{4}{5}, 0.853, 175\%, \sqrt{4}, 2.5, \sqrt{9}$$

Expressing Numeric Relationships

If a question asks to give words to a mathematical expression and says "equals," then an = sign must be included in the answer. Similarly, "less than or equal to" is expressed by the inequality symbol ≤, and "greater than or equal" to is expressed as ≥. Furthermore, "less than" is represented by <, and "greater than" is expressed by >.

Equations use the equals sign because the numeric expressions on either side of the symbol (=) are equivalent. In contrast, inequalities compare values or expressions that are unequal. Although not always true, linear equations that include a variable often have just one value for the variable that makes the statement true. Linear inequalities generally have an infinite number of values that make the statement true.

Inequalities are a concise mathematical way to express the relationship between unequal values. More specifically, they describe in what way the values are unequal. A value could be greater than (>); less than (<); greater than or equal to (≥); or less than or equal to (≤) another value. The statement "five times a number added to forty is more than sixty-five" can be expressed as $5x + 40 > 65$. Common words and phrases that express inequalities are:

Symbol	Phrase
<	is under, is below, smaller than, beneath
>	is above, is over, bigger than, exceeds
≤	no more than, at most, maximum
≥	no less than, at least, minimum

Solving Linear Inequalities

When solving a linear inequality, the solution is the set of all numbers that makes the statement true. The inequality $x + 2 \geq 6$ has a solution set of 4 and every number greater than 4 (4.0001, 5, 12, 107, etc.). Adding 2 to 4 or any number greater than 4 would result in a value that is greater than or equal to 6. Therefore, $x \geq 4$ would be the solution set.

Solution sets for linear inequalities often will be displayed using a number line. If a value is included in the set (≥ or ≤), there is a shaded dot placed on that value and an arrow extending in the direction of the solutions. For a variable $>$ or $\geq$ a number, the arrow would point right on the number line (the direction where the numbers increase); and if a variable is $<$ or $\leq$ a number, the arrow would point left (where the numbers decrease). If the value is not included in the set ($>$ or $<$), an open circle on that value would be used with an arrow in the appropriate direction.

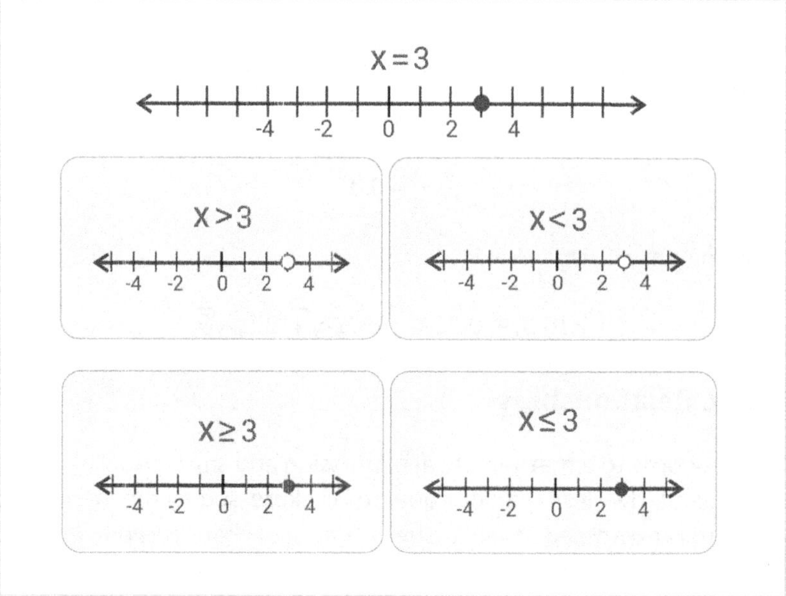

Students may be asked to write a linear inequality given a graph of its solution set. To do so, they should identify whether the value is included (shaded dot or open circle) and the direction in which the arrow is pointing.

In order to algebraically solve a linear inequality, the same steps should be followed as in solving a linear equation. The inequality symbol stays the same for all operations EXCEPT when dividing by a negative number. If dividing by a negative number while solving an inequality, the relationship reverses (the sign flips). Dividing by a positive does not change the relationship, so the sign stays the same. In other words, $>$ switches to $<$ and vice versa. An example is shown below.

Solve $-2(x + 4) \leq 22$

Distribute: $-2x - 8 \leq 22$

Add 8 to both sides: $-2x \leq 30$

Divide both sides by $-2: x \geq 15$

Mathematically Equivalent Expressions

It is helpful to be skilled at identifying values that are equivalent but that are expressed in different forms, such as a fraction, decimal, and percent, because it enables one to convert the representation of a value for easier calculation in a given problem. Manipulating values is often required when working with percentages in order to carry out calculations. The word percent means "per hundred." When dealing with percentages, it may be helpful to think of the number as a value in hundredths. For example, 15% can be expressed as "fifteen hundredths" and written as $\frac{15}{100}$ or .15.

Converting from Decimals and Fractions to Percentages

To convert a decimal to a percent, a number is multiplied by 100. To write .25 as a percent, the equation $.25 \times 100$ yields 25%. To convert a fraction to a percent, the fraction is converted to a decimal and then multiplied by 100. To convert $\frac{3}{5}$ to a decimal, the numerator (3) is divided by the denominator (5). This results in .6, which is then multiplied by 100 to get 60%.

To convert a percent to a decimal, the number is divided by 100. For example, 150% is equal to 1.5 $\left(\frac{150}{100}\right)$. To convert a percent to a fraction, the percent sign is deleted and the value is written as the numerator with a denominator of 100. For example, 2% = $\frac{2}{100}$. Fractions should be reduced: $\frac{2}{100} = \frac{1}{50}$.

Rounding Rules

As mentioned, rounding is an important concept dealing with place value. **Rounding** is the process of either bumping a number up or down, based on a certain place value.

Rounding numbers consists of:

- determining what place value the number is being rounded to
- examining the digit to the right of the desired place value to decide whether to round up or keep the digit, and
- replacing all digits to the right of the desired place value with zeros.

To round 746,311 to the nearest ten thousand, the digit in the ten thousands place should be located first. In this case, this digit is 4 (7<u>4</u>6,311). Then, the digit to its right is examined. If this digit is 5 or greater, the number will be rounded up by increasing the digit in the desired place by one. If the digit to the right of the place value being rounded is 4 or less, the number will be kept the same. For the given example, the digit being examined is a 6, which means that the number will be rounded up by increasing the digit to the left by one. Therefore, the digit 4 is changed to a 5. Finally, to write the rounded number, any digits to the left of the place value being rounded remain the same and any to its right are replaced with zeros. For the given example, rounding 746,311 to the nearest ten thousand will produce 750,000. To round 746,311 to the nearest hundred, the digit to the right of the three in the hundreds place is examined to determine whether to round up or keep the same number. In this case, that digit is a 1, so the number will be kept the same and any digits to its right will be replaced with zeros. The resulting rounded number is 746,300.

Rounding place values to the right of the decimal follows the same procedure, but digits being replaced by zeros can simply be dropped. To round 3.752891 to the nearest thousandth, the desired place value is located (3.75<u>2</u>891) and the digit to the right is examined. In this case, the digit 8 indicates that the number will be rounded up, and the 2 in the thousandths place will increase to a 3. Rounding up and replacing the digits to the right of the thousandths place produces 3.753000 which is equivalent to 3.753. Therefore, the zeros are not necessary and the rounded number should be written as 3.753.

When rounding up, if the digit to be increased is a 9, the digit to its left is increased by 1 and the digit in the desired place value is changed to a zero. For example, the number 1,598 rounded to the nearest ten is 1,600. Another example shows the number 43.72961 rounded to the nearest thousandth is 43.730 or 43.73.

Logical Connectives and Quantifiers

Logical connectives such as *and, or if,* and *then,* are often used with deductive reasoning. This type of reasoning in math involves starting with stating a general rule, and then moving forward with logic to obtain a desired conclusion. If the original statements are true, then the conclusion is true. Most of mathematics involves deductive reasoning. For example, if $x = 2$ and $y = 4$ then $x + y = 6$. Also, if x is an even number and y is an odd number, then $x + y$ is an odd number.

Quantifiers may also be encountered in mathematical problems. The quantifier *all* means that the rule applies across the board or universally or that the entire number of something is present or true. For example, *all* pentagons have five angles. In contrast, the quantifier *none* indicates that not a single one of the items or values in the statement make the statement true or fit the criteria. For example, *none* of the angles in an equilateral triangle are obtuse. The vague quantifier *some* treads the middle ground between those two extremes, and means that an unspecified number or amount of something applies or makes the statement true. For example, the whole amount or number of." For example, *some* rectangles are squares.

Filling in Missing Values in a Data Table

Missing values in a table can be calculated by determining if there is a formula to represent the relationship among values or levels in the table or if empty cells denote subtotals. For example, if a data table presents an itemized list of the type and number of items purchased and the unit price of each item, the subtotal for the cost of each type of item can be calculated by multiplying the number of that item purchased by the unit price.

Consider the table presented earlier of Walter's expenses. This time, several of the "total cost" cells are blank:

Item	Quantity	Cost Per Unit	Total Cost
Hot Coffee	200	$0.25	$50
Slow-Drip Iced Coffee	100	$0.75	
Latte	50		$50
Muffin	75	$1.00	$75
Crepe		$2.00	$90
Egg Sandwich	60	$3.00	$180
Utilities, rent, and labor			$500
Total Costs			$1,020

The total cost for slow-drip iced coffee can be calculated by multiplying the quantity (100) by the cost per unit ($0.75): $100 \times \$0.75 = \$75$. The cost per unit for a latte can be calculated by dividing the total cost ($50) by the number of lattes sold (50): $\$50 \div 50 = \$1.00$. The number of crepes sold can be found in the same manner, but this time, the total cost is divided by the unit cost: $\$90 \div \$2.00 = 45\ crepes$.

Using Information from Tables and Graphs to Solve Problems

Data can be represented in many ways. It is important to be able to organize the data into categories that could be represented using one of these methods. Equally important is the ability to read these types of diagrams and interpret their meaning.

Data in Tables

One of the most common ways to express data is in a table. The primary reason for plugging data into a table is to make interpretation more convenient. It's much easier to look at the table than to analyze results in a narrative paragraph. When analyzing a table, pay close attention to the title, variables, and data.

Let's analyze a theoretical antibiotic study. The study has 6 groups, named A through F, and each group receives a different dose of medicine. The results of the study are listed in the table below.

Results of Antibiotic Studies		
Group	**Dosage of Antibiotics in milligrams (mg)**	**Efficacy (% of participants cured)**
A	0 mg	20%
B	20 mg	40%
C	40 mg	75%
D	60 mg	95%
E	80 mg	100%
F	100 mg	100%

Tables generally list the title immediately above the data. The title should succinctly explain what is listed below. Here, "Results of Antibiotic Studies" informs the audience that the data pertains to the results of scientific study on antibiotics.

Identifying the variables at play is one of the most important parts of interpreting data. Remember, the independent variable is intentionally altered, and its change is independent of the other variables. Here, the dosage of antibiotics administered to the different groups is the independent variable. The study is intentionally manipulating the strength of the medicine to study the related results. Efficacy is the dependent variable since its results *depend* on a different variable, the dose of antibiotics. Generally, the independent variable will be listed before the dependent variable in tables.

Also play close attention to the variables' labels. Here, the dose is expressed in milligrams (mg) and efficacy in percentages (%). Keep an eye out for questions referencing data in a different unit measurement, as discussed in the next topic, or questions asking for a raw number when only the percentage is listed.

Now that the nature of the study and variables at play have been identified, the data itself needs be interpreted. Group A did not receive any of the medicine. As discussed earlier, Group A is the control, as it reflects the amount of people cured in the same timeframe without medicine. It's important to see that efficacy positively correlates with the dosage of medicine. A question using this study might ask for the lowest dose of antibiotics to achieve 100% efficacy. Although Group E and Group F both achieve 100% efficacy, it's important to note that Group E reaches 100% with a lower dose.

Data is often recorded using fractions, such as half a mile, and understanding fractions is critical because of their popular use in real-world applications. Also, it is extremely important to label values with their units when using data. For example, regarding length, the number 2 is meaningless unless it is attached to a unit. Writing 2 cm shows that the number refers to the length of an object.

Data in Graphs

Graphs provide a visual representation of data. The variables are placed on the two axes. The bottom of the graph is referred to as the horizontal axis or X-axis. The left-hand side of the graph is known as the vertical axis or Y-axis. Typically, the independent variable is placed on the X-axis, and the dependent variable is located on the Y-axis. Sometimes the X-axis is a timeline, and the dependent variables for different trials or groups have been measured throughout points in time; time is still an independent variable but is not always immediately thought of as the independent variable being studied.

The most common types of graphs are the bar graph and the line graph.

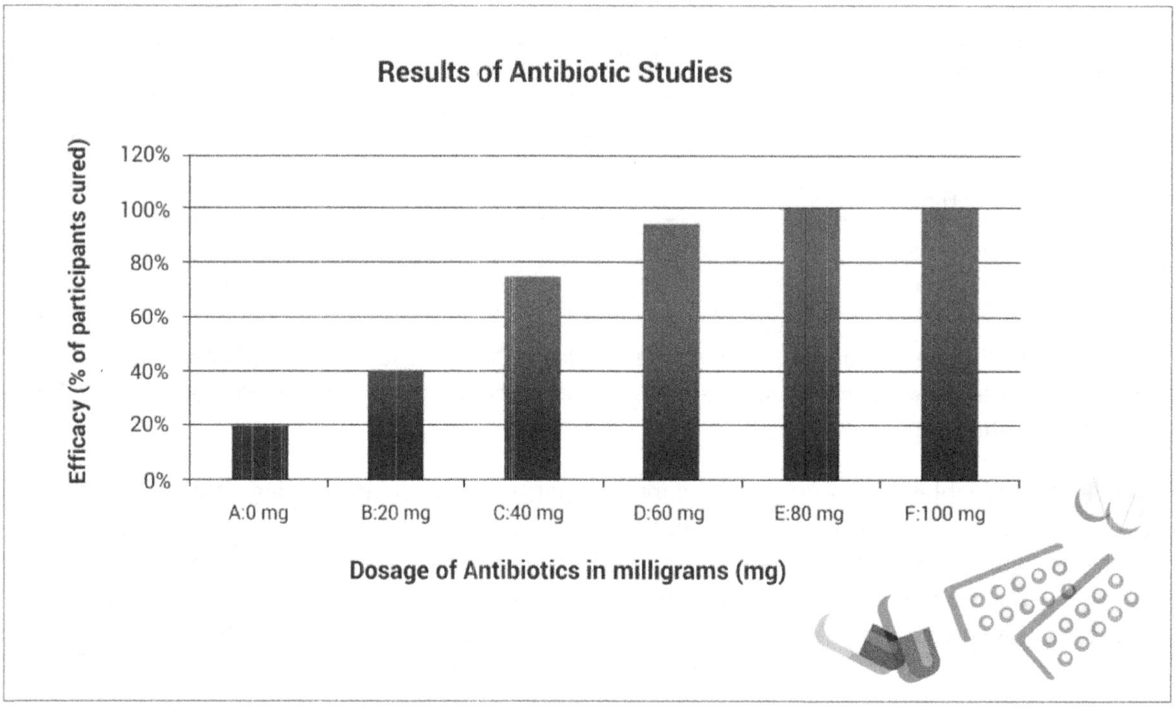

The **bar graph** above expresses the data from the table entitled "Results of Antibiotic Studies." To interpret the data for each group in the study, look at the top of their bars and read the corresponding efficacy on the Y-axis.

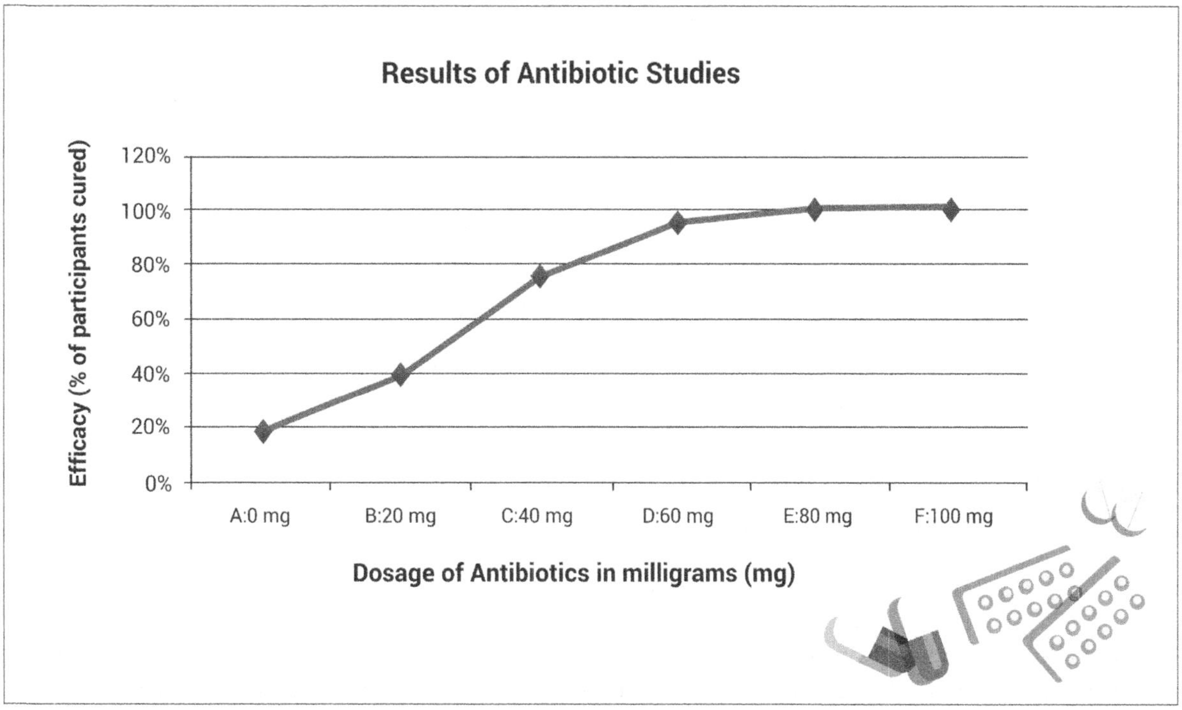

Here, the same data is expressed on a **line graph**. The points on the line correspond with each data entry. Reading the data on the line graph works like the bar graph. The data trend is measured by the slope of the line.

Data in Other Charts

Chart is a broad term that refers to a variety of ways to represent data.

To graph relations, the **Cartesian plane** is used. This means to think of the plane as being given a grid of squares, with one direction being the *x*-axis and the other direction the *y*-axis. Generally, the independent variable is placed along the horizontal axis, and the dependent variable is placed along the vertical axis. Any point on the plane can be specified by saying how far to go along the *x*-axis and how far along the *y*-axis with a pair of numbers (x, y). Specific values for these pairs can be given names such as $C = (-1, 3)$. Negative values mean to move left or down; positive values mean to move right or up. The point where the axes cross one another is called the **origin**. The origin has coordinates $(0, 0)$ and is usually called O when given a specific label.

An illustration of the Cartesian plane, along with graphs of $(2, 1)$ and $(-1, -1)$, are below.

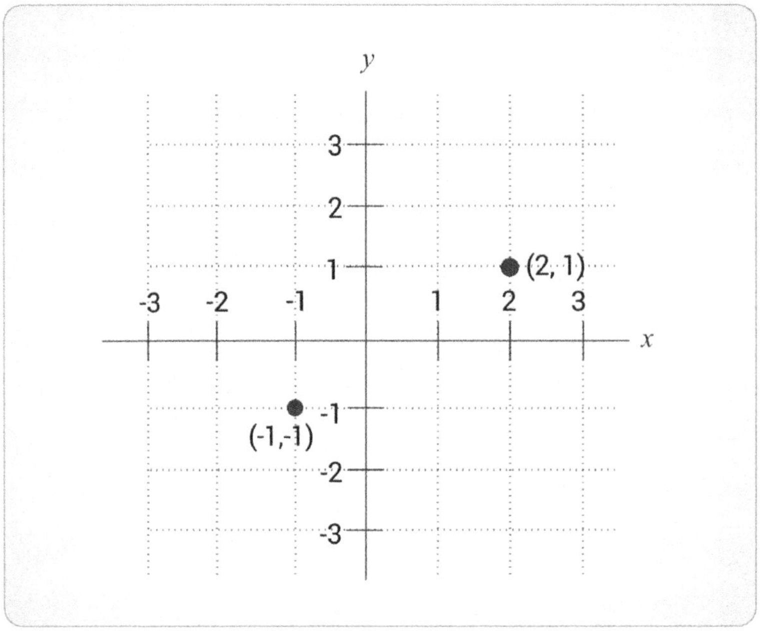

A **box plot**, also called a **box-and-whisker plot**, divides the data points into four groups and displays the five number summary for the set, as well as any outliers. The five number summary consists of:

- The lower extreme: the lowest value that is not an outlier
- The higher extreme: the highest value that is not an outlier
- The median of the set: also referred to as the second quartile or Q_2
- The first quartile or Q_1: the median of values below Q_2
- The third quartile or Q_3: the median of values above Q_2

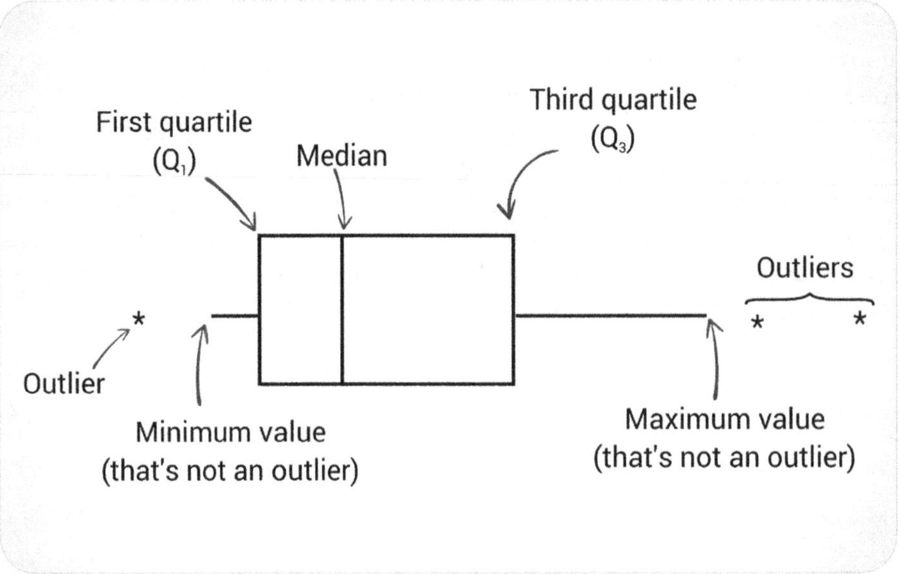

Suppose the box plot displays IQ scores for 12th grade students at a given school. The five number summary of the data consists of: lower extreme (67); upper extreme (127); Q_2 or median (100); Q_1 (91); Q_3 (108); and outliers (135 and 140). Although all data points are not known from the plot, the points are divided into four quartiles each, including 25% of the data points. Therefore, 25% of students scored between 67 and 91, 25% scored between 91 and 100, 25% scored between 100 and 108, and 25% scored between 108 and 127. These percentages include the normal values for the set and exclude the outliers. This information is useful when comparing a given score with the rest of the scores in the set.

A **line plot** is a diagram that shows quantity of data along a number line. It is a quick way to record data in a structure similar to a bar graph without needing to do the required shading of a bar graph. Here is an example of a line plot:

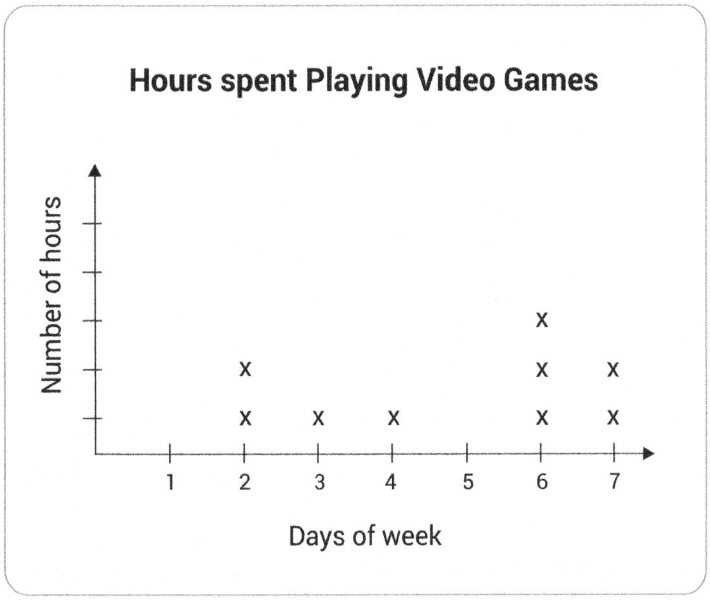

A **tally chart** is a diagram in which tally marks are utilized to represent data. Tally marks are a means of showing a quantity of objects within a specific classification. Here is an example of a tally chart:

Number of days with rain	Number of weeks
0	II
1	~~IIII~~
2	~~IIII~~ I
3	~~IIII~~ IIII
4	~~IIII~~ ~~IIII~~ ~~IIII~~
5	~~IIII~~
6	~~IIII~~ I
7	IIII

A **picture graph** is a diagram that shows pictorial representation of data being discussed. The symbols used can represent a certain number of objects. Notice how each fruit symbol in the following graph represents a count of two fruits. One drawback of picture graphs is that they can be less accurate if each symbol represents a large number. For example, if each banana symbol represented ten bananas, and students consumed 22 bananas, it may be challenging to draw and interpret two and one-fifth bananas as a frequency count of 22.

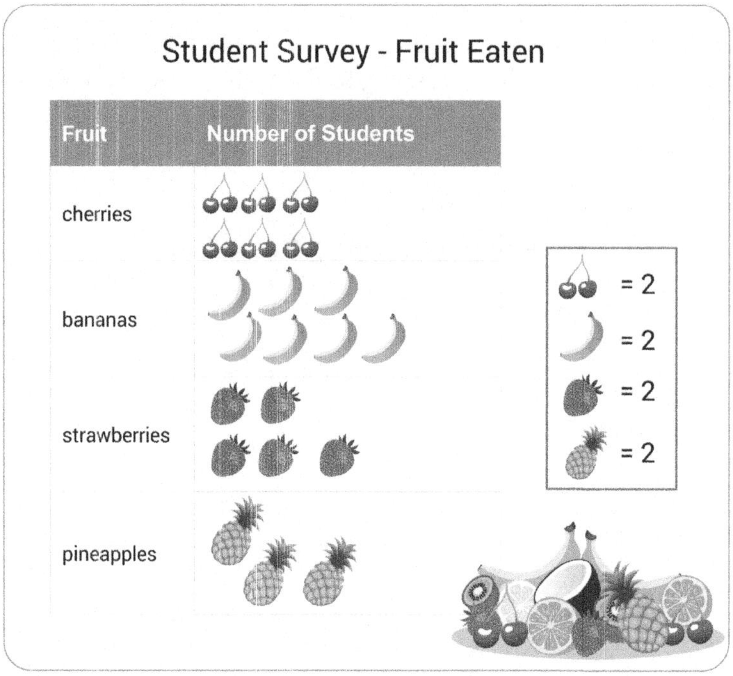

A **circle graph**, also called a **pie chart**, shows categorical data with each category representing a percentage of the whole data set. To make a circle graph, the percent of the data set for each category must be determined. To do so, the frequency of the category is divided by the total number of data points and converted to a percent. For example, if 80 people were asked what their favorite sport is and

20 responded basketball, basketball makes up 25% of the data ($\frac{20}{80}$ =.25=25%). Each category in a data set is represented by a *slice* of the circle proportionate to its percentage of the whole.

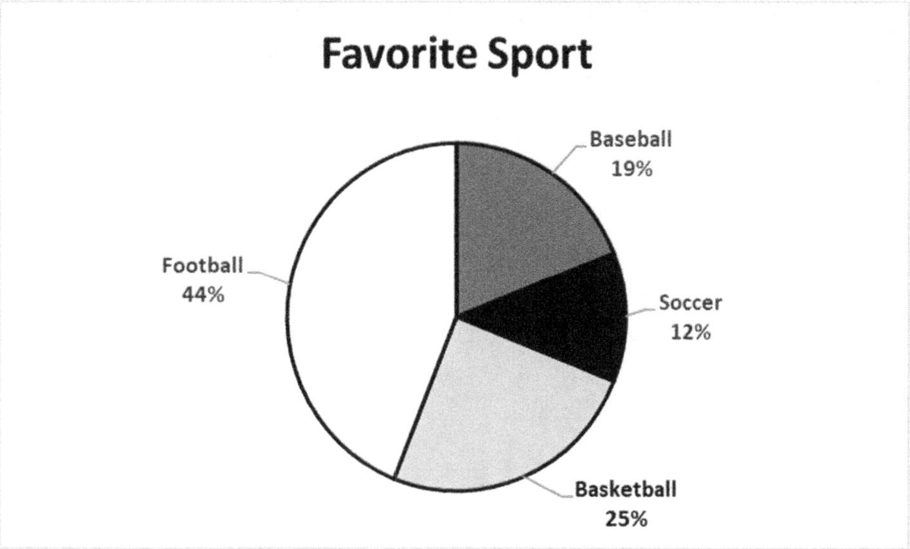

A **scatterplot** displays the relationship between two variables. Values for the independent variable, typically denoted by *x*, are paired with values for the dependent variable, typically denoted by *y*. Each set of corresponding values are written as an ordered pair (*x*, *y*). To construct the graph, a coordinate grid is labeled with the *x*-axis representing the independent variable and the *y*-axis representing the dependent variable. Each ordered pair is graphed.

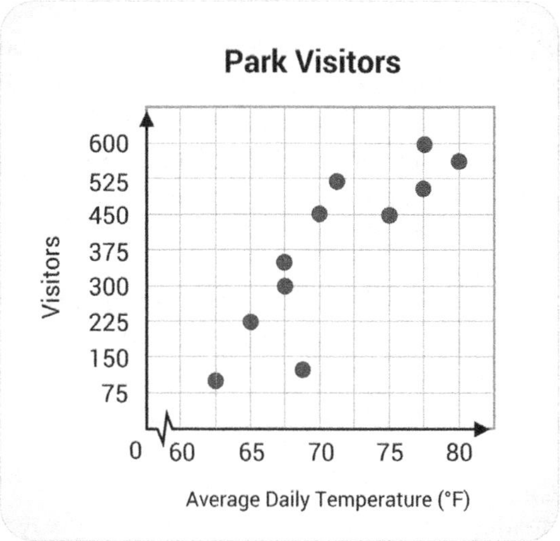

Like a scatter plot, a **line graph** compares two variables that change continuously, typically over time. Paired data values (ordered pair) are plotted on a coordinate grid with the *x*- and *y*-axis representing the two variables. A line is drawn from each point to the next, going from left to right. A double line graph simply displays two sets of data that contain values for the same two variables. The double line graph below displays the profit for given years (two variables) for Company A and Company B (two data sets).

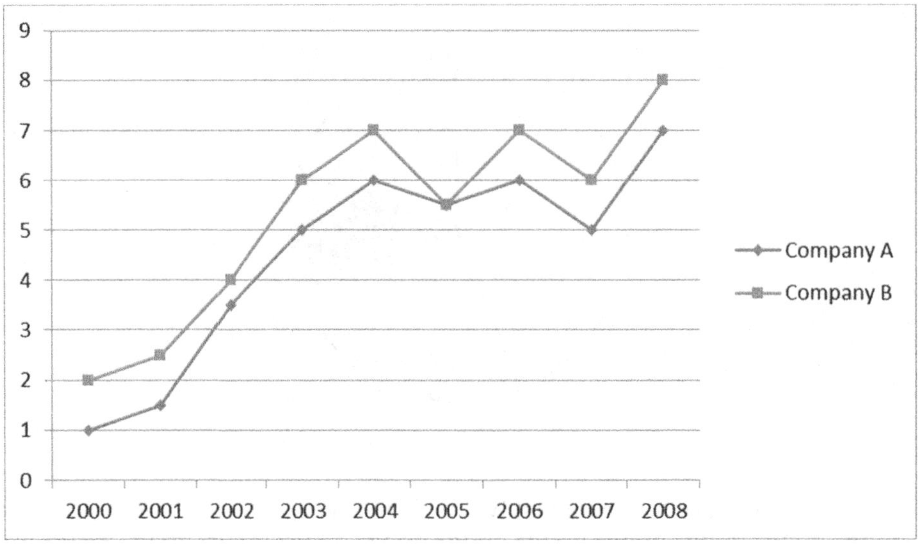

Scatter plots and line graphs can be used to display data consisting of two variables. Examples include height and weight, or distance and time. A correlation between the variables is determined by examining the points on the graph. Line graphs are used if each value for one variable pairs with a distinct value for the other variable. Line graphs show relationships between variables.

Choosing the appropriate graph to display a data set depends on what type of data is included in the set and what information must be shown. Histograms and box plots can be used for data sets consisting of individual values across a wide range. Examples include test scores and incomes. Histograms and box plots will indicate the center, spread, range, and outliers of a data set. A histogram will show the shape of the data set, while a box plot will divide the set into quartiles (25% increments), allowing for comparison between a given value and the entire set.

Scatter plots and line graphs can be used to display data consisting of two variables. Examples include height and weight, or distance and time. A correlation between the variables is determined by examining the points on the graph. Line graphs are used if each value for one variable pairs with a distinct value for the other variable. Line graphs show relationships between variables.

Drawing Conclusions Based on Graphical Displays

Comparing data sets within statistics can mean many things. The first way to compare data sets is by looking at the center and spread of each set. The **center of a data** set can mean two things: median or mean. The **median** is the value that's halfway into each data set, and it splits the data into two intervals. The **mean** is the average value of the data within a set. It's calculated by adding up all of the data in the set and dividing the total by the number of data points. Outliers can significantly impact the mean. Additionally, two completely different data sets can have the same mean. For example, a data set with values ranging from 0 to 100 and a data set with values ranging from 44 to 56 can both have means of 50. The first data set has a much wider range, which is known as the **spread** of the data. This measures how varied the data is within each set.

In an experiment, variables are the key to analyzing data, especially when data is in a graph or table. Variables can represent anything, including objects, conditions, events, and amounts of time.

Covariance is a general term referring to how two variables move in relation to each other. Take for example an employee that gets paid by the hour. For them, hours worked and total pay have a positive covariance. As hours worked increases, so does pay.

Constant variables remain unchanged by the scientist across all trials. Because they are held constant for all groups in an experiment, they aren't being measured in the experiment, and they are usually ignored. Constants can either be controlled by the scientist directly like the nutrition, water, and sunlight given to plants, or they can be selected by the scientist specifically for an experiment like using a certain animal species or choosing to investigate only people of a certain age group.

Independent variables are also controlled by the scientist, but they are the same only for each group or trial in the experiment. Each group might be composed of students that all have the same color of car or each trial may be run on different soda brands. The independent variable of an experiment is what is being indirectly tested because it causes change in the dependent variables.

Dependent variables experience change caused by the independent variable and are what is being measured or observed. For example, college acceptance rates could be a dependent variable of an experiment that sorted a large sample of high school students by an independent variable such as test scores. In this experiment, the scientist groups the high school students by the independent variable (test scores) to see how it affects the dependent variable (their college acceptance rates).

Note that most variables can be held constant in one experiment but independent or dependent in another. For example, when testing how well a fertilizer aids plant growth, its amount of sunlight should be held constant for each group of plants, but if the experiment is being done to determine the proper amount of sunlight a plant should have, the amount of sunlight is an independent variable because it is necessarily changed for each group of plants.

An **X-Y diagram**, also known as a **scatter diagram**, visually displays the relationship between two variables. The independent variable is placed on the *x-axis*, or horizontal axis, and the dependent variable is placed on the *y-axis*, or vertical axis.

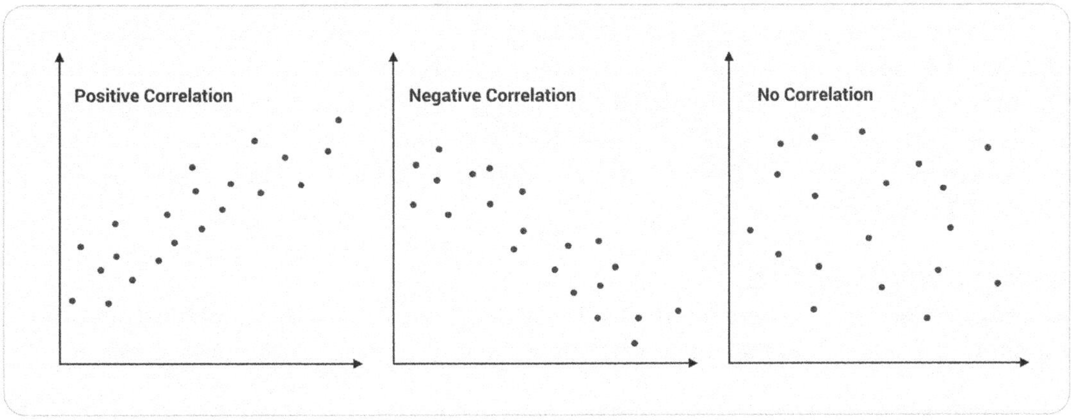

As shown in the figures above, an X-Y diagram may result in positive, negative, or no correlation between the two variables. In the first scatter plot, as the Y factor increases, the X factor increases as well. The opposite is true as well: as the X factor increases the Y factor also increases. Thus there is a positive correlation because one factor appears to positively affect the other factor

It's important to note, however, that finding a significant relationship between the dependent variable and the independent variable does not necessarily imply that there is a causal relationship between the two variables. It only means that once the independent variable is known, a fairly accurate prediction of the dependent variable can be made. This is often expressed with the phrase *correlation does not imply causation*. In other words, just because there is a relationship between two variables does not mean that one is the cause of the other. There could be other factors involved that are the real cause. For example, a positive correlation between labor hours and units produced may not equate to a cause and effect relationship between the two. Any instance of correlation only indicates how likely the presence of one variable is in the instance of another. The variables should be further analyzed to determine which, if any, other variables (i.e. quality of employee work) may contribute to the positive correlation.

As another example of the phenomenon that correlation does not imply causation, consider an experiment where the independent variable is the value of a person's house, and the dependent variable is their income. Although people in more expensive houses are expected to make more money, it is clear that their expensive houses are not the cause of them making more money. This illustrates one example of why it is important for experimenters to be careful when drawing conclusions about causation from their data.

Linear Data Fitting

The simplest type of correlation between two variables is a **linear correlation**. If the independent variable is x and the dependent variable is y, then a linear correlation means $y = mx + b$. If m is positive, then y will increase as x increases. While if m is negative, then y decreases while x increases. The variable b represents the value of y when x is 0.

As one example of such a correlation, consider a manufacturing plant. Suppose x is the number of units produced by the plant, and y is the cost to the company. In this example, b will be the cost of the plant itself. The plant will cost money even if it is never used, just by buying the machinery. For each unit produced, there will be a cost for the labor and the material. Let m represent this cost to produce one unit of the product.

For a more concrete example, suppose a computer factory costs $100,000. It requires $100 of parts and $50 of labor to make one computer. How much will it cost for a company to make 1000 computers? To figure this, let y be the amount of money the company spends, and let x be the number of computers. The cost of the factory is $100,000, so $b = 100{,}000$. On the other hand, the cost of producing a computer is the parts plus labor, or $150, so $m = 150$. Therefore, $y = 150x + 100{,}000$. Substitute 1000 for x and get $y = 150 \times 1000 + 100{,}000 = 150{,}000 + 1000 = 250{,}000$. It will cost the company $250,000 to make 1000 computers.

Interpreting Competing Data

Be careful of questions with competing studies. These questions will ask the student to interpret which of two studies shows the greater amount or the higher rate of change between two results.

Here's an example. A research facility runs studies on two different antibiotics: Drug A and Drug B. The Drug A study includes 1,000 participants and cures 600 people. The Drug B study includes 200 participants and cures 150 people. Which drug is more successful?

The first step is to determine the percentage of each drug's rate of success. Drug A was successful in curing 60% of participants, while Drug B achieved a 75% success rate. Thus, Drug B is more successful based on these studies, even though it cured fewer people.

Sample size and experiment consistency should also be considered when answering questions based on competing studies. Is one study significantly larger than the other? In the antibiotics example, the Drug A study is five times larger than Drug B. Thus, Drug B's higher efficacy (desired result) could be a result of the smaller sample size, rather than the quality of drug.

Consistency between studies is directly related to sample size. Let's say the research facility elects to conduct more studies on Drug B. In the next study, there are 400 participants, and 200 are cured. The success rate of the second study is 50%. The results are clearly inconsistent with the first study, which means more testing is needed to determine the drug's efficacy. A hallmark of mathematical or scientific research is repeatability. Studies should be consistent and repeatable, with an appropriately large sample size, before drawing extensive conclusions.

Practice Questions

1. Which of the following numbers has the greatest value?
   a. 1.4378
   b. 1.07548
   c. 1.43592
   d. 0.89409
   e. 1.43688

2. The value of 6 x 12 is the same as which of the following?
   a. 2 x 4 x 4 x 2
   b. 7 x 4 x 3
   c. 6 x 6 x 3
   d. 3 x 3 x 4 x 2
   e. 3 x 4 x 6 x 2

3. This chart indicates how many sales of CDs, vinyl records, and MP3 downloads occurred over the last year. Approximately what percentage of the total sales was from CDs?

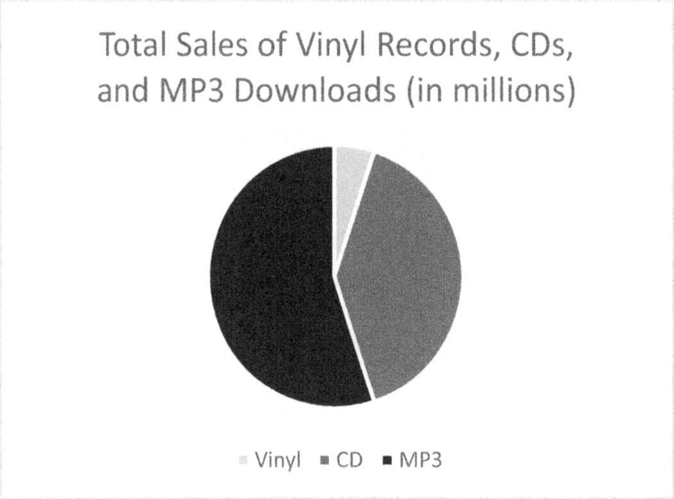

   a. 55%
   b. 25%
   c. 40%
   d. 5%
   e. 20%

4. After a 20% sale discount, Frank purchased a new refrigerator for $850. How much did he save from the original price?
   a. $170
   b. $212.50
   c. $105.75
   d. $200
   e. $150

5. A student gets an 85% on a test with 20 questions. How many answers did the student solve correctly?
   a. 16
   b. 15
   c. 18
   d. 19
   e. 17

6. Simplify the following fraction:

$$\frac{\frac{5}{7}}{\frac{9}{11}}$$

   a. $\frac{55}{63}$
   b. $\frac{7}{1000}$
   c. $\frac{13}{15}$
   d. $\frac{5}{11}$
   e. $\frac{11}{9}$

7. Johnny earns $2334.50 from his job each month. He pays $1437 for monthly expenses. Johnny is planning a vacation in 3 months' time that he estimates will cost $1750 total. How much will Johnny have left over from three months' of saving once he pays for his vacation?
   a. $948.50
   b. $584.50
   c. $852.50
   d. $942.50
   e. $952.50

8. What is $\frac{420}{98}$ rounded to the nearest integer?
   a. 3
   b. 4
   c. 5
   d. 6
   e. 7

9. Dwayne has received the following scores on his math tests: 78, 92, 83, 97. What score must Dwayne get on his next math test to have an overall average of 90?
   a. 89
   b. 98
   c. 95
   d. 100
   e. 96

10. What is the overall median of Dwayne's current scores: 78, 92, 83, 97?
   a. 19
   b. 85
   c. 83
   d. 87.5
   e. 86

11. Solve the following:

$$(\sqrt{36} \times \sqrt{16}) - 3^2$$

   a. 30
   b. 21
   c. 15
   d. 13
   e. 16

12. In Jim's school, there are 3 girls for every 2 boys. There are 650 students in total. Using this information, how many students are girls?
   a. 260
   b. 130
   c. 65
   d. 390
   e. 225

13. Five of six numbers have a sum of 25. The average of all six numbers is 6. What is the sixth number?
   a. 8
   b. 12
   c. 13
   d. 10
   e. 11

14. Kimberley earns \$10 an hour babysitting, and after 10 p.m., she earns \$12 an hour, with the amount paid being rounded to the nearest hour accordingly. On her last job, she worked from 5:30 p.m. to 11 p.m. In total, how much did Kimberley earn on her last job?
   a. \$45
   b. \$57
   c. \$62
   d. \$42
   e. \$67

15. Arrange the following numbers from least to greatest value:

$0.85, \frac{4}{5}, \frac{2}{3}, \frac{91}{100}$

a. $0.85, \frac{4}{5}, \frac{2}{3}, \frac{91}{100}$
b. $\frac{4}{5}, 0.85, \frac{91}{100}, \frac{2}{3}$
c. $\frac{2}{3}, \frac{4}{5}, 0.85, \frac{91}{100}$
d. $0.85, \frac{91}{100}, \frac{4}{5}, \frac{2}{3}$
e. $\frac{4}{5}, \frac{2}{3}, 0.85, \frac{91}{100}$

16. A ball is drawn at random from a ball pit containing 8 red balls, 7 yellow balls, 6 green balls, and 5 purple balls. What's the probability that the ball drawn is yellow?
a. $^{1}/_{26}$
b. $^{19}/_{26}$
c. $^{14}/_{26}$
d. 1
e. $^{7}/_{26}$

17. Two cards are drawn from a shuffled deck of 52 cards. What's the probability that both cards are Kings if the first card isn't replaced after it's drawn?
a. $^{1}/_{169}$
b. $^{1}/_{221}$
c. $^{1}/_{13}$
d. $^{4}/_{13}$
e. $^{1}/_{104}$

18. Four people split a bill. The first person pays for $\frac{1}{5}$, the second person pays for $\frac{1}{4}$, and the third person pays for $\frac{1}{3}$. What fraction of the bill does the fourth person pay?
a. $\frac{13}{60}$
b. $\frac{47}{60}$
c. $\frac{1}{4}$
d. $\frac{4}{15}$
e. $\frac{1}{2}$

19. Simplify the following expression:

$$4\frac{2}{3} - 3\frac{4}{9}$$

a. $1\frac{1}{3}$

b. $1\frac{2}{9}$

c. 1

d. $1\frac{2}{3}$

e. $1\frac{4}{9}$

20. A closet is filled with red, blue, and green shirts. If $\frac{1}{3}$ of the shirts are green and $\frac{2}{5}$ are red, what fraction of the shirts are blue?

a. $\frac{4}{15}$

b. $\frac{1}{5}$

c. $\frac{7}{15}$

d. $\frac{1}{2}$

e. $\frac{2}{3}$

21. Shawna buys $2\frac{1}{2}$ gallons of paint. If she uses $\frac{1}{3}$ of it on the first day, how much does she have left?

a. $1\frac{5}{6}$ gallons
b. $1\frac{1}{2}$ gallons
c. $1\frac{2}{3}$ gallons
d. 2 gallons
e. $1\frac{3}{4}$ gallons

22. Jessica buys 10 cans of paint. Red paint costs $1 per can and blue paint costs $2 per can. In total, she spends $16. How many red cans did she buy?

a. 2
b. 3
c. 4
d. 5
e. 6

23. Six people apply to work for Janice's company, but she only needs four workers. How many different groups of four employees can Janice choose?

a. 6
b. 10
c. 15
d. 36
e. 30

24. Which of the following is equivalent to the value of the digit 3 in the number 792.134?

a. 3×10
b. 3×100
c. $\frac{3}{10}$
d. $\frac{3}{100}$
e. 3×0.1

25. In the following expression, which operation should be completed first? $5 \times 6 + (5 + 4) \div 2 - 1$.

a. Multiplication
b. Addition
c. Division
d. Subtraction
e. Parentheses

26. How will the number 847.89632 be written if rounded to the nearest hundredth?

a. 847.90
b. 900
c. 847.89
d. 847.896
e. 847.895

27. The perimeter of a 6-sided polygon is 56 cm. The length of three of the sides are 9 cm each. The length of two other sides are 8 cm each. What is the length of the missing side?

a. 11 cm
b. 12 cm
c. 13 cm
d. 10 cm
e. 9 cm

28. Which of the following is a mixed number?

a. $16\frac{1}{2}$

b. 16

c. $\frac{16}{3}$

d. $\frac{1}{4}$

e. $\frac{3}{6}$

29. If you were showing your friend how to round 245.2678 to the nearest thousandth, which place value would be used to decide whether to round up or round down?

a. Ten-thousandth
b. Thousandth
c. Hundredth
d. Thousands
e. Ones

30. What is the value of *b* in this equation?

$5b - 4 = 2b + 17$

a. 13
b. 24
c. 7
d. 21
e. 14

31. Express the solution to the following problem in decimal form:

$$\frac{3}{5} \times \frac{7}{10} \div \frac{1}{2}$$

a. 0.042
b. 84%
c. 0.84
d. 0.42
e. .084

32. What is an equivalent measurement for 1.3 cm?
    a. 0.13 m
    b. 0.013 m
    c. 0.13 mm
    d. 0.013 mm
    e. 1.13 mm

33. Katie works at a clothing company and sold 192 shirts over the weekend. $\frac{1}{3}$ of the shirts that were sold were patterned, and the rest were solid. Which mathematical expression would calculate the number of solid shirts Katie sold over the weekend?
    a. $192 \times \frac{1}{3}$
    b. $192 \div \frac{1}{3}$
    c. $192 \times (1 - \frac{1}{3})$
    d. $192 \div 3$
    e. $192 \div \left(1 - \frac{1}{3}\right)$

34. Which four-sided shape is always a rectangle?
    a. Rhombus
    b. Square
    c. Parallelogram
    d. Quadrilateral
    e. Trapezoid

35. A rectangle was formed out of pipe cleaner. Its length was $\frac{1}{2}$ ft, and its width was $\frac{11}{2}$ inches. What is its area in square inches?
    a. $\frac{11}{4}$ inch^2
    b. $\frac{11}{2}$ inch^2
    c. 22 inches^2
    d. 33 inches^2
    e. 11 inches^2

36. How will $\frac{4}{5}$ be written as a percent?
    a. 40 percent
    b. 125 percent
    c. 90 percent
    d. 80 percent
    e. 85 percent

37. If Danny takes 48 minutes to walk 3 miles, how long should it take him to walk 5 miles maintaining the same speed?

a. 32 min
b. 64 min
c. 80 min
d. 96 min
e. 78 min

38. A solution needs 5 ml of saline for every 8 ml of medicine given. How much saline is needed for 45 ml of medicine?

a. $\frac{225}{8}$ ml
b. 72 ml
c. 28 ml
d. $\frac{45}{8}$ ml
e. 25 ml

39. If $\frac{5}{2} \div \frac{1}{3} = n$, then n is between:

a. 5 and 7
b. 7 and 9
c. 9 and 11
d. 3 and 5
e. 11 and 13

40. Which common denominator would be used in order to evaluate $\frac{2}{3} + \frac{4}{5}$?

a. 15
b. 3
c. 5
d. 10
e. 8

41. Which of the following equations best represents the problem below?
The width of a rectangle is 2 centimeters less than the length. If the perimeter of the rectangle is 44 centimeters, then what are the dimensions of the rectangle?

a. $2l + 2(l - 2) = 44$
b. $(l + 2) + (l + 2) + l = 48$
c. $l \times (l - 2) = 44$
d. $(l + 2) + (l + 2) + l = 44$
e. $2(l - 2) = 44$

42. A piggy bank contains 12 dollars' worth of nickels. A nickel weighs 5 grams, and the empty piggy bank weighs 1050 grams. What is the total weight of the full piggy bank?

a. 1,110 grams
b. 1,200 grams
c. 2,150 grams
d. 2,200 grams
e. 2,250 grams

43. Last year, the New York City area received approximately $27\frac{3}{4}$ inches of snow. The Denver area received approximately 3 times as much snow as New York City. How much snow fell in Denver?

a. $71\frac{3}{4}$ inches
b. $27\frac{1}{4}$ inches
c. $89\frac{1}{4}$ inches
d. $83\frac{1}{4}$ inches
e. $86\frac{1}{2}$ inches

44. Which of the following would be an instance in which ordinal numbers are used?

a. Katie scored a 9 out of 10 on her quiz.
b. Matthew finished second in the spelling bee.
c. Jacob missed one day of school last month.
d. Kim was 5 minutes late to school this morning.
e. John was on vacation for 6 days.

45. The graph shows the position of a car over a 10-second time interval. Which of the following is the correct interpretation of the graph for the interval 1 to 3 seconds?

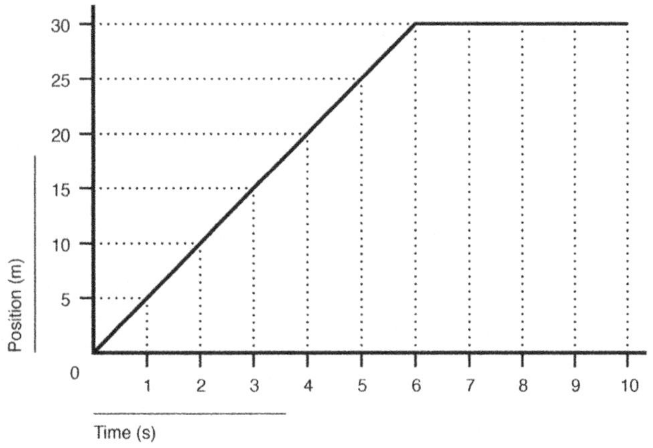

a. The car remains in the same position.
b. The car is traveling at a speed of 5m/s.
c. The car is traveling up a hill.
d. The car is traveling at 5 mph.
e. The car accelerates at a rate of 5m/s.

46. If Sarah reads at an average rate of 21 pages in four nights, how long will it take her to read 140 pages?
   a. 6 nights
   b. 26 nights
   c. 8 nights
   d. 27 nights
   e. 7 nights

47. The phone bill is calculated each month using the equation $c = 50g + 75$. The cost of the phone bill per month is represented by c, and g represents the gigabytes of data used that month. What is the value and interpretation of the slope of this equation?
   a. 75 dollars per day
   b. 75 gigabytes per day
   c. 50 dollars per day
   d. 50 dollars per gigabyte
   e. 125 dollars per gigabyte

48. How will the following number be written in standard form: $(1 \times 10^4) + (3 \times 10^3) + (7 \times 10^1) + (8 \times 10^0)$
   a. 137
   b. 13,780
   c. 1,378
   d. 8,731
   e. 13,078

49. What is the area of the regular hexagon shown below?

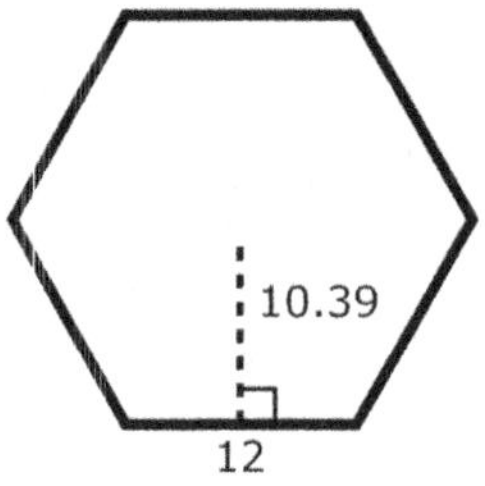

   a. 72
   b. 124.68
   c. 374.04
   d. 748.08
   e. 372.96

50. The area of a given rectangle is 24 square centimeters. If the measure of each side is multiplied by 3, what is the area of the new figure?
   a. 48 cm^2
   b. 72 cm^2
   c. 216 cm^2
   d. 13,824 cm^2
   e. 224 cm^2

Answer Explanations

1. A: Compare each numeral after the decimal point to figure out which overall number is greatest. Choices *A* (1.43785) and *C* (1.43592) both have the same tenths (4) and hundredths (3). However, the thousandths is greater in answer *A* (7), so *A* has the greatest value overall.

2. D: By grouping the four numbers in the answer into factors of the two numbers of the question (6 and 12), it can be determined that (3 x 2) x (4 x 3) = 6 x 12. Alternatively, each of the answer choices could be prime factored or multiplied out and compared to the original value. 6×12 has a value of 72 and a prime factorization of $2^3 \times 3^2$. The answer choices respectively have values of 64, 84, 108, 72, and 144 and prime factorizations of 2^6, $2^2 \times 3 \times 7$, $2^2 \times 3^3$, and $2^3 \times 3^2$, so answer *D* is the correct choice.

3. C: The sum total percentage of a pie chart must equal 100%. Since the CD sales take up less than half of the chart and more than a quarter (25%), it can be determined to be 40% overall. This can also be measured with a protractor. The angle of a circle is 360°. Since 25% of 360 would be 90° and 50% would be 180°, the angle percentage of CD sales falls in between; therefore, it would be answer *C*.

4. B: Since $850 is the price *after* a 20% discount, $850 represents 80% of the original price. To determine the original price, set up a proportion with the ratio of the sale price (850) to original price (unknown) equal to the ratio of sale percentage:

$$\frac{850}{x} = \frac{80}{100}$$

(where *x* represents the unknown original price)

To solve a proportion, cross multiply the numerators and denominators and set the products equal to each other: (850)(100) = (80)(x). Multiplying each side results in the equation 85,000=80x.

To solve for *x*, divide both sides by 80: $\frac{85{,}000}{80} = \frac{80x}{80}$, resulting in *x*=1062.5. Remember that *x* represents the original price. Subtracting the sale price from the original price ($1062.50-$850) indicates that Frank saved $212.50.

5. E: 85% of a number means that number should be multiplied by 0.85: $0.85 \times 20 = \frac{85}{100} \times \frac{20}{1}$, which can be simplified to:

$$\frac{17}{20} \times \frac{20}{1} = 17$$

6. A: First simplify the larger fraction by separating it into two. When dividing one fraction by another, remember to *invert* the second fraction and multiply the two as follows:

$$\frac{5}{7} \times \frac{11}{9}$$

The resulting fraction $\frac{55}{63}$ cannot be simplified further, so this is the answer to the problem.

7. D: First, subtract $1437 from $2334.50 to find Johnny's monthly savings; this equals $897.50. Then, multiply this amount by 3 to find out how much he will have (in three months) before he pays for his vacation: this equals \$2692.50. Finally, subtract the cost of the vacation (\$1750) from this amount to find how much Johnny will have left: \$942.50.

8. B: Dividing by 98 can be approximated by dividing by 100, which would mean shifting the decimal point of the numerator to the left by 2. The result is 4.2, which rounds to 4.

9. D: To find the average of a set of values, add the values together and then divide by the total number of values. In this case, include the unknown value of what Dwayne needs to score on his next test, in order to solve it.

$$\frac{78 + 92 + 83 + 97 + x}{5} = 90$$

Add the unknown value to the new average total, which is 5. Then multiply each side by 5 to simplify the equation, resulting in:

$78 + 92 + 83 + 97 + x = 450$
$350 + x = 450$
$x = 100$

Dwayne would need to get a perfect score of 100 in order to get an average of at least 90.

Test this answer by substituting back into the original formula.

$$\frac{78 + 92 + 83 + 97 + 100}{5} = 90$$

10. D: For an even number of total values, the *median* is calculated by finding the *mean* or average of the two middle values once all values have been arranged in ascending order from least to greatest. In this case, $(92 \ + 83) \div 2$ would equal the median 87.5, answer *D*.

11. C: Follow the *order of operations* in order to solve this problem. Solve the parentheses first, and then follow the remainder as usual.

$$(6 \times 4) - 9$$

This equals 24 – 9 or 15, answer *C*.

12. D: Three girls for every two boys can be expressed as a ratio: 3:2. This can be visualized as splitting the school into 5 groups: 3 girl groups and 2 boy groups. The number of students which are in each group can be found by dividing the total number of students by 5:

$$\frac{650 \text{ students}}{5 \text{ groups}} = \frac{130 \text{ students}}{\text{group}}$$

To find the total number of girls, multiply the number of students per group (130) by the number of girl groups in the school (3). This equals 390, Choice *D*.

13. E: If the average of all six numbers is 6, that means:

$$\frac{a+b+c+d+e+x}{6}=6$$

The sum of the first five numbers is 25, so this equation can be simplified to:

$$\frac{25+x}{6}=6$$

Multiplying both sides by 6 gives $25+x=36$, and *x*, or the sixth number, can be solved to equal 11.

14. C: Kimberley worked 4.5 hours at the rate of $10/h and 1 hour at the rate of $12/h. The problem states that her pay is rounded to the nearest hour, so the 4.5 hours would round up to 5 hours at the rate of $10/h.

$$(5h)\left(\frac{\$10}{h}\right)+(1h)\left(\frac{\$12}{h}\right)=\$50+\$12=\$62$$

15. C: The first step is to depict each number using decimals. $\frac{91}{100}$ = 0.91

Dividing the numerator by denominator of $\frac{4}{5}$ to convert it to a decimal yields 0.80, while $\frac{2}{3}$ becomes 0.66 recurring. Rearrange each expression in ascending order, as found in answer C.

16. E: The sample space is made up of $8+7+6+5=26$ balls. The probability of pulling each individual ball is $^1/_{26}$. Since there are 7 yellow balls, the probability of pulling a yellow ball is $^7/_{26}$.

17. B: For the first card drawn, the probability of a King being pulled is $\frac{4}{52}$. Since this card isn't replaced, if a King is drawn first the probability of a King being drawn second is $\frac{3}{51}$. The probability of a King being drawn in both the first and second draw is the product of the two probabilities: $\frac{4}{52}\times\frac{3}{51}=\frac{12}{2652}$. This fraction, when divided by 12, equals $\frac{1}{221}$.

18. A: To find the fraction of the bill that the first three people pay, the fractions need to be added, which means finding common denominator, which will be 60.

$$\frac{1}{5}+\frac{1}{4}+\frac{1}{3}=\frac{12}{60}+\frac{15}{60}+\frac{20}{60}=\frac{47}{60}$$

The remainder of the bill is:

$$1-\frac{47}{60}=\frac{60}{60}-\frac{47}{60}=\frac{13}{60}$$

19. B: Simplify each mixed number of the problem into a fraction by multiplying the denominator by the whole number and adding the numerator:

$$\frac{14}{3}-\frac{31}{9}$$

Since the first denominator is a multiple of the second, simplify it further by multiplying both the numerator and denominator of the first expression by 3 so that the denominators of the fractions are equal.

$$\frac{42}{9} - \frac{31}{9} = \frac{11}{9}$$

Simplifying this further, divide the numerator 11 by the denominator 9; this leaves 1 with a remainder of 2. To write this as a mixed number, place the remainder over the denominator, resulting in $1\frac{2}{9}$.

20. A: The total fraction taken up by green and red shirts will be:

$$\frac{1}{3} + \frac{2}{5} = \frac{5}{15} + \frac{6}{15} = \frac{11}{15}$$

The remaining fraction is:

$$1 - \frac{11}{15} = \frac{15}{15} - \frac{11}{15} = \frac{4}{15}$$

21. C: If she has used 1/3 of the paint, she has 2/3 remaining. $2\frac{1}{2}$ gallons are the same as $\frac{5}{2}$ gallons. The calculation is:

$$\frac{2}{3} \times \frac{5}{2} = \frac{5}{3} = 1\frac{2}{3} \text{ gallons}$$

22. C: We are trying to find x, the number of red cans. The equation can be set up like this:

$$x + 2(10 - x) = 16$$

The left x is actually multiplied by \$1, the price per red can. Since we know Jessica bought 10 total cans, $10 - x$ is the number blue cans that she bought. We multiply the number of blue cans by \$2, the price per blue can.

That should all equal \$16, the total amount of money that Jessica spent. Working that out gives us:

$$x + 20 - 2x = 16$$

$$20 - x = 16$$

$$x = 4$$

23. C: Janice will be choosing 4 employees out of a set of 6 applicants, so this will be given by the choice function. The following equation shows the choice function worked out:

$$\binom{6}{4} = \frac{6!}{4!\,(6-4)!} = \frac{6!}{4!\,(2)!}$$

$$\frac{6 \cdot 5 \cdot 4 \cdot 3 \cdot 2 \cdot 1}{4 \cdot 3 \cdot 2 \cdot 1 \cdot 2 \cdot 1} = \frac{6 \cdot 5}{2} = 15$$

24. D: $\frac{3}{100}$. Each digit to the left of the decimal point represents a higher multiple of 10 and each digit to the right of the decimal point represents a quotient of a higher multiple of 10 for the divisor. The first digit to the right of the decimal point is equal to the value ÷ 10. The second digit to the right of the decimal point is equal to the value ÷ (10×10), or the value ÷ 100.

25. E: Using the order of operations, multiplication and division are computed first from left to right. Multiplication is on the left; therefore, multiplication should be performed first.

26. A: 847.90. The hundredths place value is located two digits to the right of the decimal point (the digit 9 in the original number). The digit to the right of the place value is examined to decide whether to round up or keep the digit. In this case, the digit 6 is 5 or greater so the hundredth place is rounded up. When rounding up, if the digit to be increased is a 9, the digit to its left is increased by one and the digit in the desired place value is made a zero. Therefore, the number is rounded to 847.90.

27. C: Perimeter is found by calculating the sum of all sides of the polygon. $9+9+9+8+8+s=56$, where *s* is the missing side length. Therefore, 43 plus the missing side length is equal to 56. The missing side length is 13 cm.

28. A:$16\frac{1}{2}$. A mixed number contains both a whole number and either a fraction or a decimal. Therefore, the mixed number is $16\frac{1}{2}$.

29. A: The place value to the right of the thousandth place, which would be the ten-thousandth place, is what gets utilized. The value in the thousandth place is 7. The number in the place value to its right is greater than 4, so the 7 gets bumped up to 8. Everything to its right turns to a zero, to get 245.2680. The zero is dropped because it is part of the decimal.

30. C: To solve for the value of b, both sides of the equation need to be equalized.

Start by cancelling out the lower value of -4 by adding 4 to both sides:

$5b - 4 = 2b + 17$
$5b - 4 + 4 = 2b + 17 + 4$
$5b = 2b + 21$

The variable *b* is the same on each side, so subtract the lower 2b from each side:

$5b = 2b + 21$
$5b - 2b = 2b + 21 - 2b$
$3b = 21$

Then divide both sides by 3 to get the value of *b*:

$$3b = 21$$

$$\frac{3b}{3} = \frac{21}{3}$$

$$b = 7$$

31. C: The first step in solving this problem is expressing the result in fraction form. Separate this problem first by solving the division operation of the last two fractions. When dividing one fraction by another, invert or flip the second fraction and then multiply the numerator and denominator.

$$\frac{7}{10} \times \frac{2}{1} = \frac{14}{10}$$

Next, multiply the first fraction with this value:

$$\frac{3}{5} \times \frac{14}{10} = \frac{42}{50}$$

Decimals are expressions of 1 or 100%, so multiply both the numerator and denominator by 2 to get the fraction as an expression of 100.

$$\frac{42}{50} \times \frac{2}{2} = \frac{84}{100}$$

In decimal form, this would be expressed as 0.84.

32. B: 100 cm is equal to 1 m. 1.3 divided by 100 is 0.013. Therefore, 1.3 cm is equal to 0.013 m. Because 1 cm is equal to 10 mm, 1.3 cm is equal to 13 mm.

33. C: $\frac{1}{3}$ of the shirts sold were patterned. Therefore, $1 - \frac{1}{3} = \frac{2}{3}$ of the shirts sold were solid. Anytime "of" a quantity appears in a word problem, multiplication needs to be used. Therefore:

$$192 \times \frac{2}{3} = 192 \times \frac{2}{3} = \frac{384}{3} = 128 \text{ solid shirts were sold}$$

The entire expression is $192 \times \left(1 - \frac{1}{3}\right)$.

34. B: A rectangle is a specific type of parallelogram. It has 4 right angles. A square is a rhombus that has 4 right angles. Therefore, a square is always a rectangle because it has two sets of parallel lines and 4 right angles.

35. D: Area = length x width. The answer must be in square inches, so all values must be converted to inches. $\frac{1}{2}$ ft is equal to 6 inches. Therefore, the area of the rectangle is equal to $6 \times \frac{11}{2} = \frac{66}{2} = 33$ square inches.

36. D: 80 percent. To convert a fraction to a percent, the fraction is first converted to a decimal. To do so, the numerator is divided by the denominator: $4 \div 5 = 0.8$. To convert a decimal to a percent, the number is multiplied by 100: $0.8 \times 10 = 80\%$.

37. C: 80 min. To solve the problem, a proportion is written consisting of ratios comparing distance and time. One way to set up the proportion is: $\frac{3}{48} = \frac{5}{x}\left(\frac{distance}{time} = \frac{distance}{time}\right)$ where *x* represents the unknown value of time. To solve a proportion, the ratios are cross-multiplied:

$$(3)(x) = (5)(48) \rightarrow 3x = 240$$

The equation is solved by isolating the variable, or dividing by 3 on both sides, to produce $x = 80$.

38. A: Every 8 ml of medicine requires 5 ml. The 45 ml first needs to be split into portions of 8 ml. This results in $\frac{45}{8}$portions. Each portion requires 5 ml. Therefore:

$$\frac{45}{8} \times 5 = 45 \times \frac{5}{8} = \frac{225}{8} \text{ ml is necessary}$$

39. B: $\frac{5}{2} \div \frac{1}{3} = \frac{5}{2} \times \frac{3}{1} = \frac{15}{2} = 7.5.$

40. A: A common denominator must be found. The least common denominator is 15 because it has both 5 and 3 as factors. The fractions must be rewritten using 15 as the denominator.

41. A: The first step is to determine the unknown, which is in terms of the length, l.

The second step is to translate the problem into the equation using the perimeter of a rectangle, $P = 2l + 2w$. The width is the length minus 2 centimeters. The resulting equation is:

$$2l + 2(l - 2) = 44$$

The equation can be solved as follows:

$2l + 2l - 4 = 44$	Apply the distributive property on the left side of the equation
$4l - 4 = 44$	Combine like terms on the left side of the equation
$4l = 48$	Add 4 to both sides of the equation
$l = 12$	Divide both sides of the equation by 4

The length of the rectangle is 12 centimeters. The width is the length minus 2 centimeters, which is 10 centimeters. Checking the answers for length and width forms the following equation:

$$44 = 2(12) + 2(10)$$

The equation can be solved using the order of operations to form a true statement: $44 = 44$.

42. E: A dollar contains 20 nickels. Therefore, if there are 12 dollars' worth of nickels, there are:

$$12 \times 20 = 240 \text{ nickels}$$

Each nickel weighs 5 grams. Therefore, the weight of the nickels is:

$$240 \times 5 = 1{,}200 \text{ grams}$$

Adding in the weight of the empty piggy bank, the filled bank weighs 2,250 grams.

43. D: 3 must be multiplied times $27\frac{3}{4}$. In order to easily do this, the mixed number should be converted into an improper fraction.

$$27\frac{3}{4} = 27 \times 4 + \frac{3}{4} = \frac{111}{4}$$

Therefore, Denver had approximately:

$$3 \times \frac{111}{4} = \frac{333}{4} \text{ inches of snow}$$

The improper fraction can be converted back into a mixed number through division.

$$\frac{333}{4} = 83\frac{1}{4} \text{ inches}$$

44. B: Ordinal numbers represent a ranking. Placing second in a competition is a ranking among the other participants of the spelling bee.

45. B: The car is traveling at a speed of five meters per second. On the interval from one to three seconds, the position changes by ten meters. By making this change in position over time into a rate, the speed becomes ten meters in two seconds or five meters in one second.

46. D: This problem can be solved by setting up a proportion involving the given information and the unknown value. The proportion is:

$$\frac{21\, pages}{4\, nights} = \frac{140\, pages}{x\, nights}$$

Solving the proportion by cross-multiplying, the equation becomes $21x = 4 * 140$, where $x = 26.67$. Since it is not an exact number of nights, the answer is rounded up to 27 nights. Twenty-six nights would not give Sarah enough time.

47. D: The slope from this equation is 50, and it is interpreted as the cost per gigabyte used. Since the *g*-value represents number of gigabytes and the equation is set equal to the cost in dollars, the slope relates these two values. For every gigabyte used on the phone, the bill goes up 50 dollars.

48. E: 13,078. The power of 10 by which a digit is multiplied corresponds with the number of zeros following the digit when expressing its value in standard form.

Therefore:

$$(1 \times 10^4) + (3 \times 10^3) + (7 \times 10^1) + (8 \times 10^0) = 10{,}000 + 3{,}000 + 70 + 8 = 13{,}078$$

49. C: 374.04. The formula for finding the area of a regular polygon is $A = \frac{1}{2} \times a \times P$ where *a* is the length of the apothem (from the center to any side at a right angle), and P is the perimeter of the figure. The apothem *a* is given as 10.39, and the perimeter can be found by multiplying the length of one side by the number of sides (since the polygon is regular):

$$P = 12 \times 6 \rightarrow P = 72$$

To find the area, substitute the values for *a* and *P* into the formula:

$$A = \frac{1}{2} \times a \times P$$

$$A = \frac{1}{2} \times (10.39) \times (72) \rightarrow A = 374.04$$

50. C: 216 cm^2. Because area is a two-dimensional measurement, the dimensions are multiplied by a scale that is squared to determine the scale of the corresponding areas. The dimensions of the rectangle are multiplied by a scale of 3. Therefore, the area is multiplied by a scale of 3^2 (which is equal to 9): $24\, cm \times 9 = 216\, cm^2$.

Writing

POWER Strategy for Writing

The POWER strategy helps all writers focus and do well during the writing process.

The POWER strategy stands for the following:

- Prewriting or Planning
- Organizing
- Writing a first draft
- Evaluating the writing
- Revising and rewriting

Prewriting and Planning

During the prewriting and planning phase, writers learn to think about their audience and purpose for the writing assignment. Then they gather information they wish to include in the writing. They do this from their background knowledge or new sources.

Organizing

Next, writers decide on the organization of their writing project. There are many types of organizational structures, but the common ones are: story/narrative, informative, opinion, persuasive, compare and contrast, explanatory, and problem/solution formats.

Writing

In this step, the writers write a first draft of their project.

Evaluating

In this stage, writers reread the writing and note the sections that are strong or that need improvement.

Revising and Rewriting

Finally, the writer incorporates any changes they wish to make based on what they've read. Then writers rewrite the piece into a final draft.

Introducing, Developing, and Concluding a Text Effectively

Almost all coherent written works contain three primary parts: a beginning, middle, and end. The organizational arrangements differ widely across distinct writing modes. Persuasive and expository texts utilize an introduction, body, and conclusion whereas narrative works use an orientation, series of events/conflict, and a resolution.

Every element within a written piece relates back to the main idea, and the beginning of a persuasive or expository text generally conveys the main idea or the purpose. For a narrative piece, the beginning is the section that acquaints the reader with the characters and setting, directing them to the purpose of the writing. The main idea in narrative may be implied or addressed at the end of the piece.

Depending on the primary purpose, the arrangement of the middle will adhere to one of the basic organizational structures described in the information texts and rhetoric section. They are cause and effect, problem and solution, compare and contrast, description/spatial, sequence, and order of importance.

The ending of a text is the metaphorical wrap-up of the writing. A solid ending is crucial for effective writing as it ties together loose ends, resolves the action, highlights the main points, or repeats the central idea. A conclusion ensures that readers come away from a text understanding the author's main idea. The table below highlights the important characteristics of each part of a piece of writing.

Structure	Argumentative/Informative	Narrative
Beginning	Introduction *Purpose, main idea*	Orientation *Introduces characters, setting, necessary background*
Middle	Body *Supporting details, reasons and evidence*	Events/Conflict *Story's events that revolve around a central conflict*
End	Conclusion *Highlights main points, summarizes and paraphrases ideas, reiterates the main idea*	Resolution *The solving of the central conflict*

Elements of Effective Writing

The following are characteristics that make writing readable and effective:

- Ideas
- Organization
- Voice
- Word choice
- Sentence fluency
- Proper Writing Conventions
- Presentation

Ideas

This refers to the content of the writing. Writers should focus on the topic shown in the picture or prompt. They should narrow down and focus their idea, remembering that they only have fifteen minutes to plan and write! Then they learn to develop the idea and choose the details that best shows the idea to others.

Organization

Many writers are inclined to jump into their writing without a clear direction for where it is going. Organization helps plan out the writing so that it's successful. Your writing should have an introduction, a body, and a conclusion.

Introduction (beginning): Writers should invite the reader into their work with a good introduction. They should restate the prompt in their own words so that readers know what they are going to read about.

Body (middle): The body is where the main thoughts and ideas are put together. Thoughtful transitions between ideas and key points help keep readers interested. Writers should create logical and purposeful sequences of ideas.

Conclusion (end): Writers should include a powerful conclusion to their piece that summarizes the information but leaves the reader with something to think about.

Voice

Voice is how the writer uses words and how they use sentence structure to sound like themselves! It shows that the writing is meaningful and that the author cares about it. It is what makes the writing uniquely the author's own. It is how the reader begins to know the author and what they "sound like."

Word Choice

The right word choice helps the author connect with their audience. If the work is narrative, the words tell a story. If the work is descriptive, the words can almost make you taste, touch, and feel what you are reading! If the work is an opinion, the words give new ideas and invite thought. Writers should choose detailed vocabulary and language that is clear and lively.

Sentence Fluency

When sentences are built to fit together and move with one another to create writing that is easy to read aloud, the author has written with fluency. Sentences and paragraphs start and stop in just the right places so that the writing moves well. Sentences should have a lot of different of structures and lengths.

Proper Writing Conventions

Writers should make their writing clear and understandable through the use of proper grammar, spelling, capitalization, and punctuation.

Presentation

Writers should try to make their work inviting to the reader. Writers show they care about their writing when it is neat and readable.

Tips for the Writing Section

1. Don't panic! This section isn't scored. It is just a great way to show teachers how smart you are and how well you can tell a story and write. You can do it!

2. Use your time well. Fifteen minutes is quick! It is shorter than almost every TV show. Don't spend too much time doing any one thing. Try to brainstorm briefly and then get writing. Leave a few minutes to read it over and correct any spelling mistakes or confusing parts.

3. Be yourself! You are smart and interesting and teachers want to get to know you and your unique ideas. Don't feel pressured to use big vocabulary words if you aren't positive what they mean. You will be more understandable if you use the right word, not the fanciest word.

Conventions of Standard English Grammar, Punctuation, and Spelling

Conventions of Standard English

Educators must first be masters of the English language in order to teach it. Teachers serve several key roles in the classroom that all require that they know the conventions of grammar, punctuation, and spelling. Teachers are communicators. They must know how to structure their own language for clarity. They must also be able to interpret what the students are saying to accurately either affirm or revise it for correctness. Teachers are educators of language. They are the agents of change from poor-quality conventions to mastery of the concepts. Teachers are responsible for differentiating instruction so that students at all levels and aptitudes can succeed with language learning. Teachers need to be able to isolate gaps in skill sets and decide which skills need intervention in the classroom. Teachers are evaluators. They are responsible for making key decisions about a student's educational trajectory based on their assessment of the student's capabilities. Teachers also have great impact on how students view themselves as learners. Teachers are models. They must be superb examples of educated individuals. Just like with any other subject, people need a strong grasp of the basics of language. They will not be able to learn these things unless the teachers themselves have mastered it. Teachers foster socialization; socialization to cultural norms and to the everyday practices of the community in which they live is of utmost importance to students' lives. These processes begin at home but continue early in a child's life at school. Teachers play a key role in guiding and scaffolding students' socialization skills. If teachers are to excel in this role, they need to be adept with the use of the English language.

Understanding the Conventions of Standard English

Parts of Speech

The English language has eight parts of speech, each serving a different grammatical function.

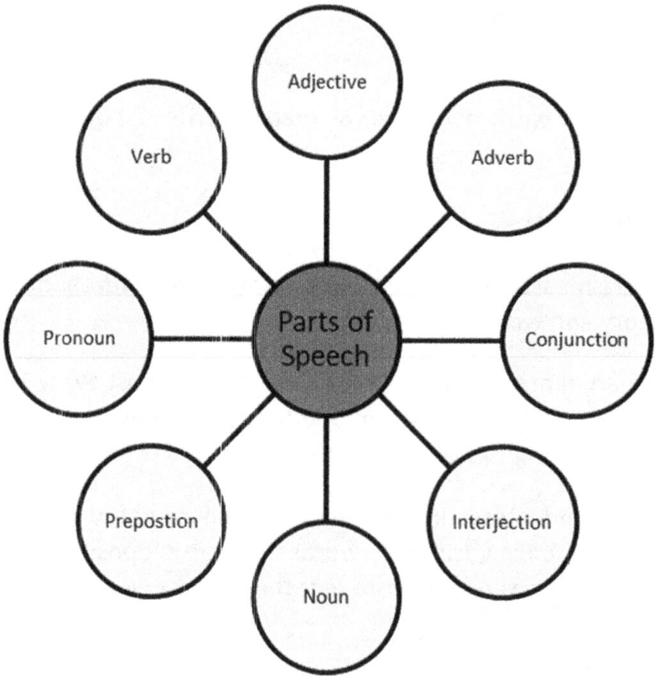

Verb

Verbs describe an action—e.g., *run, play, eat*—or a state of being—e.g., *is, are, was*. It is impossible to make a grammatically-complete sentence without a verb.

He *runs* to the store.

She *is* eight years old.

Noun

Nouns can be a person, place, or thing. They can refer to concrete objects—e.g., chair, apple, house—or abstract things—love, knowledge, friendliness.

Look at the *dog*!

Where are my *keys*?

Some nouns are *countable*, meaning they can be counted as separate entities—one chair, two chairs, three chairs. They can be either singular or plural. Other nouns, usually substances or concepts, are *uncountable*—e.g., air, information, wealth—and some nouns can be both countable and uncountable depending on how they are used.

I bought three *dresses*.

Respect is important to me.

I ate way too much *food* last night.

At the international festival, you can sample *foods* from around the world.

Proper nouns are the specific names of people, places, or things and are almost always capitalized.

Marie Curie studied at the Flying University in Warsaw, Poland.

Pronoun

Pronouns function as substitutes for nouns or noun phrases. Pronouns are often used to avoid constant repetition of a noun or to simplify sentences. *Personal pronouns* are used for people. Some pronouns are *subject pronouns*; they are used to replace the subject in a sentence—I, we, he, she, they.

Is *he* your friend?

We work together.

Object pronouns can function as the object of a sentence—me, us, him, her, them.

Give the documents to *her*.

Did you call *him* back yet?

Some pronouns can function as either the subject or the object—e.g., you, it. The subject of a sentence is the noun of the sentence that is doing or being something.

You should try it.

It tastes great.

Possessive pronouns indicate ownership. They can be used alone—mine, yours, his, hers, theirs, ours—or with a noun—my, your, his, her, their, ours. In the latter case, they function as a determiner, which is described in detail in the below section on adjectives.

This table is *ours.*

I can't find *my* phone!

Reflexive pronouns refer back to the person being spoken or written about. These pronouns end in -*self/-selves.*

I've heard that New York City is gorgeous in the autumn, but I've never seen it for *myself.*

After moving away from home, young people have to take care of *themselves.*

Indefinite pronouns are used for things that are unknown or unspecified. Some examples are *anybody, something,* and *everything.*

I'm looking for *someone* who knows how to fix computers.

I wanted to buy some shoes today, but I couldn't find *any* that I liked.

Adjective

An adjective modifies a noun, making it more precise or giving more information about it. Adjectives answer these questions: What kind? Which one?

I just bought a *red* car.

I don't like *cold* weather.

One special type of word that modifies a noun is a ***determiner.*** In fact, some grammarians classify determiners as a separate part of speech because whereas adjectives simply describe additional qualities of a noun, a determiner is often a necessary part of a noun phrase, without which the phrase is grammatically incomplete. A determiner indicates whether a noun is definite or indefinite, and can identify which noun is being discussed. It also introduces context to the noun in terms of quantity and possession. The most commonly-used determiners are articles—a, an, the.

I ordered *a* pizza.

She lives in *the* city.

Possessive pronouns discussed above, such as *my*, *your*, and *our*, are also determiners, along with *demonstratives*—this, that—and *quantifiers*—much, many, some. These determiners can take the place of an article.

Are you using *this* chair?

I need *some* coffee!

Adverb

Adverbs modify verbs, adjectives, and other adverbs. Words that end in –ly are usually adverbs. Adverbs answer these questions: When? Where? In what manner? To what degree?

She talks *quickly*.

The mountains are *incredibly* beautiful!

The students arrived *early*.

Please take your phone call *outside*.

Preposition

Prepositions show the relationship between different elements in a phrase or sentence and connect nouns or pronouns to other words in the sentence. Some examples of prepositions are words such as *after*, *at*, *behind*, *by*, *during*, *from*, *in*, *on*, *to*, and *with*.

Let's go *to* class.

Starry Night was painted *by* Vincent van Gogh *in* 1889.

Conjunction

Conjunctions join words, phrases, clauses, or sentences together, indicating the type of connection between these elements.

I like pizza, *and* I enjoy spaghetti.

I like to play baseball, *but* I'm allergic to mitts.

Some conjunctions are *coordinating*, meaning they give equal emphasis to two main clauses. Coordinating conjunctions are short, simple words that can be remembered using the mnemonic FANBOYS: for, and, nor, but, or, yet, so. Other conjunctions are *subordinating*. Subordinating conjunctions introduce dependent clauses and include words such as *because*, *since*, *before*, *after*, *if*, and *while*.

Interjection

An *interjection* is a short word that shows greeting or emotion. Examples of interjections include *wow*, *ouch*, *hey*, *oops*, *alas*, and *hey*.

Wow! Look at that sunset!

Was it your birthday yesterday? *Oops*! I forgot.

Errors in Standard English Grammar, Usage, Syntax, and Mechanics

Sentence Fragments

A *complete sentence* requires a verb and a subject that expresses a complete thought. Sometimes, the subject is omitted in the case of the implied *you*, used in sentences that are the command or imperative form—e.g., "Look!" or "Give me that." It is understood that the subject of the command is *you*, the listener or reader, so it is possible to have a structure without an explicit subject. Without these elements, though, the sentence is incomplete—it is a *sentence fragment.* While sentence fragments often occur in conversational English or creative writing, they are generally not appropriate in academic writing. Sentence fragments often occur when dependent clauses are not joined to an independent clause:

> *Sentence fragment*: Because the airline overbooked the flight.

The sentence above is a dependent clause that does not express a complete thought. What happened as a result of this cause? With the addition of an independent clause, this now becomes a complete sentence:

> *Complete sentence*: Because the airline overbooked the flight, several passengers were unable to board.

Sentences fragments may also occur through improper use of conjunctions:

> I'm going to the Bahamas for spring break. And to New York City for New Year's Eve.
>
> While the first sentence above is a complete sentence, the second one is not because it is a prepositional phrase that lacks a subject [I] and a verb [am going]. Joining the two together with the coordinating conjunction forms one grammatically-correct sentence:
>
> I'm going to the Bahamas for spring break and to New York City for New Year's Eve.

Run-ons

A *run-on* is a sentence with too many independent clauses that are improperly connected to each other:

> This winter has been very cold some farmers have suffered damage to their crops.

The sentence above has two subject-verb combinations. The first is "this winter has been"; the second is "some farmers have suffered." However, they are simply stuck next to each other without any punctuation or conjunction. Therefore, the sentence is a run-on.

Another type of run-on occurs when writers use inappropriate punctuation:

> This winter has been very cold, some farmers have suffered damage to their crops.

Though a comma has been added, this sentence is still not correct. When a comma alone is used to join two independent clauses, it is known as a ***comma splice***. Without an appropriate conjunction, a comma cannot join two independent clauses by itself.

Run-on sentences can be corrected by either dividing the independent clauses into two or more separate sentences or inserting appropriate conjunctions and/or punctuation. The run-on sentence can be amended by separating each subject-verb pair into its own sentence:

> This winter has been very cold. Some farmers have suffered damage to their crops.

The run-on can also be fixed by adding a comma and conjunction to join the two independent clauses with each other:

> This winter has been very cold, so some farmers have suffered damage to their crops.

Parallelism

Parallel structure occurs when phrases or clauses within a sentence contain the same structure. Parallelism increases readability and comprehensibility because it is easy to tell which sentence elements are paired with each other in meaning.

> Jennifer enjoys cooking, knitting, and to spend time with her cat.

This sentence is not parallel because the items in the list appear in two different forms. Some are *gerunds*, which is the verb + ing: *cooking, knitting*. The other item uses the *infinitive* form, which is to + verb: *to spend*. To create parallelism, all items in the list may reflect the same form:

> Jennifer enjoys cooking, knitting, and spending time with her cat.

All of the items in the list are now in gerund forms, so this sentence exhibits parallel structure. Here's another example:

> The company is looking for employees who are responsible and with a lot of experience.

Again, the items that are listed in this sentence are not parallel. "Responsible" is an adjective, yet "with a lot of experience" is a prepositional phrase. The sentence elements do not utilize parallel parts of speech.

> The company is looking for employees who are responsible and experienced.

"Responsible" and "experienced" are both adjectives, so this sentence now has parallel structure.

Dangling and Misplaced Modifiers

Modifiers enhance meaning by clarifying or giving greater detail about another part of a sentence. However, incorrectly-placed modifiers have the opposite effect and can cause confusion. A *misplaced modifier* is a modifier that is not located appropriately in relation to the word or phrase that it modifies:

> Because he was one of the greatest thinkers of Renaissance Italy, John idolized Leonardo da Vinci.

In this sentence, the modifier is "because he was one of the greatest thinkers of Renaissance Italy," and the noun it is intended to modify is "Leonardo da Vinci." However, due to the placement of the modifier next to the subject, John, it seems as if the sentence is stating that John was a Renaissance genius, not Da Vinci.

> John idolized Leonard da Vinci because he was one of the greatest thinkers of Renaissance Italy.

The modifier is now adjacent to the appropriate noun, clarifying which of the two men in this sentence is the greatest thinker.

Dangling modifiers modify a word or phrase that is not readily apparent in the sentence. That is, they "dangle" because they are not clearly attached to anything:

> After getting accepted to college, Amir's parents were proud.

The modifier here, "after getting accepted to college," should modify who got accepted. The noun immediately following the modifier is "Amir's parents"—but they are probably not the ones who are going to college.

> After getting accepted to college, Amir made his parents proud.

The subject of the sentence has been changed to Amir himself, and now the subject and its modifier are appropriately matched.

Inconsistent Verb Tense

Verb tense reflects when an action occurred or a state existed. For example, the tense known as *simple present* expresses something that is happening right now or that happens regularly:

> She *works* in a hospital.

Present continuous tense expresses something in progress. It is formed by to be + verb + -ing.

> Sorry, I can't go out right now. I *am doing* my homework.

Past tense is used to describe events that previously occurred. However, in conversational English, speakers often use present tense or a mix of past and present tense when relating past events because it gives the narrative a sense of immediacy. In formal written English, though, consistency in verb tense is necessary to avoid reader confusion.

> I traveled to Europe last summer. As soon as I stepped off the plane, I feel like I'm in a movie! I'm surrounded by quaint cafes and impressive architecture.

The passage above abruptly switches from past tense—*traveled, stepped*—to present tense—*feel, am surrounded.*

> I *traveled* to Europe last summer. As soon as I *stepped* off the plane, I *felt* like I was in a movie! I *was surrounded* by quaint cafes and impressive architecture.

All verbs are in past tense, so this passage now has consistent verb tense.

Split Infinitives

The *infinitive form* of a verb consists of "to + base verb"—e.g., to walk, to sleep, to approve. A *split infinitive* occurs when another word, usually an adverb, is placed between *to* and the verb:

> I decided *to simply walk* to work to get more exercise every day.

The infinitive *to walk* is split by the adverb *simply*.

> It was a mistake *to hastily approve* the project before conducting further preliminary research.

The infinitive *to approve* is split by *hastily*.

Although some grammarians still advise against split infinitives, this syntactic structure is common in both spoken and written English and is widely accepted in standard usage.

Subject-Verb Agreement

In English, verbs must agree with the subject. The form of a verb may change depending on whether the subject is singular or plural, or whether it is first, second, or third person. For example, the verb *to be* has various forms:

> I am a student.
>
> You are a student.
>
> She is a student.
>
> We are students.
>
> They are students.

Errors occur when a verb does not agree with its subject. Sometimes, the error is readily apparent:

> We is hungry.

Is is not the appropriate form of *to be* when used with the third person plural *we*.

> We are hungry.

This sentence now has correct subject-verb agreement.

However, some cases are trickier, particularly when the subject consists of a lengthy noun phrase with many modifiers:

> Students who are hoping to accompany the anthropology department on its annual summer trip to Ecuador needs to sign up by March 31st.

The verb in this sentence is *needs*. However, its subject is not the noun adjacent to it—Ecuador. The subject is the noun at the beginning of the sentence—students. Because *students* is plural, *needs* is the incorrect verb form.

> *Students* who are hoping to accompany the anthropology department on its annual summer trip to Ecuador *need* to sign up by March 31st.

This sentence now uses correct agreement between *students* and *need*.

Another case to be aware of is a *collective noun*. A collective noun refers to a group of many things or people but can be singular in itself—e.g., family, committee, army, pair team, council, jury. Whether or not a collective noun uses a singular or plural verb depends on how the noun is being used. If the noun refers to the group performing a collective action as one unit, it should use a singular verb conjugation:

> The family is moving to a new neighborhood.

The whole family is moving together in unison, so the singular verb form *is* is appropriate here.

> The committee has made its decision.

The verb *has* and the possessive pronoun *its* both reflect the word *committee* as a singular noun in the sentence above; however, when a collective noun refers to the group as individuals, it can take a plural verb:

> The newlywed pair spend every moment together.

This sentence emphasizes the love between two people in a pair, so it can use the plural verb *spend*.

> The council are all newly elected members.

The sentence refers to the council in terms of its individual members and uses the plural verb *are*.

Overall though, American English is more likely to pair a collective noun with a singular verb, while British English is more likely to pair a collective noun with a plural verb.

Grammar, Usage, Syntax, and Mechanics Choices

Colons and Semicolons

In a sentence, *colons* are used before a list, a summary or elaboration, or an explanation related to the preceding information in the sentence:

> There are two ways to reserve tickets for the performance: by phone or in person.
>
> One thing is clear: students are spending more on tuition than ever before.

As these examples show, a colon must be preceded by an independent clause. However, the information after the colon may be in the form of an independent clause or in the form of a list.

Semicolons can be used in two different ways—to join ideas or to separate them. In some cases, semicolons can be used to connect what would otherwise be stand-alone sentences. Each part of the sentence joined by a semicolon must be an independent clause. The use of a semicolon indicates that these two independent clauses are closely related to each other:

> The rising cost of childcare is one major stressor for parents; healthcare expenses are another source of anxiety.
>
> Classes have been canceled due to the snowstorm; check the school website for updates.

Semicolons can also be used to divide elements of a sentence in a more distinct way than simply using a comma. This usage is particularly useful when the items in a list are especially long and complex and contain other internal punctuation.

> Retirees have many modes of income: some survive solely off their retirement checks; others supplement their income through part time jobs, like working in a supermarket or substitute teaching; and others are financially dependent on the support of family members, friends, and spouses.

Its and It's

These pronouns are some of the most confused in the English language as most possessives contain the suffix –'s. However, for *it*, it is the opposite. *Its* is a possessive pronoun:

> The government is reassessing *its* spending plan.

It's is a contraction of the words *it is*:

> *It's* snowing outside.

Saw and Seen

Saw and *seen* are both conjugations of the verb *to see*, but they express different verb tenses. *Saw* is used in the simple past tense. *Seen* is the past participle form of *to see* and can be used in all perfect tenses.

> I seen her yesterday.

This sentence is incorrect. Because it expresses a completed event from a specified point in time in the past, it should use simple past tense:

> I *saw* her yesterday.

This sentence uses the correct verb tense. Here's how the past participle is used correctly:

> I *have seen* her before.

The meaning in this sentence is slightly changed to indicate an event from an unspecific time in the past. In this case, present perfect is the appropriate verb tense to indicate an unspecified past experience. Present perfect conjugation is created by combining *to have* + past participle.

Then and Than

Then is generally used as an adverb indicating something that happened next in a sequence or as the result of a conditional situation:

> We parked the car and *then* walked to the restaurant.

> If enough people register for the event, *then* we can begin planning.

Than is a conjunction indicating comparison:

> This watch is more expensive *than* that one.

> The bus departed later *than* I expected.

They're, Their, and There

They're is a contraction of the words *they are*:

> *They're* moving to Ohio next week.

Their is a possessive pronoun:

> The baseball players are training for *their* upcoming season.

There can function as multiple parts of speech, but it is most commonly used as an adverb indicating a location:

> Let's go to the concert! Some great bands are playing *there*.

Insure and Ensure

These terms are both verbs. *Insure* means to guarantee something against loss, harm, or damage, usually through an insurance policy that offers monetary compensation:

> The robbers made off with her prized diamond necklace, but luckily it was *insured* for one million dollars.

Ensure means to make sure, to confirm, or to be certain:

> *Ensure* that you have your passport before entering the security checkpoint.

Accept and Except

Accept is a verb meaning to take or agree to something:

> I would like to *accept* your offer of employment.

Except is a preposition that indicates exclusion:

> I've been to every state in America *except* Hawaii.

Affect and Effect

Affect is a verb meaning to influence or to have an impact on something:

> The amount of rainfall during the growing season *affects* the flavor of wine produced from these grapes.

Effect can be used as either a noun or a verb. As a noun, *effect* is synonymous with a result:

> If we implement the changes, what will the *effect* be on our profits?

As a verb, *effect* means to bring about or to make happen:

> In just a few short months, the healthy committee has *effected* real change in school nutrition.

Components of Sentences

Clauses

Clauses contain a subject and a verb. An *independent clause* can function as a complete sentence on its own, but it might also be one component of a longer sentence. *Dependent clauses* cannot stand alone as complete sentences. They rely on independent clauses to complete their meaning. Dependent clauses usually begin with a subordinating conjunction. Independent and dependent clauses are sometimes also referred to as *main clauses* and *subordinate clauses*, respectively. The following structure highlights the differences:

> Apiculturists raise honeybees because they love insects.

Apiculturists raise honeybees is an independent or main clause. The subject is *apiculturists*, and the verb is *raise*. It expresses a complete thought and could be a standalone sentence.

Because they love insects is a dependent or subordinate clause. If it were not attached to the independent clause, it would be a sentence fragment. While it contains a subject and verb—*they love*—this clause is dependent because it begins with the subordinate conjunction *because*. Thus, it does not express a complete thought on its own.

Another type of clause is a *relative clause*, and it is sometimes referred to as an *adjective clause* because it gives further description about the noun. A relative clause begins with a *relative pronoun*: *that, which, who, whom, whichever, whomever*, or *whoever.* It may also begin with a *relative adverb*: *where, why*, or *when.* Here's an example of a relative clause, functioning as an adjective:

> The strawberries that I bought yesterday are already beginning to spoil.

Here, the relative clause is *that I bought yesterday*; the relative pronoun is *that*. The subject is *I*, and the verb is *bought*. The clause modifies the subject *strawberries* by answering the question, "Which strawberries?" Here's an example of a relative clause with an adverb:

> The tutoring center is a place where students can get help with homework.

The relative clause is *where students can get help with homework*, and it gives more information about a place by describing what kind of place it is. It begins with the relative adverb *where* and contains the noun *students* along with its verb phrase *can get*.

Relative clauses may be further divided into two types: essential or nonessential. *Essential clauses* contain identifying information without which the sentence would lose significant meaning or not make sense. These are also sometimes referred to as *restrictive clauses*. The sentence above contains an example of an essential relative clause. Here is what happens when the clause is removed:

> The tutoring center is a place where students can get help with homework.
>
> The tutoring center is a place.

Without the relative clause, the sentence loses the majority of its meaning; thus, the clause is essential or restrictive.

Nonessential clauses—also referred to as *non-restrictive clauses*—offer additional information about a noun in the sentence, but they do not significantly control the overall meaning of the sentence. The following example indicates a nonessential clause:

> New York City, which is located in the northeastern part of the country, is the most populated city in America.
>
> New York City is the most populated city in America.

Even without the relative clause, the sentence is still understandable and continues to communicate its central message about New York City. Thus, it is a nonessential clause.

Punctuation differs between essential and nonessential relative clauses, too. Nonessential clauses are set apart from the sentence using commas whereas essential clauses are not separated with commas. Also, the relative pronoun *that* is generally used for essential clauses, while *which* is used for nonessential clauses. The following examples clarify this distinction:

Romeo and Juliet is my favorite play *that Shakespeare wrote*.

The relative clause *that Shakespeare wrote* contains essential, controlling information about the noun *play*, limiting it to those plays by Shakespeare. Without it, it would seem that *Romeo and Juliet* is the speaker's favorite play out of every play ever written, not simply from Shakespeare's repertoire.

Romeo and Juliet, which Shakespeare wrote, is my favorite play.

Here, the nonessential relative clause—"which Shakespeare wrote"—modifies *Romeo and Juliet*. It doesn't provide controlling information about the play, but simply offers further background details. Thus, commas are needed.

Phrases

Phrases are groups of words that do not contain the subject-verb combination required for clauses. Phrases are classified by the part of speech that begins or controls the phrase.

A *noun phrase* consists of a noun and all its modifiers—adjectives, adverbs, and determiners. Noun phrases can serve many functions in a sentence, acting as subjects, objects, and object complements:

The shallow yellow bowl sits on the top shelf.

Nina just bought *some incredibly fresh organic produce*.

Prepositional phrases are made up of a preposition and its object. The object of a preposition might be a noun, noun phrase, pronoun, or gerund. Prepositional phrases may function as either an adjective or an adverb:

Jack picked up the book *in front of him*.

The prepositional phrase *in front of him* acts as an adjective indicating which book Jack picked up.

The dog ran into the back yard.

The phrase *into the backyard* describes where the dog ran, so it acts as an adverb.

Verb phrases include all of the words in a verb group, even if they are not directly adjacent to each other:

I *should have woken up* earlier this morning.

The company **is** now *offering* membership discounts for new enrollers.

This sentence's verb phrase is *is offering*. Even though they are separated by the word *now*, they function together as a single verb phrase.

Structures of Sentences

All sentences contain the same basic elements: a subject and a verb. The *subject* is who or what the sentence is about; the *verb* describes the subject's action or condition. However, these elements, subjects and verbs, can be combined in different ways. The following graphic describes the different types of sentence structures.

Sentence Structure	Independent Clauses	Dependent Clauses
Simple	1	0
Compound	2 or more	0
Complex	1	1 or more
Compound-Complex	2 or more	1 or more

A *simple sentence* expresses a complete thought and consists of one subject and verb combination:

The children ate pizza.

The subject is *children*. The verb is *ate*.

Either the subject or the verb may be *compound*—that is, it could have more than one element:

The children and their parents ate pizza.

The children *ate pizza and watched a movie*.

All of these are still simple sentences. Despite having either compound subjects or compound verbs, each sentence still has only one subject and verb combination.

Compound sentences combine two or more simple sentences to form one sentence that has multiple subject-verb combinations:

The children ate pizza, and *their parents watched a movie*.

This structure is comprised of two independent clauses: (1) *the children ate pizza* and (2) *their parents watched a movie.* Compound sentences join different subject-verb combinations using a comma and a coordinating conjunction.

I called my mom**,** *but* she didn't answer the phone.

The weather was stormy**,** *so* we canceled our trip to the beach.

A *complex sentence* consists of an independent clause and one or more dependent clauses. Dependent clauses join a sentence using *subordinating conjunctions*. Some examples of subordinating conjunctions are *although, unless, as soon as, since, while, when, because, if,* and *before*.

I missed class yesterday *because* my mother was ill.

Before traveling to a new country, you need to exchange your money to the local currency.

The order of clauses determines their punctuation. If the dependent clause comes first, it should be separated from the independent clause with a comma. However, if the complex sentence consists of an independent clause followed by a dependent clause, then a comma is not always necessary.

A *compound-complex sentence* can be created by joining two or more independent clauses with at least one dependent clause:

> After the earthquake struck, thousands of homes were destroyed, and many families were left without a place to live.

The first independent clause in the compound structure includes a dependent clause—*after the earthquake struck*. Thus, the structure is both complex and compound.

First Essay Prompt

Directions: The Writing section of the CBEST will require test takers to write two essays based on provided prompts. The first essay will have an expressive aim, with a topic relating to the test taker's past lived experience. The second essay has a referential aim so that test takers can showcase their analytical and expository writing skills.

Please read the prompt below and answer in an essay format.

Students encounter many different courses and teachers throughout their high school and post-secondary careers. Pick a course that stands out in your memory and describe the influential impact and the elements or reasons that this course made a lasting impression on you.

Second Essay Prompt

Please read the prompt below and answer in an essay format.

Some people feel that sharing their lives on social media sites such as Facebook, Instagram, and Snapchat is fine. They share every aspect of their lives, including pictures of themselves and their families, what they ate for lunch, who they are dating, and when they are going on vacation. They even say that if it's not on social media, it didn't happen. Other people believe that sharing so much personal information is an invasion of privacy and could prove dangerous. They think sharing personal pictures and details invites predators, cyberbullying, and identity theft.

Write an essay to someone who is considering whether to participate in social media. Take a side on the issue and argue whether or not he/she should join a social media network. Use specific examples to support your argument.

Dear CBEST Test Taker,

We would like to start by thanking you for purchasing this study guide for your CBEST exam. We hope that we exceeded your expectations.

Our goal in creating this study guide was to cover all of the topics that you will see on the test. We also strove to make our practice questions as similar as possible to what you will encounter on test day. With that being said, if you found something that you feel was not up to your standards, please send us an email and let us know.

We would also like to let you know about other books in our catalog that may interest you.

CSET English

This can be found on Amazon: amazon.com/dp/1628457198

CSET Multiple Subject

amazon.com/dp/1628458739

NES Elementary Education

amazon.com/dp/1628454334

CSET Mathematics

amazon.com/dp/1628459158

We have study guides in a wide variety of fields. If the one you are looking for isn't listed above, then try searching for it on Amazon or send us an email.

Thanks Again and Happy Testing!
Product Development Team
info@studyguideteam.com

FREE Test Taking Tips DVD Offer

To help us better serve you, we have developed a Test Taking Tips DVD that we would like to give you for FREE. **This DVD covers world-class test taking tips that you can use to be even more successful when you are taking your test.**

All that we ask is that you email us your feedback about your study guide. Please let us know what you thought about it – whether that is good, bad or indifferent.

To get your **FREE Test Taking Tips DVD**, email freedvd@studyguideteam.com with "FREE DVD" in the subject line and the following information in the body of the email:

a. The title of your study guide.

b. Your product rating on a scale of 1-5, with 5 being the highest rating.

c. Your feedback about the study guide. What did you think of it?

d. Your full name and shipping address to send your free DVD.

If you have any questions or concerns, please don't hesitate to contact us at freedvd@studyguideteam.com.

Thanks again!

Made in the USA
Coppell, TX
07 September 2020

37174778R00116

THE ILLUSTRATED WOMAN

Photographs by

WILLIAM DEMICHELE

Preface

Shotsie Gorman

Book Design

Paul Miyamoto

PROTEUS PRESS

NEW YORK

Published
in the
United States by
PROTEUS PRESS, INC.
40 Broadway
Albany, New York 12202

The Illustrated Woman
First Edition

Printed in Singapore
by Palace Press

Library of Congress Catalog Card Number: 91-068444
ISBN 0-9631708-0-5

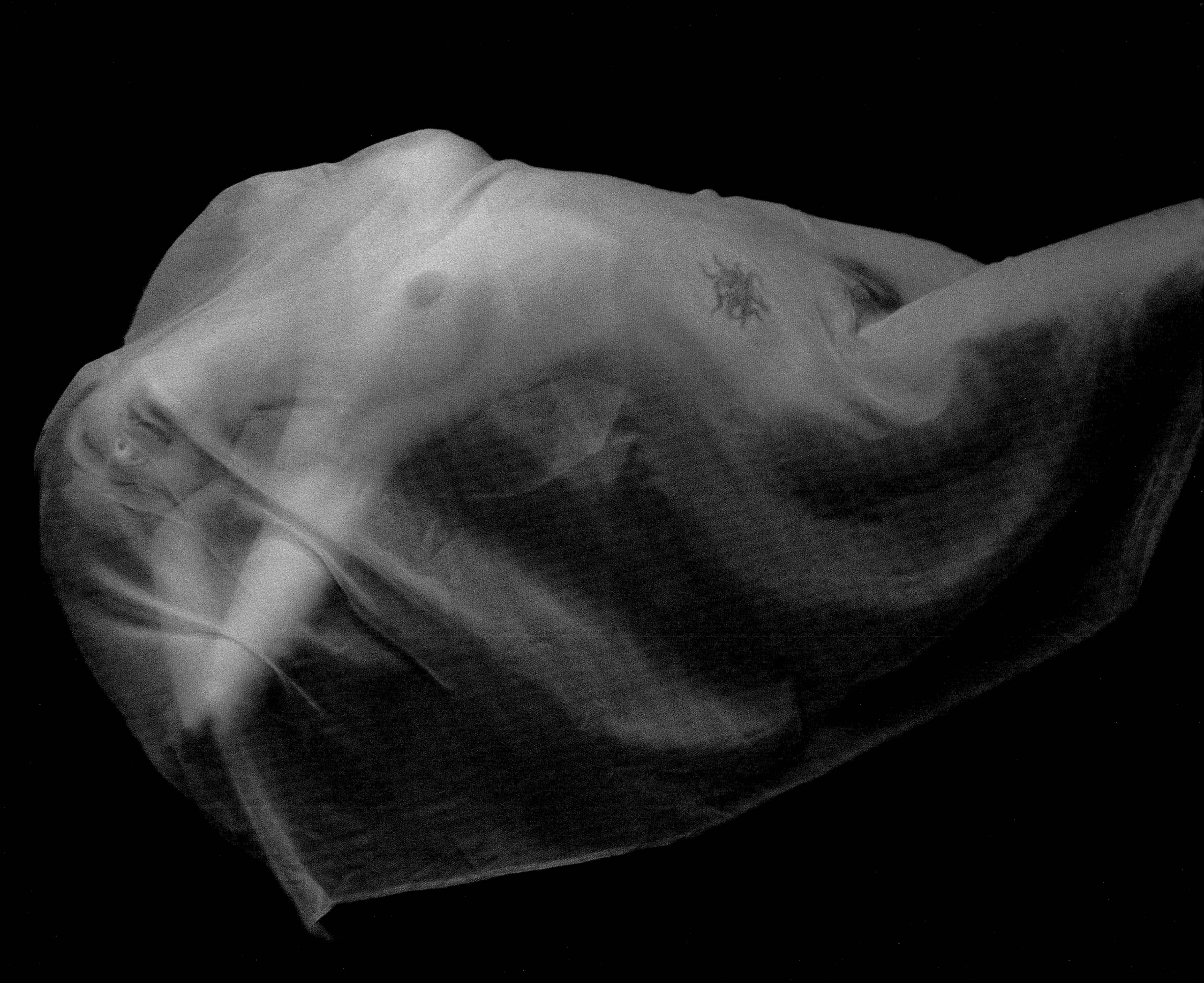

PREFACE

DURING A GALLERY EXHIBITION OF THE ILLUSTRATED WOMAN PHOTOGRAPHS, Bill DeMichele was confronted by an incensed young woman, "Did you deliberately intend to offend people with these photos?" What becomes clear with this question, beyond her indignation, is the lack of indifference when responding to photos of tattooed bodies. In the arts, tattooing and photography have few equals in their power to emotionally move the viewer. In this case, despite the clear visual beauty and sincere approach to the subject, the combination of Bill DeMichele's photography and the art of tattooing produces shocking images. What we have here, in a sense, is the classical female nude, with its long history of moral, social and political ramifications and the "bizarre" (by conventional standards), the tattooed and pierced body image. This blending carries with it enormous baggage. It is necessary to try to delineate the surrounding issues concerning these images in a clear manner. Once relieved of the misunderstandings, one can better appreciate the effort on the part of the tattooed woman and the artist, Bill DeMichele.

There is a resonance that must be noted in the response to photography that is often voiced by viewers of the tattooed person. Generally, the accepted notion is that all great photographic art validates itself both by the audience reaction and its "point of view". The photographer is inescapably tied to his or her viewpoint both literally, by the limits of the camera as a tool, and metaphorically, by the choice of image and the camera technique he or she chooses to use. The underlying excitement of these particular photos is the coming together of two potent art forms that stir immediate powerful reactions.

What follows in this book is photography and tattooing synchronizing on aesthetic, social, psychological and political spheres. The social perceptions of photography sets it apart from other traditional forms of expression, which links it on many levels to tattooing by virtue of the intense emotional response they both elicit. While many forms of expression are accepted as ephemeral, fantasy, inner visions, the photograph (regardless of its content) is perceived to "be" reality.

In that perspective, photography steps out of the realm of art and begins to be seen as a true empirical experience. Perhaps that is why there has long been a period of rejection to photography as art by the cognoscenti, and more recently, a recognized shock to its content in the general public's eye (i.e. the Mapplethorpe fiasco). In effect, what occurs is based on this understanding: the photograph is forcibly prying open the psyche by a "perceived" literal translation of the world. The photograph then becomes a visceral experience in the shadow world of our belief systems. As a result, the photograph (unlike its counterparts in the arts) must carry with it the burden of visual standards contained in the current cultural memory in a literal way. It would follow that in many cases, when one responds negatively to a photograph, one reacts on a subconscious level in fear. This fear I will call "paradigm vertigo". The image that we see before us becomes, by virtue of its confluence to the modern information media stream, a direct threat to our "comfort zone". In this, our set of psychic rules, we create blocks to certain types of expression. Dr. Peck in *The Road Less Traveled* would have called these rules our "map of reality". Albeit, mediocrity is the standard psychological "comfort zone" in our culture, as evidenced by our current lack of appreciation of the arts and our perverse loathing of diversity.

By establishing these perspectives, I am pointing out the fact that in our culture "Gross Consciousness" in a pejorative sense, rather than cultural memory, comprises our aesthetic judgement. The conventional wisdom then is being dictated via electronic media images rather than by oral traditions or written ones. These technological images tend to distort our humanity. It is this pervasive, bland and often violent influence on our minds that helps to place photography in the odd position of being caught somewhere between mass media images and the inner world of the artist. Similarly, tattooing elicits from the same uninitiated public a response of fear. It invades that "comfort zone" by forcing people to confront their own inner lives. Our society has mastered ignoring this inner world of primal emotional motivations. This is the very essence of the tattoo image. As such, we are angered by any reminders that we are just a short step from our primal past. When people see extensive tattooing on a human body for the first time, they are drawn into a nether world of swirling archetypal symbols in the strictest Jungian sense. This is disconcerting, to put it mildly, but that is the beauty and the power of tattooing as an art form—that it moves us to question. It is an enigma.

Although photography has reached the level of acceptance it deserves as an art form, tattooing is seemingly doomed to the awkward position of stepchild to the more serious arts, and in most cases a rejected family member of the folk art community. You would think the dichotomies present in tattooing and photography would ostensibly give both art forms the power to affect the modern consciousness in a positive way. But this would require stepping out of dogmatic thinking and tossing out the "map". While I have felt this power within tattooing myself, I have not witnessed evidence of that recognition in the public view, or for that matter in the tattoo world itself, and only a glimmer of it in the academic community. Given this static state, the Illustrated Woman photographs must be recognized for the groundbreaking blend that they are. Paintings with light, lighting the way of acceptance both for a woman's choice to step out of the conventional role cast for her in our society and the recognition of Tattooing as a qualified means of personal self-expression. Look with an open mind. In the end it is your decision.

SHOTSIE GORMAN

INTRODUCTION

WHEN I WAS 21, I GOT MY FIRST TATTOO. IT WAS ON MY FIRST TRIP TO THE WEST COAST, first time on the road, the first time I truly felt free. It was also the first time I truly felt lost. It was the 70's and I was hitchhiking across America. When I hit San Francisco, the first thing I saw was Lyle Tuttle's shop. After a lot of thought, I knew it was the right time for a tattoo. A small simple brand on my butt of two fish, the sign of Pisces. The process, the implications of a tattoo and the tattoo I got, all symbolized how I felt at that time. It was a personal decision; I showed no one and no one asked. Somehow it felt right, it made me feel a little prouder. I felt more like a renegade. Little did I know that, almost twenty years later, tattooing would be changing my life again.

I don't know where I saw my first tattoo. They were kind of just always around. When I was young, my favorite author was Ray Bradbury and I loved reading "The Illustrated Man". The idea of stories being told on your skin was a very mystical experience to me. When I was a teenager I walked into my first tattoo parlor. I remember seeing all the designs neatly framed on the wall. Each design had a small number and a price tag on it and there was a buzzing sound coming from the back room. Every once in a while, I would stop in and just look at the designs until the guy there would kick me out. Being in this large room, looking at all that "flash" gave me a certain feeling. I don't know what it was, but it was the same feeling I got when I went to the side show that came to town once a year.

I have never been one to ask the usual questions about tattoos, but since I got my latest tattoos (that cover both my calves and are more visible) and started showing my photographs in art exhibits, me and my pictures have heard them all. "Does it hurt?", "Are they real?", "Are they permanent?". These are the standards. "How could they?" and "Who would do such a thing?", along with all the presumptions of character, have been the eye openers for me. Suddenly, I realized my photographs are about "visual prejudice". It's funny how people give themselves away by the way they talk in front of a photograph. It's the kind of talk that is muttered under the breath or behind one's back. Suddenly, I found myself as spokesperson for the tattooed, defending their integrity as well as my own. This experience has had an effect on my pictures and this book.

I realized that women have long been subject to the pressures of physical appearance. The tattooed woman has taken this stigma and has used it to facilitate her art. Even though tattooing has gained acceptance or at least a tolerance as of late, when a woman gets tattooed she immediately gets more attention than a man. The general public is compelled to be more opinionated about a woman with body art.

A woman's reason for tattoos and body adornment varies from accentuating her body with designs to personal images that give inner strength and pleasure. But all the images and symbols that are worn on the skin of the Illustrated Woman tell a personal story. Some stories are obvious, like portraits of their children or loved ones. Others are more personal and the tattoo may mean nothing to the viewer. The most intriguing story told to me is about a woman who had her parents' names tattooed on her using their ashes after an unfortunate accident. To most people, the most fascinating aspect of tattooing is the permanence, which makes the tattoo a symbol of commitment and fortitude.

I consider the photographs in this book to be portraits. And although some of these images may differ from your definition of portrait, through this style I have tried to strip away all the cues of time and location to allow the subject to speak aloud of her statement. To let each person reveal her story not only with her tattoos, but with her body language, her expressions, her pose. I wanted to capture the attitude and presence of each person. I avoided using any overt photographic techniques or dictating the pose of the subject. These simple images of the female form are stronger than any manipulated photo technique. After starting this project, I realized how important it was that each photograph also have a dignity about it. A pride and sureness that would overcome, or at least confront, the prejudice of any viewer.

I decided to do a book of my photographs after seeing what was out there in the way of books and magazines. It seemed that most tattoo books show detailed pictures of tattoos. I personally felt that a better approach to showing tattoos would be to minimize the close-up shots and show more of the relationship of tattoos to the body. In this way, the full aesthetic is better appreciated. I believe the body, as a whole, is the canvas for any size tattoo. And the whole should be seen, or at least implied, to appreciate the full art of tattooing.

On this note, I must say it was often difficult to crop or choose some of the images over others. I am very aware that I am a photographer and not a tattoo artist. I had to constantly consider and weigh the aesthetics of the image with the content of the photograph. Several times I chose more than one photograph to show a person; some poses are cropped close or show no head (often by request of the subject) and there are a few men shown at the side of their woman. I regret not being able to show everyone I photographed, but I am happy to say that the final layout includes over a hundred different women representing the work of almost a hundred and fifty artists from around the world.

Over the past five years while working on this project I have met many people, and have made many new friends. Many of the women in this book were photographed more than once, over a period of time. I find these composites of change very interesting; it proves tattoos, while permanent, can change just like the poeple who wear them. Many of the women have told me that I am the only one to photograph them nude. Some were uncomfortable being photographed at all. I would like to thank them all for their trust, honesty and commitment to my project. The women I have photographed fit no particular stereotype. Their socioeconomic backgrounds are diverse. Their occupations range from nurses, doctors, executives and secretaries to mothers, students and laborers.

The "colored people" who look at this book, well, they understand. But, this portfolio of photographs is also for the non-inked. I would like this book to be an experience that educates, as well as amazes. To stimulate thought and conversation. To let the viewer know that tattooing is an art form that exists widely throughout the world. And that tattooing contains all the credibility, aesthetic, talent and fortitude that any art medium subscribes to.

The past five years have been a real eye opener and a growing experience for me, I hope these images can do the same for you.

BILL DEMICHELE

RACHEL EAST LANSING, MI 1989

GUY AITCHISON

DEBORAH SAN FRANCISCO, CA 1991

(PANDORA'S TOYBOX) GUY AITCHISON, (ATLANTIAN BRACELET) JULI MOON

KIRBY GLENDALE, CA 1991

(RIGHT SHOULDER) LEO ZULUETA, (CHEST) BERT RODRIQUEZ, (RIGHT BREAST) KARI BARBA

TITINE SWITZERLAND 1991

FILIP LEU

(ABOVE) HEIDI ESCONDIDO, CA 1991

PATTY KELLEY

(AT RIGHT) MAGGIE AUSTIN, TX 1989

DAVE LUM

15

GENZIANA BRAZIL 1989

MARCO LEONI

(above and at right) ISOBEL FT. MYERS, FL 1991

BILL HANNONG

DOROTHY DAYTON, KY 1991

ROBERT BENEDETTI

ELIZABETH BURKE, VA 1989

TONY BROWNING

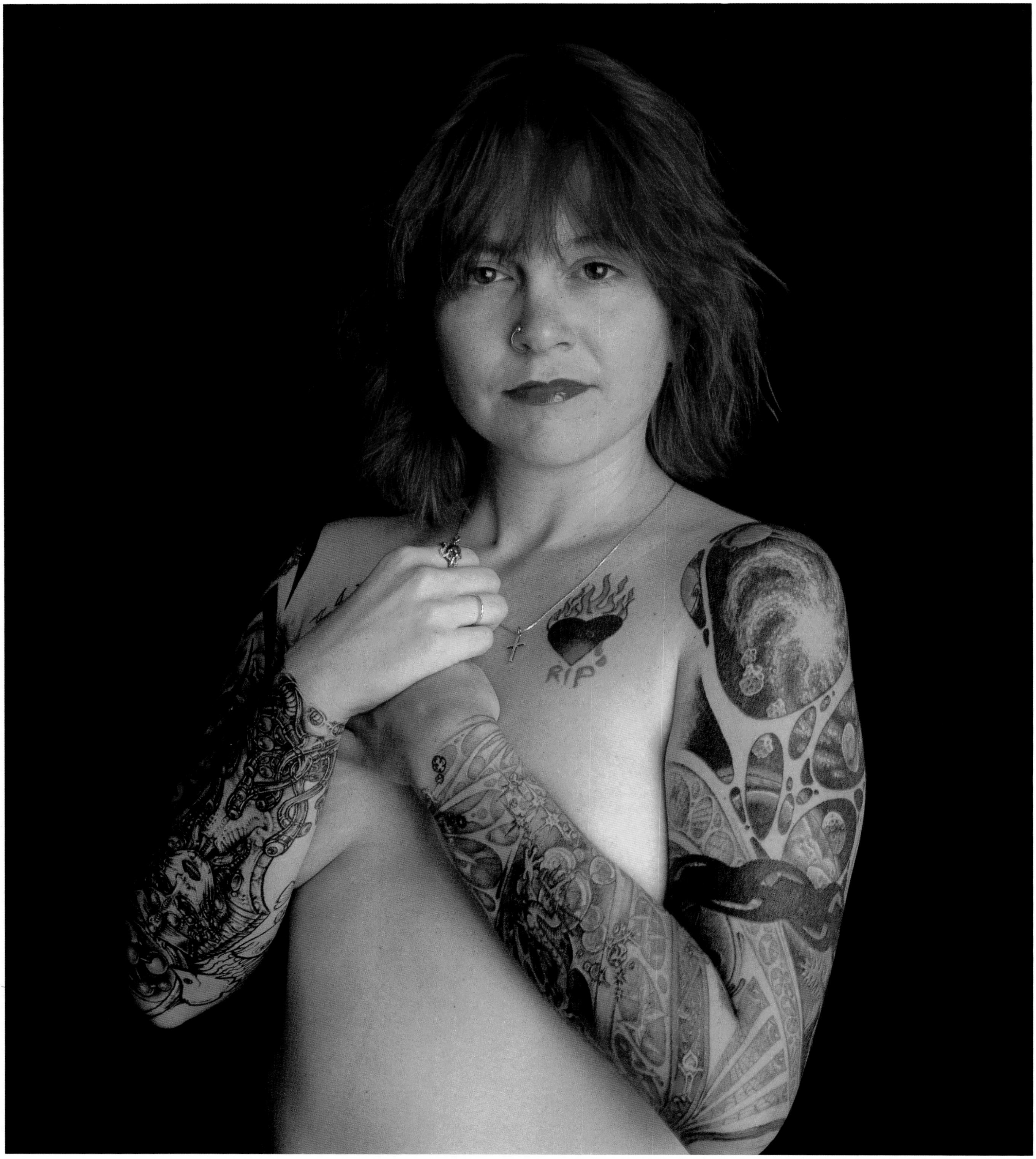

LORRI CHICAGO, IL 1990

GUY AITCHISON

LYNN SCOTTDALE, GA 1989

PAINLESS PAUL NELSON

MARIA HAMILTON, OH 1990

DANA BRUNSON

LISA CHICAGO, IL 1989

ROY BOY

TANYA BURKE, VA 1989

JAMES MARLOWE

LINDA LOS ANGELES, CA 1991

LEO ZULUETA

BETONY RICHMOND, VA 1988

UNKNOWN

SARAH FALLS CHURCH, VA 1989

JAMES MARLOWE

CAITLIN CHICO, CA 1989

FRED

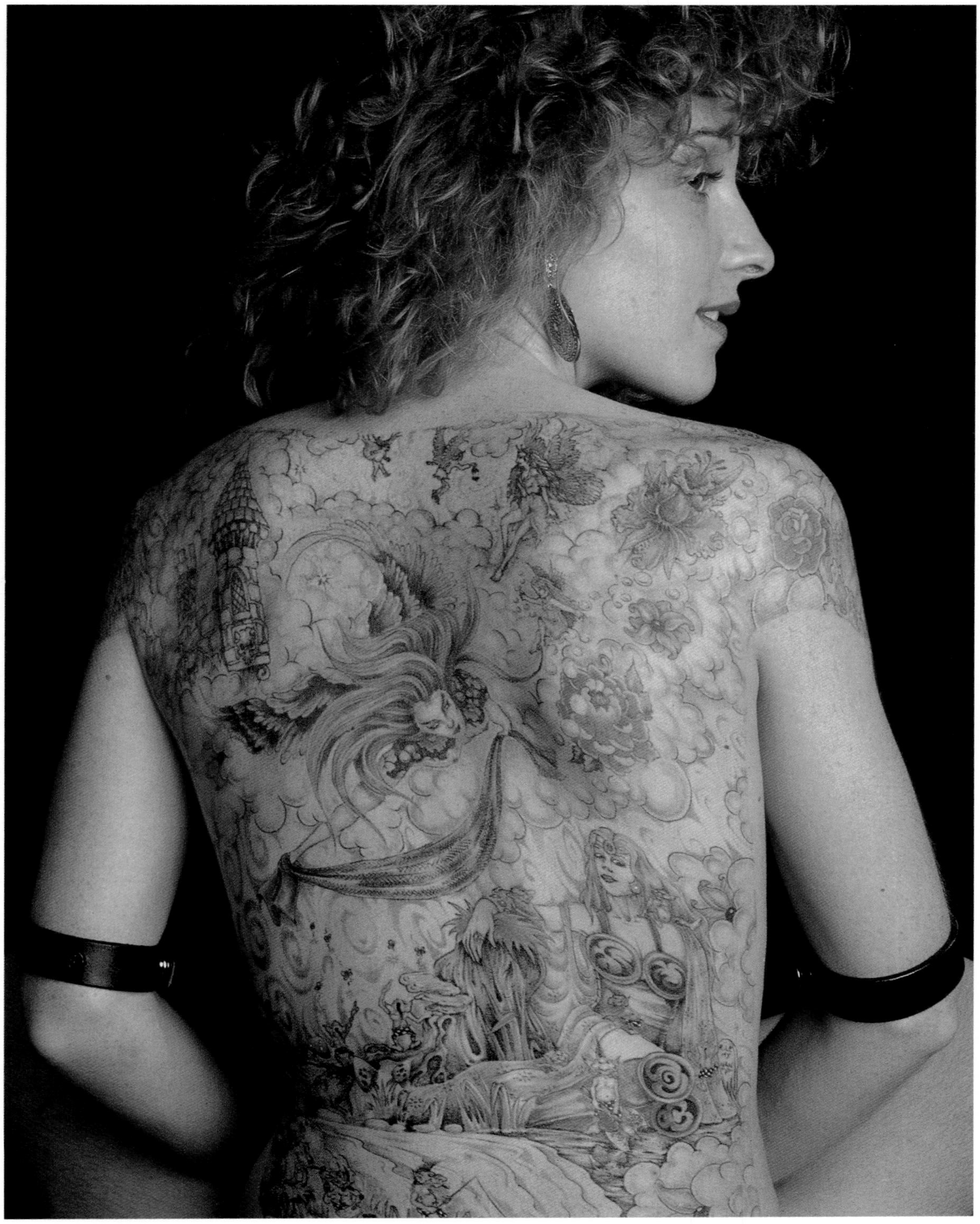

(above) CLARE ENGLAND 1990

DANNY FULLER

(at right) THERESA SAN FRANCISCO, CA 1991

(IVY BELT, CELTIC SNAKE, WHEAT) BILL SALMON
(CELTIC FISH BAND) VYVYN LAZONGA

Renate and Tom BROOKLYN, NY 1990

Mike Bakaty

CARMEN FAIRVIEW, NJ 1989

SHOTSIE GORMAN

JACQUELINE ENGLAND 1992

(FAIRIES) MICKY SHARPZ, (TIGER) IAN OF READING

(above and at right) JESSICA PHILADELPHIA, PA 1991

(Back of Legs, Right Wristband, Anklet and Back) Bee, (Right Shoulder) Buffy Herman

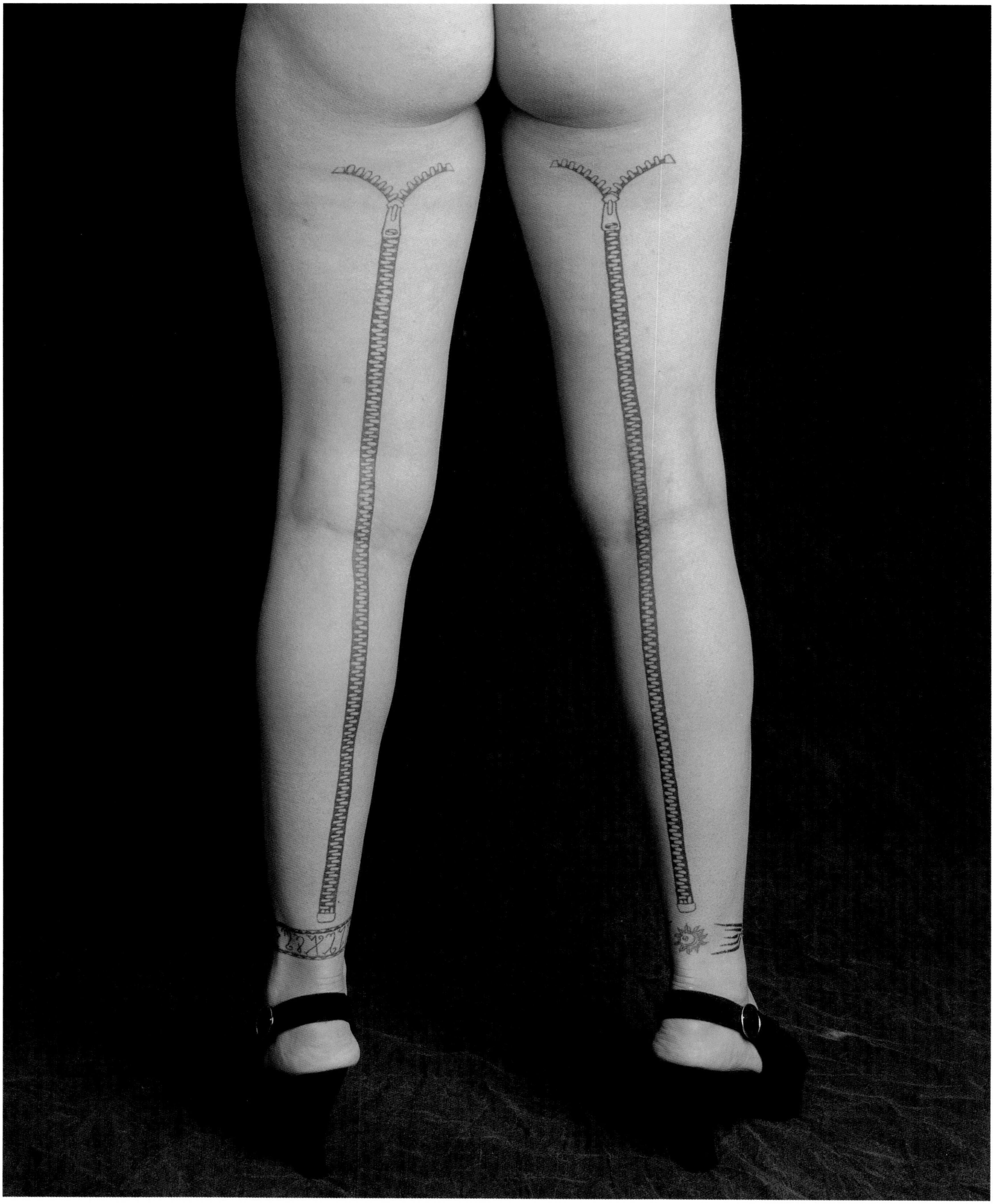

TERRI PANAMA CITY, FL 1991

TONY OLIVAS

LIN ENGLAND 1990

BRIAN CARVILLE OF WINDSOR

KELLY BREA, CA 1991

KARI BARBA

INGER RAYNHAM, MA 1988

KEVIN CRONIN

(above and at right) GLORIA NEW YORK, NY 1990

JONATHAN SHAW

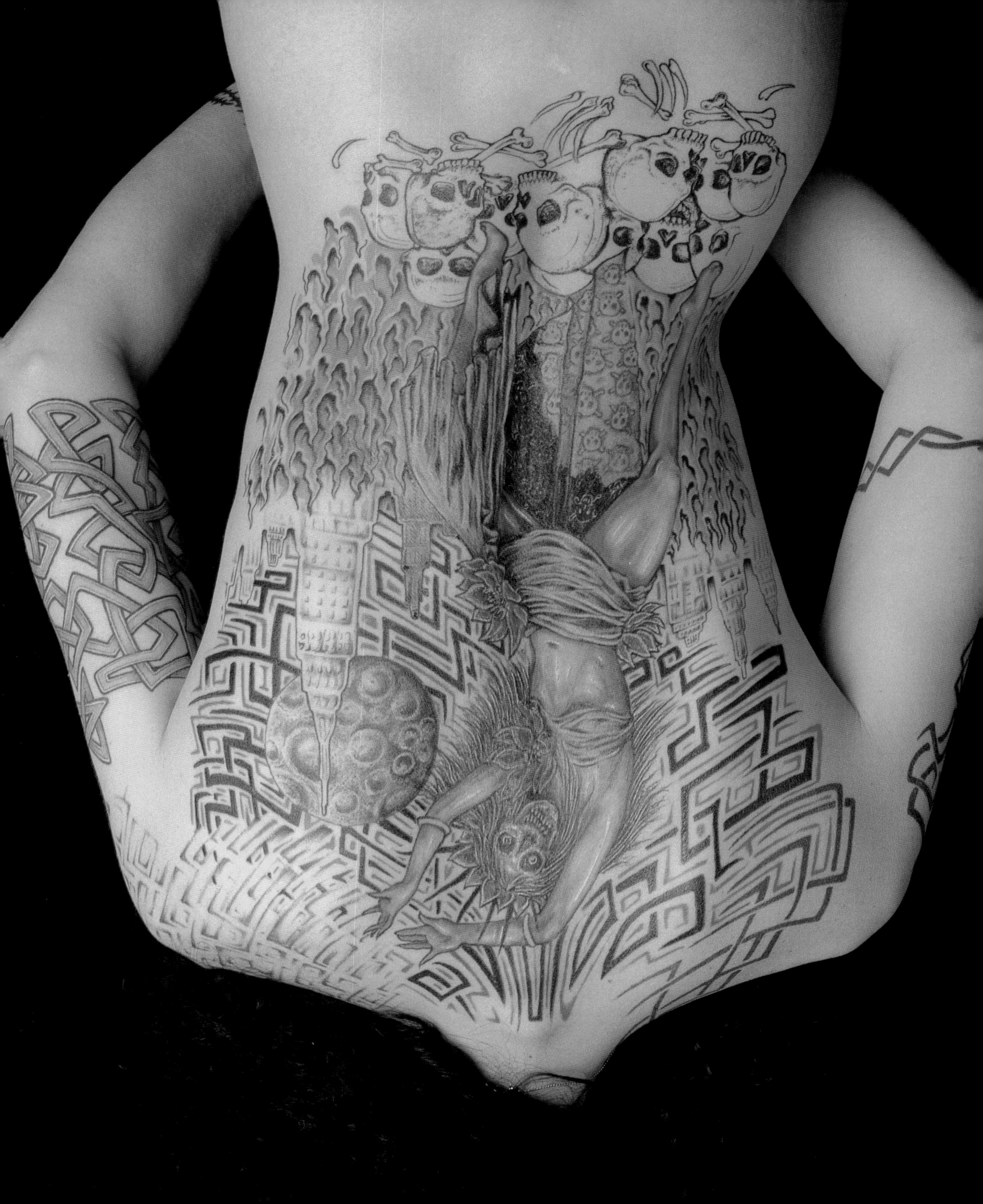

CATHY AND GILL LOS ANGELES, CA 1991

(CATHY'S TATTOOS) GILL MONTIE, (GILL'S TATTOOS) VARIOUS ARTISTS

Debbie and John youngstown, oh 1991

(Tattoos on Debbie) John Lenz, (Back, Chest and Sides of John) Debbie Lenz

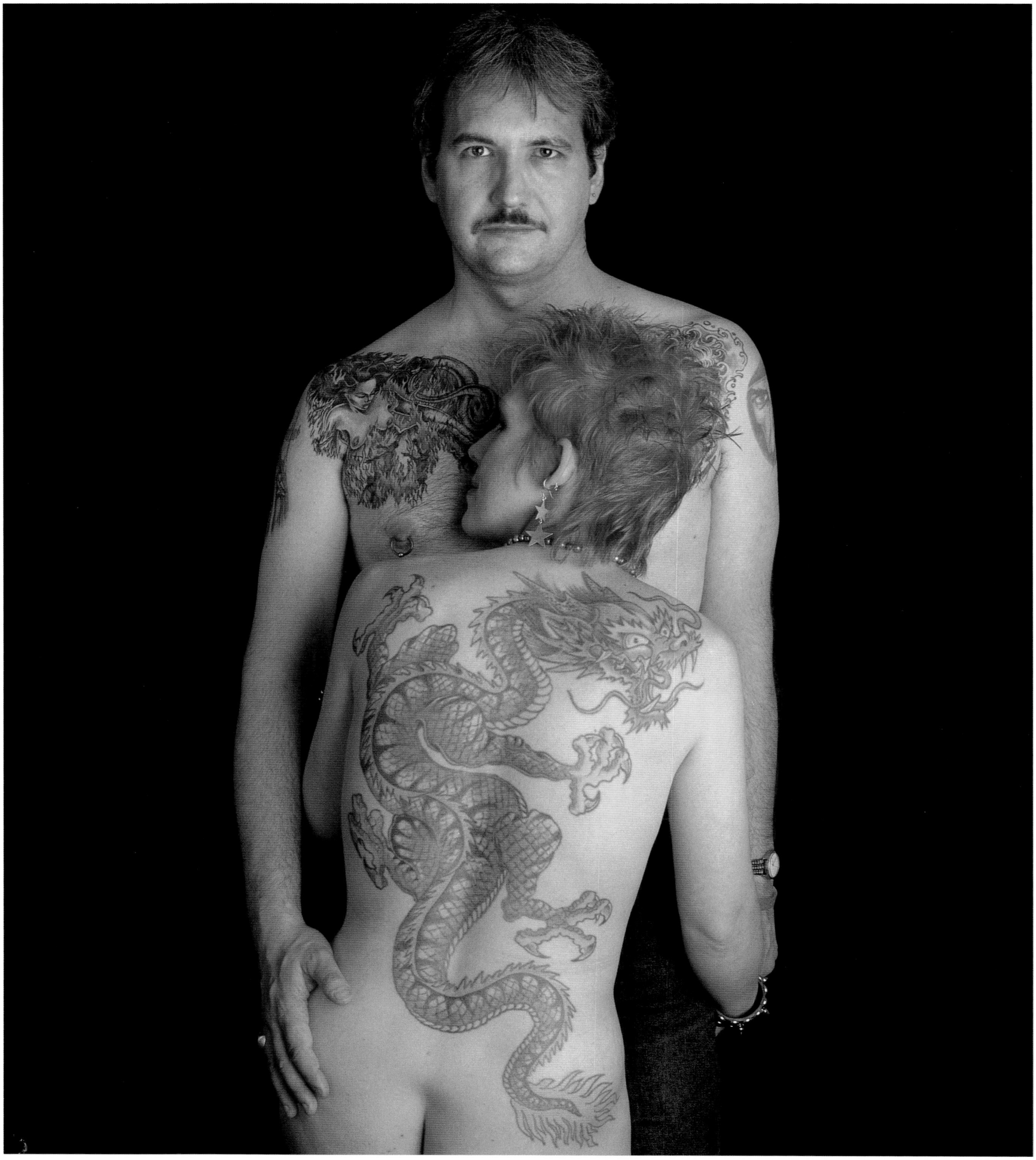

ADRIENNE AND ANTHONY FAIRFIELD, NJ 1990

(TATTOOS ON BOTH) BOB ROBERTS

(above and at right) Kay Portland, CT 1992

(Back, Sides and Chest) Bill Loika, (Belly and Thigh) Juli Moon, (Right Side Waist) Berni Luther

(AT LEFT) DEBORAH CONVERSE, TX 1991

FALLEN ANGEL

(ABOVE) MICK GLEN BURNIE, MD 1991

TOM BEASLEY, D.E. HARDY AND OTHERS

LENORE NEW YORK, NY 1992

GUY AITCHISON

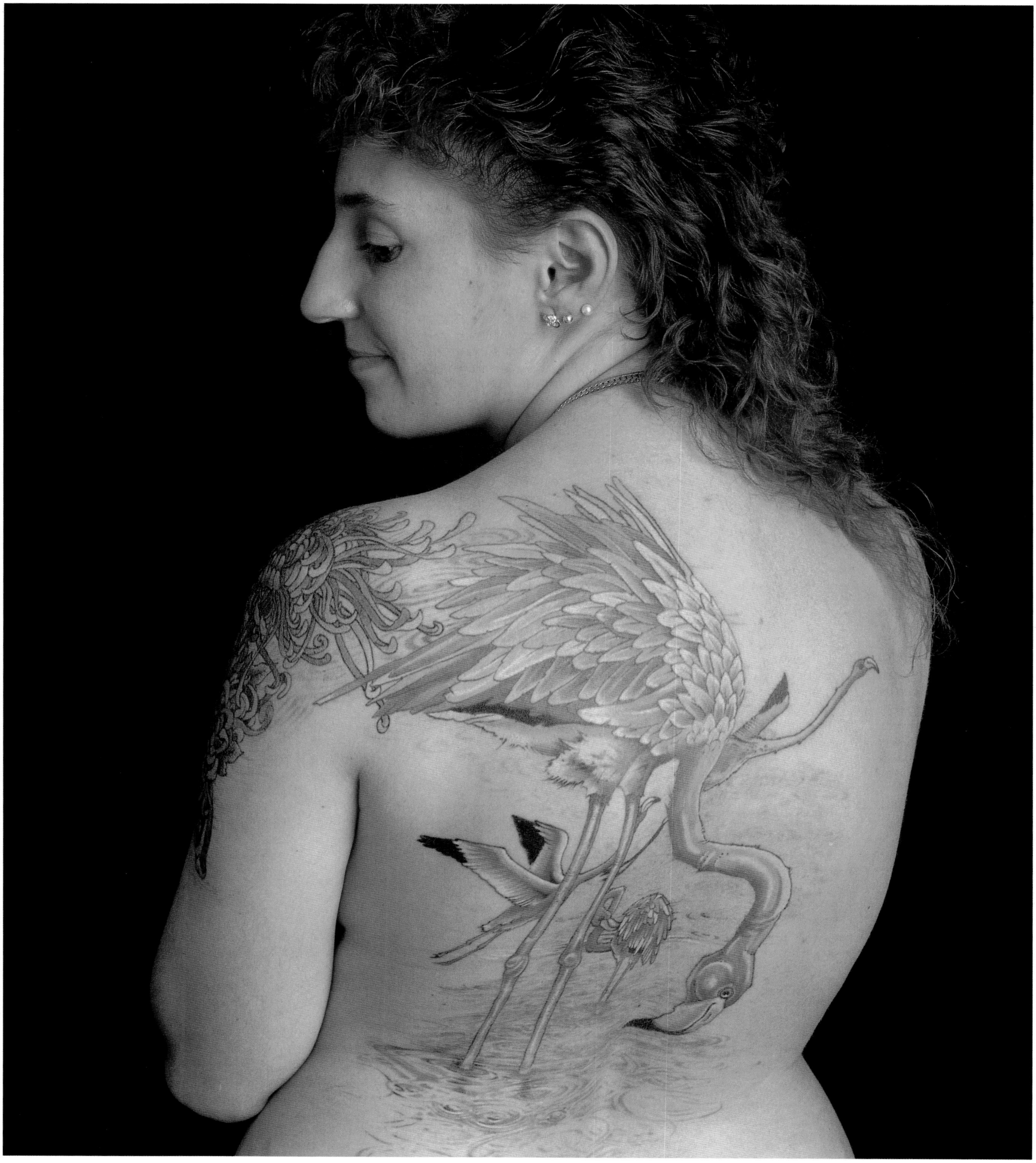

MICHELLE HALEDON, NJ 1988

SHOTSIE GORMAN

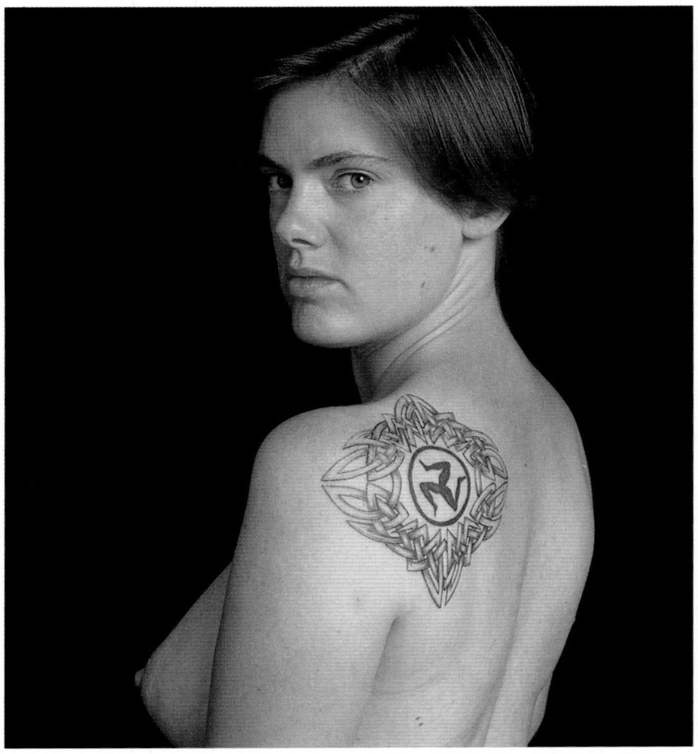

HEATHER COSTA MESA, CA 1991

JACK

JOAN CHICAGO, IL 1991

MARSHALL

DEBBIE CHICAGO, IL 1991

GUY AITCHISON

LYNN TUCSON, AZ 1991

KEELY TACKETT

SANDY woodstock, ny 1991

PAT SINATRA

(at left) MICHELLE CLAREMONT, CA 1991

KARI BARBA

(above) AHNA VENICE, CA 1991

FIP BUCHANAN

Jennifer and Joe Rural Hall, NC 1990

(Jennifer's Tattoos) Christy Smith, (Joe's Head) Bob Montagna, (Joe's Snake) Snake, (Joe's Other Tattoos) Christy Smith

(ABOVE) BROOKE SAN FRANCISCO, CA 1991

(LEFT FOREARM) TIMOTHY HOYER, (ALL OTHER TATTOOS) MARCUS

LINDSAY TRUMBULL, CT 1990

DANNY WILLIAMS, (NECK) BERNI LUTHER

DAWN LONG ISLAND CITY, NY 1990

(RIGHT ARMBAND) MIKE MCCABE

DAWN LONG ISLAND CITY, NY 1990

(RIGHT ARMBAND) MIKE MCCABE, (LEFT ARM) MARK MAHONEY

(ABOVE) MELISSA MILWAUKEE, WI 1991

GUY AITCHISON

(AT RIGHT) BARBARA BOONTON, NJ 1992

PAUL BOOTH

FRANCES NEW YORK, NY 1990

JAY GRELL

MARTHA NEW YORK, NY 1990

(WRIST) JONATHAN SHAW, (ROSE AND TRIBAL) BERNI LUTHER

MELISSA RICHMOND, VA 1990

JEFF EDEN

DEIRDRE WASHINGTON, DC 1989

TONY BROWNING, JAMES MARLOWE

CYNTHIA ARLINGTON, VA 1988

UNKNOWN

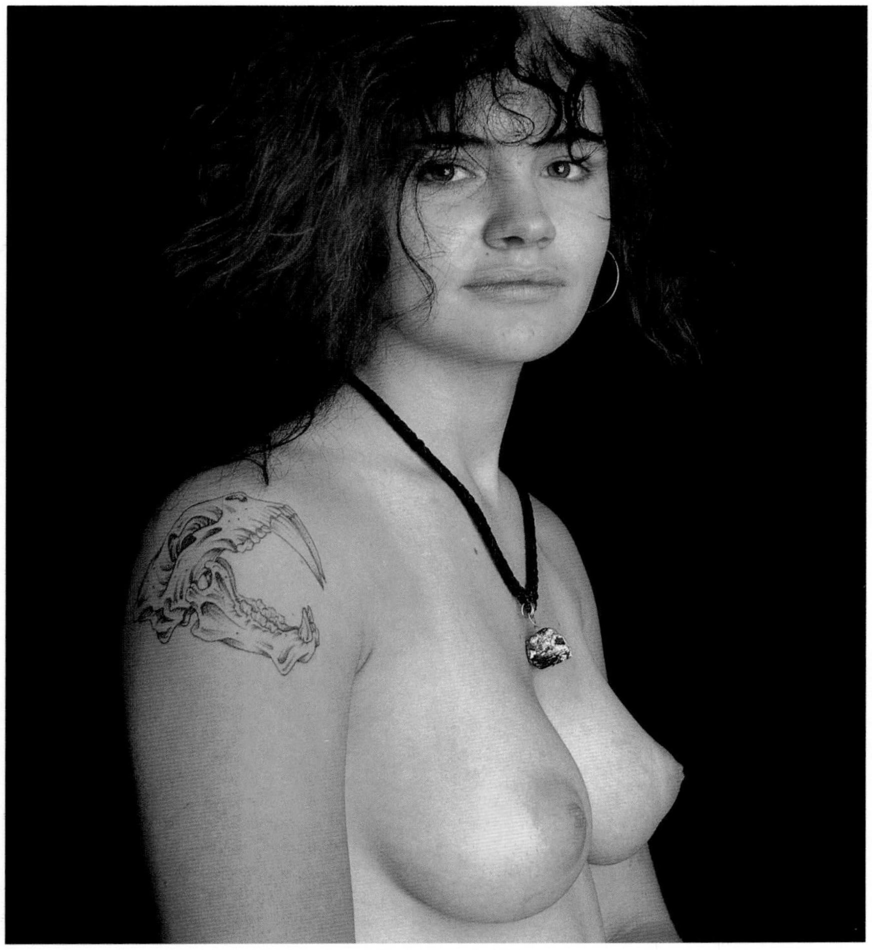

(ABOVE) LARA RICHMOND, VA 1990

JEFF EDEN

(AT RIGHT) LARA RICHMOND, VA 1991

CRAZY ACE, JASON HOBIE, RUSTY NEEDLES, ANDY NEVILLE, JOHN SARGERSON, FALLEN ANGEL, CARL HESS AND JEFF EDEN

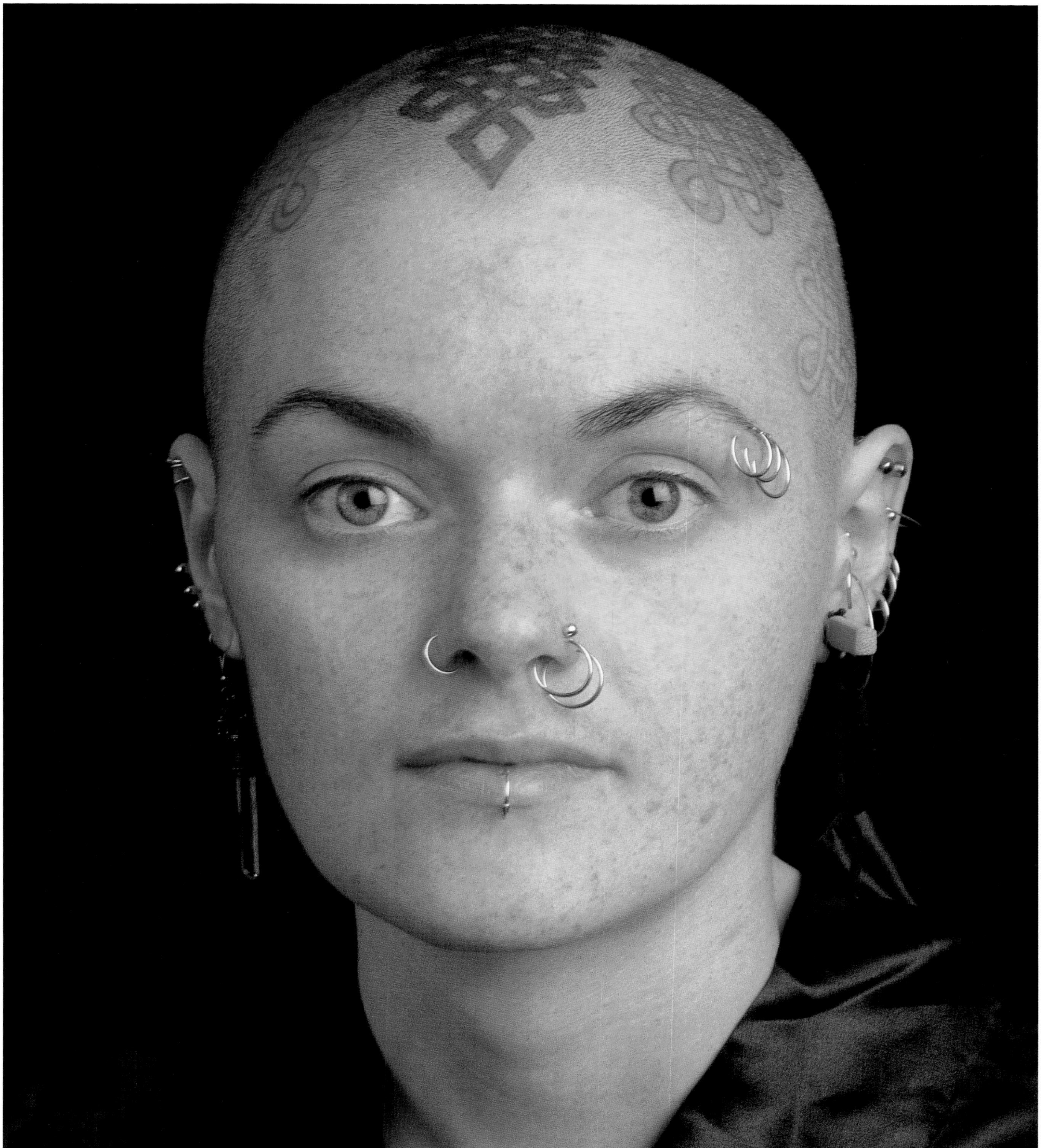

JENNIFER ALEXANDRIA, VA 1990

BILL SALMON

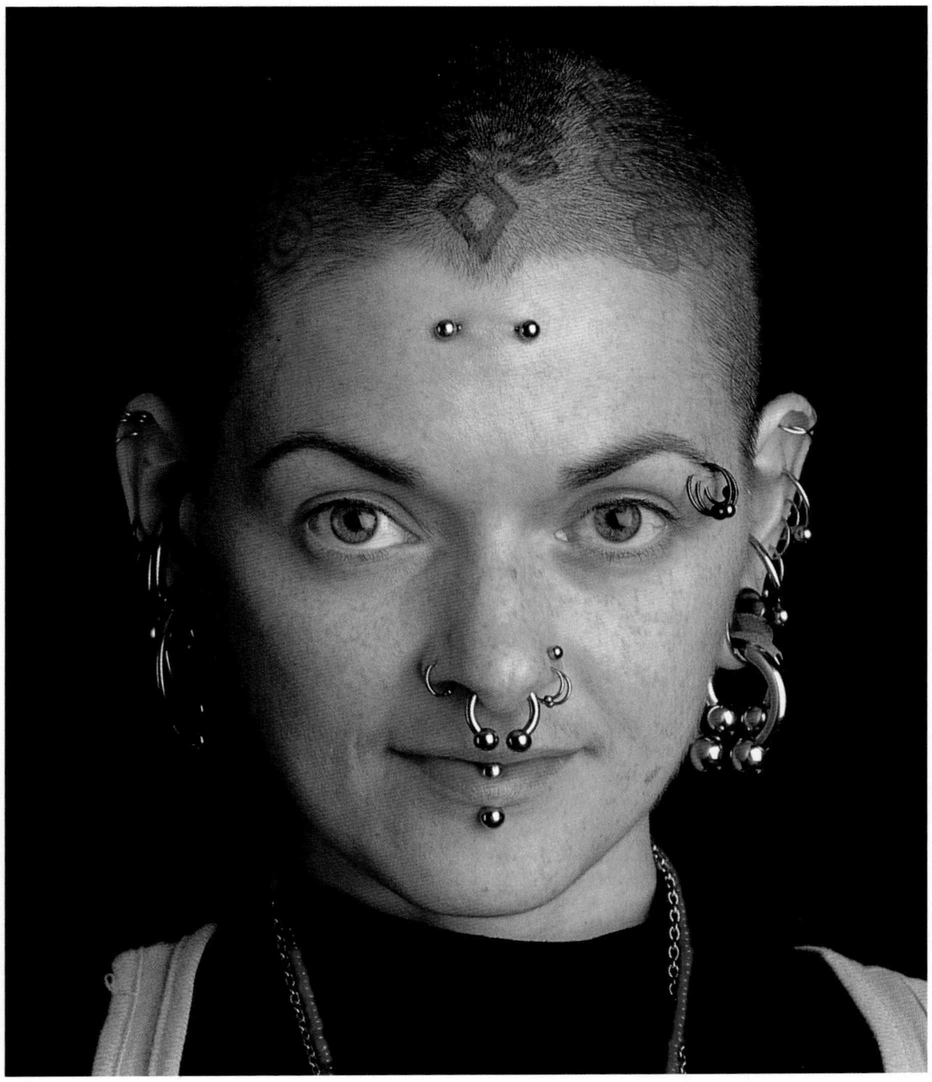

JENNIFER LOS ANGELES, CA 1991

BILL SALMON

(AT RIGHT) JENNIFER ALEXANDRIA, VA 1989

JULI MOON, ED HARDY AND TOM BEASLEY

(above) ELAYNE [ANGEL] LOS ANGELES, CA 1991

(WINGS) BOB ROBERTS, (HEART) PATTI PAVLIK

(at right) LINDA LOS ANGELES, CA 1991

(ARMS) LEO ZULUETA, (PELVIS) JILL JORDAN

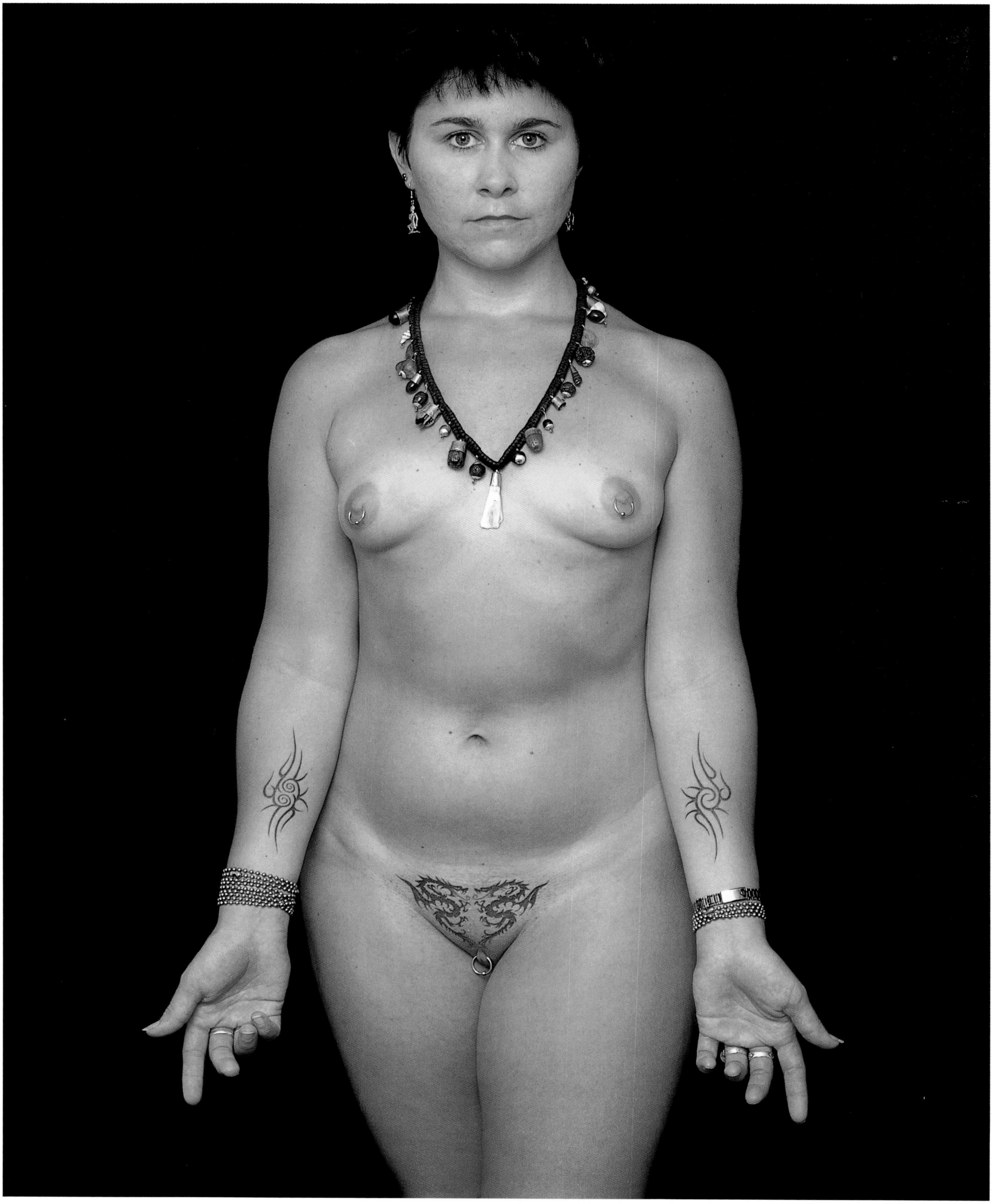

(above and at right) DRAGON LADY LOS ANGELES, CA 1991

SHOTSIE GORMAN

REBECCA DENVER, CO 1991

(CHERUB AND ANKLET) KELLY MILLER, (ALL OTHER TATTOOS) GREG KING

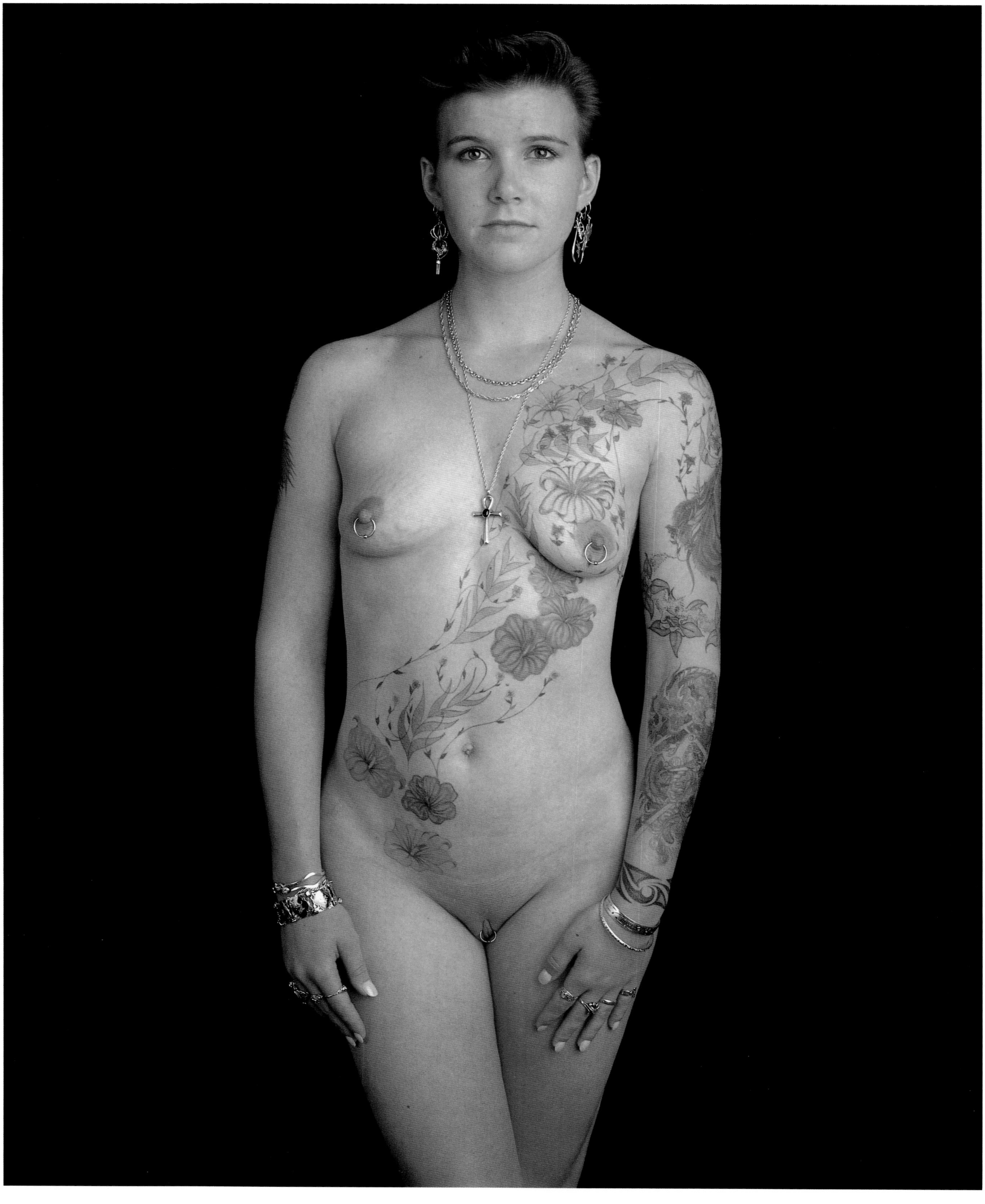

TINA SWISSVALE, PA 1991

CRAIG HELMICH

(TOP) KATHY GLOVERSVILLE, NY 1991

DREW SENESE

(BOTTOM) ANNA CHICAGO, IL 1991

DICK WARSOCKI

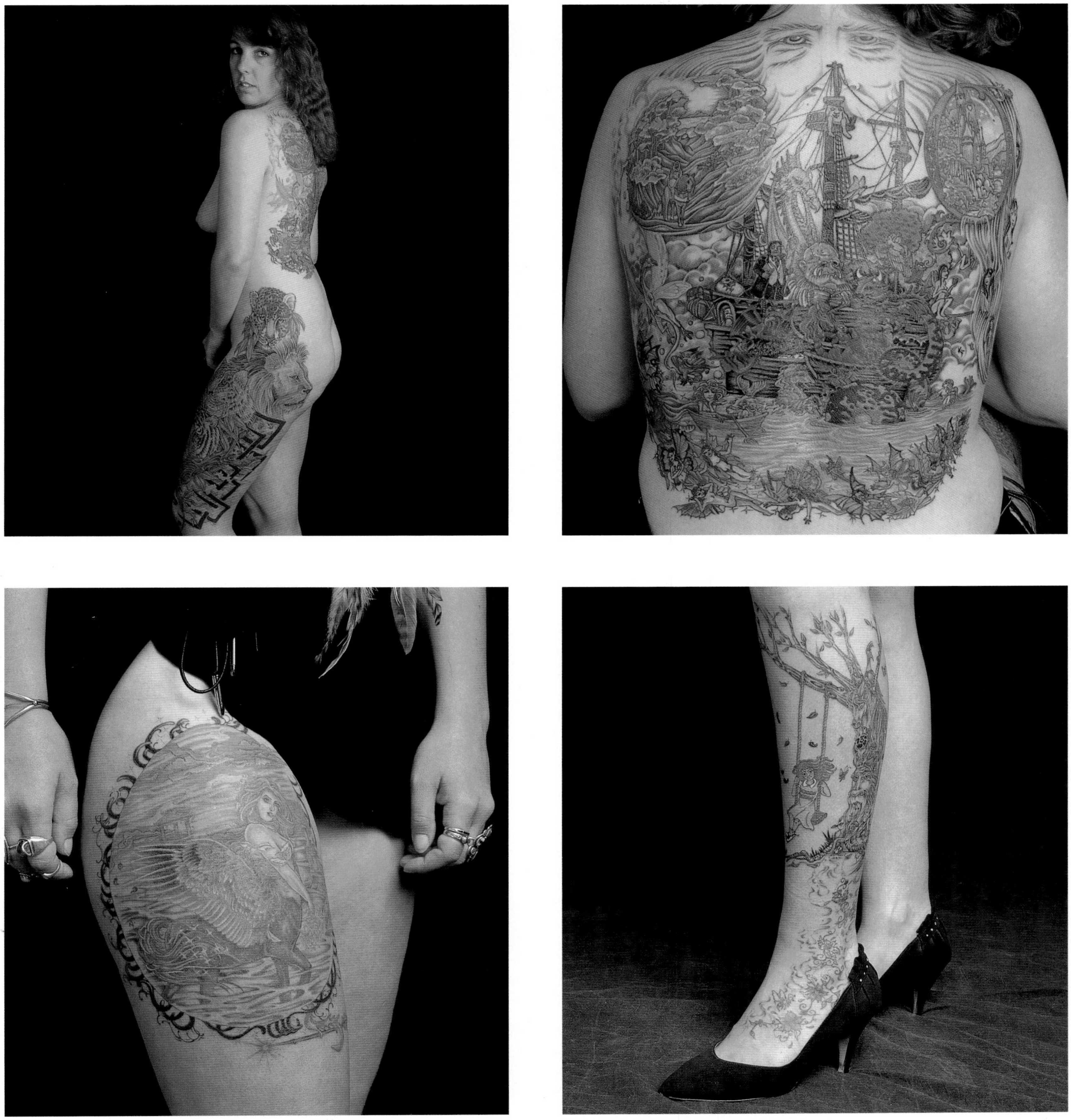

Cheryl Tucson, AZ 1991 and 1992

Keely Tackett

MICHELLE BILOXI, MS 1991

SAILOR MOSES, DICK WARSOCKI, AL BENNEDETTI, JULI MOON

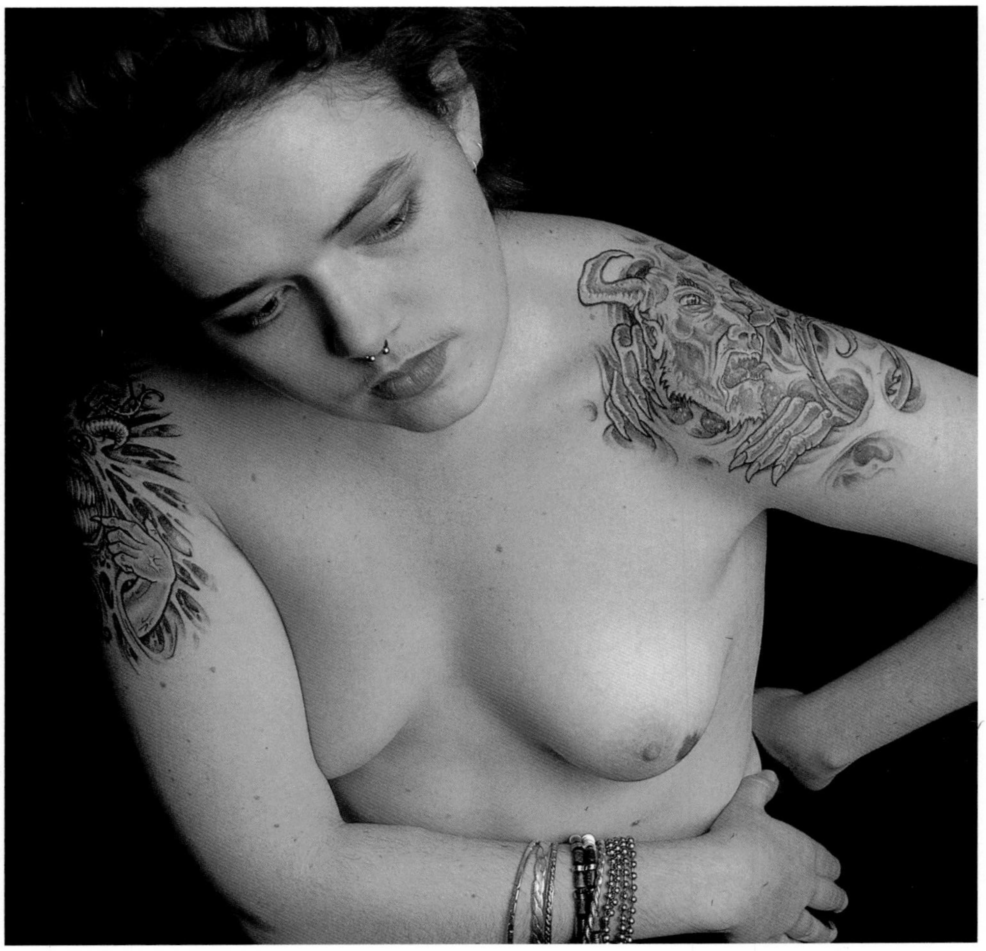

(TOP) CADY LONGMEADOW, MA 1992

GUY AITCHISON

(BOTTOM) SHELLY NEW YORK, NY 1992

ERIK LAWSON

JOLIE NORTHPORT, NY 1990

(BREAST) RICHARD STELL

LORI NEW YORK, NY 1992

(RIGHT HIP) JACK RUDY, (REAR END) EDDIE DEUTSCHE

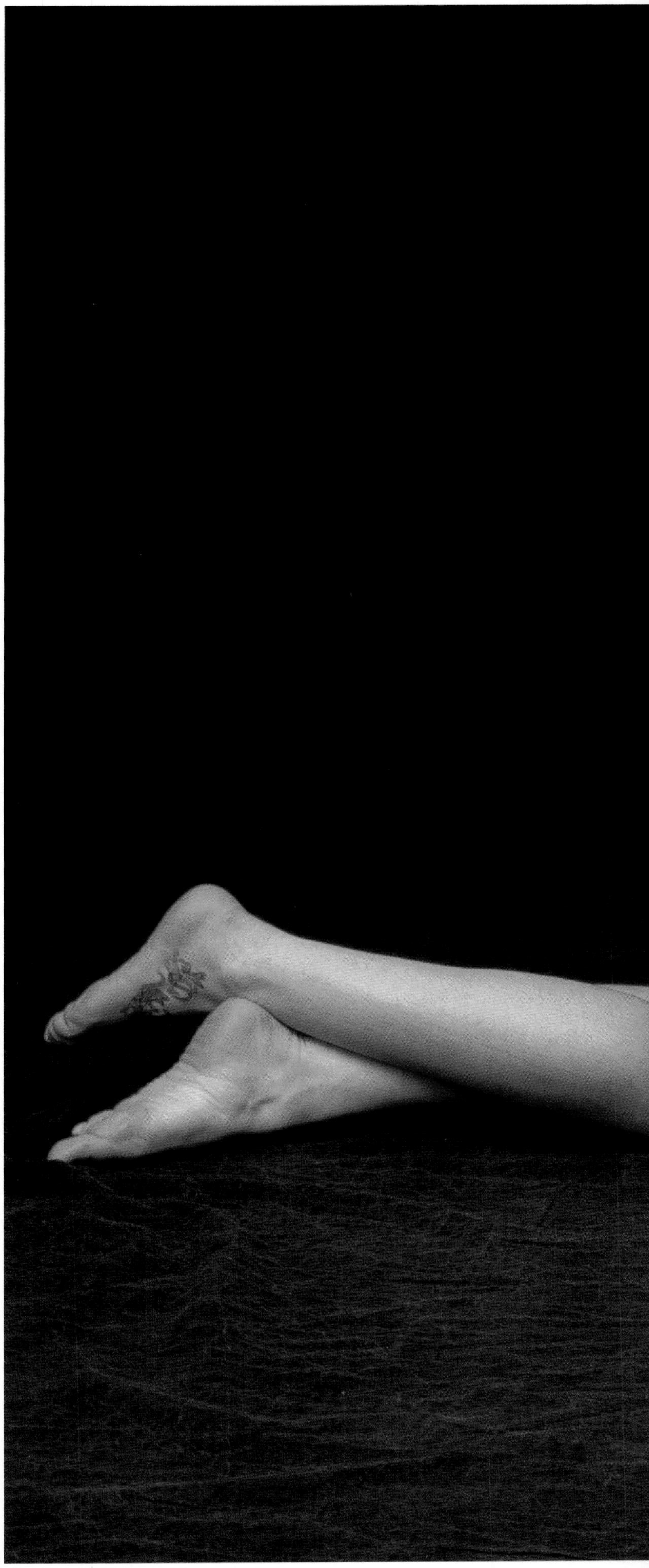

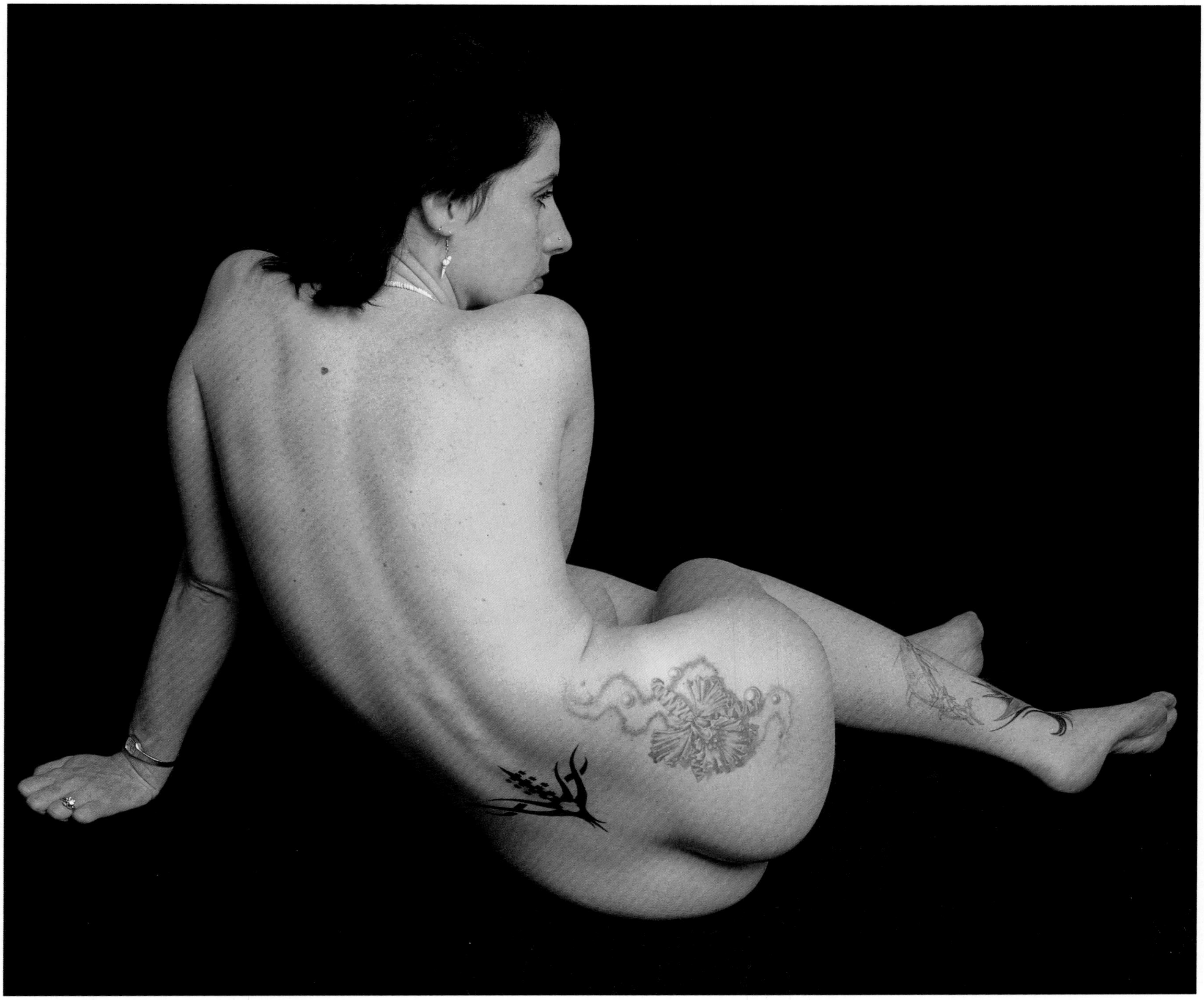

(above) PATTY SAN DIEGO, CA 1991

(ORCHID) FIP BUCHANAN, (DOLPHINS) JACK RUDY, (TRIBAL) LEO ZULUETA

(at right) JULI SEABROOK, NH 1989

TOM BEASLEY, MICKY SHARPZ, DANI FOWLER, ED HARDY

PAT CLIFTON, NJ 1989

SHOTSIE GORMAN

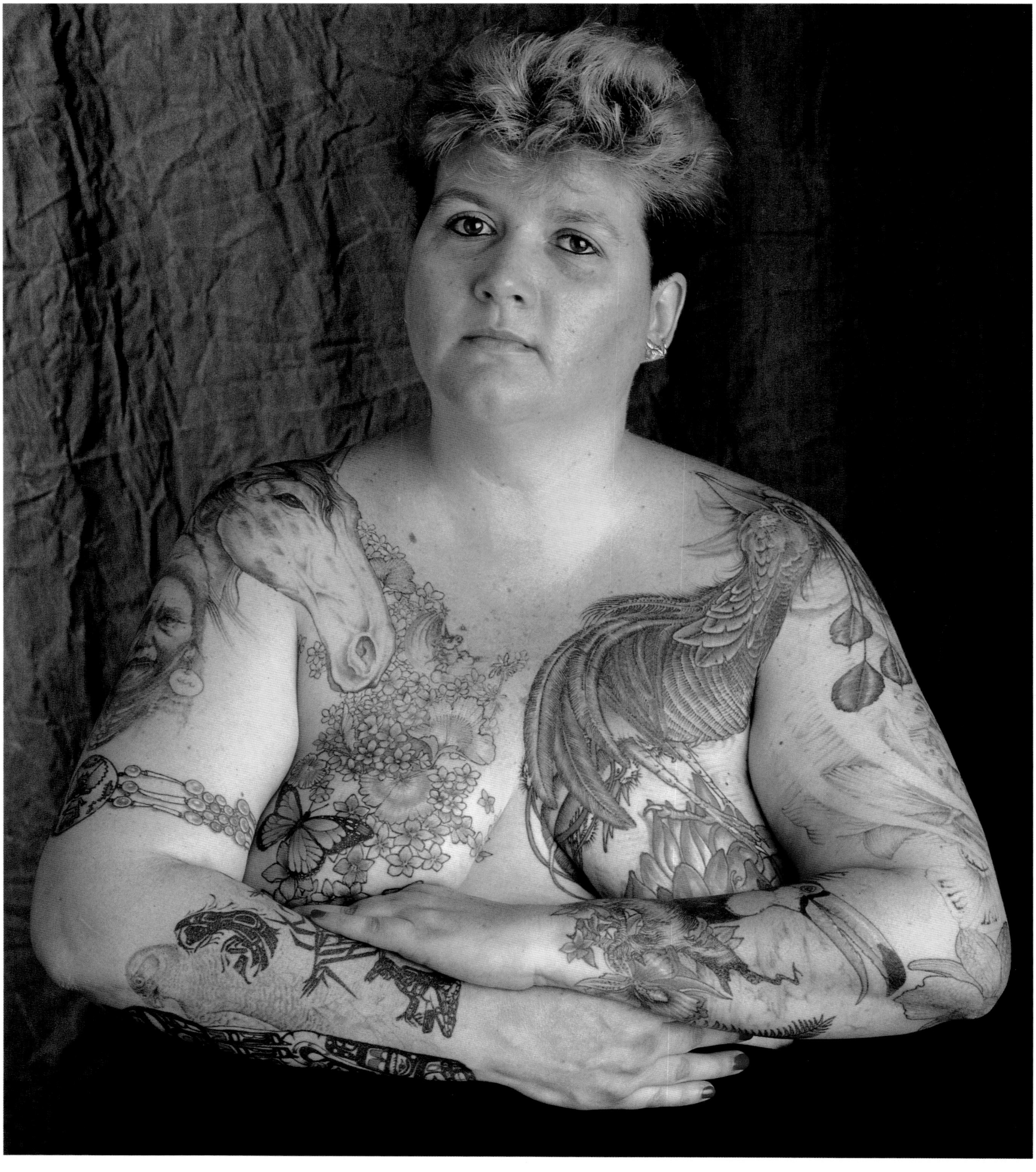

PAT clifton, nj 1989

Shotsie Gorman

DIANE HOPATCONG, NJ 1991

SPIDER WEBB

DIANE HOPATCONG, NJ 1991

(LEG) STEVE FERGUSON, (ABDOMEN) LYLE TUTTLE, (ARMBANDS) CARY BRIEF, (SHOULDER) DANIELA BRIEF

RUTH SHAMOKIN, PA 1992

JULI MOON

(ABOVE) TRACY JAMAICA PLAIN, MA 1992

(UPPER RIGHT ARM) EDDIE DEUTSCHE, (FOREARM) MARCUS, (ALL TRIBAL) AL BENEDETTI, (NECK) ANDY NEVILLE, (LEFT WRISTBAND) SUZANNE FAUSER

(AT RIGHT) DONNA NEW YORK, NY 1991

(LOWER ABDOMEN, BREASTS, CHEST) MIKE PERFETTO, (STOMACH) SEAN VASQUEZ, (LEFT ARM) SEAN VASQUEZ, MIKE MCCABE, (RIGHT ARM) SHOTSIE GORMAN, PAT SINATRA

(above) DEBRA ROCK ISLAND, IL 1992

DAVE HEYDN

(at right) JACCI NEW ORLEANS, LA 1990

(FROM BOTTOM TO TOP) DON NOLAN, HENRY GOLDFIELD, PAUL ROGERS, GREGG IRONS, BOB ROBERTS, SHOTSIE GORMAN, CLIFF RAVENS

(above, at right and overleaf) PEGGI FT. MYERS, FL 1990

(Left Foot) Bud Pierson, (Arch of Right Foot) Jim Watson, (Left Ankle) Marco Pisa, (Eyelids) Winona martin, (Right Arm and Left Arm) Gill Montie, (Right Thigh, Right Calf, Both Sides of Torso) Don Nolan

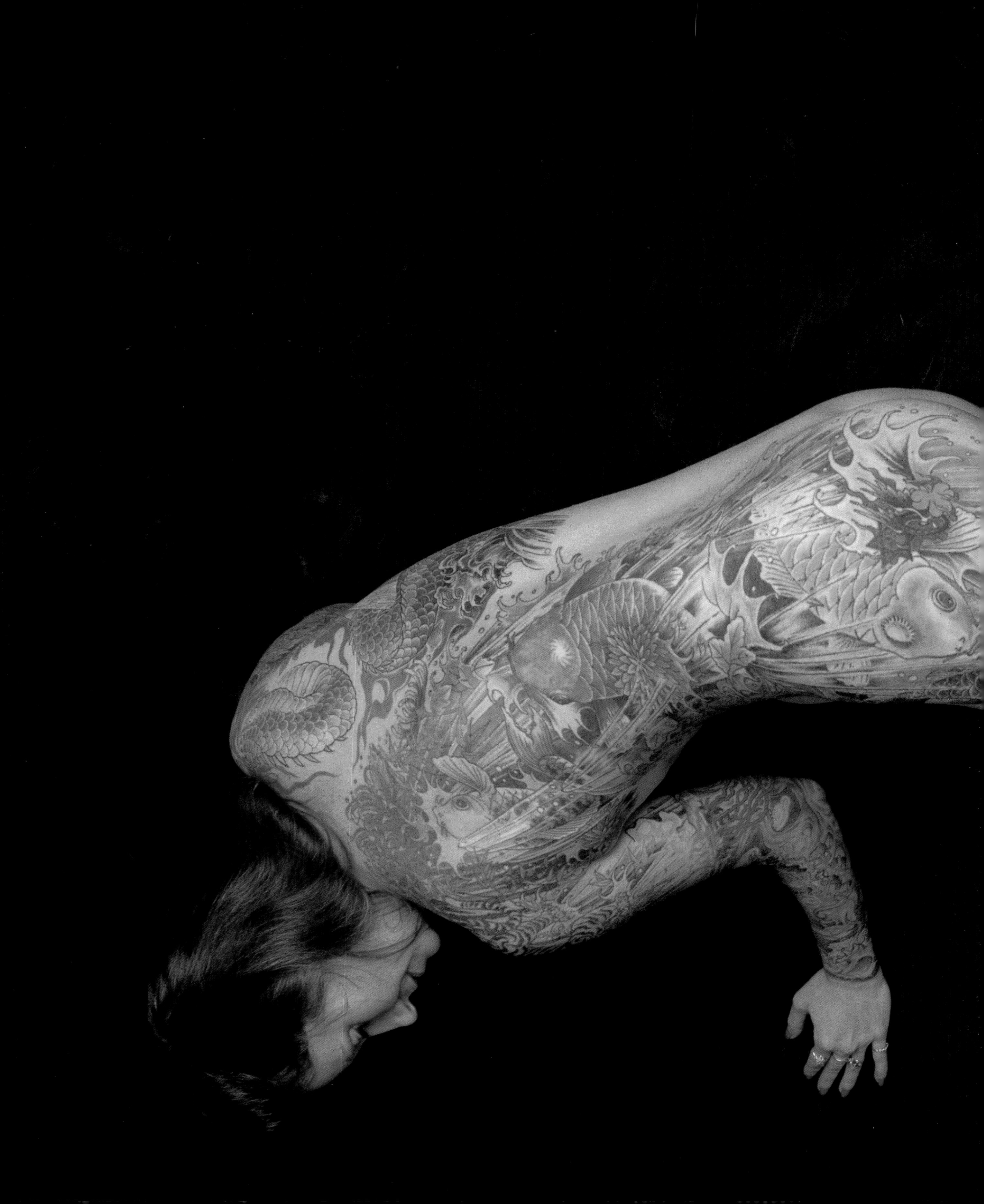

(at left) CAROLYN WAYNESBORO, PA 1992

T.L. CALHOUN, WITH THANKS TO TONEY, FINGERS, MOUSE AND BOB

(above) TAMMY FT. COLLINS, CO 1990

GREG SKIBO

SUNSHINE CORONA, CA 1991

(ARM ROSE) LIL DAVE SPELLMAN, (LEG FLORAL) RICK SPELLMAN, (HIBISCUS) GINA DWYER

JUDY EAST HARTFORD, CT 1991

(RIGHT LEG PEACOCK AND FLOWER) INKER [STEVE GABRIEL], (LEFT LEG TIGER) TOM BEASLEY, (LEFT LEG GARTER) INKER, (LEFT LEG KITTY) JACK RUDY, (LEFT HIP KITTY) DANA BRUNSON, (LEFT ARM) JACK RUDY, INKER, (RIGHT ARM LADYBUGS) INKER

GINA TUCSON, AZ 1989

DENNIS DWYER

GINA TUCSON, AZ 1991

DENNIS DWYER

NANCY PITTSBURGH, PA 1991

NANCY CONTE

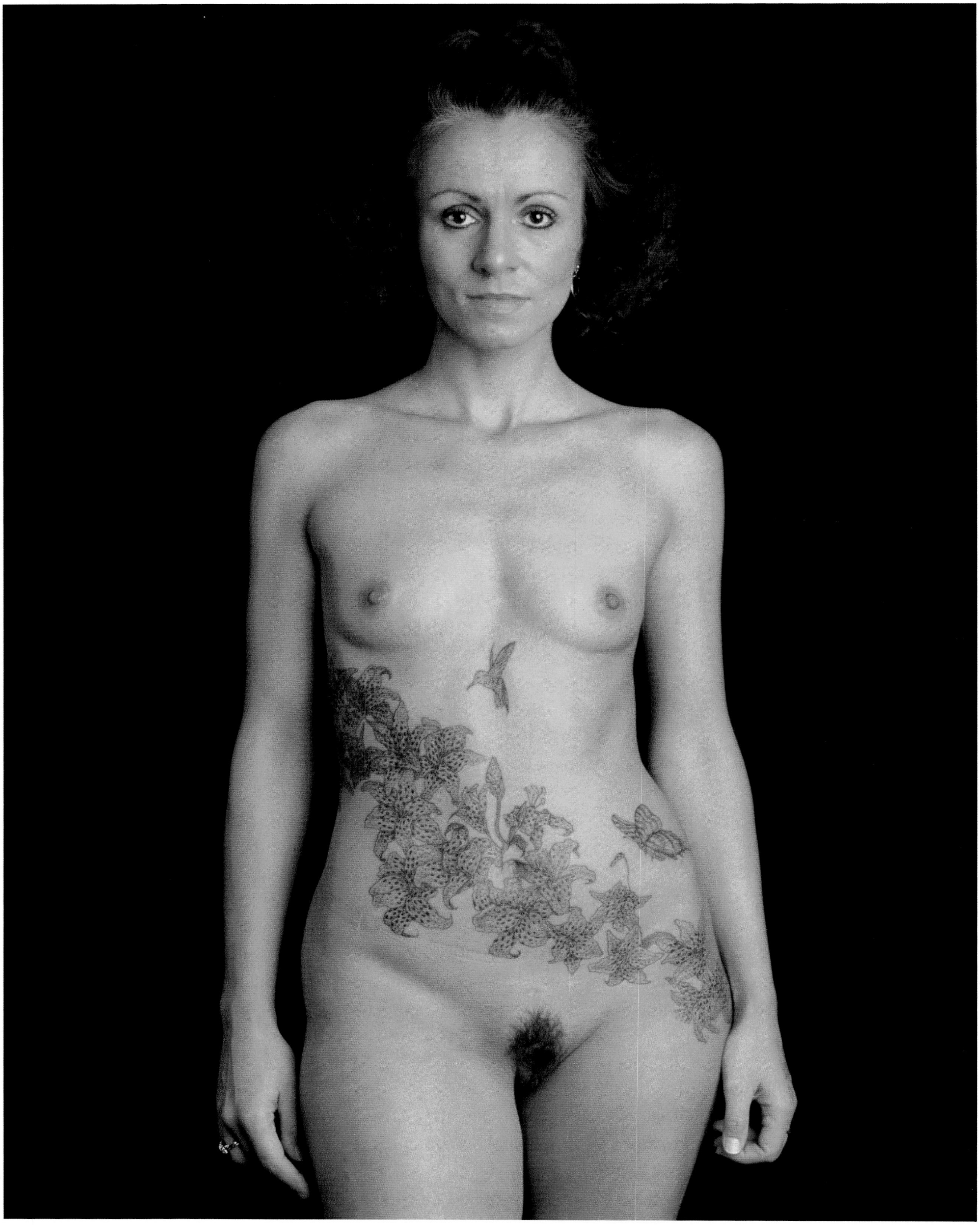

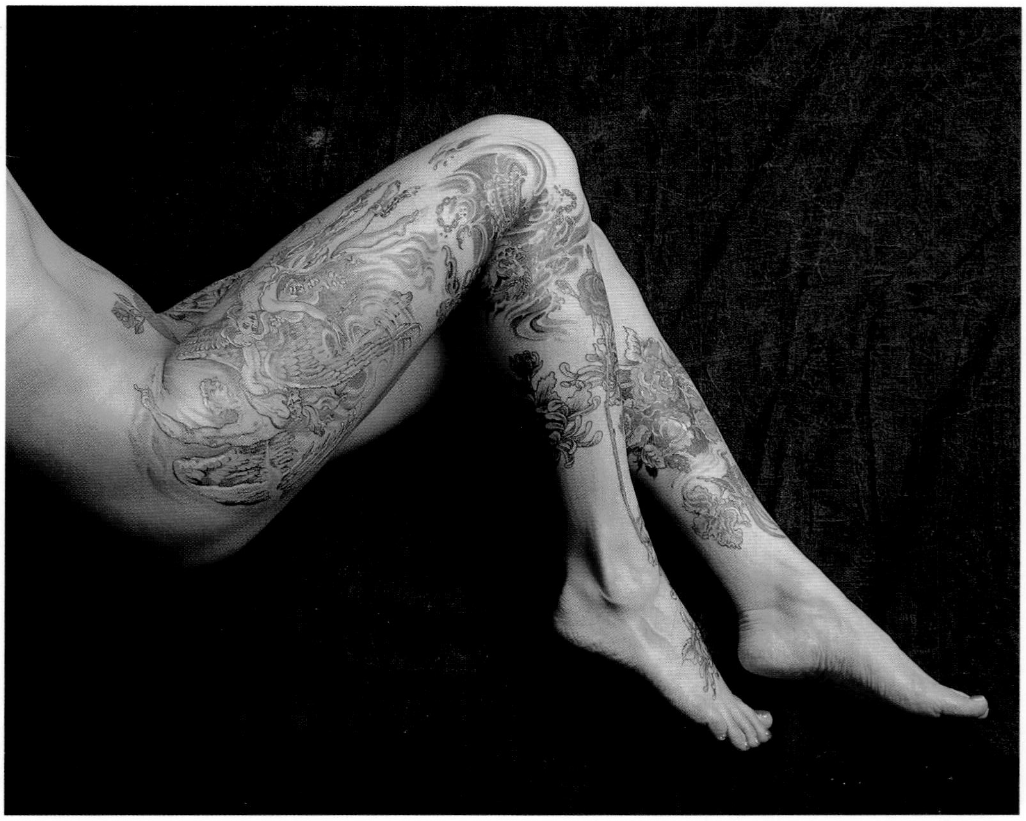

STAR LORAIN, OH 1991

MARTY HOLCOMB

Star Lorain, OH 1991

"Big Ed" Roberts

(ABOVE) ROBYNE ORLANDO, FL 1991

BUD PIERSON

(AT RIGHT) SHELLY CARSON CITY, NV 1991

KELLY MILLER

(ABOVE AND AT RIGHT) JEZO NEW YORK, NY 1991

(LEFT SHOULDER) DARREN ROSA, (RIGHT ARM) TODD VARGAS

(OVERLEAF) TERRI ROSEVILLE, CA 1990

WILD BILL HILL

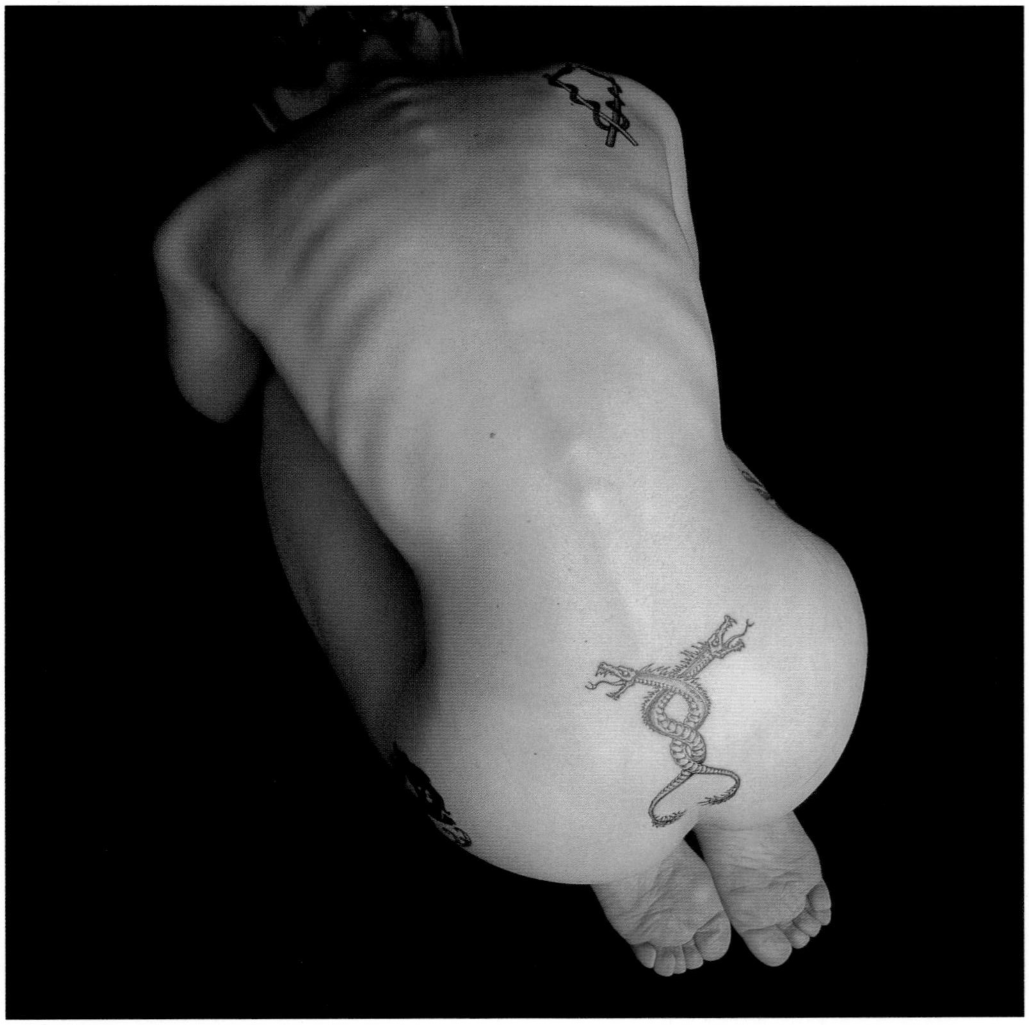

(ABOVE AND AT RIGHT) DEBARAH ELKRIDGE, MD 1990

(RIGHT SHOULDER) MARSHALL BACHELDER, (BOTTOM BACK) GUY AITCHISON, (RIGHT THIGH) TUX, (ABDOMEN) ALEX

DANIELA AUSTRIA 1990 AND 1991

(LEFT ARM) BERNI LUTHER, (RIGHT ARM) CHRIS MASON, CARY BRIEF

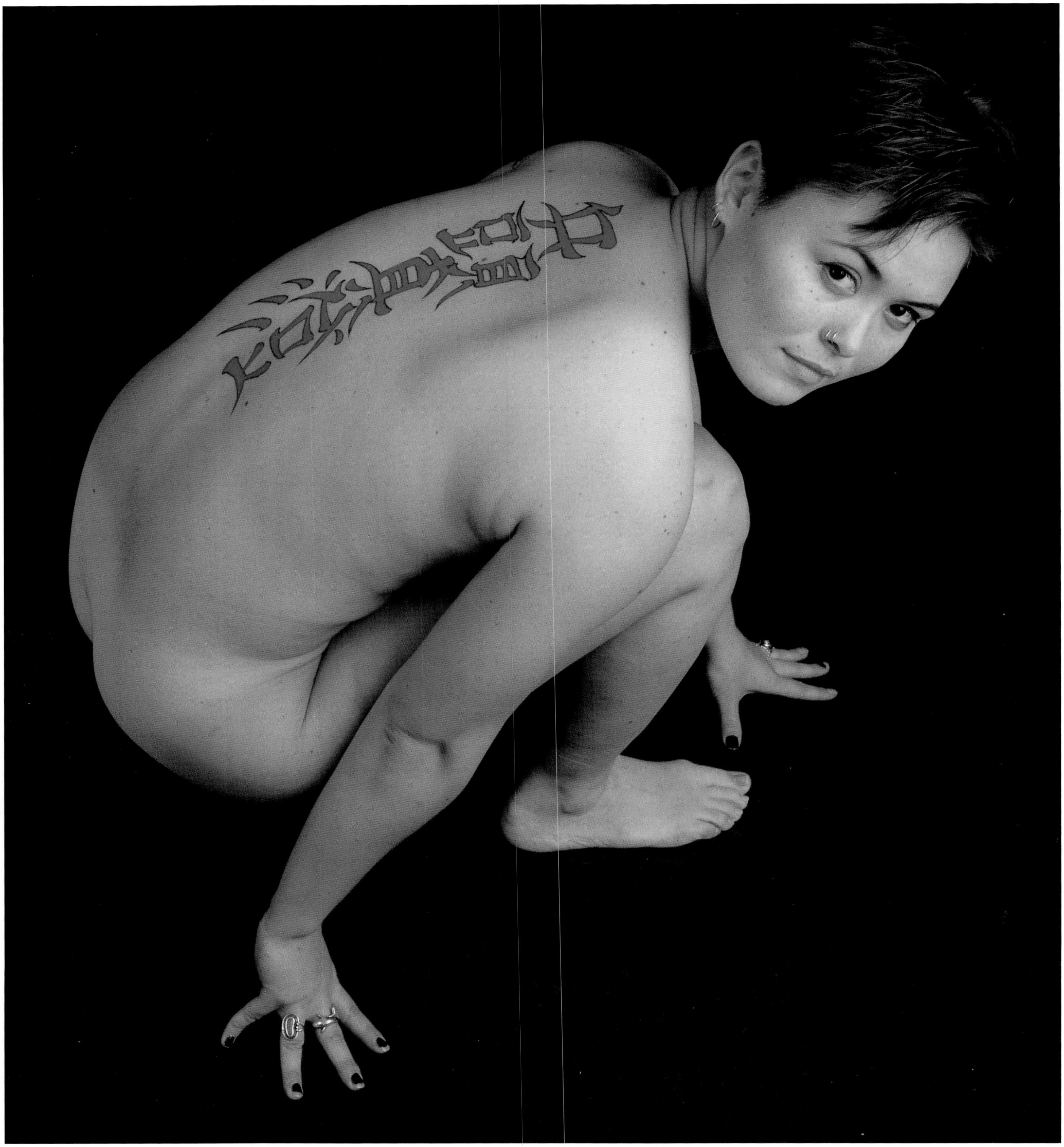

MASUMI RICHMOND, VA 1991

JEFF EDEN

(above and at right) WANDA PEORIA, IL 1991

(Back and Left Arm) Guy Aitchison, (Right Arm) Hawk

COLORADO24/7
CONNECTICUT24/7
DELAWARE24/7
FLORIDA24/7
GEORGIA24/7
KANSAS24/7
KENTUCKY24/7
LOUISIANA24/7
MAINE24/7
MARYLAND24/7
MONTANA24/7
NEBRASKA24/7
NEVADA24/7
NEW JERSEY24/7
NEW HAMPSHIRE24/7
OKLAHOMA24/7
OREGON24/7
PENNSYLVANIA24/7
RHODE ISLAND24/7
SOUTH CAROLINA24/7
VIRGINIA24/7
WASHINGTON24/7
WEST VIRGINIA24/7
WISCONSIN24/7
WYOMING24/7
Amazing Photographs of An Extraordinary State

DETROIT
This pink Caddy, unlike Aretha's, doesn't ride on the "Freeway of Love." It's a come-on for the Classic Car Wash Café—a hand car wash by day and music venue by night—on Detroit's near east side.
Photo by Mairin Chapman

Michigan 24/7 is the sequel to *The New York Times* bestseller *America 24/7* shot by tens of thousands of digital photographers across America over the course of a single week. We would like to thank the following sponsors, the wonderful people of Michigan, and the talented photojournalists who made this book possible.

Adobe

OLYMPUS

LEXAR Media

snapfish

jetBlue AIRWAYS

WEBWARE

Google

DIGITAL POND

ebay

DK

LONDON, NEW YORK, MUNICH, MELBOURNE, and DELHI

Created by Rick Smolan and David Elliot Cohen

24/7 Media, LLC
PO Box 1189
Sausalito, CA 94966-1189
www.america24-7.com

First Edition, 2004
04 05 06 07 08 10 9 8 7 6 5 4 3 2 1

Published in the United States by
DK Publishing, Inc.
375 Hudson Street
New York, NY 10014

Cataloging-in-Publication data is
available from the Library of Congress
ISBN 0-7566-0062-6

Printed in the UK by Butler & Tanner Limited

First printing, October 2004

FRANKFORT
Predawn patrol: Ultralight flyer and teacher Pat Totten banks over Point Betsie in his "motorcycle in the sky." On Lake Michigan just south of Sleeping Bear Dunes, the lighthouse at Point Betsie is one of 116 in Michigan, the most of any state.
Photo by J. Carl Ganter, MediaVia

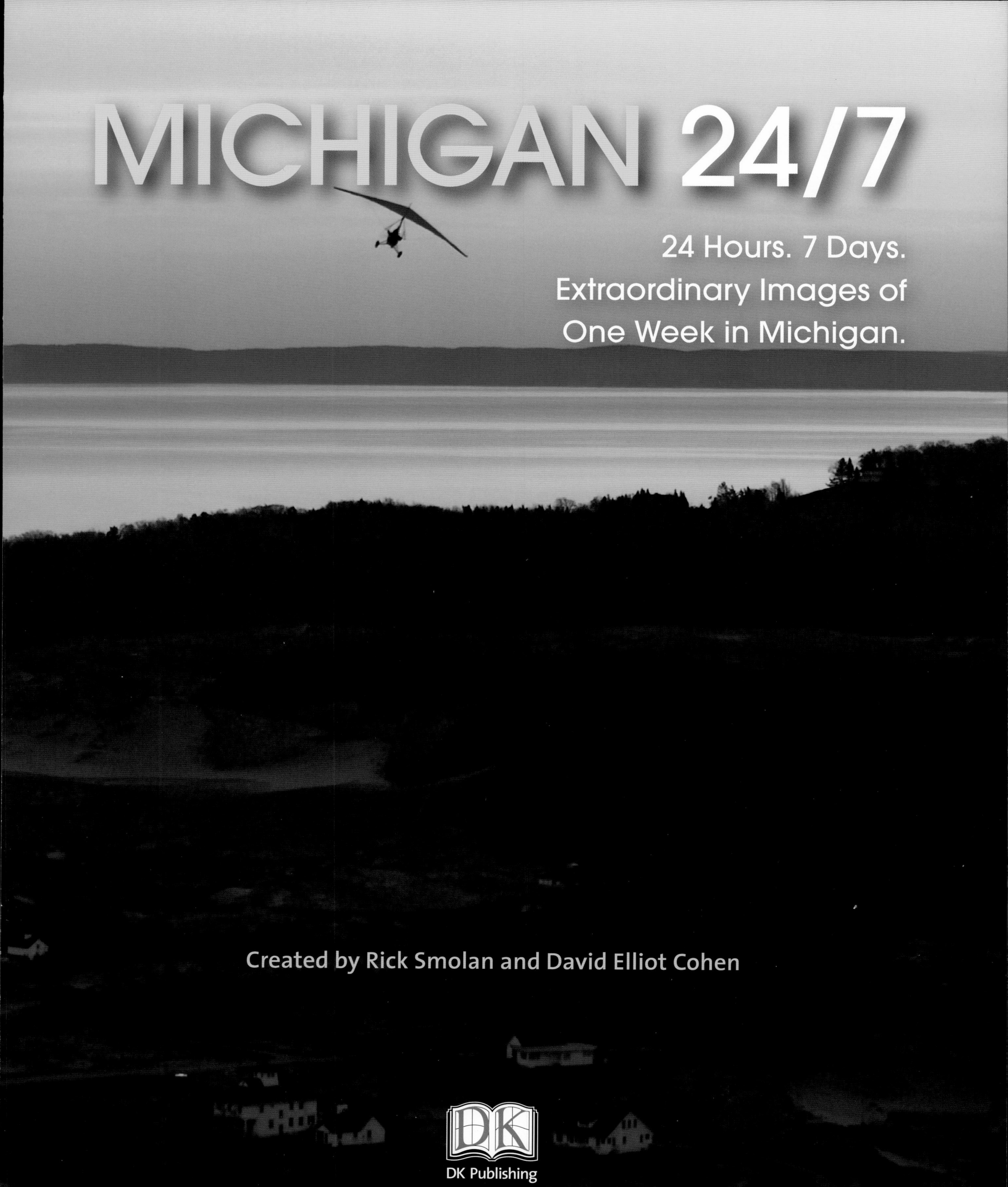

MICHIGAN 24/7

24 Hours. 7 Days.
Extraordinary Images of
One Week in Michigan.

Created by Rick Smolan and David Elliot Cohen

DK Publishing

About the America 24/7 Project

A hundred years hence, historians may pose questions such as: What was America like at the beginning of the third millennium? How did life change after 9/11 and the ensuing war on terrorism? How was America affected by its corporate scandals and the high-tech boom and bust? Could Americans still express themselves freely?

To address these questions, we created *America 24/7*, the largest collaborative photography event in history. We invited Americans to tell their stories with digital pictures. We asked them to shoot a visual memoir of their lives, families, and communities.

During one week in May 2003, more than 25,000 professionals and amateurs shot more than a million pictures. These images, sent to us via the Internet, compose a panoramic yet highly intimate view of Americans in celebration and sadness; in action and contemplation; at work, home, and school. The best of these photographs, more than 6,000, are collected in 51 volumes that make up the *America 24/7* series: the landmark national volume *America 24/7*, published to critical acclaim in 2003, and the 50 state books published in 2004.

Our decision to make *America 24/7* an all-digital project was prompted by the fact that in 2003 digital camera sales overtook film camera sales. This technological evolution allowed us to extend the project to a huge pool of photographers. We were thrilled by the response to our challenge and moved by the insight offered into American life. Sometimes, the amateurs outshot the pros—even the Pulitzer Prize winners.

The exuberant democracy of images visible throughout these books is a revelation. The message that emerges is that now, more than ever, America is a supersized idea. A dreamspace, where individuals and families from around the world are free to govern themselves, worship, read, and speak as they wish. Within its wide margins, the polyglot American nation manages to encompass an inexplicably complex yet workable whole. The pictures in this book are dedicated to that idea.

—Rick Smolan and David Elliot Cohen

American nightlight: More than a quarter of a billion people trace a nation with incandescence in this composite satellite photograph.
Photo by Craig Mayhew & Robert Simmon, NASA Goddard Flight Center/Visions of Tomorrow

Handprint of America

By Susan Ager

I live at the tip of Michigan's little finger, proud that my state is shaped like a body part. We are the handprint of America, although some say we resemble an oven mitt. We point to where we live on our palms. Glance at any map—or look at the planet from space—and you'll spot us there, in the middle of the continent, nearly surrounded by water.

But whoa! We're a state with two parts, joined by the five-mile Mackinac Bridge that we pronounce "Mackinaw." The ornery residents of the Upper Peninsula, or U.P., call themselves Yoopers and refer to the rest of us as trolls: We live beneath the bridge.

We're descendents of miners and trappers, lumberjacks and Ojibway natives, runaway slaves and soybean farmers, auto barons and men who came from Poland and Kentucky to work on Henry Ford's assembly line for five bucks a day. Rosie the Riveter was born here.

Yeah, we're tough. We've got to be. We swim in Lake Superior. We grill steaks in the snow.

Fresh water defines us. Our map is speckled with lakes so small you can swim across, while our shores border four of the five Great Lakes, too big to see across.

That gives us big ideas.

Water may define us, but gasoline pumps through our veins. We gave birth to the auto industry and pay it strict homage. We drive everywhere. You won't find subways here or carpool lanes. We drive even when we should walk, making us one of the heaviest states. At donut shops, clerks say, "You only want one?"

INTERLOCHEN
At the tail end of northern Michigan's spring thaw, the oak is the first tree in the woods to leaf out. Then come the bigtooth aspen, quaking aspen, and white ash.
Photo by J. Carl Ganter, MediaVia

We drive to Canada for dinner. Most weekends we fall in line on I-75 to drive Up North to sand dunes, Petoskey stones, and lighthouses, to U-pick apples and cherries, to rented cabins, second homes, and more than a million boats Michiganders afford on union wages.

Michiganders? That's my choice but, oh my, some of us insist on Michiganians.

That we can't agree on what to call ourselves doesn't mean a thing. We can't agree on what "opening day" means either. Baseball? Trout season? The auto show? This is telling: On November 15, when deer season opens, many Up North schools close for the day.

Clearly, we respect our instincts.

We disagree but mostly peaceably. As you'll see in these pages, we're a thickening stew of histories and ethnicities. When you work in Detroit you're likely to share the photocopier with Chaldeans, Armenians, Nigerians, Germans, and Mexicans. Detroit's supersized mayor, Kwame Kilpatrick, is barely in his 30s, wears an earring, and is energizing a city many Americans think is dull and dying. We may wish for more from Detroit but don't diss it. It's ours and it feeds us: music and coney dogs, music and *paczki*.

We see the life. We feel the spirit. You can spot a Michigander anywhere. They're rolling their shoulders and singing along with "Baby Love," "My Girl," and "R.E.S.P.E.C.T."

We know the words. We know ourselves. What's not to respect?

SUSAN AGER *is an award-winning columnist for the* Detroit Free Press. *Apart from seven years in San Francisco, she has lived in Michigan all her life.*

MACKINAC ISLAND
An employee walks up the approach to Mackinac Island's Grand Hotel on a foggy spring morning. With motorized vehicles banned on the two-by-three-mile island, there's no gridlock—transportation is by horse and buggy, bicycle, or foot.
Photo by Bruce Edwards, The Flint Journal

GLEN ARBOR
Sleeping Bear Dunes National Lakeshore stretches 35 miles and covers more than 50,000 acres along the leeward side of Lake Michigan. A legacy of the Ice Age, the dunes developed after glaciers spread southward from Canada, depositing huge piles of rock and sand when they melted.
Photo by J. Carl Ganter, MediaVia

ESSEXVILLE
The *Great Lakes Trader* barge eases past Bay City's Lafayette Street drawbridge on the Saginaw River. Settlement money from state lawsuits filed against industrial polluters has helped pay for new parks, wildlife refuges, and agricultural land in this once heavily polluted corridor.
Photo by Kent Miller, The Bay City Times

OSCODA
Amid the maple and pine treetops of Lumberman's Monument, North Carolina tourist David Stebbing looks for pileated woodpeckers, hermit thrushes, and red-breasted nuthatches. Stebbing, who was on a spring birdwatching safari around the Great Lakes, reported sighting a Kirtland's warbler not far from the monument. The warbler is found only in Michigan's jack pine forests.
Photo by Kent Miller, The Bay City Times

WARREN
Margo Pennefather gets help blowing out candles from 5-year-old granddaughter Elena Mazurkiewicz. Pennefather isn't letting another birthday slow her down. In addition to teaching reading and computer skills at the General Motors Adult Learning Center, she coordinates the education program at her church and recently earned a Master Gardener certificate from Michigan State University.
Photo by Jeffrey Sauger, Reflex News

Hearth & Home

DETROIT
Debra Robinson, who says her two children are her best friends, relishes what she calls a "bonding mood" with daughter Paula Smiley in the family's west side home. They do a lot together, including perform. Paula, aka Miz Korona, is a rap artist, and sometimes brings her mom on stage for a duet.
Photo by Donna Terek, The Detroit News

EAST LANSING
Robby Olds, 11, says he was bored with just TV, so he started taking piano lessons from his church choir director in second grade. Although his schedule is now much busier—it includes weekly tennis lessons and playing clarinet in the school band—he plans to stick with his first love. His favorite composers are Bach and Mozart.
Photo by David Olds

GROSSE POINTE WOODS
Primp and circumstance: Mother-in-law-to-be Mary Friedmann (in yellow) and stylists at the Edwin Paul Salon fuss with Katie Kimble's veil in preparation for her wedding that afternoon. The 21-year-old bride married her high school sweetheart, Aaron Friedmann, six hours later at St. Peter's Catholic Church in Mount Clemens.
Photo by J. Kyle Keener, Detroit Free Press

DEARBORN
Groom Mohamad Zaarour (in gold vest) and bride Nadia Noureddine dance their wedding night away at the Bint Jebail Cultural Center. The Detroit metropolitan area, which includes Dearborn, is home to America's largest, most influential Arab-American population.
Photos by Sylwia Kapuscinski, Detroit Free Press

DEARBORN
Bride and groom are gone, but flower girl Layal Bachrouche, 5, remains. The Bint Jebail Cultural Center is named for a town in southern Lebanon and is a gathering place for the Detroit area's 44,000 Lebanese Americans. Many came in the 1950s and 1960s for jobs; others followed to escape the ravages of war.

NOVI
On a typical morning in the Boals household, it takes both parents to get the kids fed and off to daycare. Shannon Boals, an engineering supervisor in Ford's brake department, appreciates his employer's family-friendly policies. He has every other Friday off.
Photos by Bryan Mitchell

NOVI

Sandy Boals, a Ford transmission systems engineer, took a one-year leave when she had her youngest child. When she returned to work, the company gave her a flex-time schedule. She has two days a week at home with Logan, 2, and baby Lindsay.

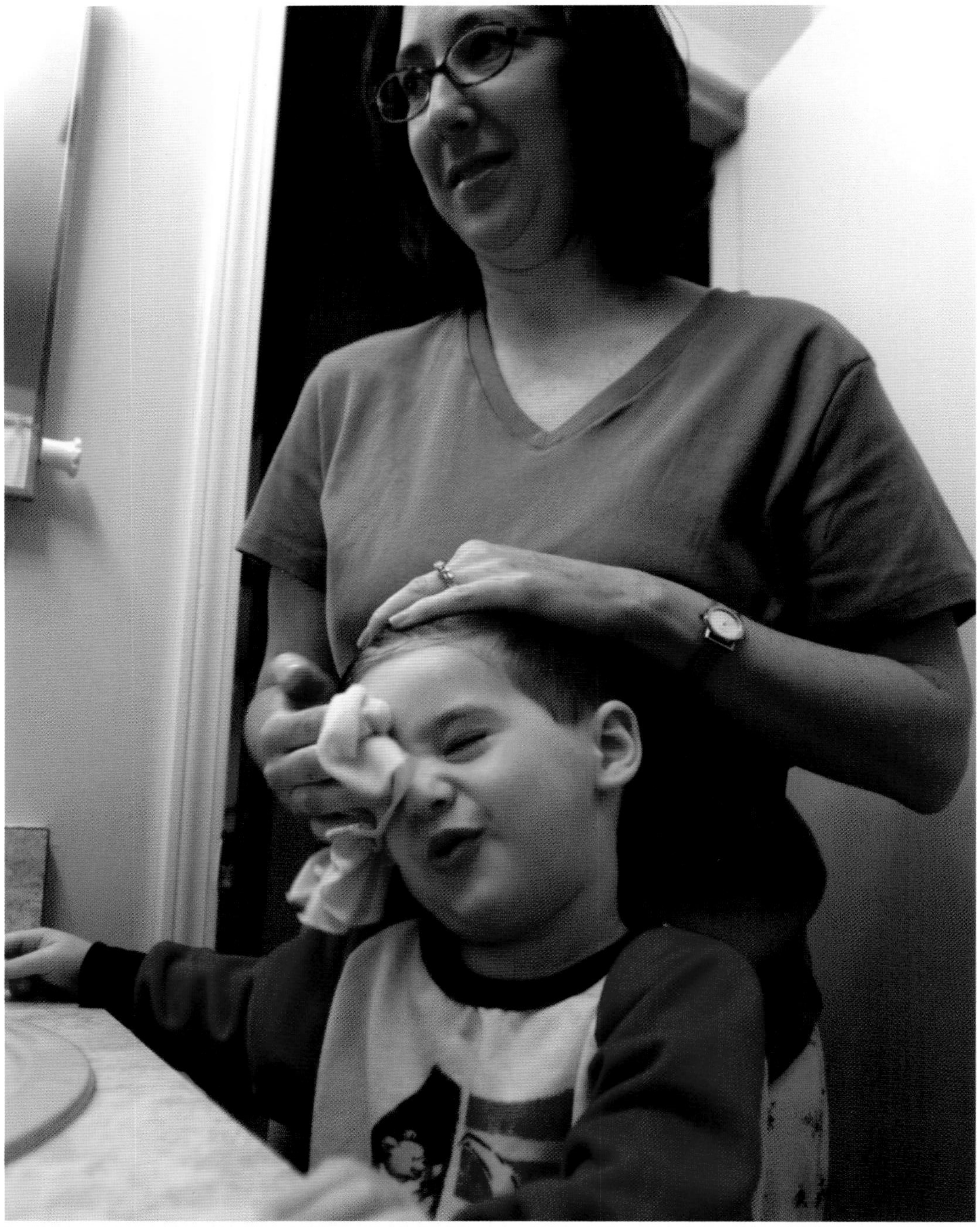

GROSSE POINTE PARK
Mother's little helper: 13-month-old Emma learned early on that the dishwasher was center stage in the Johnston kitchen and a safe haven from the overly affectionate family dogs.
Photo by Andrew Johnston, Detroit Free Press

FRANKENMUTH
After church, Harry and Eleanor Krafft host a weekly Sunday dinner for their family. Four of their five children live in the Frankenmuth area, and they bring their 10 grandchildren, including sofa wrestlers Alex Borchard, David Krafft, Aaron Krafft, and Jeremy Borchard. With everyone's busy schedules, the dinners give family members a chance to catch up and stay close.
Photo by Steve Jessmore, The Flint Journal

MIDLAND
Pam Steu calls her 10-month-old granddaughter Elaiyna a miracle baby. Elaiyna's mom, Jennifer Schwartzkopf, had a tough pregnancy, compounded by a near-fatal car accident in her fifth month. "I use any excuse to spend time with my granddaughter," says Steu.
Photos by Ryan Wood, Midland Daily News

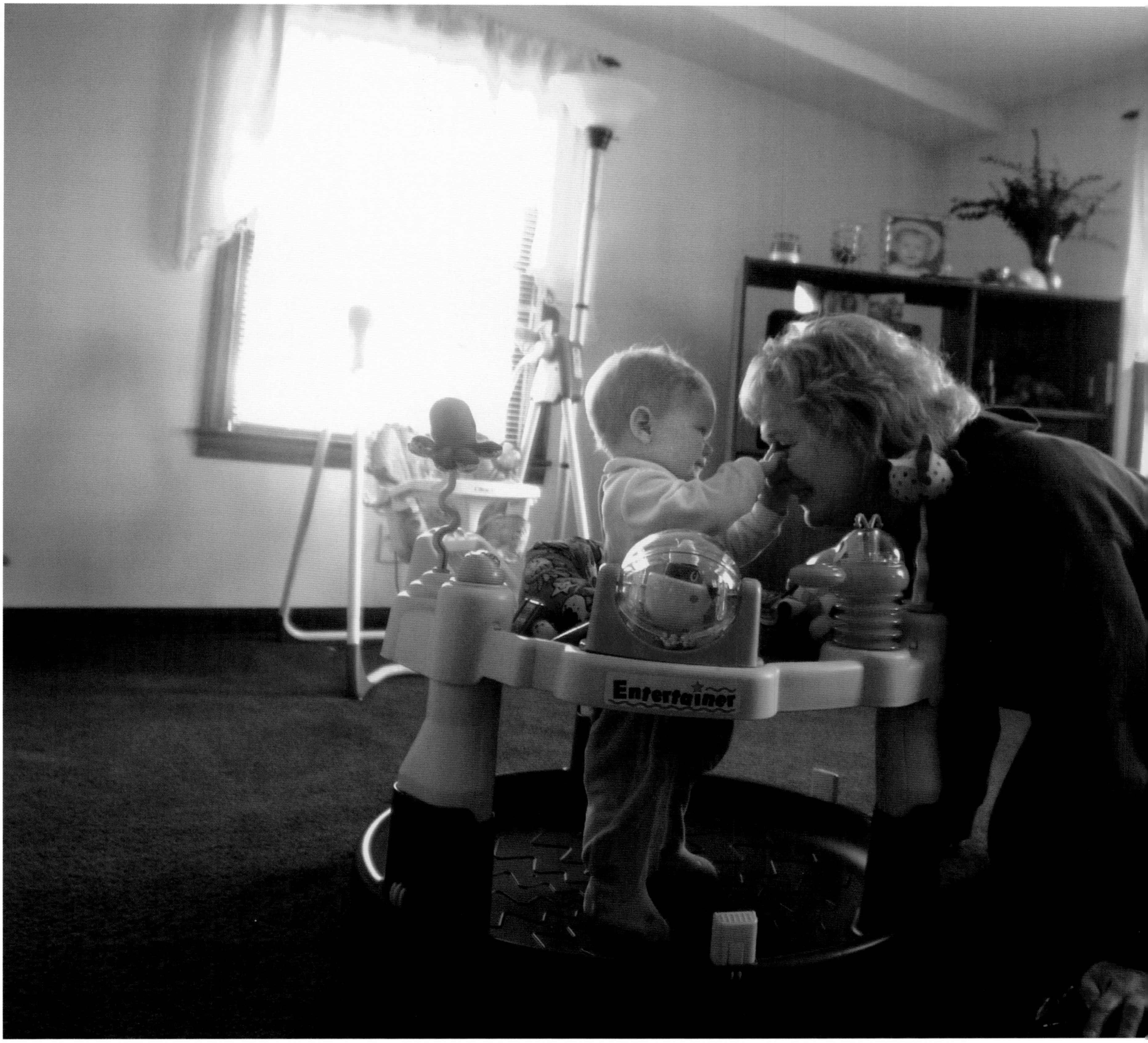

MIDLAND
Levi Marble, 15, has been living with his foster parents, Pam and Randy Steu, since he was 11. The Steus, who have taken in 40 foster children since 1994, are hopeful Levi will reunite with his family. "He and his father are working pretty hard on things. God willing, he'll be able to return home," says Pam Steu.

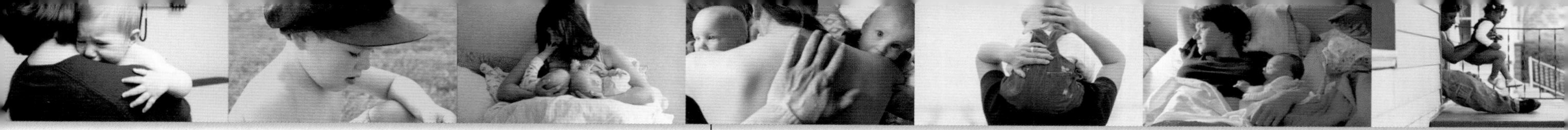

KALAMAZOO
Photographer Mark Bugnaski is a hands-on dad, much to the relief of wife Sabine Lenzner. Their 9-month-old twin daughters Zoe and Eva were "whiny and demanding all day," dad says, leaving mom in desperate need of a back rub.
Photo by Mark Bugnaski, Kalamazoo Gazette

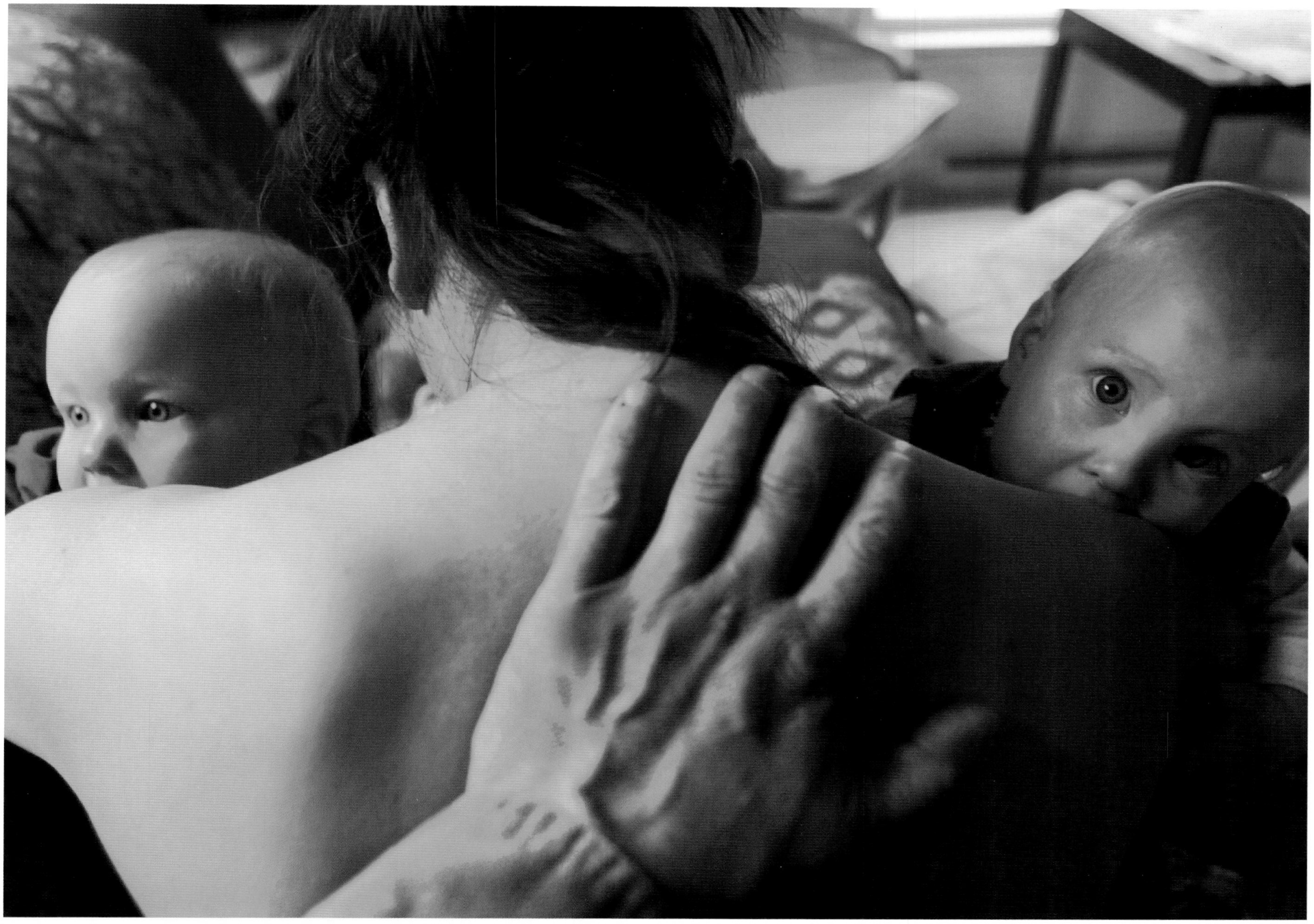

ANN ARBOR
Shamya Mason, 3, never complained during chemotherapy, surgery, and a bone marrow transplant to treat her adrenal gland cancer. Now disease free, Shamya attends preschool and watches *Blues Clues* with her cousins. "It was such a long, hard battle," says mother Sharonda Rawls. "But she's happy and healthy now."
Photo by Leisa Thompson, The Ann Arbor News

GROSSE POINTE
Right idea, wrong place: When retired teacher Karen Anderson adopted baby Sarah, now 3, from Changsha, China, in 2001, Sarah had three cavities. Now she brushes her teeth diligently—and spits in a receptacle that suits her height.
Photo by Amy Leang, Detroit Free Press

BAY CITY
Betsy Miller, 2, multitasks as dad, photographer Kent Miller, captures one step in her speedy transition from infancy to childhood.
Photo by Kent Miller, The Bay City Times

TRAVERSE CITY
Ever since she co-edited the 2003 high school yearbook, Claire Gibbons, 15, has been obsessed about picture placement in her roomful of family and friends. When she's not working on the montage, Claire sings in a garage band, plays soccer, and really pays attention in physics class.
Photo by Elizabeth Conley

EAST LANSING
Parents Sonya Pentecost, Bob Davis, Catherine Hula, Carol Luster, and Rick Hula bunch up to take pictures of their kids before the East Lansing High School prom. The parents sponsor the "post prom," an alcohol-free, all-night party at the school.
Photos by David Olds

EAST LANSING
Trying not to poke her date Jeff Roder, senior Lindsey Waters ends up sticking herself as she pins on his boutonniere. Lindsey and her girlfriend, Caroline Brooks, took hours to get ready (including the salon appointment for their hair); she says the guys took about 20 minutes.

EAST LANSING

Strapless dresses were all the rage at the prom. The style, first launched in the 1950s by Elizabeth Taylor's dress in *A Place in the Sun*, is back now. Many of the girls drove 60 miles to the Detroit suburb of Novi to purchase the perfect dress and to make sure no one else had the same one.

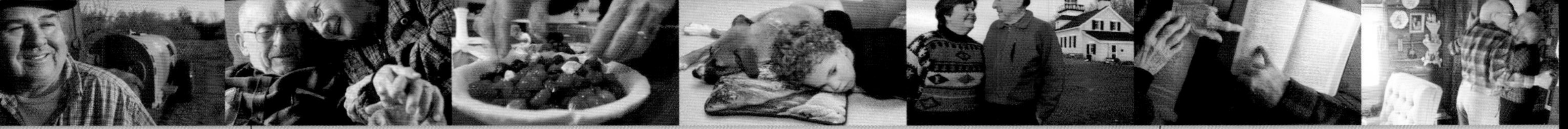

SANFORD
Newlyweds: Mirle and Alma Thompson look forward to their one-year wedding anniversary in June 2003. Mirle's sister introduced them, and three months later Mirle, 82, married Alma, 93. "We are still as much in love as we were when we met," says Alma. "That's not true," says Mirle. "We are more in love now than we were then."
Photos by Ryan Wood, Midland Daily News

SANFORD
After morning services at the Edenville Seventh-day Adventist Church, the Thompsons spend Saturday afternoon at home reading Bible verses together.

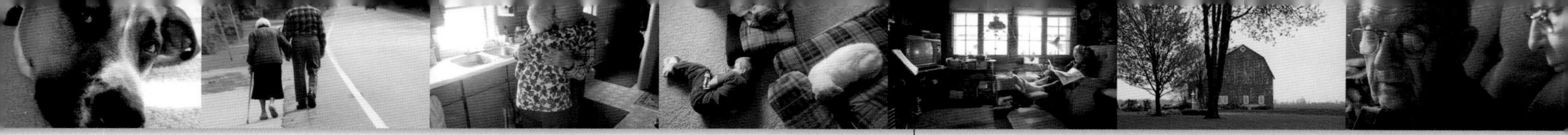

SANFORD

After retiring from a career in TV and radio repair, Mirle Thompson and his first wife Ethel permanently moved to their Sanford Lake vacation cabin. Ethel died in 1997, and the cabin fell into disorder. When Mirle married Alma, the place got fixed up.

FRANKENMUTH
Who says it's bad to play with your food? At the kids' table at Sunday dinner, the clever Alex Borchard, 5, chewed out a mask from a slice of his grandmother's homemade garlic bread.
Photo by Steve Jessmore, The Flint Journal

PORT HURON
Branching out: Missy Beck, 24, takes a break from her College and Careers church group meeting. "When I was a kid, I was a little monkey," says Beck, who's studying to be a welder at St. Clair County Community College.
Photo by Andrea Wingard

MIDLAND
Skye Curtis, 9, would read night and day if her journalist parents let her, which sometimes puts them in the awkward position of scolding her for reading too much.
Photo by Rodney Curtis

HAMTRAMCK
Homemaker Nasima Zaman Chowdhury readies daughter Nusrat, 3, for a post-lunch nap. Chowdhury and her husband, both originally from Bangladesh, moved to Hamtramck from New York City seven years ago. The resurgent Detroit suburb is known for its ethnically diverse population, hip nightlife, and tightly knit community.
Photo by Amy Leang, Detroit Free Press

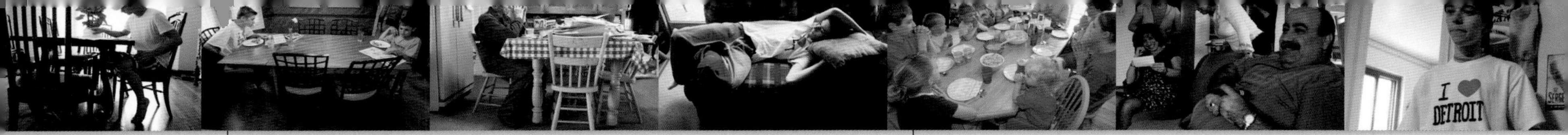

GROSSE POINTE PARK

While mom Joan Wendzinski is off with son Peter, 16, at his Sunday night soccer game, Andrew (Peter's twin) and brother John, 10, finish a pizza dinner courtesy of dad Michael, who ordered it himself.

Photo by J. Kyle Keener, Detroit Free Press

SAGINAW

"We didn't plan to have a certain number of children," says Dale Kumke. "We just welcomed them one gift at a time." He, his wife Sheila, and their nine kids say grace before dinner.

Photo by Jeff Schrier

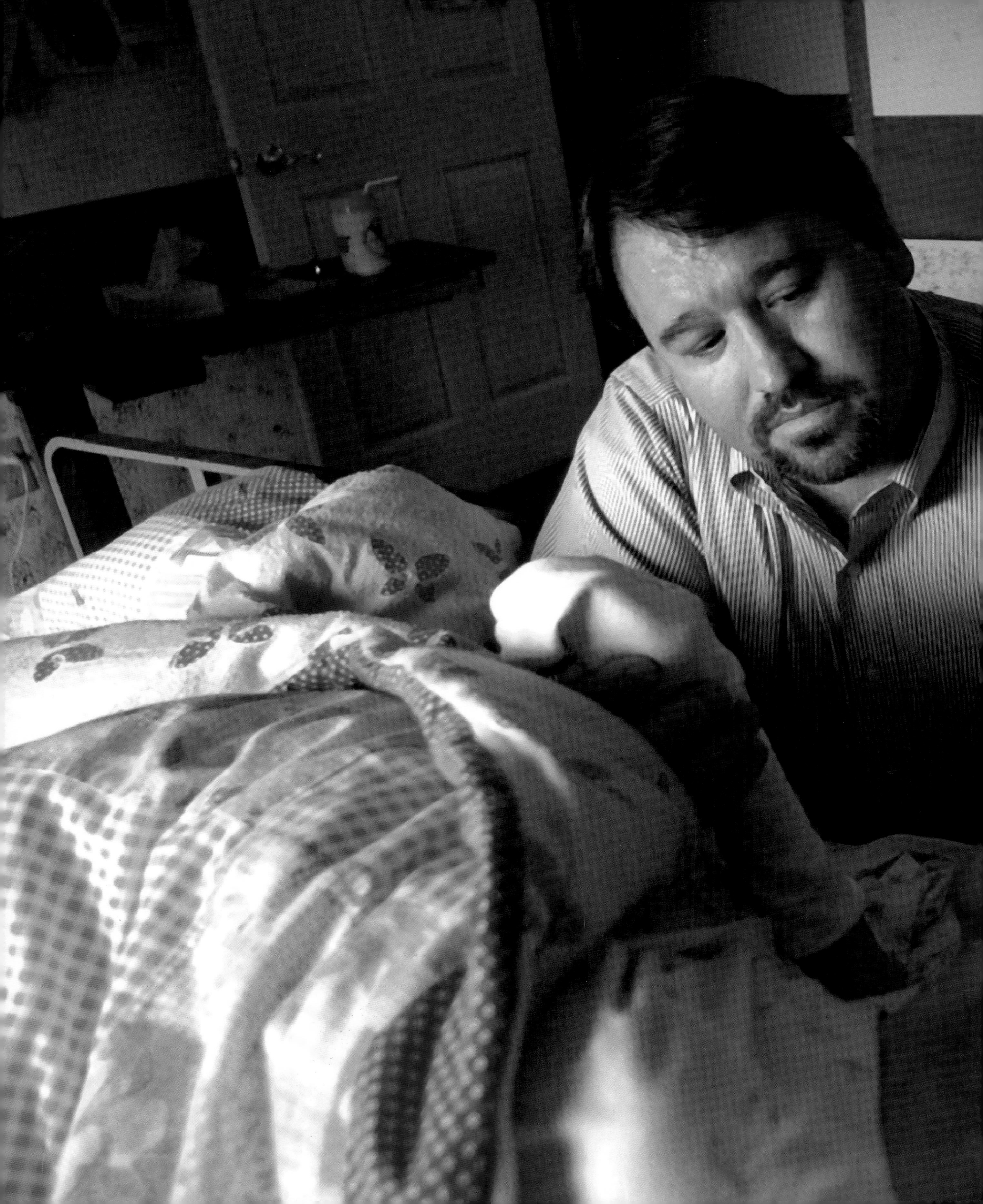

ESSEXVILLE
The decision to move octogenarian Pauline Kuhn to Brian's House hospice was made collectively by her eight children and 29 grandchildren after a stroke paralyzed her left side and impaired her memory. "She recognized me this time," says grandson Stephen Rivet of his Sunday visit to the hospice. "She said my name."
Photo by Kent Miller, The Bay City Times

FRANKENMUTH
Instead of paying strangers, Roger Weiss has his three children help with the evening milking so they can spend time together. Youngest daughter Lydia's job? Cleaning the cows' teats. The fifth (and sixth) generation of the family to work the land, the Weisses recently celebrated the farm's 150th anniversary.
Photos by Steve Jessmore, The Flint Journal

FRANKENMUTH
Margie Weiss, 12, coaxes a day-old calf to take colostrum, a cow's first milk, from a bottle at the family's dairy farm. Colostrum, which looks and smells like yogurt gone bad, is high in protein, fat, and antibodies.

EAST LANSING

In Kabul, Anisa Arib was a member of the Consul for Afghan Women. The Taliban shut down the organization in 1992, and the Rahmans fled to Uzbekistan. Ten years later, Anisa and her husband Aziz resettled in Lansing. Despite the hardships, they count themselves lucky; 52 relatives died during the Taliban regime, and their 9-year-old daughter, who is blind and deaf, is now getting the care she needs.
Photo by David Olds

FARMINGTON HILLS

Car crazy: John James, wife Sharon, daughter Carrie, and son Loren gather at home in their showcase driveway. James is CEO of James Group International, an auto-parts conglomerate. Aside from the 2003 H2 Hummer and the wood-trimmed 1947 Chrysler Town and Country convertible shown here, the family's stable is packed with antique cars, but James won't say how many.

Photo by Hugh Grannum

The year 2003 marked a turning point in the history of photography: It was the first year that digital cameras outsold film cameras. To celebrate this unprecedented sea change, the *America 24/7* project invited amateur photographers—along with students and professionals—to shoot and, via the Internet, submit digital images. Think of it as audience participation. Their visions of community are interspersed with the professional frames throughout this book. On the following four pages, however, we present a gallery produced exclusively by amateur photographers.

ROCKFORD Rosie's Diner had its minute of fame when a 60s paper-towel commercial was filmed at the counter, where "quicker picker upper" Alex Niedzwiecki relishes his shake. ***Photo by Stacy Niedzwiecki***

ROCKFORD A newborn robin, Michigan's state bird, awaits his next meal in Russ and Stacy Niedzwiecki's backyard. ***Photo by Stacy Niedzwiecki***

EELAND Darrell Vande Hoef plows his fields the old-fashioned way—with Percheron draft horses like this earling, Alex, who reluctantly returns to the barn after a day of grazing. ***Photo by Karen Fitz LaBarge***

OWELL Headed to the trampoline, 6-year-old Jenica Barrett leads the way. Four-year-old Jeremy holds on—fo

ALLEGAN Something you don't see much anymore, like full-service gas stations or change on the bus...Tyler Jackson, 8, drinks from a stream running through the Allegan woods. ***Photo by Lee Jackson***

HOLLAND Started in 1929 by a high school biology teacher, the rootsy Tulip Time Festival draws a million visitors to Holland, a diverse, fast-growing area of western Michigan. ***Photo by Joy Johnson***

ROCKFORD Casey Lenon, 3, and Claire Sundman, 4, tap their way through their song "Yes I Can" at the annual recital at the Rockford School of Dance. ***Photo by Patricia Rosengren***

BOYNE CITY Mushroom hunts, mushroom recipe cook-offs, and mushroom seminars distinguish the otherwise fairly typical annual Morel Mushroom Festival, held on the shore of Lake Charlevoix. ***Photo by Michael Meleski***

DEARBORN
Kenneth Talison sets a fast pace installing windlaces (noise mufflers) in 2,000 cars a week at the Ford Assembly Plant. Wielding his airgun to shoot screws, he can muffle a Mustang in a minute. Some fellow workers marvel, and others are dismayed. "They say I discourage them," he jokes, "because they can't shoot 'em as fast as I can."
Photo by Nancy Andrews, Detroit Free Press

Hard At Work

DETROIT
For 26 years, Ralph Skinner has worked for the Parade Company, which puts on Detroit's longstanding Thanksgiving Day parade. The senior art director freshens up these antique Italian papier-mâché figures for their big day.
Photo by Paul Bednarski

GRAND HAVEN
Night shift: Cashier Kerry Amber, 28, began working at the Meijer's superstore as a bagger when she was 16. Meijer's is open around the clock every day except Christmas. This 210,000-square-foot branch, one of 78 in Michigan, has about 500 employees.
Photos by Ken Stevens, Muskegon Chronicle

GRAND HAVEN

To be with her three children after school, Laura Dufford requested the night shift at Meijer's. "I turned into a night owl," she says. From 11 p.m. to 7:30 a.m., she unloads and stacks produce while her family sleeps. When she gets home, Dufford sleeps in two shifts: 9 to 1, and 7 to 10. In between is family time.

DANGER
WARNING
SLIPPERY FLOOR

BAY PORT
Most of the 7,000 pounds of whitefish that fisherman Richard Bacca catches and weighs for the Bay Port Fish Company is shipped to New York City's fish markets within 24 hours. But the company also caters to nostalgic Michiganders living in other states: It over-nights special orders of Great Lakes yellow perch and walleye to homesick customers in California and Arizona.
Photo by Kent Miller, The Bay City Times

BIRMINGHAM
Architect Keith Moffat, 56, is so proud of his eye-popping cowboy boots that he wears them on the job. "My boots never let me forget where I come from," says Moffat, who was raised in Texas. "And they let me know that I'm cooler than anyone else up here."
Photo by J. Kyle Keener, Detroit Free Press

LINWOOD
"The best thing about my job is that I get to watch the seasons change," says garbage jumper Demetrius Braddock. His six-hour route takes him through the Pinconning area's rural byways, where he watches nature's cycle from his perch above the truck's rear tires.
Photo by Kent Miller, The Bay City Times

SUTTONS BAY

John Crampton's Willow Vineyards produce 1,000 cases of wine—Chardonnay, Pinot Noir, Pinot Gris—a year. Michigan's wine production is growing, and the state is now the eighth largest producer in the country.

Photo by Jeff Schrier

HART

On the eastern shore of Lake Michigan, in Oceana county, the Van Sickle farm harvests about 30,000 pounds of asparagus a week. For Guadelupe Carrion Estrada and Martin Lugo Moreno, the work is intense: Each ripe stalk is snapped by hand, never cut. Michigan is the third largest asparagus grower in the country.
Photo by Ken Stevens, Muskegon Chronicle

ST. IGNACE
Maintenance worker Corey Peterson's view from the Mackinac Bridge beats any corner office in the country. He claims he can see halfway down into lower Michigan from his perch on "Mighty Mac's" main cable.
Photo by Bruce Edwards, The Flint Journal

HH

ROYAL OAK
Downtime at the penguinarium. For a zoo penguin to receive proper health care, it helps to get used to human hands. Bonnie Van Dam, head zookeeper for birds at the Detroit Zoo, grooms a receptive rockhopper. King penguins, ruling their part of the roost in the background, are less receptive to such ministrations.
Photo by Donna Terek, The Detroit News

KALAMAZOO
Once a handcrafted Heritage guitar has been stained, Ted Beville scrapes the excess color off the plastic binding. He began doing this detail-oriented finishing work 40 years ago at Gibson, which left for Nashville in 1984. Heritage's high-quality instruments—used by Roy Clark and other world-renowned musicians—sell for as much as $12,000.
Photo by Mark Bugnaski, Kalamazoo Gazette

FLINT
In the final step of a six-point oil filter inspection, Mary Brooks checks for rattles. She works at Community Industries, a Genesee County program that offers piecework to developmentally disabled clients. Brooks also picks up skills that will help her navigate the marketplace when it's time to find her own job.
Photo by Steve Jessmore, The Flint Journal

FLINT
A line repairman at the General Motors truck assembly plant and United Auto Workers Local 598 member, Roger Adolph comes from a family of autoworkers. His father and grandfather worked at Buick. Birthplace of the UAW, the city of Flint saw the first GM-UAW agreement signed in 1937 after a 44-day sitdown strike.
Photo by Steve Jessmore, The Flint Journal

MACKINAC ISLAND
Help wanted: dock porter. Must be able to balance up to 400 pounds of luggage on a bike and make 40 trips a day between Mackinac Island hotels and ferry dock. This coveted summer job pays between $600 and $800 a week in tips and salary.
Photo by Bruce Edwards, The Flint Journal

FRANKENMUTH
Founder Wally Bronner makes his rounds at Bronner's Christmas Wonderland, the world's largest Christmas store. A vocal and devout Christian, Bronner opened the store, now the size of a football field, at 25 Christmas Lane in 1945. The emporium purveys Nativity scenes, ornaments, Santa suits, and a full line of jumbo-sized commercial decorations.
Photo by Steve Jessmore, The Flint Journal

OSCODA
Technician Kenneth Webster peels off paper and plastic sheathing from a Kalitta Air Boeing 747 cargo jet after giving it a new paint job. Ten hours after Webster touched up its tail, the jet took off for Kuwait carrying mail for American soldiers stationed in Iraq.
Photo by Kent Miller, The Bay City Times

AUBURN HILLS
Generating wind speeds of up to 140 mph, the aero-acoustic wind tunnel at DaimlerChrysler's technology center is used to test standard production automobiles as well as company-sponsored race cars. The 31,000-square-foot facility cost $37.5 million and took three years to build.
Photo by Jeffrey Sauger, Reflex News

MACKINAC ISLAND
Official greeter and information czar at the Grand Hotel for the past five years, doorman Richard Houghton, 33, greets guests from his post on the famous 660-foot porch. When the hotel closes for winter at the end of October, Houghton returns to Jamaica where he works at his dad's shuttle-boat business.
Photo by Bruce Edwards, The Flint Journal

FLINT
Among his many brushes with greatness, Paul T. Spaniola of Paul's Pipe Shop on South Saginaw Street once taught the actress Susan Hayward how to smoke a pipe for a movie. A six-time world champion pipe smoker (i.e., the guy who can keep a bowl of tobacco smoking the longest), Spaniola, 90, opened his store in 1947.
Photo by Steve Jessmore, The Flint Journal

SAULT STE. MARIE
Lock and dam operator Richard Lee walks the 600-foot bulk carrier *Olympic Merit* into MacArthur Lock, one of the world-famous Soo locks at Sault Ste. Marie. First engineered in 1853, the system has gradually expanded. Each year, 11,000 vessels carrying 90 million tons of cargo pass through the locks, which connect Lake Superior to Lake Huron.
Photo by Bruce Edwards, The Flint Journal

LANSING
Michigan scored a milestone in November 2002 in electing its first female governor, Democrat Jennifer M. Granholm. The 43-year-old mother of three, shown here at a meeting with her staff, was formerly the state's attorney general.
Photo by David Olds

ESSEXVILLE
In the predawn hours, a barge called the *Great Lakes Trader* disgorges 24,000 metric tons of clinker and stone dug from a quarry in Picton, Ontario, into the Saginaw River receiving yard of Essroc Materials, Inc. The 845-foot-long vessel plies the waters of Great Lakes industrial ports, loading and unloading $9 million worth of iron, aggregate, and coal each year.
Photo by Kent Miller, The Bay City Times

GRAND HAVEN
A 47-foot U.S. Coast Guard Motor Life Boat busts through storm swells during routine training exercises. In 1988, Grand Haven was designated "Coast Guard City, USA." Every year the city hosts a national memorial service for Coast Guard seamen lost in the line of duty.
Photo by Cory Morse, Muskegon Chronicle

ST. IGNACE
During a precise "direct deployment" exercise, Aviation Survival Technician 2nd Class Shaun Legas hangs 25 feet above the Straits of Mackinac. He'll be lowered to within three feet of his rescue target.
Photo by Bruce Edwards, The Flint Journal

OTSEGO
Kelly Kujawa, a tight end with the Toledo Spitfire, cools off at halftime during a game against the Southwest Michigan Jaguars. The National Women's Football Association, formed in 2000 by sports-entertainment entrepreneur Catherine Masters, fielded 29 teams in 2003 and has more franchises in the works. Long story short: Toledo lost the game, 41-0.
Photos by Mark Bugnaski, Kalamazoo Gazette

OTSEGO
For the love of the game: The motto couldn't be more fitting for the NWFA. Players like Jennifer Schwartz receive no salary, have to pay for their uniforms, and are required to buy their own insurance.

OTSEGO
How rough is the NWFA? Ask Denise Miller. The Jaguars' rookie defensive end tore the anterior cruciate ligament in her left knee after being clipped during the game against the Spitfire. Miller, an English literature professor, had reconstructive surgery a few weeks later.

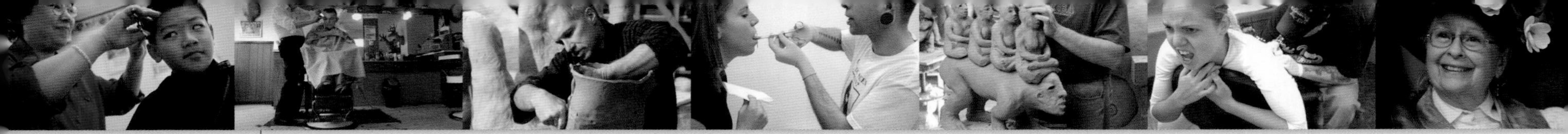

BAY CITY
At age 82, Allie Wawrzyniak cut back his barbering to three weeks a month so he could spend more time fishing and hunting. Wawrzyniak learned the trade from his father and opened his barbershop 50 years ago. Customers like Gerald Rychlicki often leave the shop with Allie's signature send-off: "There, good for another 1,000 miles."
Photo by Steve Jessmore, The Flint Journal

MADISON HEIGHTS
Marilyn Chu of Marilyn Salon uses her Dirt Devil to dust off Samuel Kwong after his trim. Chu, a Taiwanese immigrant who came to Michigan in 1971, says she is specifically trained to cut Asian hair. "Asian people all have coarse hair, and American hairdressers don't know what to do with it."
Photo by Amy Leang, Detroit Free Press

DETROIT
Lorena Sy straightens wigs at Lee's Beauty and Barber Supply. The store, which opened in 1991, is one of Detroit's oldest Korean-owned, African-American beauty supply stores. Korean Amer icans, who make up less than one percent of Detroit's population (African Americans make up 81 percent), have found a niche in the city's hair care supply industry.
Photo by Amy Leang, Detroit Free Press

ROYAL OAK
Tunnel vision: Covering more than four acres, the Detroit Zoo's Arctic Ring of Life is the world's largest polar bear exhibit. Its centerpiece is the Polar Passage, a 70-foot-long acrylic tunnel—the best view of diving and swimming polar bears this side of the North Pole.
Photo by J. Kyle Keener, Detroit Free Press

Michigan At Play

DETROIT
Debra White-Hunt, 52, dances to her own choreography in "Field of Fire," a solo piece depicting the passion of both interpersonal and religious relationships. White-Hunt's unitard and overlay are singed at the edges to "get the feeling of fire in them." As the co-founder and director of the Detroit-Windsor Dance Academy, White-Hunt mentors 500 dancers, from ages 4 to 76.
Photo by Hugh Grannum

DETROIT
Drum major Christine Williams signals partner Jamel Williams for the next sequence of an Every Eight routine—a high-energy dance of eight movements in eight seconds. The duo led Northern High School to victory in the city's Battle of the Bands competition with up-tempo renditions of R&B classics like Stevie Wonder's "All I Do."
Photo by Mandi Wright, Detroit Free Press

DETROIT

The show must go on but first a few last-minute logistical details have to be addressed. Each year, Martin Luther King High School deploys its dynamite band and auxiliary pomerettes to the Eastern Market's Flower Day celebration. On the program: "Get Ready," by the Temptations, "Black and Blue," by the Backstreet Boys, and "Together Again," by Janet Jackson.
Photo by Eric Smith

DETROIT
At the Association of Chinese Americans drop-in center in downtown Detroit, Ju Su Li (center) suffers from a streak of bad mahjongg luck. The 67-year-old Chinese immigrant, who came to the city seven years ago to be with his family, works part-time at a McDonald's to earn a little spending (or, in this case, losing) money.
Photos by Amy Leang, Detroit Free Press

DETROIT
Nick Karas, C. Katsimihas, Pete Haralambis, and Jim Papas—all regulars at Epiros Coffee House—spend Saturday afternoon drinking demitasses of coffee, watching soccer matches on TV, and playing traditional Greek card games like *koupes* and *diloti*.

Zac
Mike

BAY CITY
Heave ho! Creekside Intermediate School sixth-graders Michael Krull (first in line) and Zac Goodwin (behind him) crank on the foresail halyard aboard the *Appledore IV*, an 85-foot sailing schooner. The environmental cruise stops at research stations on Saginaw Bay to teach children about marine ecosystems.
Photos by Kent Miller, The Bay City Times

BAY CITY
The sloop *Sara Jane* follows the fleet leader on a close starboard tack during the Bay City Yacht Club's first race of the year. Saginaw Bay's shallow, protected waters and 20-knot winds make it one of Michigan's top sailing destinations.

DETROIT
Paula Smiley, aka Miz Korona, joins rap artist Deena Moore, aka ReddBone, to give a rap lesson to Smiley's niece Taniya. Miz Korona's music career received a big boost when she appeared in the movie *8 Mile*, which starred Detroit rapper Eminen. The experience put an end to her plans to be a dentist.
Photo by Donna Terek, The Detroit News

METAMORA

Hounds, please: Although these foxhounds don't actually catch their prey—the Metamora Hunt Club doesn't allow the foxes to be killed—Huntsman Pat Pearce and Master of Foxhounds Joe Kent still train the club's 60 dogs to nose out quarry that has gone to ground.

Steve Jessmore, The Flint Journal

ROCHESTER
At the starting line on the Addison Oaks Spring Classic, these professional racers wobble up to speed. The 30-mile race happens on a cross-country ski trail near Bald Mountain Recreation Area, through forest, rolling hills, and farmland.
Photo by Bryan Mitchell

BINGHAM
Chillin': Before heading off to work, carpenter John Babka sails Lake Leelanau (water temperature: 40 degrees). A former mountain biker, Babka switched to windsurfing six years ago. It's hard to find fault with his reason: "When you crash in the water, you don't break your bones."
Photo by J. Carl Ganter, MediaVia

GRAND HAVEN
Skimboarding, like its deep-end sister surfing, is said to have originated in Hawai'i. In the 1920s, lifeguards at Laguna Beach, California perfected the sport. Derek Gerencer, 18, gets set to take off on his moving board and glide across a thin slip of Lake Michigan water.
Photo by Cory Morse, Muskegon Chronicle

T
e threat: Zion Roberts boxes at Joe
's Boxing Academy, and plays football
basketball. Byrd thinks Roberts can go
e way as a boxer. The 10-year-old has
dy won two Junior Olympic golds.
by Lisa DeJong, The Flint Journal

Presents
TEAM BYRD
TUESDAY
FIGHT
NIGHT
AT THE NETWORK
4510 S. Dort Hwy.
Flint (Dort at Hemphill)
SDAY MARCH 22, 1994
8:00PM

ST. LOUIS
Hooded sniper Mike Keetch, 14, exposing his paintball marker and loader, draws down on a target during an outing with the Golden Assembly of God Church.
Photos by Jeff Schrier

ST. LOUIS
To avoid the enemy—and live paintball fire—Justin Aman, 13, sprints for cover. Despite the warlike play, safety is a big concern and all participants must wear face protection during matches.

ST. LOUIS
Teenage boys wait in ambush during a game of "capture the enemy's flag," a popular paintball wargame. The church youth group spent the day at Pine River Paintball to learn teamwork—and release some manic energy.

SAGINAW
In the zone: Thomas Livingston focuses on the perfect pitch. No longer distracted by the winter bowling season, he sharpens his "shoe" skills at American Legion Post 439.
Photos by Jeff Schrier

SAGINAW

Opening night: With bowling season officially over, horseshoe season begins. Members of American Legion Post 439 in Saginaw throw shoes every Wednesday evening at a pit next to their building. The players claim three motivating factors: fun, competition, and beer.

SAGINAW
The Tri-City Carvers, a local wood-carving group, worked for two years to create the animals for the popular Saginaw Children's Zoo Carousel, completed in 1999. Noah Wallaert of New Hudson rides a rabbit.
Photo by Jeff Schrier

DETROIT
Right after 9/11, Steven Bowen, 10, and brother Kyle, 6, along with their cousin painted the fences in front of their house on Detroit's Southwest Side. "People might be sad," says ringleader Steven. "So we thought it might make them happy to have a flag." It took them two days to semicomplete the job.
Photo by J. Kyle Keener, Detroit Free Press

FLINT
Berston Field House, the first community center in 1930s Flint to admit African Americans, provides kids with a place to play after school and during the summer. Eleven-year-old Adrian Ewing (shooting) could be the next Mateen Cleaves, Morris Peterson, or Glen Rice—all Berston alumni who made it to the NBA.
Photo by Ryan Garza, The Flint Journal

NIKE

COPPER HARBOR
A fishing boat makes its way across Lake Fannie Hooe, near Copper Harbor in the Keweenaw Peninsula. Despite its remote nature, the area was extensively disturbed by copper mining in the 19th century.
Photo by Brian Masck, The Flint Journal

QUINCY
Colten Carter, 4, looks like a pro at a goat tying competition with one end of the rope in his mouth and the other in his back pocket. The National Little Britches Rodeo Association holds events throughout the country for 8- to 18-year-olds, as well as contests for Little Wranglers (ages 5 to 7) and Trail Hands (kids under 5).
Photos by Lisa DeJong, The Flint Journal

QUINCY
Austin Grim, 5, of Lowell, got the best of this goat, and his knot stayed tied for the required six seconds. The younger kids also compete in stick pony barrel racing and mutton busting.

QUINCY
Wes Bailey, 12, shows perfect form during the bull riding competition. Though new to the sport, the Olivet resident was the number one junior bull rider in Michigan for the 2002 to 2003 season. Juniors have to stay on the bull a wrenching six seconds; pros hang on for eight.

MT. PLEASANT

Down the stretch they come! Crazy Alice, jockeyed by Jeff Wetzel, thunders down the straightaway during the Udder Race finals. Unfortunately for Holstein and rider, their mad dash to the finish line copped them only a third-place ribbon. In its fourth year at Mt. Pleasant Meadows Racetrack, the annual event claims to crown the world's fastest cow.

Photos by Steve Jessmore, The Flint Journal

MT. PLEASANT

And the winner is...Ryan Miller on The Little Witch! Not only did the crossbred Angus-Holstein vanquish her rivals, she also broke her own record as world's fastest cow, finishing the two-mile race in less than eight minutes, with an average speed of 16 mph. Her $1,700 in winnings went to her stable, the Wetzel Dairy Farm. Miller kept the trophy.

FLINT
Miles Carter started playing music in college at Prairie View A&M in Texas. He was the sax man in several jazz combos and taught elementary school music in Flint for 40 years. Carter has retired from teaching but still performs at community and church events.
Photo by Lisa DeJong, The Flint Journal

ANN ARBOR
When Katherine Weider, a television producer and musician, recently visited family in Canada, she mentioned she'd like to learn the accordion. Presto squeezo! Turned out that for 30 years her aunt had been storing a Frontalini accordion that had belonged to Weider's Czech grandfather.
Photo by Mark Einhaus

TROY
St. Joseph's Chaldean Catholic Church serves 25,000 parishioners, mostly Iraqi immigrants. Chaldean Catholicism, established in 1553 and sanctioned by Rome in 1830, is headquartered in Baghdad. It represents the largest Christian community in Iraq.
Photo by Jeffrey Sauger, Reflex News

Reason To Believe

NORTHVILLE
Many of the 800 walkers in the American Cancer Society's Race for the Cure created luminarias to honor cancer survivors, people battling the disease, or loved ones who lost that fight. More than 1,300 lights lined a route through Ford Field Park.
Photo by Steve Fecht

ANN ARBOR
Sister Martin Therese tools around on a scooter at the Sisters of Mary, Mother of Eucharist convent. The modern nunnery—built in 1999 by Domino's Pizza founder Tom Monaghan—encourages unconventional approaches to evangelism. Its Theology on Tap program sends the sisters out to local sports bars to reach young Catholics. "We turn some heads," says Sister Marie Gemma.
Photos by Leisa Thompson, The Ann Arbor News

ANN ARBOR
Pray Hard and Play Hard is the motto of the Sisters of Mary, Mother of Eucharist convent. Sister Maximilian Marie takes that dictum seriously as she skies for a spike during the nuns' daily recreation hour. Sports can get competitive at the convent but the nuns still try to support each other. "There's no trash talking," says Sister Marie Gemma.

FRANKENMUTH
Located at the edge of the Cass River, the St. Lorenz Lutheran Church was integral to the founding of Frankenmuth. The original pastor, Johann Loehe, a missionary from Bavaria, named the township in 1845 to remind settlers of their homeland in Franconia.
Photo by Steve Jessmore, The Flint Journal

LOWELL

Rev. Calvin Hill, a Methodist minister who describes himself as a "traditional Navajo following Christ," presides at the wedding of a Native American bride. His regalia features a headpiece attached by a "roach pin," from which hang prayer feathers. About 200 Navajo live in Michigan, a distinct—and transplanted—minority amid the state's "Three Fires" indigenous tribes: Ojibwe, Ottawa, and Potawatomi.

Photo by Lance Wynn, The Grand Rapids Press

NORTH MUSKEGON

Every Sunday, bible instructor Jim Wingren crams his SUV with cross, hymnals, keyboard, and collection plate and drives to North Muskegon High School to hold services in the cafeteria. Wingren cofounded the 70-member Anchor of Hope Nazarene Church because, he says, "Planting churches is the fastest way to grow Christ country."

Photo by Cory Morse, Muskegon Chronicle

DETROIT
Mormon elders Jared Johnson, 20, and Eric Blowers, 19, pray with Dorothy Stradwick on her front porch. Stradwick converted to Mormonism before she met Blowers and Johnson, who are spending two years doing missionary work in Detroit. "When I go to sleep at night, I always say God bless the Mormons too," Stradwick says.
Photo by Amy Leang, Detroit Free Press

DETROIT
After seven months of preparatory classes, Daisy Campos, 16, received her baptism, first communion, and confirmation—all in one day at St. Anne's Church. Her parents, two brothers, and sister came to witness the five-hour ceremony.
Photo by Hugh Grannum

HOLTON
The Amish community established in Holton in 1990 is considered more modern and progressive than some of Michigan's other Amish settlements. Holton's members allow furniture to be upholstered and telephones in the home—some even have voicemail.
Photo by Ken Stevens, Muskegon Chronicle

DO
NOT
PASS

HOLY BIBLE

DETROIT
Divine millinery: The tradition of African-American women and grand hats at church is unabated. Ellen Shoemaker, arriving at the Greater Grace Temple for services, bought her sculpted creation in Newark, New Jersey. Her daughter, who names all of her mother's hats, dubbed this one "Brazil."
Photos by Donna Terek, The Detroit News

DETROIT
Bernice Terry, known at Hartford Memorial Baptist Church as Mother Terry, owns more than 100 hats, almost all of her own design and making. She fashioned this bouquet from 100 silk lilies, and—for the dew drops—more than 300 Austrian crystals. Terry knows where she got her talent: "God gave it to me."

DETROIT
Kay Steen-Stoutermire is one of Hartford Memorial Baptist Church's Women With Hattitude. The group's fashion shows raise money for the church's ambitious $20 million project: a 24-hour center for Detroit's at-risk young people.

EAGLE HARBOR
Father Basil and Hegumen Nicholas founded Poorrock Abbey monastery on a remote stretch of Keweenaw Peninsula. Aiming to focus on a strict religious life, they began their order, the Holy Transfiguration Skete, in the early 1980s. The fathers say they came to the region looking for purgatory and found paradise.
Photos by Brian Masck, The Flint Journal

EAGLE HARBOR

During early morning mass at Poorrock Abbey, Hegumen Nicholas raises the chalice. The Holy Transfiguration Skete describes itself as a Catholic Monastery of the Byzantine Rite, whose members embrace "poverty, chastity, obedience, and stability of life." The term skete refers to an association of hermits belonging to the Greek Orthodox Church. A hegumen is equivalent to an abbot or a prior.

EAGLE HARBOR
Poorrock Abbey cooks up a pot of gold in its pots of jams. Its best-known jam is thimbleberry, *rubus parviflorus*, a wild forest relative of the raspberry. The monks run a sophisticated operation, with a website purveying a variety of mouth-watering wares. The two-fisted pot-stirrer is employee Rob Danis; Brother Sergius measures ingredients.
Photos by Brian Masck, The Flint Journal

EAGLE HARBOR
Poorrock Abbey produces and sells more than 60 varieties of jams, jellies, and preserves. Basics include strawberry and blueberry jams. Not-so-basics include dandelion jelly and crab apple preserves.

DETROIT
The real action at Cass Community Methodist Church takes place beyond the chancel, out where the church reaches residents of the hard-knocks Cass Corridor neighborhood. Church members operate a shelter, soup kitchen, food service for homebound seniors, and free medical clinic on Saturdays.
Photos by Hugh Grannum

DETROIT

At the Genesis Lutheran Church's 16th annual Altar Guild Tea, dancers from the Detroit-Windsor Dance Company let loose with "Shake the Foundation." The $25 tea benefits the 15 altar guilds that set up the communion service each Sunday, clean the chancel, and create the church banners.

MUSKEGON HEIGHTS
The Christ Temple Apostolic Church choir raises the roof and lifts Robin Bennett, 43, to exhaltation.
Photo by Ken Stevens, Muskegon Chronicle

MUSKEGON HEIGHTS
Services conclude with a call to come forward and be blessed. This particular Sunday, the emphasis is on children. Gwen Crenshaw, a Sunday school teacher, lays her right hand on 12-year-old Courtney Washington and her left on Antashia Williams, 4.
Photo by Ken Stevens, Muskegon Chronicle

DETROIT
"If it weren't for Cass Community Church, I'd be in jail or dead," says Keith Hill (center) who was raised by a drug-addicted mother. Hill was working a minimum-wage job at a uniform company when he began attending services. "I found a family," he says. Hill is now a program assistant at the church.
Photo by Hugh Grannum

DETROIT
Church trustee Karen Plant "passes the peace" during Sunday services. Plant, a county prosecutor, first got involved with the church by volunteering at its soup kitchen.
Photo by Hugh Grannum

MADISON HEIGHTS
Mark Perun, 36, lost his second cousin, Larry Sanko, in the World Trade Center attacks. On September 13, 2001, the custom vertical-blind maker stayed up all night to craft this flag-motif vertical blind. Perun won't sell it or make another, he says, because "it was made from the heart, not the pocketbook."
Photo by J. Kyle Keener, Detroit Free Press

Our Town

LANSING
Lansing, the capital and state's fifth-largest city, could soon become the healthiest, too. Sparrow Hospital hung signs on the lamp posts along Michigan Avenue urging folks to "Eat Fruits & Vegetables", "Be Physically Active," "Get Adequate Rest," and "Smile."
Photo by David Olds

Comerica
CONSTRUCTIO
VEHICLES
ONLY
30
BUS STOP

FRANKENMUTH
Six-year-old William Coopes attends morning kindergarten, and his next-door neighbor Lindsay goes to the afternoon session. William draws up a chair and waits patiently for his playmate's bus.
Photo by Steve Jessmore, The Flint Journal

REDFORD
Little big man: Manager Derek Farnsworth adds a Lilliputian touch to the eight-foot-tall Chippendale landmark outside his store, Royce Direct Art & Furniture Antique Reproductions on 8 Mile Road.
Photo by J. Kyle Keener, Detroit Free Press

SAGINAW
Michigander: Mother goose and her brood traipse through the dandelions beside the Saginaw River while papa brings up the rear.
Photo by B. Broadbent

WIXOM

The Neller brothers got all excited when the tinkling tones of the ice cream truck wafted through their neighborhood for the first time that spring...right before dinnertime.

Photo by Barbara Neller

DEARBORN
Haider Al-Jubury and Emad Al-Kasid are among 100,000 Iraqis now living in greater Detroit. Both came to Dearborn after the 1991 uprising against Saddam Hussein. At the Sinbad Grand Café, they discuss Al-Jubury's desire to expand his trucking business to Iraq. "It is time to introduce American business models to our country," he says.
Photo by Jeffrey Sauger, Reflex News

DETROIT

Adel Al-Hakim, 40, bestows a respectful *salaam* (greeting) on Hussein Karkhi, 71, before evening prayer at the Imam Ali Islamic Center in Detroit. After prayer, services are held to commemorate Iraqis discovered in mass graves and those still missing after being jailed during Saddam Hussein's regime.

Photo by Sylwia Kapuscinski, Detroit Free Press

DETROIT

About one in the morning at a concert at St. Andrews Hall, King Gordy and the Fat Killahz fill the stage. Gordy, in black, leads the lyric assaults, while hype man Fatt Father backs him up. The Fat Killahz, whose slogan is "ride or diet," weigh in at 300 pounds-plus. A high point in the act comes when King Gordy removes his shirt.
Photos by Donna Terek, The Detroit News

DETROIT
At a concert in St. Andrews Hall, front-row fans Monique Perry, a rapper herself, and Biba Adams, a rap reporter for *Real Detroit Weekly*, press forward to applaud a favorite: Miz Korona.

DETROIT
Contractor and car collector Steve Brunetti cruises down East Jefferson Avenue in his 1932 Auburn Boat Tail Speedster. Built to compete with the Duesenberg, the car originally went for $3,500. Today the classic fetches $100,000 or more, but Brunetti paid nothing. He got his as barter for roofing a house.
Photo by J. Kyle Keener, Detroit Free Press

LITCHFIELD
Out for a Sunday drive, members of the Model A Restorers' Club pass an Amish couple on their way to church. According to club records, there are about 75,000 Model As (produced from 1927 to 1931) on the road.
Photo by Lisa DeJong, The Flint Journal

GRAND HAVEN
Summer is still a ways off for the folks of Grand Haven on Lake Michigan, as this nasty lake-slap attests. Soon, however, the lake will calm, and prevailing westerly winds will generate the consistent, shapely surf that has made the town the surfing capital of the Great Lakes.
Photo by Ken Stevens, Muskegon Chronicle

DAVISON

Darwin Sohmer, 80, donated this mirror painting to the Davison-Richfield Senior Center, where he and his buddies meet Mondays and Thursdays to play pool. The prize is a bag of marbles—whoever wins the last game takes it home.

Photo by Steve Jessmore, The Flint Journal

BAY CITY
Urban musher Jennifer Wood-Czuprynski gathers speed on her paw-powered scooter. Czisa, a cocker spaniel and poodle mix, isn't exactly Iditarod material—she lasts only a few blocks on the tugline before she gets tired.
Photo by Kent Miller, The Bay City Times

GRAND HAVEN
Huddled against the Grand Haven Lighthouse bulwark, friends Alex Liddil, 16, and Rhea Ybarra, 18, watch a lake sunset. South Pier is a popular spot—it's where Alex and Rhea met two years before.
Photo by Cory Morse, Muskegon Chronicle

COLDWATER
It's in the genes: Michigan native Becky Harwell was taught to air dry clothes by her mother and grandmother. Harwell hopes to pass the practice on to her two daughters. She says it makes clothes smell better and last longer, and it saves energy.
Photo by Lisa DeJong, The Flint Journal

GLEN HAVEN
Raggedy Ann and Andy are relegated to being props in a rescue demonstration for children visiting the Sleeping Bear Point Lifesaving Station.
Photo by J. Carl Ganter, MediaVia

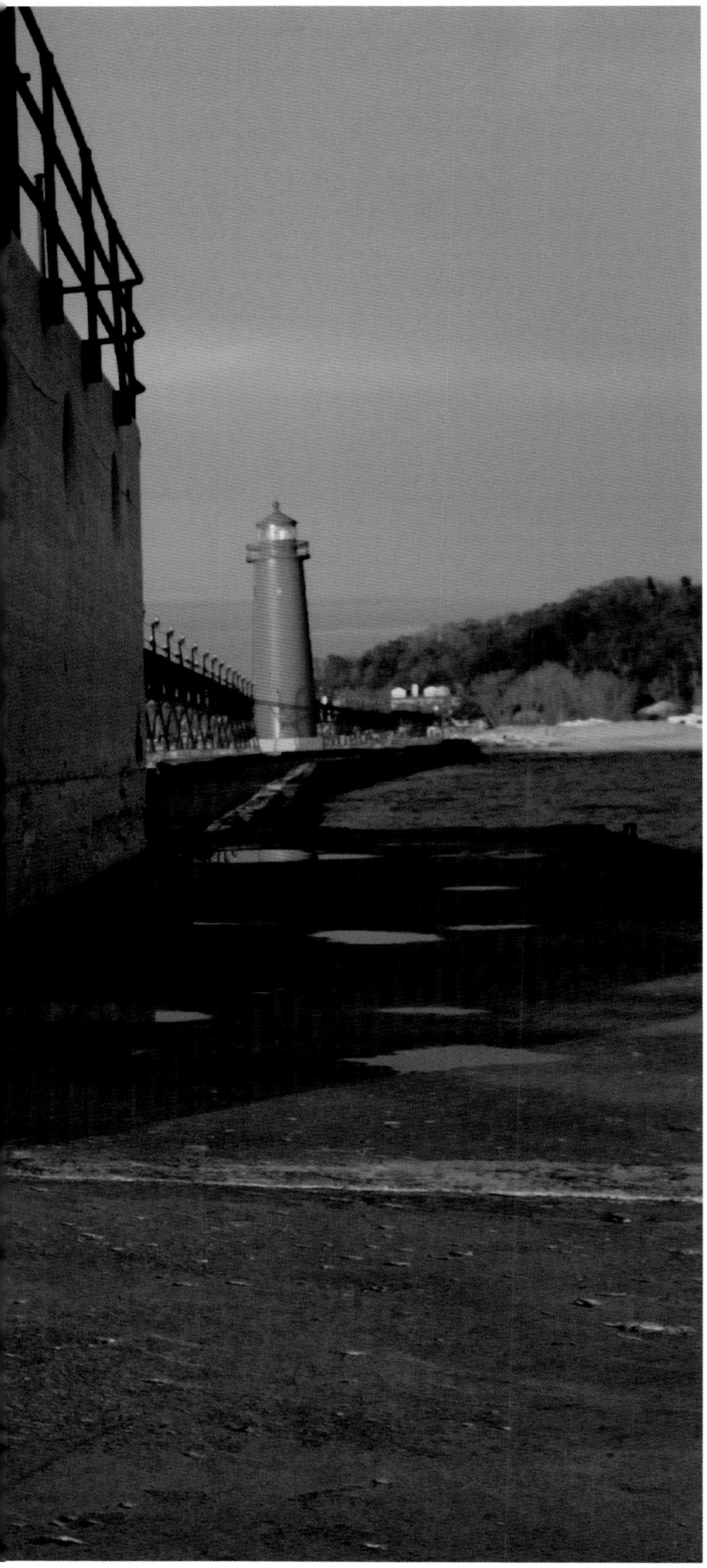

ST. IGNACE
Red, white, and moose: This familiar landmark on US-2 just north of the Mackinac Bridge got the flag treatment after 9/11.
Photo by Bruce Edwards, The Flint Journal

EAGLE HARBOR
The two flags signal that the Eagle Harbor General Store—on the Upper Peninsula's northern tip—is open for business. New owners decided that the very old store, once open only for summer vacationers, would remain open through the winter. Eagle Harbor year-rounders cheered: no more 25-mile trips through lots of snow for groceries.
Photo by Brian Masck, The Flint Journal

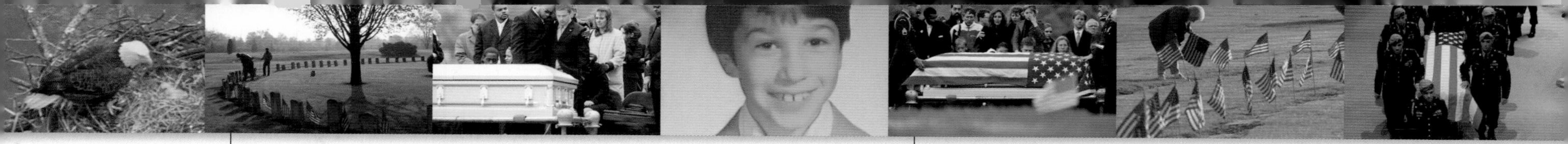

SAGINAW

Every year on the second Sunday before Memorial Day, Korean War veteran Hank Zissler, 67, and Vietnam veteran Bruce Manry, 50—along with other members of American Legion Post 22—spend the morning at Forest Lawn Cemetery, placing flags on veterans' gravestones, some of which date back to the Civil War.

Photo by Jeff Schrier

BERKLEY

Family and friends gather graveside to honor Army Sergeant Sean Reynolds at Roseland Park Cemetery. Reynolds, 25, died during the U.S.-led invasion of Iraq.

Photo by J. Kyle Keener, Detroit Free Press

ELM HALL
Cabin on a lake, hunters' lookout, chicken coop, kids' playhouse, and finally, in 1948, Elm Hall Post Office—that is the provenance of the 8 by 16 foot building that qualifies as the country's second smallest post office. "The smallest," says officer-in-charge Barb Sheets, "is 8 by 15, in Ochopee, Florida."
Photo by Jeff Schrier

48830
S. POST OFFICE
ELM HALL
POST OFFICE
Holiday Closing

ISLE ROYALE NATIONAL PARK
Day dawns at the least-visited national park in the country: Isle Royale. Beauty is a draw, accessibility is not. The 45-mile archipelago, teeming with wildlife in Lake Superior, can be reached only by plane or boat.
Photo by Brian Masck, The Flint Journal

AMBAS
BRI

DETROIT
The suspension bridge over the Detroit R
that connects Detroit and Windsor, Onta
is the busiest international border crossi
in North America. The photographer say
dashed about in a nearby park to find thi
lunar alignment.
Photo by Chip Somodevilla, Detroit Free P

ne week of May 12-18, 2003, more than 25,000 professional and amateur photographers spread out oss the nation to shoot over a million digital photographs n the goal of capturing the essence of daily life in America.

The professional photographers were equipped with obe Photoshop and Adobe Album software, Olympus 050 digital cameras, and Lexar Media's high-speed npact flash cards.

The 1,000 professional contract photographers plus ther 5,000 stringers and students sent their images via (file transfer protocol) directly to the *America 24/7* osite. Meanwhile, thousands of amateur photographers oaded their images to Snapfish's servers.

At *America 24/7*'s Mission Control headquarters, located NET in San Francisco, dozens of picture editors from the on's most prestigious publications culled the images vn to 25,000 of the very best, using Photo Mechanic by nera Bits. These photos were transferred into Webware's veMedia Digital Asset Management (DAM) system, ch served as a central image library and enabled the gners to track, search, distribute, and reformat the images the creation of the 51 books, foreign language editions, and magazine syndication, posters, and exhibitions.

Once in the DAM, images were optimized (and in some es resampled to increase image resolution) using Adobe toshop. Adobe InDesign and Adobe InCopy were used to ign and produce the 51 books, which were edited and ewed in multiple locations around the world in the form Adobe Acrobat PDFs. Epson Stylus printers were used for to proofing and to produce large-format images for ibitions. The companies providing support for the *erica 24/7* project offer many of the essential components anyone building a digital darkroom. We encourage you to

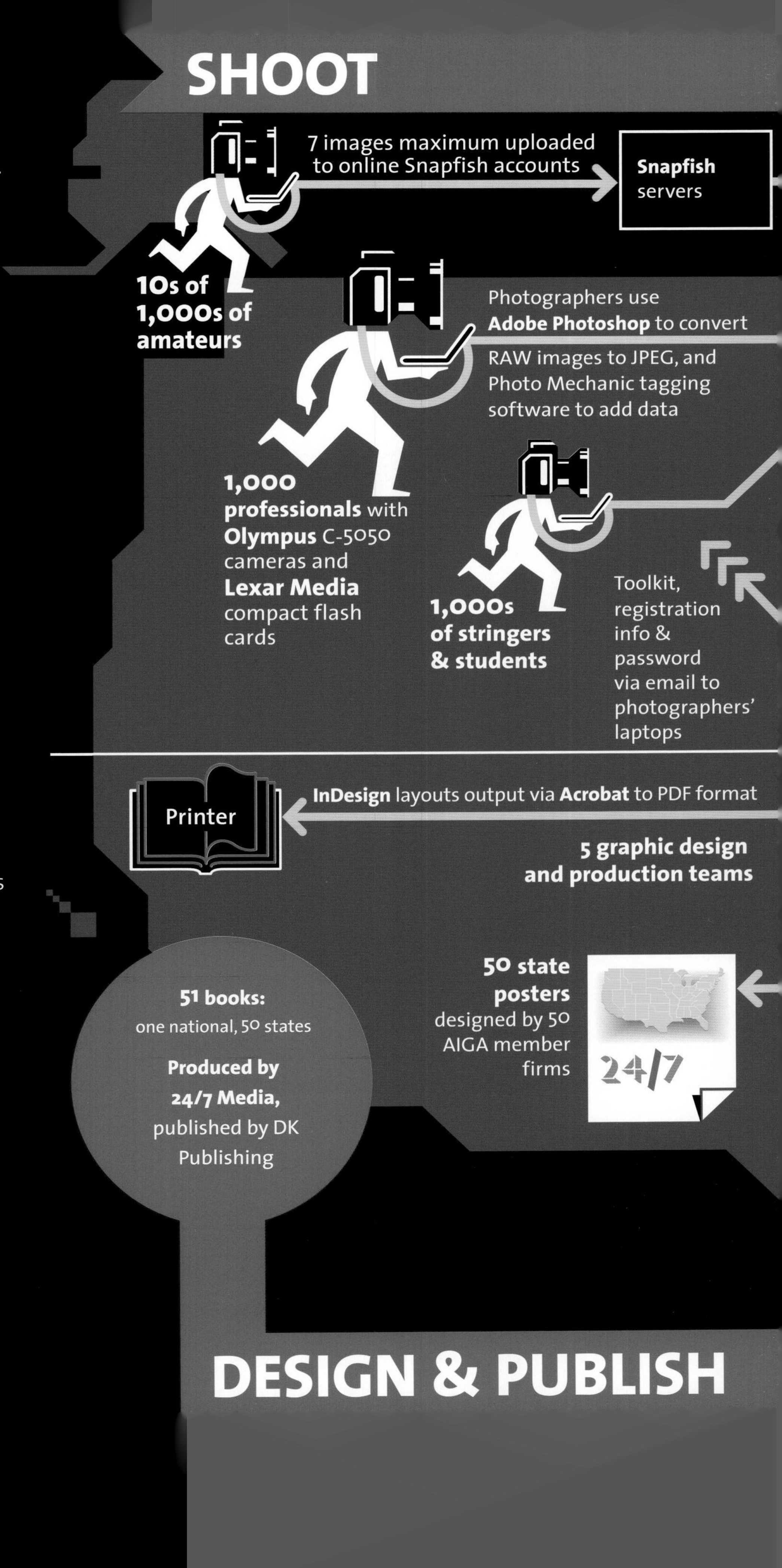

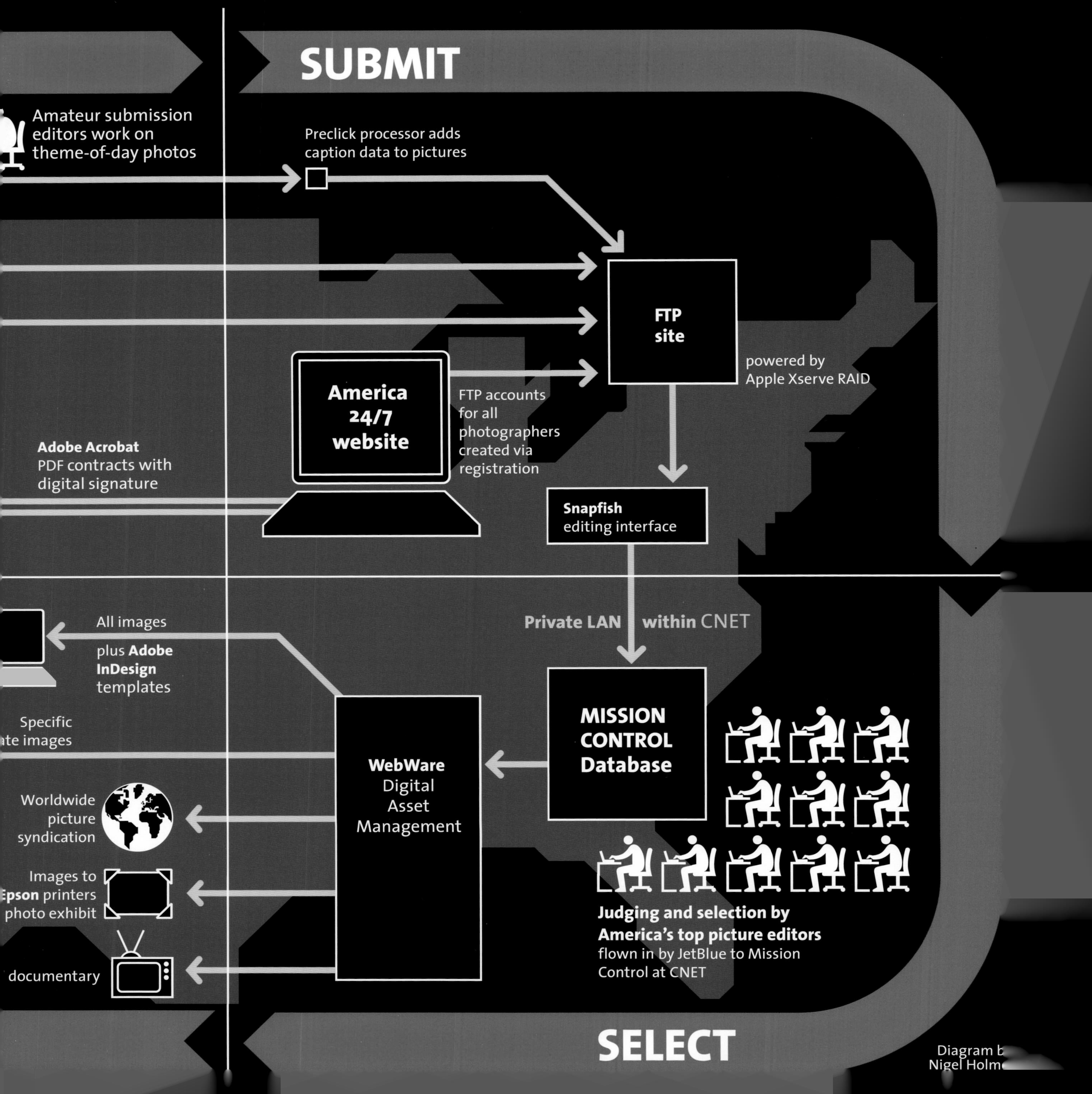
SUBMIT
Amateur submission editors work on theme-of-day photos
Preclick processor adds caption data to pictures
FTP site
powered by Apple Xserve RAID
America 24/7 website
FTP accounts for all photographers created via registration
Adobe Acrobat PDF contracts with digital signature
Snapfish editing interface
Private LAN within CNET
All images
plus Adobe InDesign templates
Specific
te images
MISSION CONTROL Database
WebWare Digital Asset Management
Worldwide picture syndication
Images to
pson printers
photo exhibit
documentary
Judging and selection by America's top picture editors flown in by JetBlue to Mission Control at CNET
SELECT
Diagram b
Nigel Holm

Participating Photographers

Coordinator: Steve Jessmore, Chief Photographer, *The Flint Journal*

Nancy Andrews, *Detroit Free Press*
Kevin Barrett
Paul Bednarski
Robert Broadbent
Mark Bugnaski, *Kalamazoo Gazette*
Mairin Chapman
Elizabeth Conley
Rodney Curtis
Lisa DeJong, *The Flint Journal*
Bill Diller, Diller Photo
Bruce Edwards, *The Flint Journal*
Mark Einhaus
Steve Fecht
J. Carl Ganter, MediaVia
Ryan Garza, *The Flint Journal*
Hugh Grannum
Lee Jackson
Steve Jessmore, *The Flint Journal*
Joy Johnson
Andrew Johnston, *Detroit Free Press*
Jose Juarez, *The Oakland Press*
Sylwia Kapuscinski, *Detroit Free Press*
J. Kyle Keener, *Detroit Free Press*
Karen Fitz LaBarge
Amy Leang, *Detroit Free Press*
Brian Masck, *The Flint Journal*
Michael Meleski
Kent Miller, *The Bay City Times*
Bryan Mitchell
Cory Morse, *Muskegon Chronicle*
Barbara Neller
Stacy Niedzwiecki
David Olds
Patricia Rosengren
Jeffrey Sauger, Reflex News
Jeff Schrier
Eric Smith
Chip Somodevilla, *Detroit Free Press*
Ken Stevens, *Muskegon Chronicle*
Donna Terek, *The Detroit News*
Leisa Thompson, *The Ann Arbor News*
Andrea Wingard
Ryan Wood, *Midland Daily News*
Mandi Wright, *Detroit Free Press*
Lance Wynn, *The Grand Rapids Press*

Thumbnail Picture Credits

Credits for thumbnail photographs are listed by the page number and are in order from left to right.

24 Jeffrey Sauger, Reflex News
Sylwia Kapuscinski, *Detroit Free Press*
Julie Dawes
J. Carl Ganter, MediaVia
J. Kyle Keener, *Detroit Free Press*
Jeffrey Sauger, Reflex News
Jeffrey Sauger, Reflex News

25 Jeffrey Sauger, Reflex News
Bruce Edwards, *The Flint Journal*
Jeffrey Sauger, Reflex News
Bruce Edwards, *The Flint Journal*
Sylwia Kapuscinski, *Detroit Free Press*
Steve Jessmore, *The Flint Journal*
Sylwia Kapuscinski, *Detroit Free Press*

26 Jeffrey Sauger, Reflex News
Cory Morse, *Muskegon Chronicle*
Bryan Mitchell
Cory Morse, *Muskegon Chronicle*
Lance Wynn, *The Grand Rapids Press*
Cory Morse, *Muskegon Chronicle*
J. Kyle Keener, *Detroit Free Press*

27 Jesse L. Mark
Lance Wynn, *The Grand Rapids Press*
Ken Stevens, *Muskegon Chronicle*
Kent Miller, *The Bay City Times*
Bryan Mitchell
Jeff Schrier
Nichol Krupp

28 Andrew Johnston, *Detroit Free Press*
Elizabeth Conley
Elizabeth Conley
Andrew Johnston, *Detroit Free Press*
Kent Miller, *The Bay City Times*
J. Carl Ganter, MediaVia
Paul Bednarski

29 J. Carl Ganter, MediaVia
Steve Jessmore, *The Flint Journal*
B. Broadbent
Ryan Wood, *Midland Daily News*
B. Broadbent
Bruce Edwards, *The Flint Journal*
Robert D. Ramey

30 Julie Dawes
J. Kyle Keener, *Detroit Free Press*
Ryan Wood, *Midland Daily News*
Bill Diller, Diller Photo
Cory Morse, *Muskegon Chronicle*
Jeff Schrier
J. Kyle Keener, *Detroit Free Press*

31 Ryan Wood, *Midland Daily News*
David Olds
Ryan Wood, *Midland Daily News*
B. Broadbent
Ryan Wood, *Midland Daily News*
Ryan Wood, *Midland Daily News*
Bryan Mitchell

32 Bryan Mitchell
Nichol Krupp
Mark Bugnaski, *Kalamazoo Gazette*
Mark Bugnaski, *Kalamazoo Gazette*
Mark Bugnaski, *Kalamazoo Gazette*
Elizabeth Conley
Cory Morse, *Muskegon Chronicle*

33 Leisa Thompson, *The Ann Arbor News*
Elizabeth Conley
Leisa Thompson, *The Ann Arbor News*
Mark Bugnaski, *Kalamazoo Gazette*
Mark Bugnaski, *Kalamazoo Gazette*
Mark Bugnaski, *Kalamazoo Gazette*
Mark Bugnaski, *Kalamazoo Gazette*

34 Linda Rae Norris
Kent Miller, *The Bay City Times*
Amy Leang, *Detroit Free Press*
Antoinette Houtman
Amy Leang, *Detroit Free Press*
Kent Miller, *The Bay City Times*
Rodney Curtis

35 Kent Miller, *The Bay City Times*
Amy Leang, *Detroit Free Press*
Kent Miller, *The Bay City Times*
Laura Rothrock Lyster
Kent Miller, *The Bay City Times*
Bill Diller, Diller Photo
Philip E. Hearn

38 Chip Somodevilla, *Detroit Free Press*
David Olds
David Olds
J. Kyle Keener, *Detroit Free Press*
David Olds
Elizabeth Conley
Chip Somodevilla, *Detroit Free Press*

39 David Olds
Chip Somodevilla, *Detroit Free Press*
Bill Diller, Diller Photo
Chip Somodevilla, *Detroit Free Press*
David Olds
Bill Diller, Diller Photo
Bill Diller, Diller Photo

40 J. Carl Ganter, MediaVia
Ryan Wood, *Midland Daily News*
J. Carl Ganter, MediaVia
Philip E. Hearn
Bruce Edwards, *The Flint Journal*
Ryan Wood, *Midland Daily News*
Ryan Wood, *Midland Daily News*

41 Philip E. Hearn
Ryan Wood, *Midland Daily News*
Ryan Wood, *Midland Daily News*
Ryan Wood, *Midland Daily News*
Ryan Wood, *Midland Daily News*
Bill Diller, Diller Photo
Ryan Wood, *Midland Daily News*

42 Mandi Wright, *Detroit Free Press*
Steve Jessmore, *The Flint Journal*
Steve Jessmore, *The Flint Journal*
J. Carl Ganter, MediaVia
J. Kyle Keener, *Detroit Free Press*
J. Kyle Keener, *Detroit Free Press*
Darron R. Silva

43 Steve Jessmore, *The Flint Journal*
Andrea Wingard
Mark Bugnaski, *Kalamazoo Gazette*
Steve Jessmore, *The Flint Journal*
Steve Jessmore, *The Flint Journal*
Steve Jessmore, *The Flint Journal*
Steve Jessmore, *The Flint Journal*

44 Amy Leang, *Detroit Free Press*
Rodney Curtis
Cory Morse, *Muskegon Chronicle*
J. Carl Ganter, MediaVia
Amy Leang, *Detroit Free Press*
J. Kyle Keener, *Detroit Free Press*
J. Kyle Keener, *Detroit Free Press*

45 J. Kyle Keener, *Detroit Free Press*
J. Kyle Keener, *Detroit Free Press*
Lance Wynn, *The Grand Rapids Press*
J. Kyle Keener, *Detroit Free Press*
Jeff Schrier
Jeffrey Sauger, Reflex News
J. Kyle Keener, *Detroit Free Press*

48 J. Carl Ganter, MediaVia
Lance Wynn, *The Grand Rapids Press*
Lance Wynn, *The Grand Rapids Press*
Lance Wynn, *The Grand Rapids Press*
Steve Jessmore, *The Flint Journal*
Lance Wynn, *The Grand Rapids Press*
Lance Wynn, *The Grand Rapids Press*

49 Leisa Thompson, *The Ann Arbor News*
Lance Wynn, *The Grand Rapids Press*
Steve Jessmore, *The Flint Journal*
Steve Jessmore, *The Flint Journal*
Steve Jessmore, *The Flint Journal*
Leisa Thompson, *The Ann Arbor News*
Steve Jessmore, *The Flint Journal*

50 Cory Morse, *Muskegon Chronicle*
Brian Masck, *The Flint Journal*
David Olds
Cory Morse, *Muskegon Chronicle*
Eric Smith
Hugh Grannum
J. Carl Ganter, MediaVia

51 Jeffrey Sauger, Reflex News
Hugh Grannum
Lance Wynn, *The Grand Rapids Press*
Jeffrey Sauger, Reflex News
Chip Somodevilla, *Detroit Free Press*
Mark Bugnaski, *Kalamazoo Gazette*
Lance Wynn, *The Grand Rapids Press*

60 J. Kyle Keener, *Detroit Free Press*
Ken Stevens, *Muskegon Chronicle*
J. Carl Ganter, MediaVia
Amy Leang, *Detroit Free Press*
J. Carl Ganter, MediaVia
Jeffrey Sauger, Reflex News
J. Carl Ganter, MediaVia

61 Ken Stevens, *Muskegon Chronicle*
Mairin Chapman
Mairin Chapman
Nancy Andrews, *Detroit Free Press*
Ken Stevens, *Muskegon Chronicle*
Steve Jessmore, *The Flint Journal*
J. Carl Ganter, MediaVia

63 Steve Jessmore, *The Flint Journal*
Kent Miller, *The Bay City Times*
Kent Miller, *The Bay City Times*
J. Kyle Keener, *Detroit Free Press*
Kent Miller, *The Bay City Times*
Kent Miller, *The Bay City Times*
Steve Jessmore, *The Flint Journal*

64 Amy Leang, *Detroit Free Press*
Bryan Mitchell
Amy Leang, *Detroit Free Press*
Jeff Schrier
Brian Masck, *The Flint Journal*
Ryan Wood, *Midland Daily News*
Chip Somodevilla, *Detroit Free Press*

65 Ken Stevens, *Muskegon Chronicle*
Lance Wynn, *The Grand Rapids Press*
Ken Stevens, *Muskegon Chronicle*
Paul Bednarski
Ken Stevens, *Muskegon Chronicle*
Ryan Wood, *Midland Daily News*
Jeff Schrier

70 Lance Wynn, *The Grand Rapids Press*
Mark Bugnaski, *Kalamazoo Gazette*
Nancy Andrews, *Detroit Free Press*
Mark Bugnaski, *Kalamazoo Gazette*
Donna Terek, *The Detroit News*
Mark Bugnaski, *Kalamazoo Gazette*
Nancy Andrews, *Detroit Free Press*

71 Steve Jessmore, *The Flint Journal*
Steve Jessmore, *The Flint Journal*
Mark Bugnaski, *Kalamazoo Gazette*
Donna Terek, *The Detroit News*
Steve Jessmore, *The Flint Journal*
Mark Bugnaski, *Kalamazoo Gazette*
Donna Terek, *The Detroit News*

72 Cory Morse, *Muskegon Chronicle*
David Olds
Bruce Edwards, *The Flint Journal*
Jeff Schrier
Mairin Chapman
Ryan Wood, *Midland Daily News*
Steve Jessmore, *The Flint Journal*

73 Ryan Wood, *Midland Daily News*
Jeff Schrier
Mairin Chapman
Steve Jessmore, *The Flint Journal*
Ryan Wood, *Midland Daily News*
Ryan Wood, *Midland Daily News*
David Olds

75 Kent Miller, *The Bay City Times*
Kent Miller, *The Bay City Times*
Kent Miller, *The Bay City Times*
Kent Miller, *The Bay City Times*
Jeffrey Sauger, Reflex News
Kent Miller, *The Bay City Times*
Kent Miller, *The Bay City Times*

76 Tyler Sipe
Cory Morse, *Muskegon Chronicle*
David Olds
Bruce Edwards, *The Flint Journal*
Hugh Grannum
Elizabeth Conley
Paul Bednarski

77 Steve Jessmore, *The Flint Journal*
Paul Bednarski
Steve Jessmore, *The Flint Journal*
Steve Jessmore, *The Flint Journal*
Paul Bednarski
Tyler Sipe
Ryan Garza, *The Flint Journal*

78 David Olds
Bruce Edwards, *The Flint Journal*
Cory Morse, *Muskegon Chronicle*
Nancy Andrews, *Detroit Free Press*
Cory Morse, *Muskegon Chronicle*
Mark Bugnaski, *Kalamazoo Gazette*
David Olds

79 Nancy Andrews, *Detroit Free Press*
Mark Bugnaski, *Kalamazoo Gazette*
Nancy Andrews, *Detroit Free Press*
Bruce Edwards, *The Flint Journal*
David Olds
Bruce Edwards, *The Flint Journal*
Bruce Edwards, *The Flint Journal*

82 Chip Somodevilla, *Detroit Free Press*
Charles Prikasky
Bruce Edwards, *The Flint Journal*
Cory Morse, *Muskegon Chronicle*
Chip Somodevilla, *Detroit Free Press*
Steve Jessmore, *The Flint Journal*
Leisa Thompson, *The Ann Arbor News*

83 Chip Somodevilla, *Detroit Free Press*
Bruce Edwards, *The Flint Journal*
Amy Leang, *Detroit Free Press*
Kent Miller, *The Bay City Times*
Bruce Edwards, *The Flint Journal*
Kent Miller, *The Bay City Times*
Chip Somodevilla, *Detroit Free Press*

84 Ken Stevens, *Muskegon Chronicle*
Mark Bugnaski, *Kalamazoo Gazette*
Mark Bugnaski, *Kalamazoo Gazette*
Ken Stevens, *Muskegon Chronicle*
Mark Bugnaski, *Kalamazoo Gazette*
Mark Bugnaski, *Kalamazoo Gazette*
Ken Stevens, *Muskegon Chronicle*

85 Mark Bugnaski, *Kalamazoo Gazette*
Mark Bugnaski, *Kalamazoo Gazette*
Mark Bugnaski, *Kalamazoo Gazette*
Ken Stevens, *Muskegon Chronicle*
Mark Bugnaski, *Kalamazoo Gazette*
Mark Bugnaski, *Kalamazoo Gazette*
Ken Stevens, *Muskegon Chronicle*

86 Amy Leang, *Detroit Free Press*
Steve Jessmore, *The Flint Journal*
David Olds
Jeff Schrier
David Olds
Jeff Schrier
J. Kyle Keener, *Detroit Free Press*

87 Steve Jessmore, *The Flint Journal*
Amy Leang, *Detroit Free Press*
Steve Jessmore, *The Flint Journal*
Steve Jessmore, *The Flint Journal*
Amy Leang, *Detroit Free Press*
Amy Leang, *Detroit Free Press*
Jeff Schrier

92 Eric Smith
Hugh Grannum
Amy Leang, *Detroit Free Press*

Mandi Wright, *Detroit Free Press*
Hugh Grannum
Amy Leang, *Detroit Free Press*
Hugh Grannum

93 Ken Stevens, *Muskegon Chronicle*
Hugh Grannum
Steve Jessmore, *The Flint Journal*
Hugh Grannum
Eric Smith
Bill Diller, Diller Photo
Joel Wintermantle

94 Amy Leang, *Detroit Free Press*
Amy Leang, *Detroit Free Press*
Cory Morse, *Muskegon Chronicle*
Bryan Mitchell
Amy Leang, *Detroit Free Press*
Julie Dawes
J. Kyle Keener, *Detroit Free Press*

95 J. Carl Ganter, MediaVia
Jeffrey Sauger, Reflex News
Amy Leang, *Detroit Free Press*
Jeff Schrier
Cory Morse, *Muskegon Chronicle*
Kent Miller, *The Bay City Times*
Steve Jessmore, *The Flint Journal*

97 Cory Morse, *Muskegon Chronicle*
Kent Miller, *The Bay City Times*
Kent Miller, *The Bay City Times*
Cory Morse, *Muskegon Chronicle*
Kent Miller, *The Bay City Times*
Kent Miller, *The Bay City Times*
Kent Miller, *The Bay City Times*

100 Steve Jessmore, *The Flint Journal*
Steve Jessmore, *The Flint Journal*
Jose Juarez, *The Oakland Press*
Antoinette Houtman
Paul Bednarski
Steve Jessmore, *The Flint Journal*
Antoinette Houtman

101 Paul Bednarski
Bruce Edwards, *The Flint Journal*
Paul Bednarski
Paul Bednarski
Steve Jessmore, *The Flint Journal*
Bruce Edwards, *The Flint Journal*
Steve Jessmore, *The Flint Journal*

102 Hugh Grannum
Jeff Schrier
Hugh Grannum
Chip Somodevilla, *Detroit Free Press*
Mark Bugnaski, *Kalamazoo Gazette*
Kent Miller, *The Bay City Times*
Ryan Garza, *The Flint Journal*

103 Steve Jessmore, *The Flint Journal*
Mark Bugnaski, *Kalamazoo Gazette*
Jose Juarez, *The Oakland Press*
Hugh Grannum
Steve Jessmore, *The Flint Journal*
Mandi Wright, *Detroit Free Press*
Steve Jessmore, *The Flint Journal*

106 Joel Wintermantle
Amy Leang, *Detroit Free Press*
Steve Jessmore, *The Flint Journal*
Donna Terek, *The Detroit News*
Lisa DeJong, *The Flint Journal*
Bryan Mitchell
Donna Terek, *The Detroit News*

107 Donna Terek, *The Detroit News*
Lisa DeJong, *The Flint Journal*
Donna Terek, *The Detroit News*
Mark Einhaus
Bruce Edwards, *The Flint Journal*
Steve Jessmore, *The Flint Journal*
Donna Terek, *The Detroit News*

108 Leisa Thompson, *The Ann Arbor News*
Steve Jessmore, *The Flint Journal*
J. Carl Ganter, MediaVia
Bryan Mitchell
J. Kyle Keener, *Detroit Free Press*
Ryan Wood, *Midland Daily News*
Mark Einhaus

109 Bruce Edwards, *The Flint Journal*
Ray Malace
Bryan Mitchell
Mark Bugnaski, *Kalamazoo Gazette*
Mark Bugnaski, *Kalamazoo Gazette*
Steve Jessmore, *The Flint Journal*
J. Kyle Keener, *Detroit Free Press*

111 Cory Morse, *Muskegon Chronicle*
J. Carl Ganter, MediaVia
J. Carl Ganter, MediaVia
Cory Morse, *Muskegon Chronicle*
Cory Morse, *Muskegon Chronicle*
Sara McGregor, *Macomb Community College*
Lance Wynn, *The Grand Rapids Press*

114 Ken Stevens, *Muskegon Chronicle*
Jeff Schrier
Ken Stevens, *Muskegon Chronicle*
Jeff Schrier
Lisa DeJong, *The Flint Journal*

Jeff Schrier
Jeff Schrier

116 Andrew Johnston, *Detroit Free Press*
Amy Leang, *Detroit Free Press*
Jeff Schrier
J. Kyle Keener, *Detroit Free Press*
J. Kyle Keener, *Detroit Free Press*
Kent Miller, *The Bay City Times*
J. Kyle Keener, *Detroit Free Press*

117 Kent Miller, *The Bay City Times*
Jeff Schrier
Joel Wintermantle
J. Kyle Keener, *Detroit Free Press*
Amy Leang, *Detroit Free Press*
Mark Einhaus
Jeff Schrier

118 J. Kyle Keener, *Detroit Free Press*
Jeff Schrier
Ryan Garza, *The Flint Journal*
J. Kyle Keener, *Detroit Free Press*
Kent Miller, *The Bay City Times*
Ryan Garza, *The Flint Journal*
Kent Miller, *The Bay City Times*

122 Lisa DeJong, *The Flint Journal*
Lisa DeJong, *The Flint Journal*
Lisa DeJong, *The Flint Journal*
Lisa DeJong, *The Flint Journal*
Lisa DeJong, *The Flint Journal*
Lisa DeJong, *The Flint Journal*
Lisa DeJong, *The Flint Journal*

125 Steve Jessmore, *The Flint Journal*
Steve Jessmore, *The Flint Journal*
Steve Jessmore, *The Flint Journal*
Steve Jessmore, *The Flint Journal*
Steve Jessmore, *The Flint Journal*
Steve Jessmore, *The Flint Journal*
Steve Jessmore, *The Flint Journal*

126 Jeff Schrier
Lisa DeJong, *The Flint Journal*
Jeff Schrier
Joel Wintermantle
Mark Einhaus
Leisa Thompson, *The Ann Arbor News*
Mark Einhaus

132 B. Broadbent
Leisa Thompson, *The Ann Arbor News*
Brian Masck, *The Flint Journal*
Brian Masck, *The Flint Journal*
Lance Wynn, *The Grand Rapids Press*
Leisa Thompson, *The Ann Arbor News*
Leisa Thompson, *The Ann Arbor News*

133 Cory Morse, *Muskegon Chronicle*
Leisa Thompson, *The Ann Arbor News*
Leisa Thompson, *The Ann Arbor News*
Leisa Thompson, *The Ann Arbor News*
Leisa Thompson, *The Ann Arbor News*
Sylwia Ziniewicz
Leisa Thompson, *The Ann Arbor News*

137 Lance Wynn, *The Grand Rapids Press*
Lance Wynn, *The Grand Rapids Press*
Cory Morse, *Muskegon Chronicle*
Lance Wynn, *The Grand Rapids Press*
Cory Morse, *Muskegon Chronicle*
Lance Wynn, *The Grand Rapids Press*
Amy Leang, *Detroit Free Press*

138 Cory Morse, *Muskegon Chronicle*
Brian Masck, *The Flint Journal*
Steve Jessmore, *The Flint Journal*
Amy Leang, *Detroit Free Press*
Lisa Toigo
Kent Miller, *The Bay City Times*
Mark Bugnaski, *Kalamazoo Gazette*

139 Mark Einhaus
Bruce Edwards, *The Flint Journal*
Steve Jessmore, *The Flint Journal*
Hugh Grannum
Steve Jessmore, *The Flint Journal*
Steve Jessmore, *The Flint Journal*
Mark Bugnaski, *The Flint Journal*

140 Jeffrey Sauger, *The Flint Journal*
Sylwia Kapuscinski, *Detroit Free Press*
Jeffrey Sauger, Reflex News
Jeffrey Sauger, Reflex News
Sylwia Kapuscinski, *Detroit Free Press*
J. Carl Ganter, MediaVia
Jeffrey Sauger, Reflex News

141 Sylwia Kapuscinski, *Detroit Free Press*
Mairin Chapman
Sylwia Kapuscinski, *Detroit Free Press*
Sylwia Kapuscinski, *Detroit Free Press*
Jeffrey Sauger, Reflex News
Sylwia Kapuscinski, *Detroit Free Press*
Jeffrey Sauger, Reflex News

145 Donna Terek, *The Detroit News*
Donna Terek, *The Detroit News*
Donna Terek, *The Detroit News*
Donna Terek, *The Detroit News*
Donna Terek, *The Detroit News*
Donna Terek, *The Detroit News*
Donna Terek, *The Detroit News*

146 Jeffrey Sauger, Reflex News
Brian Masck, *The Flint Journal*
Brian Masck, *The Flint Journal*
Jeff Schrier
Brian Masck, *The Flint Journal*
J. Carl Ganter, MediaVia
Andrew Skinner, *Oceana's Herald-Journal*

147 J. Kyle Keener, *Detroit Free Press*
Brian Masck, *The Flint Journal*
J. Carl Ganter, MediaVia
Jeffrey Sauger, Reflex News
Jeff Schrier
Bruce Edwards, *The Flint Journal*
J. Carl Ganter, MediaVia

148 Brian Masck, *The Flint Journal*
Brian Masck, *The Flint Journal*
Brian Masck, *The Flint Journal*
Brian Masck, *The Flint Journal*
Brian Masck, *The Flint Journal*
B. Broadbent
Brian Masck, *The Flint Journal*

149 J. Carl Ganter, MediaVia
Brian Masck, *The Flint Journal*
Brian Masck, *The Flint Journal*
J. Carl Ganter, MediaVia
Brian Masck, *The Flint Journal*
Brian Masck, *The Flint Journal*
Mark Einhaus

150 Hugh Grannum
Hugh Grannum
Jesse L. Mark
Kent Miller, *The Bay City Times*
Steve Fecht
Brian Masck, *The Flint Journal*
Steve Fecht

151 Hugh Grannum
Brian Masck, *The Flint Journal*
Hugh Grannum
Steve Fecht
Ken Stevens, *Muskegon Chronicle*
Steve Fecht
Mandi Wright, *Detroit Free Press*

152 Hugh Grannum
Ken Stevens, *Muskegon Chronicle*
J. Carl Ganter, MediaVia
Hugh Grannum
Ken Stevens, *Muskegon Chronicle*
Hugh Grannum
Hugh Grannum

153 J. Carl Ganter, MediaVia
Hugh Grannum
Ken Stevens, *Muskegon Chronicle*
Kent Miller, *The Bay City Times*
Hugh Grannum
Hugh Grannum
Hugh Grannum

159 Ken Stevens, *Muskegon Chronicle*
Steve Jessmore, *The Flint Journal*
Ken Stevens, *Muskegon Chronicle*
Andrew Skinner, *Oceana's Herald-Journal*
J. Kyle Keener, *Detroit Free Press*
J. Kyle Keener, *Detroit Free Press*
Sara McGregor, Macomb Community College

160 Brian Masck, *The Flint Journal*
B. Broadbent
Brian Masck, *The Flint Journal*
Brian Masck, *The Flint Journal*
Brian Masck, *The Flint Journal*
Hugh Grannum
Hugh Grannum

161 Hugh Grannum
Jeff Schrier
Brian Masck, *The Flint Journal*
Nancy Andrews, *The Flint Journal*
Barbara Neller
Hugh Grannum
Jeff Schrier

162 Jeffrey Sauger, Reflex News
Brian Masck, *The Flint Journal*
Jeffrey Sauger, Reflex News
Brian Masck, *The Flint Journal*
Jeffrey Sauger, Reflex News
J. Carl Ganter, MediaVia
J. Carl Ganter, MediaVia

163 Sylwia Kapuscinski, *Detroit Free Press*
J. Kyle Keener, *Detroit Free Press*
Sylwia Kapuscinski, *Detroit Free Press*
Bryan Mitchell
Jeffrey Sauger, Reflex News
Bill Diller, Diller Photo
Jeffrey Sauger, Reflex News

164 Donna Terek, *The Detroit News*
J. Kyle Keener, *Detroit Free Press*
J. Kyle Keener, *Detroit Free Press*
Chip Somodevilla, *Detroit Free Press*
Donna Terek, *The Detroit News*
Mairin Chapman
Nancy Andrews, *Detroit Free Press*

165 Nancy Andrews, *Detroit Free Press*
Paul Bednarski
Ray Malace

Bruce Edwards, *The Flint Journal*
Donna Terek, *The Detroit News*
Steve Jessmore, *The Flint Journal*
Donna Terek, *The Detroit News*

166 J. Kyle Keener, *Detroit Free Press*
J. Kyle Keener, *Detroit Free Press*
Steve Jessmore, *The Flint Journal*
J. Kyle Keener, *Detroit Free Press*
Nancy Andrews, *Detroit Free Press*
Kent Miller, *The Bay City Times*
Chip Somodevilla, *Detroit Free Press*

167 J. Kyle Keener, *Detroit Free Press*
Chip Somodevilla, *Detroit Free Press*
Lisa DeJong, *The Flint Journal*
Kent Miller, *The Flint Journal*
Bruce Edwards, *The Flint Journal*
Nancy Andrews, *Detroit Free Press*
Steve Jessmore, *The Flint Journal*

170 Eric Smith
Brian Masck, *The Flint Journal*
Kent Miller, *The Flint Journal*
Steve Jessmore, *The Flint Journal*
Brian Masck, *The Flint Journal*
Jesse L. Mark
Kent Miller, *The Flint Journal*

171 Kent Miller, *The Flint Journal*
Kent Miller, *The Flint Journal*
Mark Bugnaski, *Kalamazoo Gazette*
Rob Worth, Jr., Sunset Promotions, Inc.
Kent Miller, *The Bay City Times*
Steve Jessmore, *The Flint Journal*
Steve Jessmore, *The Flint Journal*

172 Brian Masck, *The Flint Journal*
Brian Masck, *The Flint Journal*
Brian Masck, *The Flint Journal*
Brian Masck, *The Flint Journal*
Cory Morse, *Muskegon Chronicle*
Brian Masck, *The Flint Journal*
Cory Morse, *Muskegon Chronicle*

173 Cory Morse, *Muskegon Chronicle*
Kent Miller, *The Bay City Times*
Lisa DeJong, *The Flint Journal*
Kent Miller, *The Bay City Times*
Bruce Edwards, *The Flint Journal*
J. Carl Ganter, MediaVia
Kent Miller, *The Bay City Times*

174 J. Kyle Keener, *Detroit Free Press*
Bruce Edwards, *The Flint Journal*
J. Kyle Keener, *Detroit Free Press*
J. Kyle Keener, *Detroit Free Press*
David Olds
Kent Miller, *The Bay City Times*
Bill Diller, Diller Photo

175 Kent Miller, *The Bay City Times*
Ray Malace
Kent Miller, *The Bay City Times*
Brian Masck, *The Flint Journal*
Ray Malace
Steve Jessmore, *The Flint Journal*
Jeff Schrier

177 Ryan Wood, *Midland Daily News*
Jeff Schrier
J. Kyle Keener, *Detroit Free Press*
J. Kyle Keener, *Detroit Free Press*
J. Kyle Keener, *Detroit Free Press*
Jeff Schrier
J. Kyle Keener, *Detroit Free Press*

178 Kent Miller, *The Bay City Times*
J. Kyle Keener, *Detroit Free Press*
Hugh Grannum
J. Kyle Keener, *Detroit Free Press*
Hugh Grannum
Philip E. Hearn
Kent Miller, *The Bay City Times*

179 Rob Worth, Jr., Sunset Promotions, Inc.
Nancy Andrews, *Detroit Free Press*
Chip Somodevilla, *Detroit Free Press*
Steve Jessmore, *The Flint Journal*
Leisa Thompson, *The Ann Arbor News*
J. Kyle Keener, *Detroit Free Press*
Steve Jessmore, *The Flint Journal*

Staff

The *America 24/7* series was imagined years ago by our friend Oscar Dystel, a publishing legend whose vision and enthusiasm have been a source of great inspiration.

We also wish to express our gratitude to our truly visionary publisher, DK.

Rick Smolan, Project Director
David Elliot Cohen, Project Director

Administrative
Katya Able, Operations Director
Gina Privitere, Communications Director
Chuck Gathard, Technology Director
Kim Shannon, Photographer Relations Director
Erin O'Connor, Photographer Relations Intern
Leslie Hunter, Partnership Director
Annie Polk, Publicity Manager
John McAlester, Website Manager
Alex Notides, Office Manager
C. Thomas Hardin, State Photography Coordinator

Design
Brad Zucroff, Creative Director
Karen Mullarkey, Photography Director
Judy Zimola, Production Manager
David Simoni, Production Designer
Mary Dias, Production Designer
Heidi Madison, Associate Picture Editor
Don McCartney, Production Designer
Diane Dempsey Murray, Production Designer
Jan Rogers, Associate Picture Editor
Bill Shore, Production Designer and Image Artist
Larry Nighswander, Senior Picture Editor
Bill Marr, Sarah Leen, Senior Picture Editors
Peter Truskier, Workflow Consultant
Jim Birkenseer, Workflow Consultant

Editorial
Maggie Canon, Managing Editor
Curt Sanburn, Senior Editor
Teresa L. Trego, Production Editor
Lea Aschkenas, Writer
Olivia Boler, Writer
Korey Capozza, Writer
Beverly Hanly, Writer
Bridgett Novak, Writer
Alison Owings, Writer
Fred Raker, Writer
Joe Wolff, Writer
Elise O'Keefe, Copy Chief
Daisy Hernández, Copy Editor
Jennifer Wolfe, Copy Editor

Infographic Design
Nigel Holmes

Literary Agent
Carol Mann, The Carol Mann Agency

Legal Counsel
Barry Reder, Coblentz, Patch, Duffy & Bass, LLP
Phil Feldman, Coblentz, Patch, Duffy & Bass, LLP
Gabe Perle, Ohlandt, Greeley, Ruggiero & Perle, LLP
Jon Hart, Dow, Lohnes & Albertson, PLLC
Mike Hays, Dow, Lohnes & Albertson, PLLC
Stephen Pollen, Warshaw Burstein, Cohen, Schlesinger & Kuh, LLP
Rick Pappas

Accounting and Finance
Rita Dulebohn, Accountant
Robert Powers, Calegari, Morris & Co. Accountants
Eugene Blumberg, Blumberg & Associates
Arthur Langhaus, KLS Professional Advisors Group, Inc.

Picture Editors
J. David Ake, Associated Press
Caren Alpert, formerly *Health* magazine
Simon Barnett, *Newsweek*
Caroline Couig, *San Jose Mercury News*
Mike Davis, formerly *National Geographic*
Michel duCille, *Washington Post*
Deborah Dragon, *Rolling Stone*
Victor Fisher, formerly Associated Press
Frank Folwell, *USA Today*
MaryAnne Golon, *Time*
Liz Grady, formerly *National Geographic*
Randall Greenwell, *San Francisco Chronicle*
C. Thomas Hardin, formerly *Louisville Courier-Journal*
Kathleen Hennessy, *San Francisco Chronicle*
Scot Jahn, *U.S. News & World Report*
Steve Jessmore, *Flint Journal*
John Kaplan, University of Florida
Kim Komenich, *San Francisco Chronicle*
Eliane Laffont, *Hachette Filipacchi Media*
Jean-Pierre Laffont, *Hachette Filipacchi Media*
Andrew Locke, MSNBC
Jose Lopez, *The New York Times*
Maria Mann, formerly AFP
Bill Marr, formerly *National Geographic*
Michele McNally, *Fortune*
James Merithew, *San Francisco Chronicle*
Eric Meskauskas, *New York Daily News*
Maddy Miller, *People* magazine
Michelle Molloy, *Newsweek*
Dolores Morrison, *New York Daily News*
Karen Mullarkey, formerly *Newsweek, Rolling Stone, Sports Illustrated*
Larry Nighswander, Ohio University School of Visual Communication
Jim Preston, *Baltimore Sun*
Sarah Rozen, formerly *Entertainment Weekly*
Mike Smith, *The New York Times*
Neal Ulevich, formerly Associated Press

Website and Digital Systems
Jeff Burchell, Applications Engineer

Television Documentary
Sandy Smolan, Producer/Director
Rick King, Producer/Director
Bill Medsker, Producer

Video News Release
Mike Cerre, Producer/Director

Digital Pond
Peter Hogg
Kris Knight
Roger Graham
Philip Bond
Frank De Pace
Lisa Li

Senior Advisors
Jennifer Erwitt, Strategic Advisor
Tom Walker, Creative Advisor
Megan Smith, Technology Advisor
Jon Kamen, Media and Partnership Advisor
Mark Greenberg, Partnership Advisor
Patti Richards, Publicity Advisor
Cotton Coulson, Mission Control Advisor

Executive Advisors
Sonia Land
George Craig
Carole Bidnick

Advisors
Chris Anderson
Samir Arora
Russell Brown
Craig Cline
Gayle Cline
Harlan Felt
George Fisher
Phillip Moffitt
Clement Mok
Laureen Seeger
Richard Saul Wurman

DK Publishing
Bill Barry
Joanna Bull
Therese Burke
Sarah Coltman
Christopher Davis
Todd Fries
Dick Heffernan
Jay Henry
Stuart Jackman
Stephanie Jackson
Chuck Lang
Sharon Lucas
Cathy Melnicki
Nicola Munro
Eunice Paterson
Andrew Welham

Colourscan
Jimmy Tsao
Eddie Chia
Richard Law
Josephine Yam
Paul Koh
Chee Cheng Yeong
Dan Kang

Chief Morale Officer
Goose, the dog